THE **POLITICS OF ACCESS**

AFRICA: MISSING VOICES SERIES

Donald I. Ray, general editor
ISSN 1703-1826 (Print) ISSN 1925-5675 (Online)

University of Calgary Press has a long history of publishing academic works on Africa. *Africa: Missing Voices* illuminates issues and topics concerning Africa that have been ignored or are missing from current global debates. This series will fill a gap in African scholarship by addressing concerns that have been long overlooked in political, social, and historical discussions about this continent.

No. 1 · **Grassroots Governance?: Chiefs in Africa and the Afro-Caribbean**
Edited by D.I. Ray and P.S. Reddy · Copublished with the International Association of Schools and Institutes of Administration (IASIA)

No. 2 · **The African Diaspora in Canada: Negotiating Identity and Belonging**
Edited by Wisdom Tettey and Korbla Puplampu

No. 3 · **A Common Hunger: Land Rights in Canada and South Africa**
by Joan G. Fairweather

No. 4 · **New Directions in African Education: Challenges and Possibilities**
Edited by S. Nombuso Dlamini

No. 5 · **Shrines in Africa: History, Politics, and Society**
Edited by Allan Charles Dawson

No. 6 · **The Land Has Changed: History, Society and Gender in Colonial Eastern Nigeria**
by Chima J. Korieh

No. 7 · **African Wars: A Defense Intelligence Perspective**
by William G. Thom

No. 8 · **Reinventing African Chieftaincy in the Age of AIDS, Gender, Governance, and Development** Edited by Donald I. Ray, Tim Quinlan, Keshav Sharma, and Tacita A.O. Clarke

No. 9 · **The Politics of Access: University Education and Nation-Building in Nigeria, 1948–2000** by Ogechi Emmanuel Anyanwu

UNIVERSITY OF
CALGARY
PRESS

THE POLITICS OF ACCESS

University Education and Nation-Building in Nigeria, 1948–2000

OGECHI EMMANUEL ANYANWU

AFRICA: MISSING VOICES SERIES
ISSN 1703-1826 (PRINT) ISSN 1925-5675 (ONLINE)

© 2011 Ogechi Emmanuel Anyanwu

University of Calgary Press
2500 University Drive NW
Calgary, Alberta
Canada T2N 1N4
www.uofcpress.com

No part of this publication may be reproduced, stored in a retrieval system or transmitted, in any form or by any means, without the prior written consent of the publisher.

LIBRARY AND ARCHIVES CANADA CATALOGUING IN PUBLICATION

Anyanwu, Ogechi Emmanuel, 1971-
  The politics of access : university education and nation-building in Nigeria, 1948-2000 / Ogechi Emmanuel Anyanwu.

(Africa: missing voices, ISSN 1703-1826 ; 9) Includes bibliographical references and index.
Issued also in electronic formats.
ISBN 978-1-55238-518-0

  1. Education, Higher—Nigeria—History—20th century. 2. Higher education and state—Nigeria. 3. Education, Higher—Nigeria—Political aspects. 4. Nation-building—Nigeria. 5. Economic development—Nigeria. I. Title. II. Series: Africa, missing voices series ; 9

LA1633.A59 2011   378.669'0904   C2011-905054-4

The University of Calgary Press acknowledges the support of the Alberta Foundation for the Arts for our publications. We acknowledge the financial support of the Government of Canada through the Canada Book Fund for our publishing activities. We acknowledge the financial support of the Canada Council for the Arts for our publishing program.

  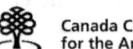

Cover design, page design, and typesetting by Melina Cusano

*To the memory of my dear mother,
Patience Anyanwu*

*To my lovely wife, Chidinma,
and daughters, Uchechi, Ozioma, and Amarachi*

Table of Contents

List of Abbreviations   xi
Acknowledgments   xiii

Introduction

Background   1
Education for Nation-Building   5
Education for Development   8
Organization   13

1: The Politics of Colonial Education

Introduction   17
Western Education and the Making of Nigeria   18
Development of Higher Education   28
Access, Economic Development, and Nation-Building   34

2: Towards Educational Reform: The Cold War, Decolonization, and the Carnegie Corporation, 1952–60

Introduction   37
Education in National Politics   38
Postwar Nigeria   46
The Ashby Commission and the Question of Relevance   59

3: The Ashby Commission, Regionalism, and University Education in the 1960s

Introduction	69
Blueprint for Change	71
Implementing Ashby's Report	79
Colonial Legacy	87
Towards Centralization	97
Conclusion	101

4: Centralization of Universities and National Integration, 1970–79: The Legacy of the Nigerian Civil War

Introduction	103
Continuing Elitism	105
Federal Control of University Education	107
Quota System and Admission Reform	115
Recession of 1978	128
Conclusion	131

5: The Second Republic and the Burden of Expansion, 1979–83: Free Education, Science and Technology, and Quota System

Introduction	135
National Open University and Universities of Technology	137
Quota System and the Challenges of Nationhood	143
State Participation in Higher Education	148
Economic Meltdown of 1983	150
Conclusion	156

6: Rationalization Policy: The IMF/World Bank and Structural Adjustment Program, 1984–90

Introduction	159
Buhari and the Search for Cost-Saving Measures	160
Babangida, IMF, and Universities	168
The World Bank and the White Paper on University Reform	172
The Impact of IMF/World Bank Policies on Universities	177
Conclusion	183

7: Crisis of Nationhood: Funding Issues, Socio-Political Instability, and Private University Education, 1990–2000

Introduction	185
Nigeria, Still a Divided Nation	186
Poor Funding, ASUU, and Military Dictatorship	191
Satellite Campuses	200
Private Universities	202
Towards a Renewed Commitment to Educational Expansion	207

Conclusion

Colonial Origins	211
The 1960s	213
Post-Civil War Nation-Building	215
Setbacks in Expansion	219
Recent Trends	221

Notes 225

Bibliography 265

Index 287

List of Abbreviations

ABU	Ahmadu Bello University
AG	Action-Group
ACEC	Advisory Committee on Education in the Colonies
AHK	Arewa House Kaduna
ASUU	Academic Staff Union of Universities
CCNY	Carnegie Corporation of New York
Cmd	Command Paper issue by the British Government
CO	Colonial Office
COFHE	Committee on the Future of Higher Education
CUE	Committee on University Entrance
CUF	Committee on University Finances
CVC	Committee of Vice-Chancellors
ETF	Education Tax Fund
Fifth NDP	Fifth National Development Plan
First NDP	First National Development Plan
Fourth NDP	Fourth National Development Plan
FNRP	First National Rolling Plan
FUT	Federal Universities of Technology
GCE	General Certificate of Education
GNPP	Great Nigeria People's Party
IMF	International Monetary Fund
IUC	Inter-University Council for Higher Education in the Colonies
JAMB	Joint Admission and Matriculation Board
JCC	Joint Consultative Council
NAE	National Archives Enugu
NAI	National Archives Ibadan

NAK	National Archives Kaduna
NAUT	Nigerian Association of University Teachers
NDA	Nigerian Defense Academy
NCE	National Council on Education
NCE	National Certificate of Education
NUC	National Universities Commission
NUNS	National Union of Nigerian Students
NYSC	National Youth Service Corps
NPN	National Party of Nigeria
NPP	Nigerian People's Party
NRB	Nigerian Education Bank
NSLB	Nigerian Student Loan Board
NPE	National Policy on Education
NOU	National Open University
NICRHEN	National Implementation Committee on the Report of the Review of Higher Education in Nigeria
NCNC	National Convention of Nigerian Citizens
NPC	National Progressive Party
PRO	Public Record Office
PRP	People's Redemption Party
PPT	Petroleum Profit Tax
PPB	Presidential Political Bureau
SAP	Structural Adjustment Program
SNPE	Seminar on a National Policy on Education
Second NDP	Second National Development Plan
Third NDP	Third National Development Plan
UME	University Matriculation Examination
UNESCO	United Nations Educational, Scientific and Cultural Organization
USAID	United States Agency for International Development
UNICEF	United Nations International Children's Emergency Fund
UPE	Universal Primary Education
UA	University of Abuja
UNN	University of Nigeria, Nsukka
UCI	University College of Ibadan
UGC	University Grants Committee
UI	University of Ibadan
UPN	United Party of Nigeria
WAEC	West African Examination Council

Acknowledgments

Many thanks to God for blessing my efforts during the period I worked on this book beyond the level of my original expectation. I am forever indebted to the two people whom I owe everything that I have achieved today: my parents, Claudius and Patience Anyanwu. Their steadfast faith and confidence in my abilities shaped me to be the person I am today. Their curiosity, loving encouragement, and kind prodding have been utterly indispensable to this project.

For years I have struggled to find words to express my gratitude to my uncle, Sir Lucius Ehieze, but I have failed. Words, it seems, are so inadequate to thank him for all his favours, too numerous to list here. Ehieze's involvement in my life made my professional career possible, and I am deeply grateful for his continued support and friendship.

I consider myself extremely fortunate for the intellectual stimulation I gained from my mentors and colleagues in Nigeria: Professors T.O.C. Ndubuizu, A.G. Anwukah, U.D. Anyanwu, C. Akujor, Aja Akpuru Aja, B.E.B. Nwoko, O.C. Nwebo, C.B. Nwachukwu, Ndu Life Njoku, John Cliff Nwadike, Okechuwku Okeke, Ngozi Uwazurike, and Barrister Okey Ehieze. They inspired me to cast my net in the right direction. My greatest intellectual debt is to Ndubuizu, the former Vice-Chancellor of Imo State University, with whom I had worked as an executive assistant. The knowledge I tapped from him regarding university education in Nigeria has informed this study in more ways than I can fully acknowledge.

Bowling Green State University (BGSU) Ohio was the place where this book began as a dissertation submitted in 2006. It was initiated under the leadership of my adviser, Dr. Apollos Nwauwa. My dissertation and this book were possible because of his competent advising and exceptionally perceptive, useful, and apt comments. This book profited from his tireless commitment to my success, and I will remain grateful to him. I would like to thank my committee members, Drs. Robert Buffington, Kefa Otiso, and Lillian Ashcraft-Eason, for assisting me throughout the period of my doctorate program beyond their duty. Special thanks are due to Buffington for reading different versions of the manuscript and offering insightful, candid criticism even after I had left BGSU. During the three years I spent at BGSU, I was blessed with Ms. DeeDee Wentland, the graduate secretary. DeeDee made the period of my graduate study worthwhile – and words are insufficient to express my gratefulness. My appreciation will be incomplete without acknowledging the support I received from Dr. Raphael Njoku from the time this project was conceived. His friendship, advice, and great insights about publishing empowered this book in many ways.

Immense appreciation and thanks are due to my chair, Dr. David Coleman, and my colleagues in the department of history at Eastern Kentucky University for creating an inspiring and conducive working environment that made this book possible. Of crucial importance to the completion of this book was Dr. Tom Appleton's assistance with my final revisions. Tom read the manuscript, made thoughtful recommendations, and responded generously to my request for his advice and time. I extend special thanks to my colleagues or mentors who made comments to papers or ideas that ultimately became part of this book: Drs. Todd Hartch, Liette Gidlow, 'Dimeji R. Togunde, Brad Wood, Ann O'Hear, Gloria Chukwu, John Lowry, Bruce MacLaren, Chris Taylor, Robert Weise, David Blaylock, Tom Otieno, Jennifer Spock, and Ebere Onwudiwe.

Over the period I worked on this book, I had the privilege of discussing many ideas surrounding social policies and politics in postcolonial Africa with Dr. Timothy Kiogora. His stalwart friendship, priceless suggestions, and exceptional insights about Africa have impacted this project significantly. For being generous with his time and serving as a dependable sounding board for my ideas and arguments, I thank him profoundly.

Material support for this research came from several sources. Initial funding came from BGSU, where I received graduate fellowship (2003–2006), non-service fellowship (fall 2005), Katzner and University Bookstore award (fall 2005), and history department grant (fall 2005). Additional funding came from Eastern Kentucky University, where I received the 2008 College of Arts and Sciences' Junior Faculty Summer Research Award, and the graduate college's University Research Committee Grants in 2006 and 2007. This book would have been impossible without the generous financial support I received from these institutions.

To gather material for this book, I travelled extensively for many years. A number of institutions, archives, and friends assisted me in this research. For their advice, interest, and help during the research stage of this book I am thankful to many. I thank Jane Gorjevsky, Curator, Carnegie Corporation Records (Columbia University Rare Book and Manuscript Library), Mrs. Constance Nnadi and staff of the National Universities Commission; staff of the Committee of Vice-Chancellors office, National Archives in Ibadan, Enugu, and Kaduna, the Federal Ministry of Education, Abuja, Arewa House, Kaduna, and Office of Statistics, Lagos. I owe my deepest gratitude to Mr. Kehinde Taiwo and Mrs. Chioma Irechukwu, both of Federal Radio Corporation of Nigeria, for making available their support in a number of ways. Their unflagging courtesy, hospitality, financial, and logistical support during my research trips to Nigeria between 2005 and 2008 were of crucial importance to the timely completion of this book. In addition, this book would have been impossible without the support I received from the following during my research trips to Nigeria: Chijioke Anyanwu (my brother), Fabian Ohaegbu, Emma Okoroafor, Kene Anyanwu, Gerald Egbuchulam, Chibunken Uwaezuoke, Chukuwma Njoku, Mr. and Engr (Mrs.) Okengwu, and Mode Anyanwu. It is also a pleasure to acknowledge those who contributed directly or indirectly to make this book possible. They include Nkeiru and Uzoma Esi, Edith and Chucks Onyeka, Chidinma Anyanwu-Ike, Chidi Alino, Dr. Lawrence Anyanwu, David and Stacy Bartholomew, Ms. Tina M. Thomas, Dr. Emma Lazarus, Festus Lazarus, Engr. Sam Lazarus, Camille Rogers, Michael Kithinji, Charles Ukanwa, and Edward Ekeanyanwu.

To the anonymous readers who reviewed the manuscript for the University of Calgary Press, I am grateful for your valuable comments and suggestions on the final drafts. I also want to convey my fathomless appreciation to the staff of the University of Calgary Press, particularly Donna Livingstone, for their enthusiastic support and professionalism. I am very appreciative of John King for editing this manuscript with care and intelligence.

An earlier version of chapter 2, entitled "The Anglo-American-Nigerian Collaboration in Nigeria's Higher Education Reform: The Cold War and Decolonization, 1948-1960," was published in the *Journal of Colonialism and Colonial History* 11, no. 3 (Winter 2010): 1–26. Reprinted with permission of The Johns Hopkins University Press. Copyright 2010 Ogechi Anyanwu and The Johns Hopkins University Press.

An earlier version of chapter 4 appeared as "Experiment with Mass University Education in Post-Civil War Nigeria, 1970–1979," in the *Journal of Nigerian Studies* 1, no. 1 (Fall 2010): 1–36. Reprinted with permission of the Nigeria Studies Association (North America) and the University of New Hampshire.

Finally, as always, I am eternally indebted to my wife, Chidinma, and daughters, Uchechi, Ozioma, and Amarachi, for their understanding and encouragement, and, more importantly, for accepting more than their fair share of family responsibilities in order to give me ample time to complete this book. I love them exceedingly.

Introduction

Background

Access to university education in Africa was inadequate during the colonial period. At independence, however, African countries departed from the elitist colonial education system by embarking on programs aimed at providing education to all, regardless of class, ethnicity, gender, or creed. Nowhere in Africa has the question of access to university education reached such a crescendo of concern and posed such a challenge to the polity than in Nigeria. This book constitutes a history of the policies and politics surrounding the push for mass university education (massification) in postcolonial Nigeria. The concept of massification as used in this study refers to Nigeria's postcolonial shift from elitist university educational system to mass education. As the most populous, oil-rich nation in Africa, with a protracted ethnic and religious conflict between the predominantly Muslim North and Christian South, the push for mass university education is central to understanding Nigeria's postcolonial socio-economic and political history. This book argues that the premise of building a modern Nigerian nation underscored the pursuit of mass university education policies by Nigeria's successive postcolonial governments. It shows the centrality of a vision of university education to the "nationalist project" in Nigeria and demonstrates that the move to mass university education was an essential social imaginary for Nigeria's vision of itself as a modern, dynamic nation state.

Through analysis of the politics that drove the massification agenda, this study bridges and recasts scholarly understanding of the challenges of national integration and socio-economic development in Nigeria's pluralistic society. It accounts for, and provides new insights on, how internal religious and ethnic/regional politics in Nigeria coalesced with external interests to shape policy initiatives on mass university education and the shifts and outcomes of the country's education policies. In illuminating Nigeria's experiment with mass education, this book enhances our understanding of the difficulties of the country's postcolonial social engineering, as well as providing a valuable glimpse into some of the similar challenges facing African countries. If we are to grasp modern Nigeria, with its intractable tensions, as well as its political instability, we must understand the dynamics of higher education policies. Thus by exploring the nature, problems, and pitfalls of the shift towards a system of mass university education throughout its colonial configuration, the immediate postcolonial adjustments, and several years of transition of military, democratic, and neo-liberal leaderships, this book provides a window into the promise and problems of Nigeria itself.

The British establishment of the first university in Nigeria, the University College of Ibadan (UCI), in 1948 was a response to decades of nationalist demand for an institution of higher education in the country. Afraid of the potential threat that educated Africans would pose to the colonial system and mindful of the financial implications of establishing universities in the colonies, colonial authorities had opposed the idea of higher education training for colonial subjects. Charles Wood, president of the Board of Control (1853–55) and secretary of state of India (1859–66) set the tone for British colonial higher education policy. In a dispatch to F.J. Halliday, lieutenant governor of Bengal, Wood had bluntly delineated the logic that ultimately shaped British colonial higher education policy:

> I do not see the advantage of rearing up a number of highly educated gentlemen at the expense of the State, whom you cannot employ, and who will naturally become depositories of discontent. If they choose to train themselves, well and good, but I

am against providing our own future detractors and opponents and grumblers.¹

The end of Second World War marked a turning point in the history of higher education in Nigeria. As part of its postwar reconstruction and development agenda, Britain came to regard university education as an important instrument, not only in the social development of her colonies, but also in training future African leaders. Thus British colonial authorities set up the Asquith and Elliot commissions to advise it on how to meet its new education vision. These commissions submitted their reports in 1945. Following the broad principles outlined by the Asquith Commission and the recommendations of the Elliot Commission, UCI was established. UCI, along with other colonial university colleges, was established based on a erroneous premise that what was suitable for Britain equally applied to the colonies. In *Universities: British, Indian, African: A Study in the Ecology of Higher Education*, Eric Ashby, a British historian, writes that

> [the] underlying British enterprise in providing higher education for her people overseas was one massive assumption: that the pattern of university education appropriate for Manchester, Exeter and Hull was *ipso facto* appropriate for Ibadan, Kampala and Singapore. If we were going to export universities to our overseas dependencies they would of course be British universities, just as the cars we export there are British cars. As with cars, so with universities: we willingly made minor modifications to suit the climate, but we proposed no radical change in design; and we did not regard it as our business to inquire whether French or American models might be more suitable.²

Soon Nigerians were disappointed with Britain's wholesale exportation of their pattern of university education to Nigeria. With an annual intake of less than 130 students, a low rate of production of (admittedly) highly trained graduates for the public and private sectors, and a lopsided curriculum and enrolment, UCI failed to satisfy the higher education needs of most Nigerians. Nationalists such as Nnamdi Azikiwe and Obafemi Awolowo thus rejected the elitist and conservative traditions of UCI and not only demanded changes in the institution's curriculum and admission policies but also intensified their push for decolonization. It was not surprising, therefore, that when Nigeria gained independence in 1960, policy-makers reconfigured university education to fulfill a new mission: the mission of nation-building and socio-economic development. Like in other African countries, colonial rule impoverished Nigeria, limiting social amenities, mobility, and economic opportunities, as well as deliberately creating discord in the country's pluralistic society. "The fundamental challenge facing universities in a postcolonial setting," as Oluwasanmi puts it, "is that of development, of bringing social and economic change rapidly into a situation which has been deprived for so long."[3] Understanding these problems and proffering solutions to them became a new task for postcolonial African universities. This book argues that attempts to engage university education to promote nation-building and facilitate socio-economic development largely shaped the shifts towards mass university education in postcolonial Nigeria.

Unlike the colonial period, the driving force behind Nigeria's postcolonial university education was hinged on Robbins's principle that "courses of higher education should be available to all who are qualified by ability and attainment to pursue them and who wish to do so."[4] Thus, the most dominant theme in the history of postcolonial university education in Nigeria is what Martin Trow, a sociologist, called the shift from elite to mass higher education.[5] Conceptually, Nigeria's massification agenda was an amalgam of three broad policies instituted by the federal government and its component units to reorganize its university education system in response to the needs of postcolonial Nigeria. First, it involved the expansion of access to university education through the establishment of more universities, the diversification of university curriculum, the centralization of university control, and the involvement of the private sector in the supply of university education. The idea was to train the country's labour force, especially in the sciences, not only to fill the vacancies created by the departing Europeans, but also to help champion future economic development and national integration.

Second, massification involved the liberalization of access to university education through measures such as state control of admission process to eliminate admission bottlenecks, the revision of the rigid British entry qualifications, the awarding of scholarships, and the granting of free university education. The purpose was to remove the historical and structural obstacles that had impeded access to university education in the colonial era. Third, massification involved the democratization of access through equal geographical distribution of universities and the introduction of an affirmative action policy (quotas) in university admission. The aim was to end the volatile and divisive educational disparity between the North and the South through equal representation of all ethnic groups in the existing institutions. The postcolonial policies of expansion, liberalization, and democratization aimed at mass university education. Although the goal of mass education was not met, these policies represented a radical departure from the elitist colonial system of higher education, which was inequitable and unrepresentative.

Education for Nation-Building

The philosophy of using mass university education to promote nation-building in Nigeria's pluralistic society was one that postcolonial governments embraced. They sought to create a nation in a society where ethnic/religious diversity, conflict, and competition had deprived it of a national identity. A nation can be viewed as a political arrangement and a cultural phenomenon aimed at developing the state. It is, according to Ernest Renan, "a soul and a spiritual principle," constituting both the past and the present, and renewing itself especially in the "present by a tangible deed: the approval, the desire, clearly expressed, to continue the communal life." For Renan, the "existence of a nation is an everyday plebiscite; it is, like the very existence of the individual, a perpetual affirmation of life."[6] Nation-building was not a factor in formulating colonial educational policies. Independence, however, created new realities and needs. Transforming the British educational system thus became necessary to meet those needs. Emile Durkheim, a French sociologist, argued that "In order for people to feel at any particular moment in time the need to change its educational system, it is necessary that new ideas and needs have emerged in which the former system is no longer adequate."[7] The broad framework for a shift in educational policy in Africa materialized in 1962 when a conference on

Development of Higher Education in Africa was held in Malagasy Republic between 3 and 12 September. Endorsing the role of universities in nation-building, the conference declared,

> African institutions of higher learning have the duty of acting as instruments for the consolidation of national unity. This they can do by resolutely opposing the efforts of tribalism and encouraging exchanges, and by throwing open the university to all students who show capacity to benefit from a university education of internationally acceptable academic standards, and by resolutely ignoring ethnic or tribal origins and political and religious discrimination.[8]

According to Richard Sklar, nation-building is a process of creating "higher loyalties that supersede parochial loyalties to subnational communities, tribes, language groups, or regions."[9] Among other things, it involves "the progressive reduction of cultural and regional tensions and discontinuities on the horizontal plane in the process of creating a homogenous territorial political community."[10] Ethnicity is "the employment or mobilization of ethnic identity and difference to gain advantage in situations of competition, conflict or cooperation."[11] Ethnicity has been "the most formidable barrier to national unity in Africa. Nearly every African state has at least one serious problem of ethnic or regional separatism."[12] Nigeria's multi-ethnic society presented a huge challenge and potential at its independence in 1960. The challenge was how to promote collective consciousness among its diverse groups in order to realize its great potentials. University education was identified as a force in uniting Nigerians in a common conscience. Durkheim stated that every society "considered at a given stage of development, has a system of education which exercises an irresistible influence on individuals."[13] Durkheim's model of nation-building posits that a society consists of individuals who are united in a *collective conscience* through the common values, norms, and rules that are partly transmitted through school. As Durkheim further noted, "Society can survive only if there exists among its members a sufficient degree of homogeneity by fixing in the child, from the beginning, the essential similarity that collective life demands."[14] Nigerian universities in a postcolonial setting were meant to reflect the nation-building process and equally contribute to it by supplying the knowledge that would constitute the basis for creating a national identity; for according to Durkheim, "it is the society as a whole and each particular social milieu that determine the ideal that education realizes."[15]

One of the most common sources of conflict between the South and the North was the educational disparity between the two areas. This gap, which began to appear in the 1840s when Christian missionaries introduced Western education to the country, widened throughout the colonial period. Due to geographical, political, and religious factors, as discussed in chapter 1, the North fell behind in Western education. The statistics of regional enrolment at UCI during the colonial period favoured southerners. For instance, out of 939 students studying in the college between 1948 and 1959, southerners numbered 865 with only 74 northerners.[16] As southerners continued to outnumber northerners in school enrolment, mutual suspicion intensified. The British resisted the northerner's demand for an affirmative action policy that would help address the gap. Such an admission policy, as they believed, "might lower academic standards, not only in terms of quality of the student's entry but in terms of the work of the staff and students throughout the college."[17]

The North-South conflicts intensified in the 1950s when it became clear to the northern elite that the more educated southerners would likely dominate the political class after independence. As the editor of a northern newspaper, *Gaskiya Ta Fi Kwabo* decried, "In all the different departments of government it is the Southerner who has the power."[18] On the eve of independence, Nigerian nationalists saw higher education reforms as an opportunity to revise the elitist British higher education system by pushing not only for expansion of human resource training but also ways of addressing the volatile educational gap between the South and the North. Against the common tendency to examine Nigeria's mass education experiment as largely designed to train human resources to fill vacancies left behind by departing European administrators, this book offers a perspective that shows that mass university education policies constituted a central element in the government's policy of addressing the historical rivalries existing among the various ethnic groups in Nigeria.[19] It reveals how the ethno-regional tensions generated by the educational disparity between the two areas defined Nigeria's postcolonial higher education politics, making, for instance, the policy of affirmative action in university admission an inevitable, attractive, yet controversial tool in the push for university expansion as well as in the promotion of national unity. Here, politics, religion, and education intersect, shedding light on Nigeria's turbulent march to nationhood. So when the viability of the idea and ideal of the Nigeria nation was tested during the Nigerian Civil War (1967–70), building "the nation anew," as Gowon termed it, became the philosophical foundation for a renewed push for mass university education in the 1970s and 1980s.[20]

Education for Development

Successive governments in Nigeria subscribed to the human capital theory as part of the nation-building project and thus embarked on an ambitious investment in educational expansion. The human capital theory gained popularity in the postwar era as policy-makers, educationists and economists increasingly accepted education as a productive investment. The theory posits that economic development of a country is contingent on capital formation achievable through investment in human beings. By improving the quality of a workforce through educational expansion, the theory argues, a country increases the productivity of citizens and thus lays the foundation for socio-economic development.[21] According to Harbison, "Education does contribute to growth but growth also makes it possible to expand and develop education. It is both the flower and the seed of economic development."[22] As many scholars have shown, human capital theory presumes that investment in education is a prerequisite to both modernization and economic growth of any society.[23] The idea that investment in education is rewarding, explains, according to Fagerlind and Saha, large government expenditure on education in both developing and developed countries.[24] A country's human resources decide the nature and pace of its socio-economic development, and, as Psacharopoulos and Woodhall state, they constitute

> the ultimate basis of wealth of nations. Capital and natural resources are passive factors of production, human beings are the active agencies who accumulate capital, exploit natural

resources, build social, economic and political organization, and carry forward national development.[25]

Postcolonial African countries, including Nigeria, anchored their mission of university education partly on the theory of human capital. This mission departed significantly from the narrow, elitist vision that characterized European higher education policy during the colonial period.[26] Access to university education in Africa was inadequate during the colonial period. Colonial authorities accorded low priority to university education because they failed to see it as an investment.[27] They were afraid of the implications of widespread production of highly educated Africans and therefore focused on training few Africans who would assist them in administering their colonies as well as occupy leadership positions after independence. Thus the admission criteria were intentionally rigorous, and, as Ashby notes, it was "more exacting than those for the universities in Scotland and Ireland, and much more exacting than the entry requirements for universities in America, Canada, and Australia."[28] To the disappointment of many Nigerians, between 1948 and 1959, only 939 students were in UCI while more than 1,911 Nigerians, who were considered unqualified by UCI standards, gained admission in American, Australian, European, and Canadian universities. The total graduates from UCI between 1950 and 1960 were only 615.[29] Worse still was the fact that course enrolment favoured liberal arts courses, neglecting courses closely aligned to the developmental needs of Nigerians, such as applied sciences, agriculture, and medical, technical, and vocational courses.[30]

The Nigerian situation was not unique; other African countries experienced similar problems. At the time of independence, only about one quarter of all professional civil service positions were held by Africans while foreigners dominated trade and industry throughout the continent.[31] Zambia, for instance, had only a hundred university graduates, while the University of East Africa that served Kenya, Tanzania, and Uganda – with a combined population of 23 million – produced only ninety-nine university graduates. At its independence in 1960, the Democratic Republic of Congo, formerly known as Zaire, had no indigenous graduate engineers, lawyers, or doctors. Few Africans were trained in agricultural science, a field most relevant to a continent known for subsistence farming. French colonies in Africa produced only four graduates in the field while there were 150 in English-speaking colonies.[32]

Since colonial university education failed to produce enough human resources to champion socio-economic transformation of the continent, independence presented African political elite with an opportunity to reconfigure university education to serve that societal need. The broad framework for a policy shift was also articulated in the 1962 conference on *Development of Higher Education in Africa*. The early 1960s was a period when many new states were emerging in Africa and thus participants at the conference focused on the new role university education would play. Faced with the choice of allowing universities to merely fulfill the narrow role that they performed in colonial Africa or take additional roles that radically distinguished them from other European institutions, as well as fit them "for greater service to the African Society," the conference declared that the "establishment and development of higher education facilities ... is basic to social and economic reconstruction of Africa."[33] It further declared that "in order to provide the high-level manpower that [Africa] will require in the process of social and economic development [they] ... will need, in the next twenty years, to increase many times the number of students in their universities."[34]

The place of education in Africa's socio-economic advancement is crucial and a host of scholars agree. In *Higher Education in Postcolonial Africa: Paradigms of Development, Decline and Dilemmas*, the authors "carefully packaged education as part of development, because this is what it really is."[35] Ashby sees universities as "absolutely essential to the economy and to the very survival of nations." He further notes that "under the patronage of modern governments, they are cultivated as intensive crops, heavily manured and expected to give a high yield to the nourishment of the state."[36] To Ajayi, university education is "a mechanism by which society generates the knowledge necessary for its own survival and sustenance, and transmits this to future generations through processes of instruction to the youth."[37] According to Chinweizu, African universities should "serve as finishing schools for those who have to lead and develop the traditions of a society."[38]

The expansion of university training had become crucial in Nigeria as early as 1957 when a constitutional conference in London established a national government and decided on 1 April 1960 as the tentative date for the country's independence. As Nigeria approached independence with only 939 students (excluding about 1,000 who were studying overseas) in UCI in 1959, nationalists blamed the college for insufficient training of the high-level human resources needed to replace the departing Europeans as well as to advance economic development. Aja Nwachuku, the federal minister of education, expressed the federal government's concern when he stated in 1959:

> If we are to approach independence with confidence and serenity, we must know that there will be adequate numbers of skilled technicians and of professional workers in all fields, who are aware and ready to accept the responsibilities attendant upon the attainment self-government.[39]

The ethos of realigning university education to address the economic challenges facing that postcolonial Nigeria was one that not only the Nigerian political elite embraced but also officials of the Carnegie Corporation, a leading philanthropic organization in the United States. Largely due to the perceived dilemma with maintaining costs and high academic standards, the colonial government had consistently resisted fundamental changes until the late 1950s when the seeming threat of the Soviet Union in Africa and the suspicion that African nationalists would seek assistance from the communists in their fight for independence opened up colonial minds to the necessity of change. The "wind of change" in the British colonies in Africa was uncontrollably fast in the postwar years. Britain's chances of maintaining friendly relations with African countries after independence would have suffered if it failed to support Nigeria's university reform.[40] Although the British were initially reluctant, the Carnegie Corporation's subtle and sustained pressure helped get the British involved in reforming the colonial education system.

Following the Second World War, Carnegie leadership believed that "a search for a new balance of power to offset the expansion of Russian influence" was America's role in the world.[41] The corporation's main mission therefore became "the effective propagation of the democratic and liberal ideals both in terms of its domestic and international connotations."[42] Led by Alan Pifer, a staff of Carnegie's international program dubbed British

Dominions and Colonies Program, and identifying Nigeria as a potential giant of Africa, Carnegie took advantage of the Cold War to advocate an alternative education system based on American models and values as a tool in containing the spread of communism in Africa.[43] Rebuffing the existing status quo in the colonies, Pifer called for expansion of all types and levels of education for Africans, especially in "agricultural, technical, and medical education and teacher training."[44] Although Pifer began his campaign in 1954, it was not until 1958 that Britain finally accepted a joint Nigerian-British-American commission to study Nigeria's higher education needs. The corporation financed the commission, named after the chair, Eric Ashby. The Ashby Commission submitted its report at Nigeria's independence in 1960; its far-reaching recommendations not only endorsed the link between university education and socio-economic development, but also provided Nigerian governments with a blueprint to guide their shift from an elite to a mass education system.[45]

Various studies by J.F. Ade Ajayi, Lameck K.H. Goma, and G. Ampah Johnson, Eric Ashby, and Apollos Nwauwa have masterfully highlighted the nationalists' demands for establishing institutions of higher learning in colonial Africa and the subsequent attempts to "Africanize" the inherited education system.[46] To extend these works, this book links a discussion of how the politics of postwar decolonization movements and the Cold War shifted Britain's long objections to higher education reform in Nigeria to attempts by nationalists to redesign the country's university system to serve the postcolonial need for rapid societal transformation. It shows how the domestic and international politics of the 1950s led to the coalescence of the interests of the Carnegie Corporation, Britain, and Nigeria, thereby laying the groundwork for Nigeria's future commitment to mass education.

Postcolonial commitment to socio-economic development facilitated university expansion not only in Nigeria but also in virtually all African countries. Demand for access to universities escalated. Enrolment surged. Financial resources were strained.[47] From less than a hundred thousand in the 1960s, students in higher education institutions in Africa increased to about 3.5 million in 2000.[48] Egypt tops the list with an enrolment figure of 1.5 million, representing an enrolment ratio of 5 per cent for the 18–22 age group. Nigeria comes second, followed by South Africa with total enrolment of about 1 million and half a million, respectively.[49] In 2009, sub-Saharan Africa alone had 4 million tertiary students. This growth, according to the World Bank, "represents one of the highest regional growth rates in the world for tertiary enrolments, averaging 8.7 per cent a year."[50] Inspired by the desire to promote economic development and often motivated by the country's oil wealth, successive Nigerian governments between 1960 and 2000 embarked on an unprecedented expansion of university education in that every four to five years in the 1960s, 1970s, and 1980s, enrolment in all the universities doubled (but slowed down in the 1990s due to economic decline).[51] Yet, the gross enrolment ratio for the 18–25 age group was approximately 5 per cent, slightly above the overall average enrolment ratio in Africa, which was 3 per cent.[52]

As this book demonstrates, the overall context of Nigerian economy and politics dictated continuities, discontinuities, and outcomes of mass university education policies. The need for rapid modernization of the economy shaped the emphasis on science and technology since independence, particularly from the 1960s to the early 1980s. This found expression in many official pronouncements. For instance, in his address at UCI (now University of Ibadan) in 1970, Yakubu Gowon, Nigeria's head of state, 1966–75, posed this challenge to Nigerian universities: "It is perhaps not too much to hope … that if it ever becomes necessary for the human race to transfer en masse to some other planets, like Mars, our scientists and technologists would be ready with the necessary means of transport for Nigerian citizens!"[53] While the sudden oil wealth of the 1970s and 1980s facilitated the proliferation of universities, official corruption, mismanagement of resources, and politicization of university education combined to truncate not only university expansion but also economic development.[54] Thus, the economic decline and political crisis of the late 1980s and 1990s diverted interests in university expansion as well as occasioned efforts by the military regimes to consolidate power at all cost while pursuing IMF/World Bank-sanctioned rationalization policies.

Organization

This book consists of seven chapters. Chapter 1 discusses the aims and objectives of Western education as conceived by the British colonial authorities, highlighting the multi-ethnic and religious settings in which Nigeria's quest for mass education emerged. It examines the forces responsible for the successful demand for the establishment of UCI in 1948, as well as the struggle to increase enrolment at the college. This chapter also gives a sense of how the disparities in school entrance between the South and the North exacerbated the existing regional tensions and rivalries, thereby making future consideration of affirmative action both unavoidable and contentious in Nigeria's nation-building project.

Due to their disappointment with the unmet demand for university education, nationalists, largely inspired by regional loyalties, campaigned for mass education and a reform of the elitist British higher education policies in Nigeria. Their demand received a boost from Carnegie Corporation officials, who campaigned for reforming the elitist British system of university education as a means of extending America's influence in Africa's emerging nations.

Chapter 2 shows how a combination of domestic and external forces resulted in the setting up of the Ashby Commission whose recommendations directed postcolonial Nigerian governments in their efforts to achieve national integration and socio-economic development in Nigeria through university expansion. As this chapter reveals, the coalescence of the interests of Carnegie, Britain, and Nigeria formed not only the cornerstone of a new era in Anglo-American collaboration in Nigerian higher education reform but also a prelude to Nigeria's postcolonial program to engage mass university education policies in the service of societal transformation.

Based on the recommendations of the Ashby Commission for "massive" and "unconventional" expansion of university education, the newly independent government, led by Alhaji Tafawa Balewa and with assistance from various international donors, embarked on the first push for mass university education, 1960–70. During this period, student enrolment in all the Nigerian universities jumped from 939 students to 9,695 students.[55] Chapter 3 discusses the aims and objectives of higher education as conceived by policy-makers during the first decade of Nigeria's independence, the expansion of facilities and access, and the ways in which regional rivalries, flawed admission policies, and the Nigerian civil war (1967–70) truncated university expansion.

In order to satisfy the rising demand for university education as well as to advance national unity after the civil war, the federal government, under the successive military regimes of Yakubu Gowon, Murtala Mohammed, and Olusegun Obasanjo, effectively took control of all the universities, federal and regional, in order to achieve uniform development. Chapter 4 shows how Nigeria's oil-rich economy and post-civil war reconciliatory mood shaped the unprecedented expansion of university education during the second push for mass education, 1970–79.

After thirteen years of military rule, a democratic government under President Shehu Shagari came to power in 1979. Eager to fulfill their electoral promises and keep Nigerians united, the newly elected officials at the federal and state levels, as chapter 5 shows, pushed for the liberalization and democratization of university education. In keeping with the vision of socio-economic development and nation-building, the Shagari administration established universities of science and technology, introduced free education and affirmative action, initiated the National Open University scheme, and allowed states to participate in educational expansion. Some of these policies were ambitious and in some ways controversial. They were made with the hopes that the increase in oil revenue will continue to generate revenue to funds these social programs. But the mismanagement of the economy and rampant corruption not only compromised mass education attempts but also threatened nation-building and economic development during the third attempt at mass university education, 1979–83.

Chapter 6 examines how the depressed economy inherited by the military regimes of Mohammed Buhari and Ibrahim Babangida required them to rethink educational expansion. Here, the premise of mass university education for nation-building and economic development faded, despite official government pronouncements to the contrary. Repositioning university education to aid economic recovery assumed great importance. This chapter shows how the involvement of the World Bank and the IMF in Nigeria's economic policies constrained the government to implement the highly consequential policy of rationalization during the fourth attempt at cautious massification, 1984–90.

After seven years of underfunding for the universities, Nigeria's oil revenue improved dramatically in 1990 because of the first Gulf War. Yet, efforts to address the question of mass university education, as chapter 7 demonstrates, were overshadowed by echoes of political instability and frequent changes of governments in the 1990s, coupled with the mismanagement of oil revenue during the fifth push for massification, 1990–2000. As the military governments wrestled with the tension generated by the surge in demand for university education, the radicalization of labour unions in the universities, and the controversy surrounding affirmative action, the deregulation of the university system seemed logical and attractive. Given the short supply of university places, the establishment of private universities, earlier resisted by various regimes in Nigeria, became "a normal and commendable supply response to a huge and growing demand for university education."[56] This chapter demonstrates that the emergence of private university education not only underscores the problems of public universities and the short supply of university education but also represents a new direction in the push for mass university education.

Faced with the challenge of promoting nation-building and socio-economic development, successive postcolonial governments in Nigeria had affirmed their commitment to mass university education. Still, there was a wide gulf between what was stated and what was practised and achieved. Although Nigerian governments often claimed success in the midst of policy failure, the 5 per cent enrolment ratio for the 18–22 age group in 2000, the sustained deterioration of universities facilities, the prevailing crisis of nationhood and economic development, the radicalization of anti-government academic unions in the universities, and the consequent instability in the system, especially in the 1980s and 1990s, eloquently shows that mass university education program failed to produce the intended outcomes. This work presents a picture of complex interlocking relationships between politics, economics and education in the push and outcomes of mass university education policies in postcolonial Nigeria. It is a compendium of useful information and insights into the many policy shifts and turns in the optimism and betrayal of Nigerian education. More importantly, it provides valuable insight into the challenges of nation-building in Nigeria's pluralistic society.

The Politics of Colonial Education

> The overriding complaint was that there was not enough education – of any kind – for the masses of the people. The key to the understanding of the whole problem of education in Africa is the appreciation of the fact that the whole region thirsts for knowledge. The wealthy and the poor, the aristocrats and the lowest peasants, Christians, Moslems and the "pagans" cry for it.
> – Kenneth O. Dike, 1962

Introduction

Nigeria's passion for higher education in the twentieth century was never in doubt; what was at issue was the provision of such education in sufficient quantities. Mass education was the priority neither of the European missionaries nor of the British colonial administrators. Consequently, throughout the colonial period, unmet demands for educational opportunities as well as the short supply of trained personnel for public and private sector services characterized British education policy. Dissatisfied with this situation, nationalists pushed not only for the expansion of primary and secondary school education but also demanded for an institution of higher learning in the country. Although a higher institution was established, access remained a problem. Besides, southerners outnumbered northerners in school enrolment, thus the existing mutual suspicion between the two areas. This chapter examines the origins and objectives of Western education during the colonial period, the forces leading to the successful demand for the establishment of the University College of Ibadan (UCI) in 1948, and the causes and implications of regional education imbalance. It shows how the short supply of university education and the tensions and conflicts generated by the educational disparity between the North and the South largely shaped Nigeria's postcolonial higher education politics, making a mass education program an attractive political tool in pursuing economic development and fostering national integration.

Western Education and the Making of Nigeria

Missionaries introduced Western education in Africa. Before the advent of Western education in Nigeria, two types of education systems existed: the traditional educational system transmitted informally through everyday living and the formal Islamic system that was introduced in the northern part of Nigeria as early as the fifteenth century. Under these systems, educational opportunity was open and available to all members of the society. Precolonial education "acted as an important method of transmission of cultural identity" and inculcated "in children the behavior and knowledge needed for the part they were to play in society."[1] As Paul Desalmand shows, precolonial education in Nigeria was provided by all members of the society; it was directly related to the needs of the society; and it was the concern of everyone and comprehensive in character.[2]

Intrinsically, indigenous education systems provided four basic educational competencies that UNESCO later adopted and promoted: learning to know, learning to do, learning to be, and learning to live together.[3] Intended to continue from 'womb to tomb,' they provided lower and higher levels of knowledge in history, identity, culture, and religion, among other areas, so as to develop the total personality of individuals from childhood to adulthood (learning to know and learning to be). In addition, they provided practical skills in agriculture, animal husbandry, hunting, and crafts, among others (learning to do). Finally, they inculcated a sense of civic duty in members of society for the sake of peace and order (learning to live together). However, the advent of Western education through European missionaries and mission schools in the 1840s changed the dynamics of the pre-existing education systems. Although those educational systems operated side by side with the Western system, over time the new education system, introduced by the missionaries and imposed on Nigeria by the British colonial government, came to become the foremost tool of social mobility.

Formal schools came into existence in Nigeria with the arrival of Thomas Birch Freeman in 1842.[4] Earlier, the Portuguese traders, who, in the early 1500s, visited Benin in southeast Nigeria, and São Thomé, off the coast of Nigeria, saw education as an important tool in the spread of Christianity. Missionaries who visited the Oba of Benin in 1515 taught his sons and the sons of other chiefs the Christian faith. The activities of missionaries during this period, however, were limited to a few trading centres, and with the growth of the transatlantic slave trade in the sixteenth and seventeenth centuries, "the legitimate trading centers declined and made no educational impact upon the people living in the interior of the country."[5] Missionary activity in Africa gathered momentum in the mid-nineteenth century as a by-product of the transatlantic slave trade. As part of the British strategy to stop the slave trade, Thomas Fowell Buxton, a prominent member of the British parliament and vice president of the Church Missionary Society (CMS), urged the cooperation of the government and the missionary societies in the 'deliverance' of Africa. As Buxton advocated,

> Let missionaries and schoolmasters, the plough and the spade, go together and agriculture will flourish; the avenues to legitimate commerce will be opened; confidence between man and man will be inspired; whilst civilization will advance as the natural effect and Christianity operate as the proximate cause, of this happy change.[6]

Largely influenced by Buxton's urging, European missionaries, traders, and explores flocked into Africa. By the mid-1800s, a number of missionary bodies had made inroads into Nigeria.[7] Eager to convert the natives to Christianity, these missionary bodies established schools in which they emphasized religious instruction. As Father Wauter, a Catholic missionary in Western Nigeria, pointedly stated, "We knew the best way to make conversion in 'pagan' countries was to open school.... So, when the district of Ekiti-Ondo was opened ... we started schools even before there was any church or mission house."[8] Because the natives could not read or write in English, the establishment of schools became a priority for European missionaries, and, as Elias Shrent, a missionary, puts it, "I have a low opinion of Christians who are not able to read their bible."[9] Inspired by the calling to spread Christianity, missionaries encouraged a policy of conversion through village schools. Admission to mission schools usually led to the conversion of the pupils to the new religion.

The curriculum of mission schools emphasized the four *R*s (religion, reading, writing, and arithmetic) and therefore produced "the much needed evangelists, clerks and teachers for the colonial society."[10] Mostly, the education provided by the missionaries was not relevant to the immediate needs of the people. In the report of the Phelps-Stocks commission on education in Africa, Thomas Jesse Jones states that missionary education failed to "realize the full significance of education in the development of the African people." He further states that, in "limiting education to class room instruction in book, missionaries were following the ideals prevailing in their home country ... [and] have therefore been strangely indifferent to the economic value of agriculture, and little concerned with the health and morals of the people."[11] Yet, the missionaries laid the foundation for both the future development of education and the emergence of the political elite in Nigeria, a fact that many scholars recognize. In *Christian Missions in Nigeria, 1841–1891*, Ajayi thoroughly discusses the role played by missionaries in the spread of Christianity and Western education in Nigeria, especially in the south. These missionaries, as Ajayi stresses, shaped the emergence of a new class and therefore played a critical role in the country's political history.[12] According to him, "in their linguistic and educational work, in their economic policies, and above all, in the class of Western-educated they were seeking to create, [missionary] influence covered the whole country."[13] British consuls, who had increasingly established effective political control of the region, modified or broadened the educational curriculum of mission schools to suit colonial objectives.

The establishment of colonial administration in Nigeria began shortly after the Berlin Conference of 1884–85. Britain had acquired political influence in many parts of Nigeria through treaties of protection with local rulers and later through conquest. Before 1900, the British had carved out the following territories in Nigeria: the Colony and Protectorate of Lagos (1886); the Niger Coast Protectorate (1893); and the Northern Protectorate (1900). In 1906, the Niger Coast Protectorate merged with the Colony and Protectorate of Lagos to become the Southern Protectorate. Modern Nigeria came into existence in 1914 when the British amalgamated the diverse peoples in the Southern and Northern Protectorates in an artificial political entity called Nigeria. A modern nation-state was born, composed of more than 250 ethnic groups, with diverse religions, languages, and cultures. Sir Frederick Lugard emerged as the first governor-general (1914–19). The unification of these two areas was not borne out of pressure from the local political groups. It was more or less an attempt to create a modern Nigeria for Britain's administrative convenience. As Osadolor states,

> Lugard considered it unnecessary to carve up a territory undivided by natural boundaries, more so since one portion (the South) was wealthy enough to commit resources to even "unimportant" programmes while the other portion (the North), could not balance its budget necessitating the British taxpayer being called upon to bear the larger share of even the cost of its administration. This partly explains the amalgamation, an act which provoked bitter controversy at the time, arousing the resentment of educated elites and of some British administrators. It, nevertheless, saddled the country with an issue – the relationship between North and South – that has dominated its politics to this day.[14]

The political, social, economic, and even educational problems that dominated Nigeria's history since the amalgamation of 1914 came to be dubbed "The National Question." This question, as the postcolonial governments articulated, was concerned "with the problems that arise when a country, such as Nigeria, is made up of many language/ethnic groups that are at different levels of development hence the need to solve these problems, and find an equitable basis for the peaceful and harmonious co-existence of these groups."[15] That process was not easy and many Nigerians saw the union as a mistake; prominent among them was Tafawa Balewa, who later became the country's first prime minister. In a statement on the floor of the Federal House of Representatives, Lagos, Balewa declared that "Since the amalgamation of southern and northern provinces in 1914, Nigeria has existed as one country only on paper.... It is still far from being united. Nigerian unity is only a British intention for the country."[16] Obafemi Awolowo, leading southern nationalists, echoed Balewa's sentiment when he wrote that "Nigeria is not a nation. It is a mere geographical expression. There are no 'Nigerians' in the same sense there are 'English' or 'Welsh' or 'French'. The word Nigeria is merely a distinctive appellation to distinguish those who lived within the boundaries of Nigeria from those who do not."[17]

Having effectively established a colonial government, the control of education became crucial in administering Nigeria. Colonial authorities initially allowed missionaries to dominate the education sector, but they increasingly came to understand the importance of consolidating imperial rule through education. This meant direct government involvement. Accordingly, the British promulgated the 1882 Colonial Educational Ordinance for West Africa (revised in 1887 and 1905). The education ordinance stipulated, among other things, that "the subject of teaching shall be the reading and writing of the English language."[18] It regulated educational activities and practices in Nigeria and provided the colonialists with the opportunity to justify colonialism, which included bringing to the colonized people the "blessings of civilization" and creating a body of literate, obedient, organized, and productive natives who would be indispensable in the exploitation of Nigeria's resources. In addition to the religious instruction provided by missionary education, the British encouraged the reading and writing of the English language, which they considered a proper medium of communication and reporting to the imperial government as well as a powerful tool for cultural assimilation. Other subjects included arithmetic and British history and geography. The British educational philosophy sought to create a group of Nigerians sufficiently literate and skilled to achieve further integration of the colonized into the mainstream of the colonial economy and administration as clerks, messengers, and interpreters. A British educator, H.S. Scott, stated that the government's view of education was creating "useful citizens," which means "literally citizens who would be of use to us. The conception was one of exploitation and development for the benefit of the people of Great Britain – it was to this purpose that such education as given was directed."[19]

Due financial constraints as well as traditions obtainable in Europe, both the missionaries and colonial authorities did not invest in educational expansion in response to many Nigerians who yearned for Western education. In a letter in which he complained about the depressing nature of his work, a CMS mission secretary wrote:

> My work is pathetic in the extreme low, in one aspect: almost every week I have to turn away deputations from both near and distant begging us to come teach them.[20]

Meanwhile, the division of Nigeria into three unequal regions in 1939 by Henry Bourdillon, Nigeria's governor-general between 1935 and 1940, set the stage for conflict between the North and the South. For administrative purposes, Bourdillon divided the country into Northern, Western, and Eastern regions, with Lagos as the administrative centre. The boundaries of these regions were conterminous with the three largest ethnic groups: the northern region with the Hausa-Fulani, the western region with the Yoruba, and the eastern region with the Igbo. The deficiencies in this division marked the beginning of the fear of domination that characterised Nigeria's political history and mostly reinforced by the educational disparity between the predominantly Christian South and the Muslim North. The North had 729,815 square kilometres of territory and about 16.8 million people. The figures for the other regions were as follows: the east had 119,308 sq km and 7.9 million people; the west contained 117,524 sq km and about 6.1 million people. Lagos was 70 sq km and 273,000 people. As these figures show, the North held 75 per cent of the land mass as well as 54 per cent of the population. Because the North was bigger than the two other regions put together (as shown in Map 1), southern elites feared potential northern domination after independence: hence the unavoidable regional rivalry, a situation for which the British bear primary responsibility. As Apollos Nwauwa puts it, "While it could be said that under British rule efforts toward unity were begun with the formation of Nigeria on the outbreak of World War 1, paradoxically, it was the same British who sowed

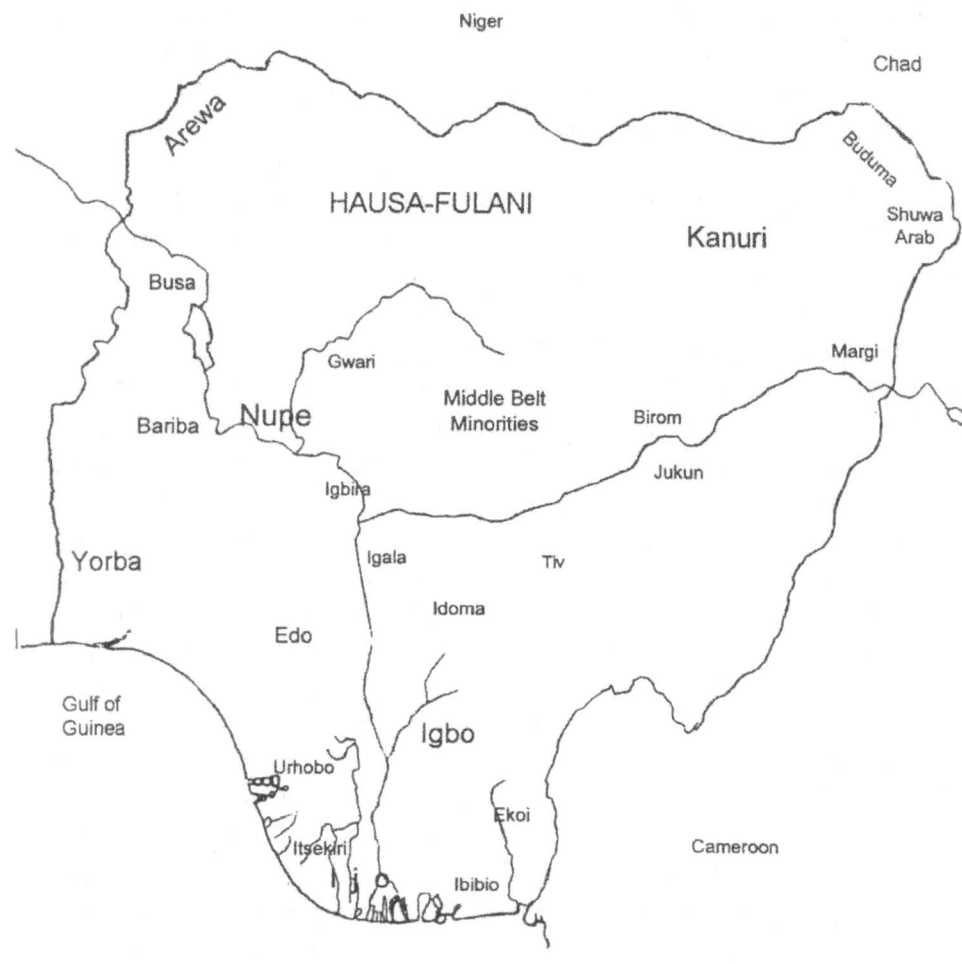

Map of Nigeria showing major ethnic groups.
(Courtesy of R.C. Njoku.)

the seeds of disunity when [they] divided Nigeria into the three unequal and ill-fated regions."[21]

The geographical, political, and religious factors that shaped the history of educational development in Nigeria laid the foundation to the North-South educational gap. According to Dike, this disparity "has been the result of the differences in timing and intensity of impact of modern education on the two sections of the country."[22] Missionaries first settled in the coastal regions in the south before they moved into the interior. While southerners were the first to embrace Christianity and Western education, northerners pursued Islamic/Arabic education and in many cases resisted the new education, a situation that was worsened by the Puddah system in the North where women and girls were deprived of access to Western education.[23] However, Islamic schools had provided a source of learning for Muslims for centuries before European incursion in Africa. In 1900 when the Protectorate of Northern Nigeria was established, there were, according to Lord Lugard, about 250,000 students in the 20,000 Koranic schools.[24]

Although proximity to the coast gave southerners advantage in educational attainment over northerners, "the more important factor was the hostility of the natural rulers of the North to Christian teaching and the Western type of education, and the British policy of supporting them in this opposition."[25] Throughout the colonial period, missionaries controlled primary and secondary education. According to Coleman, "As late as 1942, they controlled 99 percent of the schools, and more than 97 percent of the students in [Africa] were enrolled in mission school."[26] Given the missionary hold on education, the spread of Christianity and Western education became interwoven. Murray brilliantly summarized it in *The School in the Bush* thus,

> To all intents and purposes the school is the Church. Right away in the bush or in the forest the two are one, and the village teacher is also the village evangelists. An appreciation of this fact is cardinal in all considerations of African education.[27]

The "general antipathy for Western-style education" among the predominantly Muslim North created and maintained the educational gap between the two areas, especially since Western education not only became the yardstick to measure individual achievements but also a model for future socio-political development in colonial and postcolonial Nigeria.[28] Of course, the North would have been educationally advantaged than the south, had Islamic education been adopted as the only means of social mobility in Nigeria. There were 1,100 primary school pupils in the North in 1914 while the south had 35,700. As pressure for educational opportunities in the south increased in the 1920s, many community and private schools emerged, largely financed by local contributions. As shown in Tables 1.1 and 1.2, in spite of having more population than the other regions combined, the northern region had far less community schools. This is because southerners not only embraced mission education but also raised money to build schools in order to supplement the limited education provided by the missionaries. Northerners, on the other hand, saw no reason for that. In "Educational Imbalance: Its Extent, History, Dangers and Correction in Nigeria," Jubril Aminu, a former executive secretary of the Nigerian Universities Commission (NUC) and federal minister of education sums the major cause of the North-South educational gap thus:

> The first and foremost cause is the fact that Western Education came much earlier in the South than in the North. Even in the South, the early efforts were made by Christian Missionaries. The concomitant proselytizing activities of those educationists rendered them unacceptable in the Muslim North.[29]

In his desire to forestall potential conflict between mission schools and the Muslim North, Lord Lugard pledged (at the inauguration of the Protectorate of Northern Nigeria on 1 January 1900) to abide by the agreement with the emirs that included, among other things, preventing missionary work in the North.[30] This policy remained for much of the colonial period, and even when the government established experimental schools in the North, the pace of growth was slow. The schools were open only to the sons of chiefs. These schools, the colonists hoped, would help "turn out future [northern] leaders" who would be instrumental in the successful implementation of British indirect rule.[31]

Table 1.1: Ethnic/Community Schools Up to 1969.

Period	Northern Region	Eastern Region	Western Region	Mid-West Region	Total
Up to 1959	3	11	15	1	30
1960–69	10	12	13	2	37
Total	13	23	28	3	67

Source: J.M. Kosemani, "The Ethnic Factor in Educational Disparity in Nigeria," *Bensu Journal of Education* 3, no. 1 (1992): 15.

Table 1.2: Private Schools in Nigeria Up to 1969.

Period	Northern Region	Eastern Region	Western Region	Mid-West Region	Total
Up to 1959	2	9	9	5	25
1960–69	0	10	24	15	49
Total	2	19	33	20	74

Source: J.M. Kosemani, "The Ethnic Factor in Educational Disparity in Nigeria," *Bensu Journal of Education* 3, no. 1 (1992): 16a.

Given the educational disparity, regional competition and conflict was inevitable. As early as 1944, the *Daily Service* newspaper predicted "an era of wholesome rivalry" among the dominant ethnic groups: Igbo, Yoruba, and Hausa.[32] Adeyemo Alakija, the president of the Egbe Omo Oduduwa (a pan-Yoruba organization in the west), in a direct declaration of what he saw as the Yoruba role in Nigerian politics, noted in 1948 a great future for Yoruba children in which "they will hold their own among other tribes of Nigeria" and resist being "relegated to the background in the future."[33] Similarly, on the anticipated role of the Igbos, Nnamdi Azikiwe urged them not to shrink from their responsibility as leaders.[34] The Hausa ethnic group in the North similarly expressed apprehension over the likely domination of the more-educated Christian south, comprising the east and west. Abubakar Tafawa Balewa, who later became the first prime minister of independent Nigeria, expressed concern over steady migration of southerners to the North, whose presence he believed threatened to displace northerners in the colonial civil service.[35] Because southerners had more Western-educated people, the editor of the *Gaskiya Ta Fi Kwabo* newspaper warned against early independence for Nigeria. According to the paper, if the British granted Nigeria early independence, southerners would dominate the country:

> It is the southerner who has the power in the north. They have control of the railway stations; of the Post Offices; of Government Hospitals; of the canteens; the majority employed in the Kaduna Secretariat and in the Public Works Department are all Southerners.[36]

Development of Higher Education

West African intellectuals such as Edward Blyden, James Horton, J.E. Casely-Hayford, and Nnamdi Azikiwe had been demanding the establishment of universities in Africa since the second half of the nineteenth century.[37] Except for Fourah Bay College in Sierra Leone, founded by the Church Missionary Society in 1827 to train Africans as schoolmasters, catechists, and clergymen, nothing was done until 1934 when Yaba Higher College, a vocational institution, was established in Nigeria.[38] The British hoped the institution would train Nigerians to meet the need for a lower cadre of officials for the colonial service. Admission to Yaba was accordingly dependent on the availability of positions in the civil service. The college offered courses in engineering, medicine, agriculture, education, and arts, leading to diploma awards. Since the college did not award degrees, the promotion opportunities of its graduates were limited. Because graduates of the college were rated as inferior in terms of income and rank, nationalists attacked the college, and, according to Dike, they did not regard the institution "as an adequate answer to their higher education aspirations."[39] Nationalists therefore intensified their demands for a degree-awarding institution in the colony similar to those available in England – to obtain degrees that they hoped would qualify them for senior service positions.

As Kenneth Mellanby recalled, Nigerians showed passionate desires "to be given the opportunity to qualify for senior service posts."[40]

Despite the demands for a local university in Africa, Britain did not immediately change its policy for strategic and practical reasons. First, the British sought to avoid producing graduates who would demand to occupy the few available higher posts in government. As Lord Hailey stressed, "The considerations which decide the character of higher education are largely political, for the type of instruction given depends on the view held of the place in society which the educated African may be expected to fill."[41] Since there were few positions for African fill, it did not make sense for the British to produce educated men who would become, as Charles Wood bluntly stated, "depositories of discontent ... detractors and opponents and grumblers."[42]

Under the system of indirect rule, introduced by the British to govern their colonies in Africa, there was no place for highly educated Nigerians. The system of indirect rule, especially before the Second World War, involved the retention of the traditional pre-colonial political institutions, utilizing 'illiterate' indigenous rulers in governance while excluding highly educated Nigerians who had obtained their degrees abroad. Bad blood ensued. European visitors to Nigeria commented on the tension and animosity between colonialists and Nigerians who had obtained higher education overseas. According to one observer, the relationship was "delicate and difficult."[43] Likewise, Charles Roden Buxton, an English philanthropist and politician, stated that "Few white people have a good word to say for the educated Africans."[44] This situation was not surprising. Since British policy alienated educated Nigerians, they strongly opposed colonialism, and colonial officials had good reasons to dread them, especially the so-called 'radicals' who received higher education training in the United States. As James Coleman confirmed, "It was the educated who ... provoked disturbances in the provinces, published vituperative articles in the local press, and made life miserable and insecure for British administrators. There was nothing a district officer, a resident, or a governor dreaded more than political disturbances and unrest during his tour of duty."[45] In these circumstances, colonial authorities frowned on the idea of establishing universities in Nigeria to either train or to expand the educated elite, as the nationalists demanded. Given the strong opposition to the colonial government emanating from the educated elite, "the expansion of the educated class remained an anathema."[46]

Second, the colonial director of education, E.R.J. Hussey, did not want to hurry the establishment of universities in the colonies in order to maintain the high standard of British higher education. Instead, he proposed a three-stage scheme in the 1930s: the production of candidates for available positions in the public and private sector by West African colleges; the later affiliation of these colleges with an English university for the purpose of granting external degrees; and, finally, the granting of local autonomy to the colleges. Consideration of academic standards underscored this proposal. As Hussey declared, "We must at all cost avoid giving what we proclaim to be a university degree unless we can safeguard standards."[47]

Third, faced with the economic recession of the 1930s, the British, who had not provided adequate funding to Yaba, could not contemplate shouldering the additional financial burden of another higher education institution. In the 1930s, the return that the British government obtained from Nigeria's primary products was extremely low, and there were very limited funds available for other development projects. In fact, during the Second World War, a lack of sufficient funds compelled the British to reduce their funding allocations to Yaba while many members of the institution's slender staff were conscripted for war service. Worse of all, in 1939, the army took over Yaba's buildings and converted them to a military hospital. As a result, the engineering students moved to the CMS Grammar School (equivalent to a secondary school in the United States) in Lagos, while other departments relocated to Achimota College, in the Gold Coast (now Ghana).[48] Faced with resource constraints, establishing a university in Nigeria was the least priority of the British. Many Nigerians to their frustration travelled overseas for university training.[49]

Last, another common excuse in objecting to establishing universities in the colonies was the slow expansion of primary and secondary school education in most territories since the 1900s. West African governors had insisted that the pyramidal growth of primary and secondary education should be accomplished first before a university was contemplated.[50] In contrast, however, the report submitted to the Advisory Committee on Education in the Colonies (ACEC) in 1940 by the Mouat Jones subcommittee that reviewed the recommendations of West African governors stated that university education should progress together with other lower levels of education. Employing the analogy of a volcano that "built up its cone in all stages at once," the sub-committee stressed the relationships between primary, secondary, and university educational structures.[51] In December 1940, the ACEC endorsed the recommendations of the Mouat Jones sub-committee and asked the secretary of state to appoint a commission to review the university question. This step was a turning point in Africa's education development and occurred in the context of the Second World War. In fact, as Nwauwa notes, "from the late November 1942, when Allied victory became more likely, colonial development and welfare programmes were revived along with the university question."[52] Britain had finally realized that it needed to establish a university to facilitate the training of leaders in the colonies who would carry out colonial development schemes that, according to Oliver Stanley (the secretary of state for the colonies between 1942 and 1945), had suffered due to shortage of trained personnel.[53]

Second World War politics shaped Britain's overseas higher education policies. Britain needed the continued support from its colonies to wage a successful war against Nazism and Fascism and thus decided to embark on social programs designed to appease the increasingly agitated nationalists in the colonies who yearned not only for the establishment of institutions of higher learning but also for socio-economic development. In effect, the British Parliament passed the Colonial Development and Welfare Act in 1940 that aimed at addressing, among other things, the long-felt educational needs of its colonies. Supporting the initiative, Malcolm MacDonald, a member of the British parliament and later secretary of state for the colonies between 1938 and 1940, noted the contributions of overseas colonies in the Second World War "by gifts of treasure, by production of essential foodstuffs and raw materials, and by the eager raising of Colonial military units far in excess of anything that they did at a similar period in the last war."[54] In a sense, the Act sought to appease the colonies notwithstanding MacDonald's insistence that it was not "a bribe or reward for the colonies' support in this supreme crisis."[55]

In line with the new colonial attitude occasioned by the Second World War, the British appointed the Elliot and Asquith Commissions in 1943 to examine the university question for Africans. The reports of both commissions appeared simultaneously in 1945 and addressed various aspects of the university question; they constituted the blueprint for the development of university education in Nigeria as well as in other British colonies. The Asquith Commission, appointed to articulate the fundamental principles needed to guide the promotion of teaching and research in higher education and the development of university colleges in the British colonies, called for the creation of universities overseas to produce local leaders as a precondition for independence. It recommended a residential university college in a special relationship with the University of London and insisted on high academic standards in student admissions and staffing.[56] Anticipating the eventual independence of the British colonies overseas, the commission hoped the institution would help "produce men and women with the standards of public service and capacity for leadership which self-rule required."[57]

While the Asquith report supported the idea of developing higher education in Africa in anticipation of imminent independence, it did not view full independence as imminent. Even though the British encouraged constitutional developments in Nigeria from 1946 to 1954 with the purpose of granting self-government, they did not anticipate the immediate independence of Nigeria. Thus, it would be quite deceptive to equate self-government, as conceptualized by the British, with full independence. In the British tradition, internal self-government or responsible government meant government with full responsibility for local affairs. This explains why as late as 1955, the British Cabinet, troubled by the political implications of the terms 'self-government' and 'independence,' resolved that the term 'self-government' should be used in all references to the constitutional development of the colonies, stating that the term "independence in this context should be discontinued."[58] Clearly, the British were playing games in the face of U.S. and UN disapproval of imperialism as the Cold War heated up.

The Elliot Commission, on the other hand, had a limited mandate. Unlike the Asquith Commission, the Elliot Commission was established to "report on the organization and facilities of the existing centers of higher education in British West Africa and make recommendations regarding future university development in that area."[59] The commission acknowledged that "the need for educated Africans in West Africa in general already far outruns the supply, present and potential."⁶⁰ To this end, it specifically recommended the establishment of a university in Nigeria whose students would obtain degrees from the University of London.⁶¹ However, the commission did not envisage mass university education, as was the practice in Europe; instead, they espoused education for the few who would take over leadership positions at independence. The minority members of the Elliot Commission, Julian Huxley and Creech Jones, were even more conservative and short-sighted when they insisted that there would be enough students for only one university in the whole British West Africa.⁶²

The report issued by the Elliot Commission was a turning point in Nigeria's higher education. Following its recommendations – and in line with the broad principles outlined by the Asquith Commission – UCI was established in 1948. Nigerians hailed the institution as a fulfillment of years of demands for the establishment of a higher institution in Nigeria. As the Elliot Commission suggested, the college immediately entered into a special relationship with the University of London and was "by and large a sort of a carbon copy of the newer university institutions in Britain, most of which were at one stage or the other god-fathered by London University."⁶³ The curriculum was not modified to meet Nigeria's peculiar needs. The emphasis was on arts courses such as history, classics, and English, and pure science courses such as chemistry, physics, and mathematics. The students prepared for and wrote the University of London degree examinations. The Inter-University Council for Higher Education, a body that monitored higher education development in the colonies, appointed all the academic and administrative officers of the college from London on behalf of the University of London. Undeniably, the college was run according to an educational philosophy in line with the British or classical model of a university, which viewed a university as an ivory tower preoccupied with the training of the elite.

The quality of education obtained at UCI, as Ashby pointed out, was "beyond reproach," as the institution set "standards in Nigeria at a level which would be a credit to any country in the world."⁶⁴ In defence of the standards of an institution whose degree was internationally recognized, S.O. Awokoya, the minister of education in the Western Region, said: "We don't want another Yaba."⁶⁵ Similarly, a suggestion made by several critics of UCI that Nigeria should adopt the Egyptian pattern of higher education, characterized by easy entrance, diverse classes, non-residential students, and night classes, was rejected, as captured in the editorial pages of the Lagos *Daily Times*.[66] This is not surprising, since the Nigerian elite would have frowned upon any university that was not designed according to the pattern obtainable in London. They would have accused the British of running a 'slummy' second-rate university in Nigeria.

Access, Economic Development, and Nation-Building

Colonial authorities did not see education as an investment nor did they relate it to African needs. By the late 1940s, it became clear to many Nigerians that, given its narrow curriculum and lack of facilities, UCI would not satisfy the demand for places or address the human resource needs of the country. The curriculum was to a certain extent inappropriate. In the sciences, for instance, UCI emphasized pure science subjects such as mathematics, physics, and chemistry, and neglected applied science courses. Ten years after its founding, the college was not offering courses in engineering, economics, law, geology, anthropology, sociology, or public administration, and it took eight years to establish a department of education.[67] As Tai Solarin further notes,

> During the first ten years of the existence of our first university, agriculture was not taught, even though anybody could have thought it should have been the first subject on the curriculum. Between 1948 and for almost ten years later, medicine did not appear on the curriculum of our premier university ... when anybody could have expected medicine to be the second faculty. What then were the subjects that glowed on the curriculum of the first university? English Language and Literature, Latin and Greek, and Religious Studies.[68]

Worse still was that admission to Ibadan, which was obtained through either direct entry or concessional admission, was highly restrictive.[69] The entrance examination at Ibadan was highly competitive and more demanding than in many overseas universities.[70] Many students who were classified as non-university material and were denied admission owing to the stringent admission policy of Ibadan ironically proceeded to America and Europe where they successfully pursued university education, often graduating with distinctions. To worsen the admission problem at UCI, the annual intake of students in the college was not decided by the number of qualified candidates or even by the country's needs, but principally by the availability of "sleeping accommodation [at] the elite residential halls in the College."[71] Moreover, the North-South educational gap, especially in university enrolment, continued to favour southerners. Between 1948 and 1952, the percentage of students coming from the regions shows that 97 per cent of students at UCI came from the western and eastern regions while only 3 per cent were from the North.[72] This gap was bound to create potential tension in regional relations. Collectively, the narrow curriculum, lopsided regional enrolment, the exacting entrance requirements, and the few spaces in the residential halls constrained enrolment at UCI. Thus, by 1954, there were only 406 students, forcing many qualified candidates, who were denied the opportunity to obtain university education at Ibadan, to travel overseas. As shown in Table 1.3, more Nigerians studied abroad than at UCI.

Dissatisfied with the university's failure to satisfy increasing demand for university education, the new institution came under attack by Nigerian nationalists, who saw it as "conservative, cautious, elitist, and ill-equipped for pioneering a new University in an alien culture."[73] E.E. Esau, the general secretary of the Nigerian Union of Teachers, called for the expansion of Ibadan's curriculum by suggesting the establishment of a faculty of education to train teachers.[74] Editorials in one of the leading newspapers in Nigeria supported Esau's call.[75] In the same way, Dr. Nnamdi Azikiwe, a leading nationalist from the east, questioned the narrow curriculum of the institution, a curriculum that was not only unrelated to the needs of the society but restricted student intake as well. According to Azikiwe, Nigeria could not "afford to produce or to encourage the continued production of upper class parasites who shall prey upon a stagnant sterile class of workers and peasants."[76] He argued that the number of students the college trained did not match the amount of public expenditure on the institution and thus dismissed UCI as "a million pound baby simply because it knows that whenever it cries it will be accorded a million pound

Table 1.3: Nigerian Students in Universities (1948–53).

Year	UCI	UK	USA and Canada	Total
1948–49	210	510	32	752
1949–50	298	719	104	1,121
1950–51	322	938	301	1,561
1951–52	338	1,190	361	1,889
1952–53	367	1,316	370	2,317

Source: A.B. Fafunwa, *A History of Nigerian Higher Education* (Yaba, Nigeria: Macmillan, 1971), 19–20.

kiss."[77] From time to time, columns in newspapers spoke out against UCI. One called on the institution to end the "rigid method of selection of candidates for entrance to the University."[78] Another noted that Ibadan was not established "to compete with [the] standards of British institutions."[79] There were suggestions that the entrance qualifications should be lowered to hasten Nigerianization.[80]

The demands for the expansion of access to UCI in the 1940s and 1950s reflect Nigeria's yearnings for higher education and growing dissatisfaction with the elitist British higher education policy. With the exception of the establishment of three colleges of arts, sciences, and technology, the British resisted fundamental changes to their education policy. The colleges did not have university status, and they conducted their courses in arts and sciences at the intermediate level only. The British seemed to have won the day, but the forces at work were too strong to allow the status quo to remain. As nationalists continued their campaign for the expansion of university opportunities, and as Nigeria moved towards independence, the politics of the Cold War and the dynamics of decolonization gradually coincided in the 1950s to make a shift towards massification of university education a crucial element in the country's postcolonial attempts at foster economic development and promote nation-building.

2

Towards Educational Reform: The Cold War, Decolonization, and the Carnegie Corporation, 1952–60

> Educational development is imperative and urgent. It must be treated as a national emergency, second only to war. It must move with the momentum of a revolution.
> – S.O. Awokoya, 1952

Introduction

Nationalists' campaigns for colonial reform and independence in the 1950s resulted in two constitutional reviews that, for the first time in the country's history, placed education under the control of Nigerian politicians. While the South used that opportunity to pursue universal education policies at the primary and secondary education levels, the North was rather slow. The educational gap between the two regions thus widened. As Nigeria marched towards independence without the University College of Ibadan (UCI) producing adequate human resources needed for postcolonial economic development, reforming the elitist British educational system became critical. The British resistance to fundamental changes in the early 1950s increasingly eased when the perceived threat of communism in Africa and the politics of decolonization caused them to accept nationalists' aspirations aimed at realigning the country's university education to address the challenges of economic development and nation-building. It was in the context of promoting those two goals of university education that the Carnegie Corporation of New York came to play a fundamental role in Nigeria's educational development in the 1950s.

This chapter examines the mass education schemes undertaken by the federal and regional governments in the 1950s, the regional rivalries that threatened the Nigerian project, the increasing nationalist agitation for greater access to UCI, and the support of the Carnegie Corporation for tertiary education. It shows how the coalescence of domestic and external forces laid the foundation for the postcolonial governments' determination to use mass university education to reorganize the country's elitist higher education system. Intended to provide full opportunities to all, accelerate economic development, and unify Nigeria's pluralistic society, these policies provide a glimpse of the ways in which education, politics, and societal forces intersected to shape Nigeria's turbulent march to nationhood.

Education in National Politics

Since the introduction of Western education in the 1840s, the educational disparity between the Muslim North and the Christian South had been a potential source of conflict. Although mutual misunderstanding existed between the North and the South, the British maintained peace in the country through a centralized system of administration. Yet, largely due to the diversities of the two areas, the colonial authorities decided to move the country from a unitary to a federal state after the Second World War. The Richards Constitution of 1946 marked the beginning of that shift. The constitution created regional houses of assembly but denied politicians the power to legislate for their own regions.[1] This policy led to regional agitation for administrative autonomy. Because the British imposed this constitution on the regions without consultation, nationalists criticized it and demanded changes that would grant more power to the regional assemblies.

The first attempt at constitutional change occurred in 1950. John Macpherson, who was appointed governor in 1948, yielded to the nationalists' demands for a re-examination of the Richards Constitution by convening a constitutional conference in January 1950 in Ibadan. Delegates to the conference unanimously agreed on greater regional autonomy and settled for a federal system in which the regions would share power with the central government and have representatives at the national congress. By settling on a federal arrangement, the regions highlighted the ethnic divisions and tensions in the country and demonstrated a unanimous desire to safeguard their sovereignty. This, however, constituted a crucial obstacle to the prospects of building a united nation.

Although the regions agreed on a federal structure, they disagreed on the ratio of representation of each region. Conscious of their disadvantage in terms of Western education, and determined to use their bigger population to counterbalance supposed Southern domination, delegates representing the Northern Region at the Ibadan constitutional conference demanded a 50–50 representation ratio in the central legislature between the North and the South (eastern and western regions). In their defence, Mallam Sani Dingyadi, a spokesperson for the North, admitted that the South feared that the North would dictate policies for the rest of the country if given 50 per cent representation in the House of Representatives.[2] He stressed, however, that the North would feel the same way if the three regions got equal representation. According to him, since the South had a common religion, with the same standard of education, they were more likely to arrive at a common cause and thus shift the country's balance of power to their advantage. On the other hand, he lamented that

> the North has a different religion and different standards of education, so the North must stand alone by itself. Therefore, in any matter of importance one would find the East, West, Lagos … on one side leaving the North on the other side. Therefore, I do not think it is fair and cannot tolerate it that equal representation should be given to each region. What we would recommend is at least one-half representation for the North and one-half for what I call the South.[3]

In contrast, Chief Obanikoro, the spokesperson for the Western Region, together with Alvan Ikoku who represented the Eastern Region disagreed, stating that if the North had its way, this would amount to "placing the fate of the two regions at the mercy of the North."[4] They recognized that "the population of the North is larger than that of the other two regions. But if the principle is one of federation and not of domination, the basis of representation at the centre must be regional."[5] Apparently, the fear of domination, stirred by regional educational disparity, manifested itself prominently for the first time in Nigeria's history. However, at the end of the debate, the preference of the North prevailed without which the Emir of Zaria had threatened to "ask for separation from the rest of Nigeria."[6]

Based on the agreements reached at the constitutional convention, the Macpherson Constitution emerged in 1951. Unlike the preceding constitutions, the 1951 document came into being after extensive consultation with the people of Nigeria as a whole. Initiated by Sir John Macpherson, governor-general of Nigeria (1948–54), the constitution established central and regional legislative councils as well as a central executive council for the country.[7] The regional legislatures legislated only with respect to certain specified areas affecting their regions, namely, agriculture, education (primary and secondary), local government, and public health, while the central legislature was responsible for all other legislative areas. In 1952, elections were conducted, and regional political parties with clear majorities emerged to advocate the course of social and economic advancement for their respective regions. In the eastern region, the National Council of Nigeria and the Cameroons (NCNC) (which became the National Council of Nigerian Citizens after 1960) dominated the Eastern Region with the Igbo as its major ethnic base. Nnamdi Azikiwe was one of the founding members of the party. The Action Group (AG) emerged in the Western Region, led by Obafemi Awolowo and with its membership mostly from the Yoruba ethnic group. The Northern People's Congress (NPC), a northern party was led by Ahmadu Bello and was dominated by the Hausa and Fulani ethnic groups.

Education was uppermost in the minds of the newly elected regional leaders who felt that the British had failed to invest in education. According to K.O. Dike, "The nationalist realized that no impression can be made on the colossal ignorance of the country until education, of all types, permeates every sector of the community, and until it is available to the majority of the people."[8] The British government refused to introduce mass education schemes, notwithstanding high demand for education. In fact, the British education report in 1951 stated that "while universal primary education is one of the essential aims of educational policy, it is not the only, nor is it necessarily the most urgent aim."⁹ The neglect of education was deliberate; colonial authorities did not see education as an investment; otherwise, they would have allocated adequate resources to expand it. The percentage of government investment on education remained low for the greater part of the colonial period. For instance, from 1898 to 1923, expenditure on education was less than 2 per cent of the revenue. While the total revenue for 1923 was £6,509,244, only 1.5 per cent (£100,063) was spent on education. The revenue in 1936 was £6,585.458 but only £231,983 (3.5 per cent) was allocated to education. The cumulated result was that at the outbreak of the Second World War, only 12 per cent of Nigerian children of school age were in schools.¹⁰

Contrary to the educational assumptions of the colonial authorities, nationalists thought of expansion of the system as urgent because they recognized the role of education in the society. Given the popular faith in the power of education as "the motor of social development," it was understandable, as rightly captured in *Education and Nation Building in Africa*, "why the control and planning of education became, often even before independence[,] a political issue of crucial magnitude."¹¹ Motivated by the powers granted by the Macpherson Constitution, Obafemi Awolowo, the Action Group leader who won the first election to the Western House of Assembly in 1952, promised free universal primary education. In July of the same year, the minister of education in the region, S.O. Awokoya, presented to the House of Assembly a sessional paper on the region's educational policy that was a radical departure from the British policy. It insisted on the imperative and urgency of educational expansion, which it hoped should "move with the momentum of a revolution."¹² Thus the educational policy of the region, which reflected the position of the Action Group, was "one of expansion and reorientation [implying] an all-out expansion of all types of educational institutions [so] that in a few years time, it should be possible to have universal education for all children of school age in the Western Region."¹³

The bold steps taken by the Action Group government in the west largely influenced the NCNC-led party in the Eastern Region to contemplate a similar policy. In 1953, the region's minister of education, R.I. Uzoma, articulated only a modest mass education policy, which involved cost-sharing between the region and the local governments.[14] However, in that year, the NCNC witnessed a leadership overhaul, with Nnamdi Azikiwe replacing Eyo Ita as the leader of the party, while I.U. Akpabio took over from Uzoma as the minister of education. Azikiwe rejected the modest proposal of his predecessor and proposed an eight-year free education plan instead. In 1953, over half a million of the region's children of primary age were in school.[15] In the report of its 1953 mission in Nigeria, the World Bank observed that the "intense and widespread desire in Nigeria for education is encouraging ... [and the] enthusiasm for education in much of Nigeria amounts to a blind faith that schooling ... is a passport to employment and affluence."[16] As the report highlighted,

> The people of Nigeria are anxious to live better and hence to produce more goods, in greater variety; they want to become better educated; they show a growing willingness to modify those institutions which hold back economic progress and accept methods of social, economic and political organization which elsewhere have proved conducive to such progress.[17]

While the Eastern and Western regions made aggressive attempts at expanding educational opportunities, the North was rather cautious in pushing for expansion. The issue with the North was their general antipathy towards Western education As noted in chapter 1, missionary control of education through most of the colonial era meant that demands for education and desires for Christianity intersected. The South received the missionaries and their education. The Muslims, who dominated the North, perceived Western education as synonymous with Christianity and therefore resisted it. Most children from ages four to twelve attended compulsory Koranic schools. The influential local authority officials, including the emirs and the chiefs, saw no useful purpose in sending their children to Western educational institutions; indeed, they were afraid it would corrupt them. Thus, while the Koranic schools attracted the vast majority of children, the Western educational institutions in the region remained virtually empty.[18]

Unlike other regions, the North did not introduce universal education scheme. The major practical problem confronting the North in terms of expanding its education program was the inadequate number of teachers and the low entrance of northerners in UCI. Consequently, the region pursued a policy of cautious planning and maximizing efficiency through teacher training while advocating for affirmative action in university admission, which the British rejected. As the Inter-University Council report in 1952 declared, "the college while admitting every woman and northern candidate qualified for university work should resist any proposal to accept or introduce a quota system." As the report stressed, "a quota system of admission might lower academic standards, not only in terms of quality of the student's entry but in terms of the work of the staff and students throughout the college. It would damage the college and would not assist the object it was designed to serve."[19]

Commenting on the insufficient supply of university education, the World Bank Mission stressed "that Nigeria needs many times more college graduates than even the most optimistic plans could provide."[20] As the mission recommended, "every effort [should] be made to increase enrolment at the university, presently around 400, as quickly as possible.... At the same time the University College should offer a greater variety of courses ... related more directly to the economic advancement of the Nigerian people than it has been thus far."[21] The World Bank echoed the Elliot Commission's view on the development of higher education in West Africa, which argued that "the need for highly trained Africans is too great to be met in any way other than by training them in their own country."[22] The World Bank report was an indictment of UCI. It added great impetus to the nationalists' opposition to the limited opportunities provided by UCI and propelled them to agitate for changes in the institution's admission policies. Though few, if any, educational changes were made immediately, the constitutional changes in 1954 paved the way for a major milestone in Nigeria's higher education development.

The year 1954 was remarkable in the history of higher education in Nigeria because the Lyttleton Constitution placed legislative power over higher education in the hands of both the federal and regional governments. Named after Oliver Lyttleton, the secretary for the colonies, who chaired the constitutional review committee, the constitution officially fashioned Nigeria into a federation of three regions, with Lagos as the federal capital territory. It defined the relations between the federation and the regions in the distribution of legislative powers, as outlined in the legislative lists: the Exclusive List (subjects exclusively reserved for the central government), the Residual List (subjects exclusively reserved for the regions), and the Concurrent List (subjects shared by the central and regional governments).[23] Under this constitution, regional governments could legislate on the subject of primary and secondary education, which the constitution placed on the Residual List. In response to these changes, the three regions and Lagos enacted education laws that became the basis for mass education at the primary and secondary school levels.[24] In addition, the constitution placed higher education on the Concurrent Legislative List, giving both the central and regional governments authority to establish and run higher education institutions.

In line with the provision of Lyttleton Constitution, the Eastern Region went beyond the pursuit of mass primary and secondary education to initiate plans to establish a university in the region. The government of the region was conscious of the new constitutional powers granted to the regions under the 1954 Lyttleton Constitution, inspired by the World Bank's advice on the need to expand the opportunities for university education, and was still disappointed with the elitist nature of UCI. Consequently, the region seized the moment and began to push for the establishment of a regional university. Nnamdi Azikiwe, who had been a vocal critic of UCI, and who had since 1920 nursed the ambition of establishing a Nigerian university, championed the idea. Azikiwe led a delegation to Europe and America to attract investors to the Eastern Region and to seek the advice and backing on the feasibility of establishing a university in eastern Nigeria. He also introduced a motion in the Eastern House of Assembly in May 1955 seeking to create the University of Nigeria to meet the needs where UCI had failed. As Azikiwe stated,

> Such a higher institution of learning should not only be cultural, according to the classical concepts of universities, but it should also be vocational in its objective and Nigerian in content. We should not offer any apologies for making such a progressive move. After all, we must do for ourselves what others hesitate to do for us.[25]

In addition, the proposed bill called for the establishment of twenty diploma-conferring institutes. Azikiwe reasoned that if the institutes were organized to operate *pari passu* with the university, the region would have embarked upon "an historic renaissance in the fields of academic, cultural, professional and technical education on the same lines as the leading countries of the world."[26] In formulating the policy of the region for the establishment of the University of Nigeria, Azikiwe noted that the government was obliged to make a radical departure from the restrictive practices and long-held elitist traditions of UCI. In contrast to UCI, the proposed university was intended to achieve the following goals, as Azikiwe later recollected:

> It will not only blend professional cum vocational higher education, but it will create an atmosphere of social equality between the two types of students. It will adapt the "land-grant college" philosophy of higher education with the classical tradition in an African environment. It will cater for a larger student body to specialize on a variety of courses, whilst maintaining the highest academic standards. It will not restrict the number of its students purely on the basis of the potential absorption of its graduates into vacant jobs within the territorial limits of Nigeria. It will spread its activities over a wide range of fields of human endeavor to enable the average student to specialize on the basis of his aptitude.[27]

The idea of a university in the Eastern Region, dedicated to accomplish the above objectives, was unique and revolutionary because it sought to remove the obstacles that had hindered access to university education. In a sense, it was a desire for mass university education, educational expediency, and nationalism – coupled with Azikiwe's connections – that fundamentally drove the push for a new university. Azikiwe and other supporters of the American system, such as Ita Eyo, Nwafor Orizu, Mbonu Ojike, and others, received university training in the United States and were united in their opposition to the British elitist system. Apollos Nwauwa has shown how the influence of American-trained university graduates facilitated the establishment of universities in Africa, including Nigeria.[28] These supporters of American-style higher education did not stop when UCI was established in 1948. Rather, they continued as crusaders for American practical education, as contrasted to the British literary tradition. For instance, Professor Eyo Ita, a veteran teacher and a former leader of the opposition in the Eastern House of Assembly, supported the idea of establishing a vocational university education as obtainable in the American universities to challenge UCI's elitism. He predicted that a day would come when all states in Nigeria would own a university.[29]

Attraction to the U.S. system of education among American-educated Nigerians was one of the major reasons for the post-Second World War migration of hundreds of Nigerians to the United States. At the same time, their bias in favour of American educational ideals and radical nationalism contributed to the dislike of both the British and the British-educated Nigerians toward American education and American-educated Nigerians.[30] Nevertheless, on 18 May 1955, the Eastern House of Assembly passed into law the bill establishing the University of Nigeria.[31] The first practical financial step towards putting into effect the plan contained in the bill was the government's decision to direct the Eastern Nigeria Marketing Board to lay aside £500,000 annually from 13 December 1955 to the end of 1964. This fund was expected to amount to £5 million by the end of 1964.[32] On paper, the University of Nigeria was born in 1955, and, as the region continued to raise funds for the proposed university, the politics of the Cold War and decolonization created circumstances that made broader higher education reform unavoidable.

Postwar Nigeria

The postwar world was a remarkable period in the history of Africa, a period when international events commingled with domestic situation to produce changes not only in the political scene but also in educational arena. Between 1945 and 1949, Soviet-backed communist governments came to power in some eastern European countries such as Poland, East Germany, Czechoslovakia, Hungary, Bulgaria, Albania, Yugoslavia, and Romania. Joseph Stalin's policy of spreading communism globally threatened Western democracies, most notably the United States and Britain. The Cold War was raging and the Western and the Eastern blocs both looked to influence events in Africa, a continent they considered a strategic ally in their ideological confrontation.[33] On the domestic front, nationalists, angered by the failure of the colonial powers to fulfill their wartime promises, coupled with acute food shortages and unemployment in the colonies, had intensified their demands for social change. In the 1950s, the politics of decolonization and the Cold War helped to link the interests of Carnegie, Britain, and Nigeria for higher education, producing a policy shift in which the push for mass university education was now conceived as a tool in facilitating both socio-economic development and nation-building. The resulting Anglo-American-Nigerian collaboration in Nigerian higher education expansion produced a blueprint in 1960 that shaped the direction of postcolonial higher education in Nigeria.

In the context of the Cold War and decolonization, Britain sought to crack down on the radical and rebellious Nigerian nationalists, who they suspected received support from communist governments, as well as Nigerians travelling to communist countries for higher education studies. The "fear of cold war communist intervention in Africa and a determination to resist the 'extremist' nationalists," as Roger Fieldhouse notes, "created a very different atmosphere in the West African territories after 1948."[34] Communist-inclined Nigerian nationalists saw communism as a powerful tool in ending colonial rule and as a model in building a West Africa Union.[35] The growing conviction to fight colonial repressive measure more forcefully lay at the centre of the formation of the Zikist Movement in Nigeria. Newspapers such as the *West African Pilot* and the *Daily Comet* openly supported the workers strike led by Michael Imoudu in 22 June 1945 and attracted the wrath of colonial authorities who banned them. Other leftist elements in Nigeria, such Nduka Eze, Unasu Amosu, Osita Agwuna, Raji Abdallah, Ogedegbe Macaulay, and J.J. Odufuwa, served jail terms for engaging in what colonial authorities regarded as subversive activities.

In *Britain, Leftist Nationalists and the Transfer of Power in Nigeria, 1945–1965*, Tijani discusses the activities of leftist groups in Nigeria who received financial support from the Eastern bloc and the British measures to suppress them.[36] Tijani argues that the Criminal Code Ordinance in 1950, which criminalized seditious activities, was occasioned by the Zikists'

"Call for a Revolution," a call to Nigerians to defect from the colonial security forces, the discovery of weapons at the Kaduna and Lagos offices of the Zikist Movement, and "the increasing volume of communist revolutionary newsletters, and funding of leftists-led trade union organizations by the World Federation of Trade Unions (WFTU)."[37] So threatened were the colonial authorities in Nigeria by communism that they banned thirty-three books, pamphlets, and other publications that carried communist propaganda in early 1955 and clamped down on Nduka Eze and those associated with the Scholarship Board.[38] Strict conditions were imposed on Nigerians travelling to communist countries for studies or conferences as nationals of communist countries were denied visas to Nigeria.[39] The fear of communism made future cooperation between the British and Nigerian elites in educational issues inevitable. Yet, while the British continued to suppress communist elements in Nigeria, Carnegie Corporation, inspired by a desire to contain the spread of communist ideas in Africa, began a campaign for educational expansion in Nigeria.

The Cold War and decolonization presented Carnegie Corporation with an opportunity to push for the reform of the elitist British educational system aimed at extending American social values in the emerging African nations. The corporation believed that this approach would be a strategic tool in forestalling a potential Soviet influence in the continent, as well as challenging Britain's power in Africa by offering Africans an alternative, more inclusive higher education system. Carnegie's interest in educational expansion in Africa was reinforced after the end of the Second World War as a strategic tool in successfully fighting the Cold War. America's largest foundations, the Carnegie Corporation, the Rockefeller Foundation, and the Ford Foundation, had assisted the United States in furthering its interests worldwide during the ideological war with the Soviet Union. These foundations emphasized education by funding programs linking the educational systems of the new African nations to the "values, modus operandi, and institutions of the United States."[40] This was part of the United States' Cold War agenda, designed to assist in the process of decolonizing European colonies in Africa in order to establish strong socio-economic and political ties with emerging countries in Africa. Failing to do that, Carnegie thought that the USSR, intent on internationalizing communism, would establish a stronghold in Africa.

Alan Pifer was a staff member of the Carnegie Corporation's international program called British Dominions and Colonies Program (BDC), who championed the course of educational expansion in Nigeria on behalf of the corporation. He disbursed funds to help the British colonies in Africa expand their educational facilities and opportunities. Established in the 1920s with $10 million as its budget, the BDC program aimed at providing assistance to British overseas colonies. Before the Second World War, the program focused on bringing Africans to the United States, an approach that failed to address human resource shortages in the continent. After the war, Carnegie decided to change this policy. With close to $2 million in accumulated revenue, Carnegie decided to devote greater attention to British colonies in Africa, believing "that the speed and nature of developments in the British Colonies afford opportunities now for assistance from a private Foundation which could be particularly productive and timely."[41] Pifer was the man to accomplish Carnegie's objectives.

Pifer joined Carnegie in 1953 after working as the executive secretary of the U.S. Educational Commission in Britain and administering the Fulbright Program of educational exchange for five years. He had travelled extensively to Africa. As I have argued elsewhere, Pifer's "years in the Fulbright Program helped him forge a close relationship with top colonial officials in London, and through his trips to Africa, he had not only made friends with colonial officials but also garnered greater understanding of both colonial politics and nationalists' aspirations."[42] Pifer believed that "American aid, if wisely given, cannot be regarded as anything but beneficial – indeed urgent.... Education, of course is the key. There is no aspect of African life which is not affected by it."[43]

To discuss the steps needed to intervene in Africa's educational development, Carnegie Corporation officials met on 11 May 1954 in New York. In attendance were Alan Pifer and Steve Stackpole, executive assistants in the British Dominions and Colonies Program; Walter Adams, secretary of the Inter-University Council; and Sally Chilvers, secretary of the Colonial Social and Science Research Council.[44] At the meeting, Pifer and Stackpole stated that the focus of Carnegie assistance in the British colonies would henceforth be universities, university colleges, and research institutions, with the intention of changing British policy on higher education. Pifer specifically proposed that the first step toward amending these reports was to conduct a broad survey of higher education in Africa, preferably in Nigeria. In a memo to staff, Pifer explained the reasons why he chose Nigeria for the study:

> It was realized, however, that a general study of all colonial education was impracticable. Nigeria, therefore, as the largest, most important territory and the one with possibly the greatest likelihood of future disorganization in its higher education system was selected as the place where the study should be made.[45]

In a letter to Stackpole, Pifer wrote that his "own view, shared by Adams, is that too many people have been resting on the Asquith and Elliot Reports for too long. A lot has happened in the African colonies in the past ten years."[46] He advocated a review of the Asquith Commission with a view to determining UCI's relevance to the Nigeria's professional, agricultural, technical, and general education.[47]

Pifer used every opportunity he had to pursue this project. For instance, between 16 and 18 June 1955, when the principals of six Asquith university institutions, including UCI, met informally at a conference at the University College of the West Indies, Jamaica, to re-evaluate the principle of elitism that the Asquith Commission had endorsed, Pifer used the forum to advance his reform agenda. At the end of the conference, it was decided that alternative patterns of higher education, such as the idea of "mass" university education in Puerto Rico and the democratization of access to higher education in the United States, were possible models for British colonies in Africa.[48] The delegates concurred on the need to set up a commission to study strategies to expand education in Africa, beginning with Nigeria. The pact reached at the Jamaica Conference and the proposal to establish a university in eastern Nigeria according to the American pattern threatened the elitist British system of higher education.

Resistant to any attempt to reform British higher education policy, Dan Maxwell, the assistant secretary of the Inter-University Council, informed Pifer in October 1955 that the colonial office had suspended the implementation of the Jamaica resolution. The reasons he gave were as follows: events in the colonies were moving so fast that the study might not keep up with them; the Asquith principles should not be reviewed but instead interpreted, modified, and applied to each region; the best people to conduct the study would not spare the time for it; a delegation from the University of London had gone to West Africa to assess the capacity of the universities to cope with engineering courses; and the premier of the Eastern Region had proposed the establishment of the University of Nigeria. As Maxwell concluded, "until the results of these delegations and discussions have been made known and digested, the review idea has been put into cold storage."[49] Though the British shelved the idea of reforming the prevailing system, Pifer did not give up. He continued to press on, albeit diplomatically. His cause received a boost as more and more people in Nigeria questioned whether the existing higher educational facilities were suitable to the needs of developing country such as Nigeria.

Of all the regions, the North was most apprehensive of colonial educational shortcomings. That trepidation was demonstrated in 1956 when Anthony Enahoro, a southerner and a member of the House of Representatives, called for Nigeria's independence in 1956. Northern political leaders rejected it. They were afraid of perceived southern domination due to their educational lead. In refusing the motion, Ahmadu Bello, the Sarduana of Sokoto, stated that the northerners "were late in assimilating Western education yet within a short time we will catch up with [other] Regions, and share their lot.... We want to be realistic and consolidate our gains."[50] Indeed, the shortages of highly educated people in Nigeria provided the context in which Nigerian leaders sought to reform the educational system, especially in 1957 when the demands for independence reached a crescendo. In that year, a constitutional conference held in London, among other things, created a 'national government,' with elections scheduled for 11 December 1959 and a target date for independence tentatively scheduled for April 1960. Independence meant that Nigerians would have to take over the top bureaucratic positions previously held by expatriates, mostly British. As many expatriate civil servants consequently began to leave the country due to impending independence, labour shortages loomed for Nigeria's would-be leaders. Given this fact, the national government under Balewa contemplated measures to train Nigerians in preparation for the challenges of independence.

In pursuit of the Nigerianization policy, the national government appointed an officer specifically to push for the training and recruitment of Nigerians for public service positions.[51] In addition, the government selected a special committee of the House of Representatives in March 1958, which commented harshly on previous plans to train Nigerians: on unwarranted concessions accorded to expatriate officers, lack of progress in placing Nigerians in senior posts, and insufficient production of graduates from UCI.[52] Nevertheless, the government continued to train Nigerians, particularly for senior civil service positions, through the awarding of scholarships. As a result, the government increased the number of scholarships for Nigerian students to 101 in the UK, 44 in the United States, and one in India.[53]

The regional governments were equally engaged in efforts to train high-level personnel abroad in readiness for independence. The government of the Western Region sponsored 312 students from western Nigeria for training abroad, while about 2,639 private students studied in overseas higher institutions.[54] The government spent about £140,000 annually to support these students. Similarly, the Eastern Region awarded overseas post-secondary scholarships to 549 students, while 735 private students studied abroad.[55] The Northern Region did not make similar efforts. Although the region nursed the ambition of establishing a university, it was handicapped by an insufficient number of applicants due to its long antipathy to Western education. Sir John Lockwood, the permanent secretary in the federal Ministry of Education, recounted that as far back as 1957, "the Premier and the Ministry of Education of the Northern Region had left me under no illusions about their hopes. They told me at Kaduna last January [1956] that as soon as there were enough potential candidates from their region, they would wish to have a university (of their own)."[56] Nevertheless, the massive educational advances made by the governments in the Eastern and Western Regions, coupled with generous scholarship awards, ensured that either southerners or expatriates dominated federal and regional government jobs, and perhaps the same applied to jobs in the private sector. The situation was indeed very disturbing because, as a Nigerianization officer put it:

> It is believed that only one per cent of the staff of the (federal) service is of Northern origin, and it is doubtful whether, among the senior posts, the percentage is as high as this. The size of the

problem can be estimated when it is realized that Northerners constitute approximately 55 percent of the population of the federation.[57]

Since southerners filled the available posts in the federal civil service, northerners interpreted 'Nigerianization' as synonymous with 'southernization.' In response, the Public Service Commission of the Northern Region initiated a 'Northernization' policy in December 1957 as a counterpoise to the 'Nigerianization' policy. The policy stated that "if a qualified Northerner is available, he is given priority in recruitment; if no Northerner is available, an expatriate may be recruited or a non-Northerner on contract terms."[58] The policy was intended to help fill the public service in the North with northerners by discriminating against southerners, who were, indeed, the targets. Headlines like "Northernization: More Southerners Sacked," dominated daily newspapers in the South, which had harsh words for the policy.[59] The discomfort and fear in the North, arising from the educational imbalance between it and the South, underscore the Northernization policy. Because the regions were autonomous entities, the central government was too weak to prevent the resulting bitter regional competition and rivalry. As Robin Hallett noted:

> The relations of the Regions one with another are haunted by fear and suspicion; the North apprehensive of the South hurries forward its policy of Northernization; the South is half-afraid, half-contemptuous, and almost wholly ignorant of the North. Then look how weak the Federal Government is.[60]

The artificial division of Nigeria into three regions with substantial regional autonomy satisfied colonial administrative strategy but compromised the chances of building one nation out of the various antagonistic nations inhabiting Nigeria. Some colonial officials recognized this problem. Sir Alan Burns, Nigeria's governor-general from 1942 to 1943, noted that "there is no Nigerian nation.... The very name of Nigeria was invented by the British to describe a country inhabited by a medley of formerly warring tribes with no common culture, and united only in so far as they are governed by a single power."[61] Also, Lord Milverton (formerly Arthur Richards), Nigeria's governor-general from 1943 to 1948, maintained that Nigeria was more of a geographical expression than a nation.[62] In addition, an American social scientist, Martin Kilson, who conducted research on the rise of nationalism in Nigeria, concluded that "the chances for a viable, united Nigerian nation-state are rather slim indeed."[63] Educational disparity between the North and South further worsened that chance. The importance, therefore, to build a united nation through expansion of education was one that Pifer understood. During his visit to Nigeria, Pifer realized that the major source of regional tension was located in the North, a region he noted that was "educationally and economically the most backward part of the country and yet with its eighteen million people holding the whip hand politically over the Eastern and Western regions."[64] Unresolved regional tensions, Pifer warned, would undermine national security and potentially "give the Russians their first big chance in Africa."[65] He stressed that the prospect of a cohesive and strong Nigeria presented "the few counterbalancing forces" against the Soviet Union.[66]

From 1954, when the Carnegie Corporation held its first meeting on the subject of reforming higher education in the British colonies, pressures on the British government to expand opportunities for university education continued to grow. When the principals of university colleges in the British colonies met again in Salisbury in 1957 to discuss the type of university required in rapidly developing countries, they favoured the U.S. comprehensive system. Yet, Pifer knew that for his reform agenda to succeed, he needed British cooperation before Nigeria's independence because he was uncertain of succeeding in reforming the system after independence. Moreover, involving the British would ensure that Nigerians accept the American system of education that was less respected by the British-educated Nigerians. Thus, Pifer continued to push for Anglo-American cooperation.

The increasing fear of communist infiltration in Nigeria, the need to maintain friendly relations with a postcolonial Nigeria, and Pifer's consistent push for educational reform, coupled with Carnegie's readiness to provide financial support to conduct a study of Nigeria's educational needs, caused the British to allow a re-examination of their educational tradition. Sir Christopher Cox, educational advisor to the Colonial Office, after discussing the proposed study with Carnegie Corporation, committed Britain to the idea of holding an Anglo-American conference to discuss further cooperation between the UK and the United States in providing assistance to former British colonies in Africa that had achieved independence and to British colonies that were about to achieve independence. Pifer's resolve had been manifested in his consistent impact at conferences and his many informal meetings and communications with colonial administrators and educators since 1954. In addition, the United States had put pressure on Britain in general to speed up decolonization as part of its Cold War agenda.[67] Thus, the British agreement to hold a conference at which the specifics of educational reform were to be discussed was a turning point in Anglo-American participation in Nigeria's educational reform.

Carnegie consequently sponsored the Greenbrier Conference, which met from 21 to 25 May 1958, at White Springs, West Virginia, with participants invited from universities, foundations, businesses, and government agencies in the UK and United States. At the end of the conference, the delegates agreed on the need to conduct a joint British-Nigerian-American study of Nigeria's higher education needs.[68] This new partnership between the British and the United States in African education emerged in the context of the Cold War and decolonization and apparently recognized the need to forge closer relations with Africans in order to prevent them from shifting their allegiance to the communist bloc. At the conference, Pifer spoke on the need to get Nigerians on board, stressing that "we must not try to settle issues which affect the African leaders more vitally than anyone else by discussing them on a purely Anglo-American basis without the participation of the African leaders themselves."[69] But as of 1958, Nigerians were not involved in the Anglo-American deliberations. One problem was that no one in Nigeria had advocated a national study to reform the higher education system, a fact acknowledged by Cox in his letter to Pifer in July 1958, "at present I cannot clearly see an initiative of this kind coming from the Nigerian Government, or from ourselves unless we have carried the various parties concerned in Nigeria."[70]

Given the heightened wave of Nigerian nationalism in the late 1950s, any proposal coming from non-Nigerians would have been considered suspicious. Pifer and the British were therefore very uncomfortable with the idea of taking the initiative themselves. Undeterred, however, Pifer undertook a trip to Nigeria in November 1958 to sell the idea to the government officials subtly at the federal and regional levels. His goal was to get Nigerian officials to 'initiate' the study on their own. Before Pifer went to Nigeria, he stopped in London on 20 October 1958 and met with Cox, Thompson, and Sutton at the Colonial Office. At the meeting, the British expressed concern that the head of government of the Eastern Region, Azikiwe, would likely resist the proposed study because he would view it as an attempt to obstruct the implementation of his plans for the University of Nigeria.[71] Aware of what he was up against in Nigeria, Pifer informed the governor-general, Sir James Wilson Robertson, and the deputy governor-general, Sir Ralph Grey, of the purpose of his trip, and requested them to talk informally with key government officials about his impending visit. The idea was to create an atmosphere that would be receptive to Pifer's idea. In turn, top colonial officers in Nigeria approached the federal minister of education, Aja Nwachukwu, with the information that Carnegie might be interested in funding a study of post-secondary education and that Nwachukwu should use Pifer's imminent visit to appeal to him to sponsor the scheme. Nwachukuwu agreed. In November 1958, Pifer arrived in Nigeria. In a letter to Stackpole, he noted, "Shortly after I arrived in Lagos, the Federal Minister of Education proposed the survey to me and asked for Carnegie assistance to finance it."[72] Nwachukuwu's readiness to welcome Carnegie as a sponsor of higher education reforms in Nigeria was the consummation of Pifer's long years of sustained effort to involve America in the development of education in British colonies in Africa through the corporation. To Pifer, this was a dream come true.

Pifer's interest in Nigeria's higher education reform was not completely altruistic; it was an opportunity to extend American influence in Africa's most populous nation. While in Nigeria, Pifer presented a lecture at the Philosophical Society of the University College of Ibadan, on 16 November 1958, where he articulated America's goals in what he described as the "sixth period" of the "great American discovery of Africa."[73] According to Pifer, American interests in Africa during this period were academic, philanthropic, strategic, and economic. The establishment of formal and informal African studies programs in nine universities and one theological seminary, and the formation of the African Studies Association in 1956, Pifer stressed, indicated growing American attention to Africa.[74] Pifer noted that Carnegie was primarily in Africa to advance higher education and research.⁷⁵ Pointing out why Africa was important to the United States, he stressed that "a continent that occupies a fifth of the earth's surface cannot be without interest to us [America] and of course to the whole Western world."⁷⁶ In keeping with America's strategy, particularly in the context of the Cold War, Pifer further noted that "an unfriendly Africa would be a direct threat to our security."⁷⁷ The United States was mindful of the great natural endowments in Africa and therefore desired "the continent's minerals and raw materials" and saw no reason "why equitable arrangements cannot be made for us to buy our share of these, and we believe that in so doing we can help Africans develop their resources for their own ends."⁷⁸ Revealing why he selected Nigeria for the study, Pifer stressed that the country had a great potential as "the twelfth largest independent nation in the world and the third largest in the Commonwealth."⁷⁹ Pifer spoke the minds of American policy-makers and showed that American involvement was aimed at furthering their own interests while meeting the aspirations of Nigeria. These interests, as I have argued elsewhere, "are not necessarily contradictory. They are, indeed, complementary, for a strong, stable and united Nigeria presented – at least in the mind of Pifer – a future investment opportunity for American businesses."⁸⁰

To assess how the regions would receive the proposal, Pifer and Nwachukuwu toured the three regions in December 1958. The reaction was positive. It was clear from the 1958 tour that the three regions, which had functioned more or less independently since the time of the Macpherson Constitution, were willing to cooperate in educational matters, especially since the educational expansion will help them produce the needed human resources to develop their regions. The enthusiasm expressed by the regions was by no means surprising, because they had made earlier efforts along the lines of expanding educational opportunities and facilities at the primary and secondary school levels. From 1952 when universal free education was introduced in the Western Region to 1959, school facilities expanded to such an extent that primary school enrolment rose from 811,432 in 1955 to 1,080,303 in 1959, while enrolment in secondary grammar schools rose from 10,935 during the same period to 22,374.⁸¹ In the Eastern Region, primary school admission rose from 742,542 during the same period to 1,378,403, and secondary grammar school students rose from 10,584 to 15,789.⁸²

Though the North did not introduce universal free education, primary school enrolment nevertheless increased from 168,521 to 205,912, and secondary grammar school enrolment from 2,671 to 4,683 during the same period.[83] Similarly, when the 'national government' under Balewa enacted the Education (Lagos) Act of 1957 for the federal capital, Lagos, primary school students grew from 37,038 to 66,320, and secondary grammar school admission grew from 3,157 to 4,804 during the period between 1957 and 1959.[84] By 1959, about 2,775,938 students were registered in various primary schools all over the country while 47,650 students were in secondary grammar schools.[85] According to Fafunwa, "more primary and secondary schools were built and more children enrolled at the two levels between 1951 and 1959 than during the one-hundred years of British rule."[86]

Disappointingly, the existing university turned out an insufficient number of graduates. Data on student registration at UCI reveal that, by 1959, a total number of 939 students studied in UCI: 359 from the Eastern Region; 484 from the Western Region; 74 from the Northern Region; 7 from Lagos; and 17 from Cameroon.[87] The mass primary and secondary education schemes pursued since 1952, the Nigerianization policy, the critique of UCI's elitism, the initiative of the Eastern Region, and the demands for more universities and more opportunities underscored Nigeria's longing for mass education. This explains, quite explicitly, why Pifer's campaign to review the existing rigid educational system enjoyed wide support among Nigerian leaders. It was apparent in December 1958 that a commission would be set up to revisit the foundations of British higher education policy in Nigeria and articulate ways and means of expanding facilities to achieve mass access. This is because, by that date, the interests of Carnegie, Britain, and Nigeria in higher education reform had coalesced and formed not only the cornerstone of a new era in Anglo-American collaboration in Nigerian higher education expansion but also a prelude to Nigeria's postcolonial commitment to mass university education as well. One major objective that united Carnegie, British, and official Nigerian thinking – though for different reasons – was the achievement of a shift from elite to mass university education. For Carnegie, it was an opportunity to use education as a means to further American involvement in the emerging African nations, though its success depended, in essence, on British endorsement. It was also a way to challenge British influence in Africa by offering Africans an alternative higher education system based on the American model. In the eyes of the British, the pace of change in the colonies in the late 1950s was uncontrollably fast, and, for that reason, failure to identify with and plan together with these colonies would greatly jeopardize British chances of friendly relations with African countries after these countries had attained their independence. Besides, Britain was concerned that American readiness to assist Azikiwe in his bid to found a university in the east would compromise British influence in Africa's most populous nation. Yet, Britain had no choice but to cooperate since Azikiwe and other pro-American element in Nigeria campaigned for education that was more inclusive and Carnegie was ready to provide funds.

For Nigeria, the proposed study was an unprecedented and a revolutionary opportunity to advance the course of mass university education as a practical and desirable alternative to the elitist system of British higher education. Emergent policy-makers in Nigeria were well informed on the need to satisfy the mounting demand for university opportunities, imbued as they were with the idea of accelerating the training of a skilled labour force for postcolonial economic development and encouraged by the prospects of addressing the regional educational imbalance in order to promote national unity. Therefore, the study – the first inter-regional and international collaboration in Nigeria – became a critical step in the process of integrating Nigeria's pluralistic societies into a united nation. Besides, not only did the proposed study provide a glimpse of how education, politics, and economics intersected, but it also shed light on how massification policies became crucial ingredients in Nigeria's march to nationhood.

The Ashby Commission and the Question of Relevance

Carnegie's major contribution to postcolonial higher education development was its direct involvement in initiating, sponsoring, and shaping the recommendations of the Ashby Commission. Stimulated by the federal and regional governments' mass education programs, Nigeria's primary and secondary school registration soared phenomenally in the 1950s. No similar trend, however, existed at the university level. Although Nigerians yearned for more opportunities for university education, the government had not assessed the extent of the need. So, when the interest of Nigerian governments in favour of massification coincided with those of the Carnegie Corporation and the British colonial government in 1958, Nigerian federal government officials seized the opportunity to call for the appointment of a commission to assess the higher educational needs of Nigeria. This was what Pifer campaigned for since 1954.

Although it was obvious by December 1958 that a commission would be appointed to re-examine Nigeria's higher education needs, its membership and terms of reference had not yet been figured out. Pifer's early step was to recommend a notable British scholar and admirer of American system, Eric Ashby, to chair the commission because of his prestige in the British higher educational system as well as his familiarity with and admiration of American patterns of education.[88] Pifer's choice of Ashby was strategic. It aimed at protecting American interest in the final recommendations of the commission as well as guaranteeing that Nigerians would accept the American system of education they hitherto considered as inferior. More importantly, Pifer wished to avoid the possible charge by both the British and Nigerians that the commission was in reality a blatant piece of American interference and a strike against British hegemony in Africa. Thus, Carnegie had to tread carefully and diplomatically. Ashby's leadership, therefore, reassured the British, even though the new 'kids' on the block were, in fact, the Americans.

In his correspondence with V.H.K. Littlewood, the permanent secretary of the federal ministry of education, Pifer conveyed his discussions with British officials in London on the importance of conducting certain professional studies prior to the commission's work. Based on his discussion with Ashby, whom he met in Belfast in December 1958, he suggested that an economist should study the Nigerian economy to determine its capacity to support the expansion of post-secondary education; that an education specialist should organize and supervise the collection of educational statistics; and that an Islamic educator should prepare a paper on Islamic studies in Nigeria and its possible relationship to the development of higher education in the Northern Region.[89]

Nigerians were absent at this stage of the study at which the design of the commission and its membership were discussed. The understanding between Pifer and Lockwood was that either Carnegie or the Inter-University

Council would appoint the commission and have it submit its report before Nigeria's independence (now scheduled for 1 October 1960). However, when Ashby agreed to head the commission, he demonstrated a better understanding of the politics of nationalism by insisting that the Nigerian government should appoint the commission and be intimately involved in the whole process. In addition, he objected to the schedule that required the commission to submit its report before independence, stressing that if the independent Nigerian government were to accept the commission's report, it must reflect the views and initiative of Nigerians. As he cautioned,

> Is it not conceivable that the fact that the report was published before independence would give some Nigerian leaders an excuse for disregarding it? In brief, I considered whether the report of this commission wouldn't be better as a first product of an independent Nigeria rather than the last fling of advice to a British colony.[90]

Pifer accepted Ashby's suggestions, and in a letter to Lockwood, Pifer expressed his desire to see that the survey was "fully regarded in Nigeria as a Nigerian affair and if the commission were appointed by Carnegie Corporation or I.U.C., it would tend to be regarded as something imposed from outside."[91]

Another area of focus was the nature of the recommendations that the commission would make. The discussion centred on whether the commission's report should link the purposes of higher education directly to economic development by emphasizing training relevant high-level personnel. This developmental dimension echoed the prevailing trend of thought among Western economists who believed that higher education had a critical role to play in socio-economic development of any society.[92] Carnegie held the notion that education was a tool for modernization, and it hoped that the commission would investigate the interconnection of high-level labour needs, educational development in Nigeria, and economic development. In a memorandum addressed to the deputy governor-general of Nigeria, Sir Ralph Grey, Pifer stressed the economic implications of the commission's tasks and indicated that Carnegie planned to offer assistance to the Nigerian government specifically "to reorganize its system of higher education in order to make education a direct factor in economic development."[93] Similarly, in a memo to Ashby, Pifer emphasized that since economic development would be of immense importance to Nigerians, the commission should "concentrate on how to develop the personnel for leading positions as a basis for planning of national economic development."[94] Sir Christopher Cox, the advisor to the British Ministry of Overseas Development, supported Pifer but stressed that "the commission should deal partly with economic development and partly with solution of [the immediate] manpower problems of Nigeria."[95]

In promoting national development in postcolonial Nigeria, the training of a high-level workforce was fundamental. Yet Aja Nwachukwu lamented over shortages of "adequate numbers of skilled technicians and of professional workers in all fields," as the country prepares for independence.[96] Mindful of the human resource shortages in Nigeria, and motivated by the support for change, the federal and regional governments moved speedily to propose the immediate appointment of the commission to study the higher education needs of Nigeria. Consequently, in March 1959, the governor-general of Nigeria, James Robertson, sent a dispatch to the secretary of state for the colonies, Lennox Boyd, to inform the Colonial Office that the Nigerian governments welcomed the idea of a commission to study post-secondary education. The dispatch further stated that the education minister had also accepted the recommendation of the colonial advisor on education, Cox, that Eric Ashby should head the commission.[97] Acknowledging the importance of the proposed commission, Robertson declared that

> the number of educated young Nigerians produced from these sources is significant, but they are in no way adequate to the needs of the country. It is the view of the government that there must over the coming years be a considerable expansion of facilities for higher education in Nigeria. That the need exists and that it is urgent is not doubted; but its extent has not yet been studied and no programme has been drawn up for meeting it.[98]

The education minister in concurrence of the government of the regions announced the appointment of the Commission on Post-Secondary and

Higher Education on 27 April 1959. The terms of reference of the commission, usually referred to as the Ashby Commission, were principally "[t]o conduct an investigation into Nigeria's needs in the field of post-secondary and higher education over the next twenty years, and in the light of the Commission's findings to make recommendations as to how these needs can be met."[99] The members of the commission consisted of three Nigerians (one from each region), three Americans, and three Britons.[100] The commission, as Pifer had suggested, invited five experts to prepare papers on certain aspects of the commission's work.[101] Although the commission was a joint Nigerian, U.S., and UK operation, Carnegie funded it.

The inaugural meeting of the commission was held on 4 May 1959 in Lagos.[102] This was the beginning of an extensive study, involving meetings and regional field trips. The Ashby Commission was a milestone in the history of education in Nigeria. For the first time, Nigeria, the UK, and the United States came together to re-examine the principles that guided British higher education policies in Nigeria with a view to adjusting them to serve the current and future needs of a country advancing towards independence. As J.F. Ade Ajayi and others have noted, international involvement "interacted with the politics of independence to usher in a new age of higher education in Nigeria."[103] Besides this, it was the first time that the Northern, Western, and Eastern Regions had consented to a collective project in educational matters. Earlier, they had independently pursued their education policies without accepting federal coordination.

Should the anticipated recommendations emphasize courses in applied sciences in order to achieve economic development, or should they call for an expansion of access to university education with emphasis on the liberal arts? This question dominated discussions until September 1960 when the commission submitted its report. Lockwood, a British member of the Ashby Commission, hoped that "whatever the final recommendation, Nigerian universities should not continue to follow the pattern of the University of London."[104] He noted that such changes did not mean a departure from "what we regard as reasonable demands upon students," and he recommended that Nigeria should incorporate the Scottish model because "if it had the benefit of considerable infiltration of American-type courses it would probably be especially beneficial for meeting some of the special needs of Nigeria."[105] An American member of the commission,

Francis Kepple, dean of Harvard's Graduate School of Education, insisted that Nigeria should modify the tradition embodied in the Asquith report by "making opportunities for higher education more widely available, and by changing its content so as to approximate the pattern of American land-grant colleges."[106] This thinking implied that the recommendation of the commission on university reform would emphasize courses in the vocational and applied sciences that were vital to Nigeria's economic development as opposed to the existing emphasis on liberal education.

On the other hand, a British member of the commission, G.E. Watts, an educationist, argued that recommending only the training of a technical labour force for purposes of economic development would be a futile exercise as it was unlikely in the "foreseeable future that a considerable number of Nigerians would be attracted to it."[107] However, he urged the commission to stress that an adequate supply of applied scientists, engineers, technologists, technicians, and artisans was indispensable for economic development. The main issue, according to Watts, was to find "some blend of the British and American system which might be acceptable and effective in Nigeria."[108] Eric Ashby, in retrospect, believed that the best way to achieve Watts's goal was "not to go slow on education but to ruthlessly ensure that education is relevant, even if it means a radical departure from the forms and patterns associated with education in modern industrial societies."[109] He affirmed that

> The recommendations ... had on the one hand to be sufficiently deeply rooted in the existing pattern of Nigerian education to be acceptable and practicable ... on the other hand the recommendations had to promote adaptation, to stimulate innovation and prevent Nigerian higher education from congealing into a neo-British mould.[110]

Although there was a consensus among members of the commission and Nigerians on the expansion of educational facilities, some members of the commission and faculty of UCI opposed the idea of closely associating higher education with economic development through an emphasis on the sciences. Kenneth Dike, the principal of UCI and a member of the Ashby Commission, argued that the proposed curriculum reform in favour of science courses should not affect established institutions like UCI. He further stressed that "progress in science, medicine, and technology should tend to follow rather than precede education."[111] He therefore urged the commission to allow UCI to continue with "the higher education of the elite," who would be leaders of thought.[112] Likewise, John Fergusson, the head of classical education at UCI, maintained that Nigerian university education should be limited to the act of nurturing and producing the "men and women with standards of public service and capacity for leadership which self-rule requires."[113] Onabamiro, a member of the commission, believed that the unwarranted prominence given to science and technology would endanger education standards, suggesting that the "special relations existing between UCI and universities abroad – preferably the UK – should be maintained."[114]

In addition, some members of UCI's senate expressed considerable fear that the proposed curriculum changes would interfere with the high standards of the college and could counteract the influence of the college on the future pattern of higher education in Nigeria.[115] Even the Joint Consultative Committee on Education (JCC), the most influential body in the formulation of policy in the 1960s, opposed any adjustment in the existing pattern, objectives, or curriculum, basing its objections on the need to preserve academic standards.[116] Undeniably, the strong opposition to curriculum changes from the academic community, who constituted a small percentage of the Nigerian population, highlighted the pervasive influence of the elitist British tradition; many scholars who had studied under the British system selfishly defended liberal education even when an emphasis on applied courses was vital to economic development. As Sime rightly noted, "The upholders of traditional education in the humanities often hold views biased by their own success, a success which was achieved in the absence of any real competition from other disciplines."[117]

Whether there was to be an emphasis on applied science courses or on liberal arts courses, the three regions were eager to pursue the expansion of university facilities and the opportunities to train personnel who would fill senior positions in the civil service. They were less concerned with whether or not at the national level the federal government emphasized science and technology courses in the university education curriculum. Alhaji Isa Kaita, the regional minister of education in the Northern

Region, expressed his government's overriding concern to see the creation of a university in Zaria to help produce the skilled labour the region desperately needed.[118] Political leaders in the Western Region wanted an end to limited opportunities at UCI, which was why the region had advanced a plan to found its own university.[119] In the Eastern Region, Jerome Udoji, the secretary to the premier, indicated that the educational concern of his government was to enable the regional government to meet their administrative needs by producing local candidates for employment in various branches of the public service.[120]

The regions' overriding need for an educated labour force showed that UCI did not train enough Nigerian personnel for public service. Nigerian nationalists and government officials had since 1948 bemoaned the inadequate opportunities and facilities to ensure mass access to university education in spite of the high demand. Mass education experiments in the 1950s produced potential candidates for higher education and whetted appetites for more education. Sir Ronald Gould, a British schoolteacher and trade unionist who conducted a three-week tour of Nigeria in 1960, observed that "the demand for education … at all levels seems to be insatiable.… Everybody sees its desirability and even its necessity."[121] However, since opportunities for access to education were limited, many Nigerians who had the means continued to travel overseas for higher studies. By August 1960, there were at least 47,500 overseas students in Britain. Out of the 8,500 students from West Africa studying overseas, Nigeria topped the list with 6,000 students.[122]

The lack of adequate opportunities for Nigerians who desired university training was a common criticism of the British higher education system, and the call for massification of university education in place of elitist education dominated newspapers throughout the 1960s. American educational policy, based on the maximum development of every individual to the limit of his capacity, reverberated in the discussions and constituted a crucial reference point in the public quest for unlimited access to university education.[123] Notably, Olalekan Are, a former UCI student, specifically dismissed UCI as "a waste of taxpayers' money." He reminded the government of the belief in the United States that every qualified candidate was capable of learning. According to him, what UCI needed was the U.S. land grant college policy, which held: "admit and give education to all qualified candidates. Never refuse any qualified student."[124] He further argued that if this policy were implemented, UCI would handle 10,000 students, as opposed to less than a thousand. He made the following recommendations:

> The UCI entrance examination should be open to all persons irrespective of their grades in the West African School Certificate. Students should be paired up in every room and off-campus students should be encouraged as from 1960–61 session. The idea of all students being in residence must be forgotten in the interest of the nations' needs and progress. The building of more staff quarters should be discouraged so as to have enough room for future college expansion.... Money should be made available to students who cannot afford the college fees.[125]

Are's suggestions highlighted the factors that had limited access to university education for many Nigerians. These factors, as Dr. S.D. Onabamiro stated, were absent from the American system because American higher education broadly reflects "the fundamental democratic principles governing the structure of its society, and are a sharp reaction to the traditional European conception of university which used to be an exclusive preserve of the aristocracy, the upper classes, the rich and the privileged."[126] Instead of shutting out capable prospective students, according to Onabamiro, the general principle governing admission into American higher education "prefers to err on the side of taking in people who may not be able to go through the courses."[127] In their letters to the editor of the *Daily Times*, Orotayo Kitchie and J.A.O. Odupitan supported the call for expansion. Kitchie strongly appealed to the government to respond to the universal yearning for education by eligible candidates and to abandon the policy of education for the few.[128] As Odupitan stated, the government "must make haste to expand the existing scheme to suit our outlook; abandon forthwith the bogus idea of education for the very few who could afford it; [and encourage] more afternoon and evening classes.... Call it cheap education or whatever you like, but we are sure to have education at its best for the masses."[129]

Public sentiment in favour of educational expansion was rife as Nigeria even approached independence. They highlighted the growing belief that Nigeria's modernization and nation-building would be possible only through mass access to university education. Members of the Ashby Commission, who travelled to all the regions, were attentive to public opinion on education and, as shown in chapter 3, they echoed it in their report submitted to the federal government in September 1960. The implementation of the report produced by the commission marked a turning point in Nigeria's higher education, economic development, and nation-building. As the Prime Minister, Abubakar Tafawa Balewa noted, the report was "simply most important piece of business facing Nigeria" stressing that "the country's very future depends on it."[130]

3

The Ashby Commission, Regionalism, and University Education in the 1960s

> Our program for higher education should include a chance for the man who was not chosen in the early days of small numbers.
> – Francis Keppel, 1959

Introduction

The 1960s was a period of optimism in Africa. This was not surprising; most African countries had successfully fought to end colonial rule. To postcolonial African people, education, as shown in *Education and Nation Building in Africa*, held "the key that will open the door to a better life and the higher living standards they were promised as the reward of the struggle for nation liberation."[1] Rising expectation naturally weighed heavily on the shoulders of Africa's new leadership. Educational expansion, as a passport to future socio-economic development and nation-building, was the premise that shaped and directed the socio-economic policies of these leaders. Access to education in colonial Nigeria was highly limited, and although policy-makers in Africa recognized that educational expansion would be expensive, they believed it was a rewarding investment.

Julius Nyerere, the president of Tanzania, envisioned that universities must "join with the people of East Africa in the struggle to build a nation worthy of the opportunity we have won."[2] Félix Houphouët-Boigny, the president of Côte d'Ivoire, wished to engage universities in realizing the expectations of modern economy. As he rightly stated, the "problems of political, economic, and cultural development of our societies, and rising of the standard of living constitute immediate objectives ... require us to enlist the help of all the institutions of our states."[3] In his address at the inauguration of Haile Selassie 1 University in 1961, Emperor Haile Selassie, the president of Ethiopia stressed that "universities today stand as the most promising hope for constructive solutions to the problems that beset the modern world ... and the money spent in coordinating, strengthening, and expanding higher education in Ethiopia is well invested."[4] The period following political independence in most developing countries, especially those in Africa, was characterized by rapid expansion of access to education at all levels. In *Education and Social Transition in the Third World*, Carnoy and Samoff noted that

> the leadership in these societies does not just mouth rhetoric about changing and developing education. They expand it more rapidly and reach out to more people of all ages than in any previous efforts in history. They mobilize entire populations to achieve universal literacy over a short period and invent new ways to expand and deliver all levels of schooling to their citizenry.[5]

Nigeria gained independence from Britain in 1960, and Nigerian leaders shared the prevailing conviction in Africa that investment in university would help modernize their country. In an inaugural address delivered on his installation as the first chancellor of UCI, the prime minister, Abubakar Tafawa Balewa, declared that in this age of rapid technological development in the Western world, "the key to a nation's economic well-being is likely to be the amount of effort that is put into scientific research and education."[6] Earlier in 1959, the Ashby Commission was set up to help chart the course for the country's educational expansion. Based on its prediction of Nigeria in 1980 as a nation "taking its place in a technological civilization, with its own airways, its organs of mass-communication, its research institutes," the commission submitted bold proposals of educational expansion to the Balewa administration in September 1960, fittingly titled *Investment in Education: The Report of the Commission on Post-School Certificate and Higher Education*.[7]

The proposals addressed six interconnected issues, revolving around the necessity of expanding educational facilities and opportunities in order to advance both economic development and national integration; to commit available financial resources as well as secure international assistance to meet that objective; and finally, to create institutions to implement, evaluate, and monitor performance. Here, education, national needs, and external forces intersected, shedding light on how education policies shaped modern Nigeria during the period of first attempt at mass university education (1960–70). Although the goal of using mass university education to meet the country's needs for economic development and nation-building was not met during the 1960s due to regional rivalries, flawed admission, and science policies, as well as the Nigerian civil war (1967–70), the modest progress made during this period laid the foundation to future ambitious attempts at educational expansion.

Ashby recommendations guided the government in departing from the British system and employing educational expansion to serve Nigeria's needs. The commission's bold approach to educational planning differed significantly from the cautious and modest approach that had characterized colonial educational planning. Britain's policy on education, which offered £50 million to the colonies under the Colonial Development and Welfare Act of 1940, provided for controlled educational expansion within 'financial limits.' In contrast, Ashby suggested that financial limits should not hinder expansion. For the commission, education was an investment for which financing must be sought from Nigerian as well as external sources. It was no longer, as the commission insisted, a matter of budgeting according to what the country could afford but a matter of budgeting according to its future needs.[8]

Blueprint for Change

Unlike previous colonial educational reports and policies, the Ashby report acknowledged the link between investment in education and economic development, declaring that the training of a labour force in the universities, especially in the sciences, was a vital component of economic development. As the report noted, "of all Nigeria's resources her young people are the most valuable; expenditure upon their education should be a first charge upon the nation's finances."[9] Accordingly, it recommended that the minimum need over the next ten years was 80,000 people with higher education, 30,000 of whom would be in senior positions, "managerial, professional and administration."[10] To attain the target, the report recommended "an annual flow of at least 2,000 graduates from universities" in place of the present flow of "300 from Ibadan and perhaps 600 from overseas."[11] This projection was based on the submission of F.H. Harbison, an economist and human capital theorists who conducted a special study of Nigeria's labour needs at the post-secondary level. In Harbison's report, published in full as chapter 1 of the Ashby's report, he stressed that the training of human resources was indispensable for Nigeria's economic development and was a matter of urgency. Harbison argued that

> Of all the resources required for economic development, high-level manpower requires the longest 'lead-time' for creation. Modern dams, power stations, textile factories, or steel mills could be constructed within a few years. But it takes between 10 and 15 years to develop the managers, the administrators, and the engineers to operate them. Schools and college buildings can be erected in a matter of months; but it requires decades to develop high-level teachers and professors.[12]

Second, to meet the commission's estimate of the required workforce, it was necessary to build more facilities to absorb demand. Thus, the report proposed three additional universities, to be located in Lagos and the Eastern and Northern regions. The one in Lagos would operate day and evening courses leading to degrees in commerce, business administration, economics, and social science, including courses at the graduate level in higher management studies.[13] In the east, the University of Nigeria at Nsukka would be integrated with the Enugu branch of the Nigerian College of Arts, Science and Technology, while the buildings of the Nigerian College of Arts, Science and Technology in Zaria would become the nucleus for the northern university. The huge land mass and population of Nigeria were major factors in the spread of universities to all regions. As the report noted, "the distances in Nigeria, the variety of people which comprise her population ... all point to the need for at least one university in each Region."[14]

With UCI located in the West, all the regions would have a university but regional politics propelled politicians in the West to seek the creation of another university they would control since the federal government controlled UCI. The report, however, rejected the idea of another university in the Western Region but anticipated a time when there would be "a need for more than one university in each region."[15] As the commission revised its recommendations for submission, the education minister in the Western Region informed the commission that the region had decided to establish a university with regional funds.[16] Nevertheless, the commission insisted in its recommendation that the federal government should not extend financial assistance to more than one university in each region.[17] In support of his region, S.O. Onabamiro, who represented the Western Region in the commission, disagreed with the majority report and issued a minority report where he proposed the establishment of two universities in all the regions, which would bring the number of universities to seven.[18]

To ensure a steady supply of candidates for university education, the commission's report stressed the need to maintain a healthy educational pyramid with the primary school at the base, followed by secondary schools, and with post-secondary schools at the apex. The report observed that, while the pyramid in the South (East and West) was broad at the primary and secondary levels, it constricted far too sharply at the university level. In the North, the pyramid was slim at all levels. The report strongly urged that a proper balance of primary, secondary, and post-secondary education should guide subsequent educational programs.[19] It suggested the creation of 600 more secondary schools, an enlargement of existing secondary schools to facilitate a massive intake, and an increase in secondary school admission from 12,000 per annum since 1958 to more than 30,000 in 1970.[20]

Furthermore, the report suggested an increase of sixth forms to expand the number of university aspirants. The British introduced the sixth form in 1956 as a two- to three-year intermediary period of study between secondary school and university, leading to the Higher School Certificate

(HSC) or General Certificate "A" Level. It was a requirement for direct entry into UCI. Few secondary schools had the facilities and personnel for sixth form education. Besides, it was easier to gain admission to the university with 'O' Levels than with 'A' Levels. The commission recognized this problem by recommending an increase in the number of sixth forms from 22 to 110 to provide a sufficient stream of potential university students. It noted that 29,000 children would complete secondary school certificates; about 21,000 of them should seek employment, and about 8,000 should go for further training.[21]

Third, to enhance access to universities, the report emphasized the overriding need for greater flexibility and diversity in university education to accommodate the diverse interests of potential candidates. It suggested greater diversification of the university curriculum to include courses often neglected in UCI such as African studies, commerce and business administration, teaching, engineering, medicine and veterinary science, agriculture, law, and extension services. The report acknowledged that the British system of university education as obtainable suited the British because in Britain there were many alternative routes to professional training, "and the prestige of these alternative routes is such that thousands of young people prefer to take them rather than go to the university."[22] That system, however, did not suit Nigeria. According to the report,

> In a country where these alternative routes are missing or carry less prestige, the British university system is too inflexible and too academic to meet national needs. We think it is unlikely that in Nigeria these alternative routes will, in the foreseeable future, acquire the prestige which universities already have. Accordingly, a much greater diversity of demand is likely to be made on Nigerian universities than on their British counterparts.[23]

The report revealed its admiration for the American system of higher education when it identified the American land-grant universities as models for the diversification of university studies in Nigeria. According to the report, "the land-grant universities of the United States have had to fulfill functions similar to those which Nigerian universities are now called upon to fulfill, and the best of them have done so without in any way surrendering their integrity."[24] Although the report did not impose either the American or the British system of education on Nigeria, it argued that "neither kind of university should be exported unchanged to Nigeria; but both kinds have something to teach this country, and the lessons to be learnt from America include diversity and flexibility."[25]

To promote mass access to university education, the Ashby Commission recognized the importance of scholarship awards. In the past, lack of funds had prevented many bright students from accepting places offered them by UCI. According to Kenneth Dike, the principal of the college, the university asked more than 101 students who had failed to pay their fees to withdraw at the end of the 1959/60 session.[26] The Ashby Commission thus recommended "that grants should be made from regional or federal funds to all students who are accepted for admission to Nigerian universities and who are not able to pay for their university education themselves."[27]

Fourth, the commission was sensitive to the role of educational opportunities and facilities in promoting national cohesion. When Nigeria attained independence in 1960, the question of unity and balanced educational development for the equitable training of personnel, earlier subordinated to academic standards during the colonial period, assumed great importance. The commission envisaged that federal appointments would continue to generate controversy because the North was disadvantaged in terms of available high-level personnel as compared with other regions. The North did not stand a chance if strict academic merit determined appointments at the federal and regional levels of government. Therefore, the recommendation to establish a university in the North served to provide more opportunities for northerners to catch up with the South. Acknowledging the existence of strong regional loyalties as well as inter-regional rivalry, the commission warned: "It would be a disaster if each university were to serve only its own region."[28] The report called for a uniform admission policy for all the universities, based on merit without discriminating against any region or ethnic group, but cautioned that

> the borders between Regions must never become barriers to the migration of brains. Nigeria's intellectual life, and her economy, will suffer unless there is free migration of both staff and

students from one Region to another. We know that we are echoing the convictions of Nigerian leaders when we say that one of the purposes of education in this country is to promote cohesion between her Regions. Universities should be a powerful instrument for this purpose: it is their duty to respond.[29]

Fifth, since the funds required for university expansion were enormous, the commission suggested that, for the country to meet the ambitious targets contained in the report, Nigerians must be prepared to accord education first priority; to make sacrifices for it as well as to seek external assistance. The report noted that the proposal was a "stupendous undertaking" and therefore "Nigerian people will haveto forgo other things they want so that every available penny is invested in education. Even this will not be enough. Countries outside Nigeria will have to be enlisted to help with men and money. Nigerian education must for a time become an international enterprise."[30]

Sixth, the commission recommended the establishment of two interregional institutions to ensure the successful implementation of government policies. The first was the National Universities Commission, whose function was to secure and distribute funds to universities, co-ordinate the activities of the universities, and provide cohesion for the whole system of higher education in the country. The second was the Inter-Regional Manpower Board, which was charged with the duty to continuously review the labour needs of the country and to formulate programs for effective staff development. Since the 1960 Constitution granted autonomy to the regions, these bodies were designed to co-ordinate the activities of all the universities to ensure uniform development.

The Ashby Commission's proposal was based on the need to invest in mass education for economic development and nation-building. As the report noted, "it would be a grave disservice to Nigeria to make modest, cautious proposals, likely to fall within her budget, for such proposals would be totally inadequate to maintain even the present rate of economic growth."[31] By broadening its terms of reference to include the need for primary, secondary, technical, and teacher education, the commission recognized the pyramidal structure of education, with all levels of the pyramid being connected. Its vision for education ultimately became a blueprint for educational development in Nigeria. Throughout the 1960s, government was mindful of the commission's proposals as they aimed to reshape the direction of societal change; to correct the educational imbalances between the North and the South; to diversify the university education system; and to expand, improve, and democratize university facilities and opportunities. By attempting to reconfigure and reconceptualize the inherited system of higher education to serve Nigeria's postcolonial needs for a high-level labour force, economic and technological development, and national integration, the Ashby report presented a strategy for Nigeria's circumstances in the 1960s and beyond.

While the federal government considered the ramifications of the Ashby report submitted to it in September 1960, the Eastern Region went ahead to open the University of Nigeria, Nsukka (UNN) on 7 October 1960. The university started with the faculty of arts, but enrolment surged when broad and wide-ranging courses in the faculties of agriculture, applied sciences, and vocational studies were offered.[32] Dr. George Johnson, the first acting principal of the university, noted that the purpose of curriculum diversity was to "develop professional and practical curricula which produce citizens who are broadly educated and at the same time equipped with specialized knowledge which will enable them engage in productive work in a rapidly changing society."[33]

Since the Eastern Region founded UNN by taking advantage of the provision of 1954 as well as the independence constitution (which placed higher education on the Concurrent Legislative List), the Western Region pressed ahead with its plan to establish a regional university. As far back as 1958, the Action Group had been quite critical of the elitist character of UCI, and the regional government wanted an institution that would symbolize its idea of a university.[34] However, Ashby's report did not recommend the establishment of a university in the region because UCI, though a federal university, was located in the west and was expected to meet the higher education needs of the entire region. Given the fact that the region had made plans since 1958 to establish a university in the area and the minority report authored by Onabamiro favoured more than one university in each region, the region forged ahead with the idea of a regional university despite the majority report, citing regional interests as a motivating factor.

Although UCI was located in the Western Region, government officials in the region argued that the institution catered to broad national interests. They therefore sought to establish another university in the region that would serve only regional interests. The idea of a regional university was, perhaps, an attempt to afford the region full control of one university, a privilege that they anticipated the other regions would soon enjoy. Thus, in 1960, the government of the Western Region set up a university planning committee and later appointed a team that studied the systems of higher education in the United States, Mexico, Brazil, and Israel. Since the constitution permitted regional ownership of institutions of higher education on their own financial responsibility, the federal government did not stop the region from pursuing its plan. Subsequently, the region passed legislation authorizing the setting up of the University of Ife.

The ethnic/regional rivalries that had been a common feature of Nigeria's political life since the British created the three regional governments in 1939 manifested in the Western Region's quest to own a university. In the white paper released in 1960, the government accused the Ashby commission of neglecting it in its recommendations for new universities in Nigeria. It noted that while the commission recommended the establishment of universities other regions, it failed to do the same for the Western Region. The sentiments expressed in the white paper clearly revealed the intense mutual suspicion and ethnic rivalry that characterized inter-regional relations in Nigeria, especially when it presented the likely implications of not owning a university. According to the paper, the Eastern Region would own

> its own Regional University, as well as continue to enjoy its quota of admissions into the University College, Ibadan. The Northern Region might also have a new University College in Kano, the Ahmadu Bello College, as well as continue to enjoy its own quota of admissions into the University College, Ibadan, with the consolation, of course, that students from this Region might also be admitted into the Federal University Institutions in other parts of the Country.[35]

The allusion to a quota system (an affirmative action policy) of admission, supposedly applied to UCI as part of the justification for establishing a regional university in the Western Region, was both erroneous and propagandistic. The institution, in fact, did not have a quota policy for the regions following the 1952 report of the Inter-University Council. Indeed, the driving force behind the Western Region's plan to establish a university was to prevent other regions from surpassing it in training workforce. Protecting the interests of the region in the context of regional competition was a fundamental driving force, and it was evident in the white paper's concluding remarks:

> The Government has seriously considered the present position and the new situation that might arise, and regards it as its duty to take the proper measure to safeguard the interest of the people of Western Nigeria in the provision of facilities for higher education. It is in order to meet the challenge of the situation that the Government has decided to build a new university.[36]

Implementing Ashby's Report

The federal government accepted the recommendations of the Ashby Commission in 1960 "in principle as a sound analysis of the present position, and [declared] that their recommendation, with some amendments, should constitute the basis for the development of post-School Certificate and Higher Education in Nigeria for the next ten years."[37] In announcing this conclusion, the federal government proclaimed its determination to pursue an energetic policy of higher educational development and the promotion of nation-building and the economic development of the nation. As the government declared, "Nigeria must aim to make and sustain an educational effort more than three times as great as is already being made now."[38] To achieve this, it proclaimed its readiness "to play its full part in the implementation of these proposals [hoping that] … Regional Governments will be willing to shoulder their share of the financial burden of implementing the proposals."[39]

Where the federal government found the commission's recommendations to be somewhat conservative, it favoured a more radical approach. For instance, it extended the proposals by recommending a target enrolment of 10,000 students as against the 7,500 suggested by the Ashby Commission.[40] In addition, it stated government readiness to raise the number of sixth form streams to 350 in order to increase the number of students preparing for the Higher School Certificate (HSC) or the General Certificate of Education ('A' Level) to over 10,000.[41] The paper also accepted the Western Region's plans to establish a university.

The endorsement of the Ashby report was a turning point in the development of higher education in Nigeria; it formed the basis for the launching of the First National Development Plan (First NDP) for the period between 1962 and 1968. Education planning, for the first time in the country's history, was made to constitute a strategic part of national development planning. Prior to this plan, there was no comprehensive development plan. The colonial development plan was limited to the development of the agricultural sector only in terms of promoting some cash crops and the building of transport and communication systems; it neglected industrial, human resource development and nation-building. The overall national educational goal, as articulated in the First NDP, was the "democratization of education at all levels, and for all Nigerians, irrespective of their geographical location, religious persuasion, and age."[42] The plan further declared that Nigeria's "virile population has scarcely yet been developed to a degree sufficient to alleviate the poverty of the bulk of the people."[43] For the period of the First NDP, the government earmarked a total expenditure of £45 to £65 million for the implementation of the federal and regional governments' programs in the education sector. This amount, which represented about 60 per cent of the total expenditure for the First NDP, was enormous. However, the federal government was hoping to attract external funds to support this ambitious plan.[44]

To finance its expensive educational goals – and in fulfillment of the Ashby Commission's suggestion – the federal government sought external financial support. External donors committed an estimated amount of £10 million for university education in Nigeria from 1960 to 1964 in the form of foundation grants for research, endowment, and buildings. For instance, USAID provided over £1 million to UNN, the initial principal and first two vice-chancellors (G.M. Johnson 1960–64, and Glen Taggart 1964–66), and thirty professors and teachers biennially, with equipment and technical assistance especially in the central administration and agriculture. Furthermore, the Rockefeller Foundation supported agricultural and medical research and staff development at Ibadan; the Nuffield Foundation supported research facilities; the Carnegie Corporation supported education projects and institutes of education in the universities that emerged in 1960s; and the Netherlands government allocated grants to develop the faculty of engineering at UNN. UNESCO provided general assistance at Lagos, especially in the school of business administration, in collaboration with USAID; and the West German government awarded scholarships to students at various universities.[45] This external generosity demonstrated the commitment of Western countries to consolidate their hold on Nigeria in its fight against communism.

To ensure the realization of Nigeria's needs for a trained labour force, and acting on the recommendation of the Ashby Commission, the federal government composed the National Manpower Board (NMB) and the National Universities Commission (NUC) in 1962. It appointed Dr. T.M. Yesufu, a senior labour officer in the Federal Ministry of Labour, as the secretary of the NMB. The board's responsibility was to "determine periodically the nation's man-power needs in all occupations, and formulate programmes for effective man-power development throughout the federation through university expansion, scholarships, and fellowships."[46] Ideally, the recommendations of the NMB would have shaped the development plan, but the federal government launched the First NDP before forming the NMB. The shortage of high-level personnel was a central causative factor. In his speech at the first meeting of the NMB on 4 December 1962, the minister of economic development noted that "it has taken so long to constitute the Board because of a number of difficulties, one of which emphasizes the importance of your work: namely, that qualified persons were not easily available for appointment to the specialist post in the manpower Secretariat."[47] During the third meeting of the board, the minister reiterated the problem when he stated that "there are critical shortages in capital formation and high-level manpower. The two are intricately intertwined: capital is needed for manpower development but capital will be wasted if there is no adequate manpower to make optimum use of it."[48]

In line with the Ashby report, the federal government also set up the NUC under Okoi Arikpo as the executive secretary and charged it with the duty, among others, "to inquire into and advise the government on financial needs both recurrent and capital of university education in Nigeria." It was also required "to consult with the universities and other relevant bodies to plan the balanced and coordinated development of the universities in order to ensure that they are fully adequate to meet the national needs." The commission was to "receive annually a block grant from the federal government and allocate it to universities with such conditions as the commission may think advisable."[49] The federal government's prioritization of higher education in the First NDP and the emergence of both the NMB and NUC testified to the importance it attached to the expansion of university education in Nigeria. As Bello Salim aptly observed, the implementation of the Ashby report "started Nigeria's march towards general access to university education."[50]

Furthermore, in keeping with the commission's suggestions, the government of the North under the leadership of its first premier, Ahmadu Bello, invited a delegation from the Inter-University Council for Higher Education Overseas in April 1961 to seek their advice on the proposed university for the region. The delegation observed that besides providing the much-needed labour force, establishing a university in the North would stimulate all forms of education in the region, and it stressed the need for extra-mural studies to guarantee a supply of university candidates.[51] Following the advice of the delegation, the House of Assembly passed the law that established the Provisional Council for the proposed university in November 1961, and in June 1962 it established Ahmadu Bello University (ABU), located in Zaria. The North funded ABU, although the federal government gave the university the old site of the Nigerian College of Arts, Science, and Technology in Zaria, which was valued at £2.6 million. Formal lectures began on 4 October 1962 with 400 students spread through the faculties of Arts and Education, Pure Science, Social Science, Technology, and Agriculture and Forestry.

Acting also on the recommendations of the Ashby Commission, the federal government sought help from the United Nations Educational, Scientific, and Cultural Organization (UNESCO) in planning the University of Lagos. The UNESCO advisory committee for the establishment of the University of Lagos, appointed in June 1961, submitted its report in September of the same year. The report favoured opening the university with faculties of medicine, law, and commerce as well as faculties of arts, science, education, and engineering, and the Institute of African Studies. It also recommended the development of evening classes in all faculties, especially those of law and commerce.[52] In April 1962, the federal parliament passed a law establishing the University of Lagos (UNILAG), and, on 22 October 1962, the university opened with a student population of 100.[53] Since it was a federal university, the federal government provided 100 per cent funding for UNILAG. Similarly, on 24 October 1962, the University of Ife, Ile-Ife, established by the Western Region, opened with 244 students. The region wholly funded Ife, although the federal government gave the university the site of the old Nigerian College of Arts, Science, and Technology, valued at £1.5 million. The students were admitted into five faculties: agriculture, arts, economics and social science, law, and science, including pharmacy. Later courses in medical sciences, education, and agricultural engineering were added to the curriculum.[54]

By 1962, two years after independence, five universities had emerged in Nigeria, including UCI, which in 1962 severed its relationship with the University of London to become an autonomous degree-awarding institution called University of Ibadan (UI). The three regions owned and financed their respective universities at Nsukka, Ife, and Zaria, while the federal government owned and financed the universities in Lagos and Ibadan. During the 1961/62 session, there were 3,235 students were in all Nigerian universities, the highest enrolment in sub-Saharan Africa.[55] The determining factors for the establishment of regional universities were political and regional interests. The regions determined what kind of universities they wanted and where they were located. While the federal government yielded to the ambitions of the regions, it was equally acting in accordance with the conviction that education would open the road to social and economic development as well as respect for the regions whose power the constitution recognized.

With the increase in the number of universities, it became necessary to set up a forum for the vice-chancellors of these institutions to come together and discuss issues of common concern. That forum, called the

Committee of Vice-Chancellors (CVC), was founded in 1962 on the initiation of K.O. Dike. Fashioned after the Committee of Vice-Chancellors of the United Kingdom, which was a powerful non-statutory body, the CVC, as defined by Dr. Jubril Aminu, was "an informal, non-statutory body set up by the Universities to advise themselves on matters of mutual interest."[56] The forum brought vice-chancellors together in a loose, non-statutory organization with moral power based on the consensus of the members in order to make decisions for the smooth and uniform development of universities. However, its decisions were advisory; the federal and regional governments were not bound by them because there was no force of law to back them. Nevertheless, the CVC became a formidable force in shaping and influencing government policies on university education throughout the rest of the twentieth century, notably in the 1970s – as shown in chapter 4.

Like the CVC, the NUC had no statutory power. It was an administrative unit in the Cabinet Office and thus functioned in an advisory capacity and lacked power to enforce its decisions, especially as the regional governments jealously guarded their autonomy over their universities. This rendered the NUC ineffective in fulfilling the aims and objectives the government envisaged. In carrying out its duties, however, the NUC visited all universities between October 1962 and May 1963.[57] At each university, the commission had discussions with members of the governing councils, the senates, the deans of faculties, the non-professional academic staff, the administration, the non-academic staff, and the students. The commission submitted its report in 1963 to the federal government. The report addressed university funding and enrolment issues. First, it proposed that the federal government should be responsible for 50 per cent of the total recurrent and capital expenditure of the three regional universities at Nsukka, Ife, and Zaria, while federal universities in Lagos and Ibadan should continue to receive 100 per cent subsidies.

Second, based on the projection of student numbers submitted by various universities, the commission projected an enrolment of 10,000 full-time students by 1967–68, spread according to the following order of disciplines: agriculture, forestry, and fisheries, 1,250 students; pure science, 2,830; veterinary science, 300; medicine, 1,000; engineering, 2,000; arts, 1,420; and others (business, social studies, and management), 1,000.[58] The suggestion for higher intake in science courses represented the view of the Ashby Commission as well as the need for the universities to respond to government desire for rapid economic development. The NUC report noted that since the sixth form facilities did not adequately train potential university candidates, it was necessary to offer preliminary courses in Nigerian universities, especially for science courses, to provide opportunities for all Nigerians. At the same time, it stressed that the government should continue to expand the sixth form facilities in Lagos and the regions.[59]

Furthermore, the commission acknowledged the increasing demand for university education among Nigerians but observed that at every university it visited "a large number of candidates competing for admission into university are insufficiently equipped for it."[60] According to the report, many students who secured admission into university had inadequate financial resources to complete their education: "they start on a degree course with just enough money to carry them through one session in the hope that once they are in the university a scholarship or bursary would be made available to them. When this hope fails, they leave the university without completing their course and their place is wasted."[61] The commission therefore recommended automatic scholarships for all indigent students.

The federal government released its white paper in 1964, detailing its decisions on the NUC report. In the paper, it decided to give the three regional universities 50 per cent of their capital grant of £17.63 million. While UNN and Ife received 30 per cent of their recurrent grant of £30 million, ABU received 50 per cent. Justifying this disproportionate allocation, the federal government noted that "75 percent of students in ABU came from outside the North whilst the North had not at present got as many students in other universities and that was likely to be the position for some time to come."[62] Besides, it noted that the financial relief for the North would enable it to "make available more funds for the provision of sixth forms in secondary schools and thus increase the number of potential entrants in Northern Nigeria."[63] The white paper accepted the NUC report on awarding scholarships to all students and on enrolment in science courses but added that, out of the projected student population of 10,000, "7,580 should be taking courses in pure and applied sciences in view of the shortage of qualified Nigerians in those fields of study."[64]

The financial allocations in favour of the North demonstrate the federal government's awareness of the low number of high-level personnel from the region and its willingness to address it in the interests of promoting national unity. The data on registered high-level personnel by region show that the North, despite its large population, had the lowest number: the North, 54 (4.3%); the Federal Territory, 79 (6.3%); the East, 468 (37.0%); the West, 499 (39.5%), and the Mid-West 162 (12.8%).[65] These data show the regional imbalance that would remain a source of tension between the South and the North.

Why did the federal government favour courses in science and technology? The federal government's decision to train Nigerians in science and technology was a manifestation of the trend of thinking in the 1960s. The political elite and some scholars believed that the wonders of the Western world emanated from the sciences. Therefore, to sustain independence as well as justify it to Nigerians, the government hoped to train Nigerians in relevant skills vital in modernizing the economy. As a Nigerian scholar, Biobaku noted, "a developing country must modernize its economy in order to ensure growth and make its independence a reality."[66] The key, of course, was the provision of educated men trained in all disciplines but most importantly in science and technology. Moreover, university education was, unavoidably, in the frontline of government's efforts at modernization, and, as such, the emphasis on personnel training in science and technology served as a constant reinforcement of the need for investment in university education and the expansion of opportunities. In a convocation speech at UI in 1962, Nnamdi Azikiwe, the governor-general of Nigeria, gave this advice to graduating students: "In a technological age, the men who shape our destinies are men who create, and creation does not happen behind the desk or at the telephone but in the workshops of the firm, the laboratory and the virgin bush."[67]

Azikiwe was not alone in linking higher education to the practical needs of Nigerian society. Balewa had also noted that the federal government emphasized science education to provide Nigerians with the kind of education that would produce citizens who "know how to think; and knowing how, do it."[68] He stressed that the best test of Nigerian universities would be in the "success with which they help the community to build the education they need to cope with their changing needs."[69] The pronouncement of these leaders underscored the importance the federal government accorded to science education because of its place in facilitating the economic and technological development of the country. Yet the lingering educational legacy threatened the realization of mass university education and science education in the 1960s.

Colonial Legacy

Meeting the goal of economic development and nation-building in Nigeria through a policy shift towards mass education was farfetched in the 1960s. Indeed, the prevailing admission practices, inadequate sixth form facilities, insufficient and politicized scholarship awards, and regional political rivalries, as well as national conflict and the civil war undermined that goal. Thus, educational practices were in many cases reminiscent of colonial traditions. While political leaders professed their determination to realign postcolonial universities to meet specific national needs, their actions, just like those of colonial administrators, were often divorced from their words. In a sense, the elitism that characterized colonial higher education largely remained.

The admission practices of Nigerian universities, with few exceptions, followed the pattern of those of UCI in colonial Nigeria. In terms of admission requirements, the universities of Ibadan, Ife, Lagos, and Ahmadu Bello admitted candidates with the A-Level qualification or its equivalents. Candidates were required to pass five subjects at the General Certificate of Education (GCE), two of which had to be at Advanced Level, or four subjects, three of which had to be at Advanced Level. Students usually took these exams after completing a two-year program in secondary schools that had sixth forms; they were typically admitted by direct entry, spending only three years at university. These four universities also provided opportunities for concessional admission, which was available for candidates fresh from high school. Such candidates were required to have passed the GCE (Ordinary Level) in five subjects, including English and mathematics. They also sat for an entrance examination, and, if successful, took a one-year preliminary course before proceeding to a degree course. Those admitted by this method were primarily in the sciences, medicine, and technology, due to insufficient enrolment in those courses.

The University of Nigeria, Nsukka, retained the same admission policy as that which obtained in UI, Ife, Lagos, and ABU in terms of direct entry requirements and course duration. In addition, students admitted by entrance examination took four years to obtain a degree in most subjects, excluding engineering, which took five. However, UNN differed from the others by requiring a minimum entrance qualification of passes in six subjects at GCE Ordinary Level (or five credits in the West African School Certificate), provided that students passed these subjects at one sitting and included a language and either mathematics or an approved science subject. The primary entrance qualification into Lagos, UI, Ife, and ABU was quite similar to that required for entrance into United Kingdom universities, whereas UNN's policy resembled the policy governing admission to universities in the United States of America. It was largely because of UNN's flexibility that its student enrolment rivalled those of UI, a much older institution. In fact, in the 1964/65 academic session, student enrolment at UNN was 2,482 while in other universities the numbers were lower: UI (2,284), ABU (719), Ife (659), and UNILAG (659).[70]

One of the main driving forces behind the idea of concessional admission in UN, Ife, Lagos, and ABU and the Ordinary Level requirement at UNN was the lack of a sufficient number of sixth-form schools and teachers, especially in the science subjects. This situation clearly resulted in a huge shortage of students qualified for university education, especially in the sciences. Statistics from 1962 to 1968 reveal that students in the humanities outnumbered those in other fields, including the sciences.

These numbers fell below government expectations. The labour force projections indicated that at least 60 per cent of Nigeria's work force should have received at least a basic training in science and technology. As shown in Table 3.1, the enrolment situation was almost reversed, with an average of almost 60 per cent of students in the universities admitted in the liberal arts or social sciences. This statistic showed that the postcolonial curriculum reform had not yet met the expectations of the federal government, and a survey conducted by Fafunwa in 1964 confirmed the general dissatisfaction of Nigerians with the prevailing system of education.[71] Disturbed by the report of this survey, the Joint Consultative Committee at its 1964

Table 3.1: Enrolment by Discipline.

Years	Humanities (%)	Science (%)
1962/63	56	44
1963/64	57	43
1964/65	59	41
1965/66	56	44
1966/67	54	46
1967/68	57	43

Source: Annual Review of Nigerian Universities: Academic Year 1967–68 (Lagos: Federal Ministry of Information, 1968), 27.

bi-annual meeting scheduled a national conference in 1965 to discuss the problem and come up with a national philosophy to guide educational development. But due to political unrest and the eventual outbreak of war, the conference date was postponed indefinitely.

Why did the universities' enrolments fail to satisfy government's expectations? K.O. Dike, the vice-chancellor of University of UN, stated that, besides the lack of adequate funds, which frustrated the introduction of courses in the applied sciences, such as engineering and food technology, the government's efforts to encourage the study of sciences at the primary and secondary school levels were inadequate. The result was that the majority of university applicants sought courses in the humanities. To meet the admission target in the sciences, Dike believed that government should begin at the primary and secondary school levels, for

> until that is done, it would be difficult, indeed unrealistic, to accord the applied sciences the degree of emphasis that is now being demanded, no matter how strenuously the universities may be urged to alter their emphasis. If the schools persist in turning out a majority of students whose training is literary, the universities cannot turn out technologically minded students from such material.[72]

The sixth form was increasing being perceived by Nigerians as a blind copy of the British system and was thus blamed for the insufficient preparation of candidates for higher education in science disciplines. Most countries, except the United Kingdom and the former British African colonies, followed a four-year university course, which required passes in an examination at the Ordinary Level or its equivalent. Countries such as the USSR, the United States, Canada, Australia, India, and New Zealand required a good secondary school certificate and/or a pass in a university entrance examination.[73] Nigerian universities, except UNN, however, maintained an admission policy that required passes at Advanced Level GCE. Only in secondary schools with sixth forms could students prepare to take the advanced level exam. At independence, there were few such schools, which was why the Ashby Commission recommended their expansion to ensure an adequate supply of candidates for university education. Although the number of sixth formers qualified for direct entry into universities increased rapidly from 289 in 1960 to 1,190 in 1966, "university places available outpaced sixth form production by at least four times."[74] Six years after releasing the report of the commission he chaired, Eric Ashby regretted the commission's decision on sixth form:

> It may turn out that this was an unwise decision. The consequences are already unfortunate: a valuable opportunity to provide flexibility in the educational system has been lost, and one university [UNN] has found it advisable to circumvent the rigidities of the British pattern of schooling by admitting students at O level.[75]

Because the sixth form constituted a bottleneck to university expansion, the call to abolish it grew. Arikpo, the secretary of NUC, pointed out that the sixth form system was not in the best interest of Nigeria on either economic or educational grounds. He noted that the "inability to recruit qualified teachers, and the shortage of capital and recurrent funds, placed severe limitations both on increasing the number of sixth forms, and on improving those that already exist."[76] Similarly, an editorial in the *West African Journal of Education* stated that the heavy capital and recurrent cost involved in sixth form expansion was unjustifiable, especially "at a time when the staffing of the whole secondary school system cannot be regarded as satisfactory."[77] It stressed that the "time has now arrived for a systematic evaluation of the sixth form and its place, if any, in the total educational system."[78]

In response to the growing campaign against the sixth form, the federal government set up a commission under the joint auspices of the NUC and the CVC to "review the place of the sixth form as preparation for university admission and for entry to other vocations" and to determine whether or not "the sixth form as now constituted does provide a satisfactory preparation for university admission."[79] The commission was required either to make recommendations for its improvement "both in quantity and quality (content, structure and breadth) [or] to recommend alternative measures for the preparation of University entrants so as to maintain high academic standards in Nigerian universities."[80] In its report, submitted in 1967, the commission observed that "there were not enough sixth form students at the HSC level to feed the universities and the universities had to rely on private students who sat for the GCE Advanced Level and school leavers from the fifth form who took the School Certificate examination."[81] The commission noted that "the sixth form as presently organized is wasteful and uneconomical" and therefore called for its abolition as an integral part of the secondary school.[82] However, the commission advocated the temporary maintenance of concessional admission into universities, especially in the sciences, to remedy students' deficiencies. This, it suggested, would be in the interest of national needs as long as "there continues to exist an insufficient supply of inadequately qualified entrants in the field of science and technology."[83] Until the 1970s, this recommendation was not implemented, largely due to the civil war.

Another factor that affected access to universities was the candidates' financial constraints. Data on government scholarship awards from 1960 to 1965 reveal that the federal government sponsored 895 students in the five existing universities; the regional governments, 1,245 students; other bodies, 1,042; and private students, 3,525. This brought the student population in all Nigerian universities to 6,707.[84] Compared to the demand for places, however, this number was small. It was ironic, as Dike observed, that in a land crying out for trained men and women with governments that established more universities to meet this national emergency, these governments were "unwilling to award automatic scholarships to deserving students to enable them accept places offered them at Ibadan."[85] For instance, during the 1962/63 session in UI, as Dike shows, 921 students gained admission but only 670 accepted the offer, mostly due to financial reasons. About 40 per cent of them were private students, and, according to Dike, judging from experience, many of them "may not pay their fees and therefore run the risk of expulsion."[86]

The most formidable obstacle to the postcolonial goal of using mass university education to forge a united Nigeria as well as advance economic development was the country's unending inter-regional power tussle, which began in 1914 and has grown in intensity ever since. The university system was not immune to the national crisis that engulfed the country from 1964 to 1969. Since 1960, the fear of domination and deprivation had strained the relationship between the three regions. It was partly due to this fear that the independence constitution upheld the regional autonomy established during the colonial period. The first civilian administration in Nigeria, often termed the First Republic, operated a parliamentary system of government and a decentralized federation. That system emphasized regional autonomy as a way of allaying fears of domination and deprivation. Yet, national issues were purely viewed from parochial regional lenses. For instance, the first census conducted in postcolonial Nigeria in 1962 was cancelled due to heated controversy and accusations of falsifications in many areas. The second exercise, which took place in 1963, suffered the same fate. Although the census result was officially accepted, the South viewed the population of 25.86 million allocated to it and 29.80 million for the North as an insidious attempt by the North to gain national political advantage. Since population determined federal financial allocations and the number of political seats allocated to each region at the federal legislature, it was not surprising that census results would be a subject of high interest and debate.[87] Worse still was that the lingering crisis following the disputed elections of 1964 and the alleged massive corruption of political leaders at the federal and regional levels resulted in a military coup in January 1966 in which mostly prominent northern politicians, including Prime Minister Balewa, were killed. An Igbo major, Kaduna Nzeogwu, led the coup.

Although the coup was unsuccessful, the North was apprehensive of southern domination, as Major General J.T.U. Aguiyi-Ironsi, an Igbo, who was the top-ranking military officer, became the head of state. Northern misgiving was confirmed when Aguiyi-Ironsi's government adopted a unitary system of government for the country, a system that stripped the three regions of their autonomy. The new government identified education as a source of disunity and thus promulgated *Decree No. 1*, dubbed the "Unification Decree," which, among other things, aimed at reappraising educational policies to ensure high and uniform standards throughout the country as well as to re-orient universities to serve the genuine needs of the people.[88] The North, which had been educationally disadvantaged since the colonial period, had held strongly to political power at the federal level and maintained autonomy at the regional levels as a tool to overcome its educational imbalance. Aguiyi-Ironsi's centralization posture terrified northerners. As Welch and Smith put it:

> Despite its size, the North feared the southern regions. This fear sprang largely from the limited educational and economic opportunities in the region. Preference for recruitment into the Northern Civil Service was given [to] Northerners, even with lower educational qualifications. Abolition of such preferences would close the major avenue by which Northerners could advance themselves.[89]

Largely inspired by the fear of losing the autonomy and potential privileges northerners enjoyed (including in university education), another coup, spearheaded by northern military officers, overthrew Aguiyi-Ironsi's regime on 29 July 1966, six months after that regime came to power. Lieutenant Colonel (later General) Gowon, one of the leaders of the coup that saw the brutal assassination of Aguiyi-Ironsi, became the new head of state. Gowon suspended Aguiyi-Ironsi's unitary decree; a move the Igbos interpreted to mean that there was no basis for Nigerian unity. Colonel Odumegwu Ojukwu, the military governor of the East refused to accept Gowon's accession to power. The nation-building agenda of postcolonial Nigeria seemed threatened. To address the problem, Gowon convened the Ad Hoc Constitutional Conference in September to discuss a political arrangement in Nigeria that would be acceptable to all the regions. The North, which pushed for a confederal system along with the Eastern Region at this conference, later supported a strong federal system along with the Western Region. The Eastern Region remained alone. Efforts at reconciliation, which occurred at many meetings, in and outside Nigeria, failed; worsened, of course, by the indiscriminate killing of Igbos in the North. About 80–100,000 Igbos were killed in the North between May and September 1966 in the wake of the Nzeogwu-led coup.[90] Gowon's inability to end the revenge killing of Igbo people in the North caused the Igbos to lose faith in the nation-building project, thereby providing the grounds for the Eastern Region to contemplate seceding from the country.

The financial and administrative autonomy enjoyed by the regions played a critical role in the political tension that engulfed Nigeria. In 1960, oil revenue contributed only 1 per cent of federal government revenue. It jumped to 18 per cent in 1966.[91] Since the Eastern Region, which was the custodian to majority of Nigerian oil reserves, threatened secession, the federal government realized the revenue implications and thus moved to reduce the powers of the regions.[92] Mainly in order to weaken the attempt at secession, as well as to curry the support of minorities in the regions, the federal government promulgated the decree titled *States (Creation and Transitional Provision) Decree No. 14 of 1967*.[93] This decree divided the country into twelve states. Before the decree, there were four regions, the Northern, Eastern, Western, and Midwest (created in 1964). With this decree, six states were created out of the Northern Region (North Central, North Eastern, North Western, Kano, Benue-Plateau, and Kwara); three were carved out of the Eastern Region (East-Central, South Eastern, and Rivers); two were formed out of the Western Region (Lagos and Western); and the Midwest Region became the Midwestern State.[94] Ojukwu resisted these geo-political changes, arguing that it was the responsibility of the regions to create states. These changes, however, did not prevent Ojukwu from pursuing the region's secessionist agenda. On 30 May 1967, Emeka Ojukwu proclaimed the independent Republic of Biafra. Swiftly the federal government declared war on the former Eastern region. A civil war ensued, lasting from 1967 to 1970. The nation-building project that mass education policies aimed to affirm was tested and failed. Various scholars have acknowledged the devastation of the war and its impact on virtually all the future political decisions in Nigeria.[95]

The civil war had implications for educational expansion. The nation-building agenda of mass university education failed as it did not prevent the war. The war diverted funds that would have aided educational growth, disrupted academic activities, especially in the east where school activities stopped, and further worsened the lingering regional competition and mistrust. Nowhere was the regional conflict more manifest, at least in the late 1960s, than the controversy surrounding the establishment of the Indigent Students Scheme. The scheme, initiated in 1967 by Obafemi Awolowo, was designed to address the financial hindrances to mass university education. In *Blue Print for Post-War Reconstruction*, Awolowo, who was the federal commissioner for finance and deputy chair of the federal executive council, stated that Nigeria was still "deficient in high-level manpower" partly because there were talented Nigerians who are "unable to obtain secondary as well as university education, simply because their parents are too poor to find the money."[96] To remedy this situation, the federal government decided to provide money to those who were "unable to pay their fees."[97]

The implementation of the policy made the North uncomfortable. Northern leaders perceived the program as a deliberate ploy by the South to use the country's national resources to sustain its lead in education. This caused resentment in the North, even among intellectuals. Ibrahim Tahir, a lecturer at ABU, argued against the scheme on the ground that it benefited one ethnic group in the South more than others.[98] Northern opposition to the scheme reached a crescendo when the vice-chancellor of Ahmadu Bello University, Ishaya Audu, called on the federal government to scrap the scheme and replace it with a loan scheme because only five students from the North benefited from it as opposed to numerous students from the South.[99] Commenting on the statement credited to Audu, the Indigent Student Association of the University of Ibadan said that it was "ironical that some intellectuals who had attained their present academic status through virtually free primary, post-primary and all higher learning now rejected the way by which they climbed."[100] The student body declared that Audu was "arousing Northern movement against the South."[101] Although the federal minister of education, Wenike Briggs, dismissed Audu's statements as "unfortunate" and reiterated the government's support of the scheme, the federal government still went ahead and cancelled the scheme in 1969.[102] Since the head of state, Gowon, came from the North, it took little effort to persuade him to scrap the policy presumably to demonstrate his sympathy for the North.

Nigeria's postcolonial mass education policy of decolonizing the elitist British legacies in Nigeria's higher education made great progress in terms of enrolment (at least when compared to the colonial period). Yet it failed to satisfy rising demands for university education, let alone facilitate economic development and national unity. Between 1959 and 1969, student enrolment in Nigerian universities jumped from 939 to 9,695 students, excluding those at UNN, which was closed during the civil war.[103] That was a huge figure, even surpassing Ashby's proposed figures. When the Ashby Commission submitted its report in 1960, Nigerians perceived it as proposing a radical increase. However, the actual development of schools exceeded Ashby's recommendation of 7,500 students. Yet, in terms of the percentage of Nigerian in universities, the number was disappointingly low. While only 0.2 to 0.3 per cent of northerners were in the existing universities, for the rest of the country it was 0.5 to 0.6 per cent.[104]

Although the period marked a significant improvement over the elitist British pattern, it also revealed a failure to accommodate the increasing demand for university education. For instance, at the University of Ife, while 10,518 students sought for admission between 1966 and 1969, only 1,924 were successful. At the University of Ibadan, while 14,048 students applied for admission between 1964 and 1970, only 2,882 secured places.[105] Similarly, educational expansion did not translate to high enrolment of students in the science and technology courses as anticipated in the first NDP. Moreover, even though government officers, policy-makers, and other proponents of change emphasized applied sciences and vocational subjects, the actual implementation of this policy, with the exception of UNN, did not support their pronouncements. In reality, there were fewer demands for graduates in the sciences compared to the humanities, law, and liberal arts. It seemed that politicians were interested in producing graduates to fill positions in the regional and federal civil service regardless of the course of study. Therefore, candidates made demands for liberal courses to which the universities responded. In addition, prominent Nigerians in leadership positions, including Azikiwe and Awolowo, were not scientists.

The kind of role models they provided favoured arts, humanities, and law. Also, high-level positions in the civil service went 'crazy' for BA holders and occasionally BSc holders. There was an unfounded notion that the best administrators were those who majored in liberal arts, social sciences, humanities, and law. Naturally, Nigerian parents pushed their children to emulate their leaders and follow their academic path.

The absence of an effective demand for science and technology courses also resulted from the fact that the government, as Dike argued, failed to invest in secondary school education in order to produce the required candidates for science courses. Moreover, the sixth form, inherited from the British, continued to hinder access. Even though the geographical spread of universities was intended to promote national unity, the implementation of some educational policies such as the Indigent Students Scheme clearly exposed the animosities that existed between the North and the South. Worse still, the civil war not only truncated the process of nation-building but also halted the expansion of educational facilities and opportunities. Given these problems, policy-makers and other Nigerians alike felt that the aims and objectives of university education remained unrealized. The 1960s therefore witnessed what Adaralegbe described as

> a constant babble of voices as educators, parents, government functionaries, the laymen, scholars, and the press (with conflicting ideas) speak of the ills of our educational system and particularly the inadequacy of the school curriculum to develop individual Nigerians and the nation at the rate and tempo to put us on the World map.[106]

Towards Centralization

The desire for a centralized and uniform coordination, expansion, and reform of universities was one of the major legacies of the civil war. That desire encouraged Gown to set up two commissions whose recommendations, apparently shaped by the experience of the civil war, dictated the country's future educational direction, especially in the 1970s. The first commission was asked to review the country's revenue allocation formula.

One of the implications of the creation of twelve states in 1966 was the importance of changing the pre-existing revenue allocation formula in which the former regional governments had considerable financial autonomy. In light of the new military posture favouring a more centralized control of all the states in the country, the federal government was compelled to set up a committee in 1968 to examine and suggest changes to the existing system of revenue allocation in the country. The committee, headed by I.O. Dina and dubbed the "Dina Committee," submitted its report in 1969. Basing its recommendations on the need to maintain unity, it requested the federal government to take custody of the revenue hitherto controlled by the former regions. The report stated:

> The existence of a multiplicity of taxing and spending authorities with regard to the same revenue source or expenditure function not only generates major administrative problems, but also reduces the effectiveness of any fiscal coordination effort. This weakness is particularly manifest under planning conditions which require a positive integration of development planning and fiscal administration. The logic of planning renders invalid the dichotomy between public finance and development finance, and demands that revenue allocation be seen as an integral part of the later. Once it is accepted that the overwhelming social urge is for accelerated economic development as a major prerequisite for expansion of welfare services, then the point must be sustained that financial relations become only meaningful in the context of integrated development planning.[107]

In this spirit, the report proposed that all Nigerian universities be financed 100 per cent by the federal government.[108] State officials, who wanted to have some degree of autonomy in financial matters, expressed strong opposition to the committee's recommendations. At their meeting in 1969, the commissioners of finance of all the states rejected the report.[109] Yet, as shown in chapter 4, and against the objections of the states, the committee's recommendations guided the federal government's post-1970 socioeconomic policies, including university control and expansion.

The next attempt by Gowon to reposition education in order to realize its objectives was made in 1969. Since fighting had subsided during the civil war, the federal government through the chief federal adviser on education and head of the Nigerian Educational Research Council (NERC), S.J. Cookey, summoned a National Curriculum Conference (NCC) to study, among other things, the problems of higher education in Nigeria and search for solutions with a view to repositioning it to satisfy Nigeria's needs and expectations.[110] Initiated by a group of highly influential American-educated Nigerians, including Babs Fafunwa and Adeneji Adaralegbe, co-sponsored by the federal government and some international organizations, and chaired by Cookey, the NCC was held in Lagos in September 1969.[111] The NCC attracted more than 150 participants, including experts and professionals, as well as representatives of trade unions, farmers, town unions, women's organizations, religious bodies, teachers' associations, university teachers and administrators, youth clubs, businesspersons, and government officials. The NCC was not for education specialists alone; the broad spectrum of participants represented the end users of education. As Cookey observed, "it was necessary also to hear the views of the masses of people who are not directly engaged in teaching or educational activities, for they surely have a say in any decisions to be taken about the structure and content of Nigerian education."[112]

The mood in the country was one of dissatisfaction with the prevailing system of education. The federal commissioner for education, W.O. Briggs, captured that mood by admitting the failure of the current educational system but then reaffirmed government support for mass education, science education, and education for national unity. According to Briggs, mass education was crucial so that "the masses of our people to understand the modern world in which they live, and take a lively, active and appreciative interest in the wonderful discoveries and inventions of man not only our youths but also adults."[113] Regarding science, Briggs stressed that the present system of education had failed "because it has tended to produce an educated class of 'pen-pushers,' and because it did not lay the foundations of economic freedom by providing the manual skills and expertise for successful industrial and agricultural development."[114] As he argued, "one of the consequences of this modern age of technology ... is the rising tide of automation."[115] Thus, for Nigeria "to meet the needs of the machines age, our workers must be flexible and versatile so as to be able to cope with the supervision, operations, repair, and maintenance of complicated and delicate equipment."[116] Furthermore, Briggs stressed that education was supposed to teach the principles of citizenship in order to promote national unity. He asked, "Could a better system of education have prevented it [civil war]? Can education remove its causes in our society and ensure stability? My answer to this question would be yes, for good education would include in its programme training for citizenship."[117]

The federal government received the report of the conference in October 1969. Unlike the Ashby report, the document sought for the abolition of the sixth form, which Cookey described as "a blind copy of the British system; too narrow and inflexible."[118] In its place, it recommended a 6-3-3-4 system of education as provided in America. This involved six years of primary school; a two-tier system of secondary schooling divided into a three-year junior high school and a three-year senior high school with a direct transition to a restructured four-year university course.[119] The document also emphasized the need to "educate [Nigerians] on a mass scale," and unlike the Ashby Commission, proposed free education at all levels "to all those who can benefit from it."[120] The report further cautioned that the modern Nigerian university should not remain an ivory tower any longer, even if it wished to do so; instead, the "Nigerian university must serve as an agent and instrument of change in bringing the fruits of modern technology and our rich cultural heritage to as many Nigerians as possible."[121] Even more important in light of the ethnic tension that caused the civil war, the report recommended that universities should take part in the process of national development and serve as a catalyst for national unity and change.[122]

The major themes of the conference were educational expansion, self-reliance, national unity, and economic development. In calling for a restructuring of the Nigerian educational system along the lines of the American system, the report reflected the particular and active American influence of its conveners and sponsors. Since 1960, the American system of education had continued to be attractive to Nigerians. The British system, earlier held in high regard, increasingly lost its appeal. The climate that produced the recommendations reflected sensitivity to America's lead in landing the first man on the moon on 20 July 1969. This event dramatically heightened Nigeria's admiration of American degrees, and, as captured by E.O. Fagbamiye, "If the award of such degrees would ensure a technological break-through for Nigeria, many Nigerians would gladly support such awards."[123]

Conclusion

The 1960s witnessed a noteworthy shift towards educational expansion following the recommendations of the Ashby Commission's report and motivated by the politics of economic development and nation-building. Five autonomous universities emerged, geographically spread to promote (though unsuccessful) national unity; scholarship awards (though inadequate) were extended by the various governments; science education was emphasized (without results); and the curriculum was diversified, leading to an increase in student population to 9,695. The smooth implementation of the massification program during this period was compromised by regional rivalries, financial constraints, the sixth form, the low demand for science courses, the military overthrow of the civilian government, and the civil war. The experience of the civil war, however, set the tone for the post-civil war expansion of university education, ushering in the second attempt at mass education in which rebuilding the country's economy and national spirit became an overriding social policy.

4

Centralization of Universities and National Integration, 1970–79: The Legacy of the Nigerian Civil War

> The universities should be a vehicle for the promotion of national consciousness, unity, understanding and peace.... Education is a recognized factor of unity in a nation, but unfortunately we still have within our nation educational disparity which tends to undermine the desires and efforts to achieve true unity; because there can only be true unity where educational opportunities and resultant facilities, amenities and benefits are evenly distributed.
>
> – OLUSEGUN OBASANJO, 1976

Introduction

Most postcolonial African countries wrestled with the problem of uniting members of their pluralistic societies in what Emile Durkheim calls a *conscience collective*. Social solidarity within a society, as Durkheim notes, is possible "if there exists among its members a sufficient degree of homogeneity by fixing in the child, from beginning, the essential similarity that collective life demands."[1] At its independence in 1960, Nigeria was a state devoid of a national identity. As many studies have shown, the diverse ethnic groups within Nigeria had divergent and conflicting interests, often claiming different heritage, language, and culture.[2] The British indirect rule system of administration that entrenched separate ethnic and regional identities worsened the historical rivalries and hostilities among the country's nationalities. These problems crystallized in the Nigerian Civil War (1967–70). The war highlighted the rivalries that characterized Nigeria's pluralistic society and questioned the viability of the 'nationalists' project. Yet, it rekindled the federal government's determination to explore ways of uniting the country's diverse groups together as a nation, one of which was by closing the educational gap existing between the North and the South.

Given the bitter experiences of the war, the overriding emphasis of the postwar social programs, including education, was, understandably, to keep the country together. The end of the civil war on 12 January 1970 was thus a turning point in the country's educational history; it marked a rebirth of the Nigerian nation and ushered in a new era typified by the implementation of far-reaching educational programs. Notably, the question of national unity and integration based on balanced educational development featured prominently in the mass university education experiments of the 1970s. The ideal of a nation, reinforced after the civil war, formed the philosophical foundation for post-1970 push for massification of university education. The military head of state, Yakubu Gowon, set the nation-building tone in his victory speech at the end of the war when he affirmed his administration's desire to foster national "reintegration, reconciliation, and reconstruction," requesting Nigerians to help "rebuild the nation anew."[3] Since the government could not affirm a non-existent collective conscience, it was prepared, among other things, to use mass university education policies to create one – an essential step in nation-building.

Throughout the 1970s, therefore, the successive military governments of Gowon (1966–75), Murtala Mohammed (1975–76), and Olusegun Obasanjo (1976–79) assumed an exclusive control of university education as a strategic tool to facilitate national unity and economic development. This historic shift in the country's educational development had more to do with the legacy of the civil war and the federal government's desire to assert control over the nation state. In a sense, the shift in the nature of the Nigerian state caused a major shift in the country's educational management.

Continuing Elitism

The civil war exacerbated the existing shortages in university places, interrupting the goal of mass university education. It affected all levels of educational activities, especially in the eastern states where educational facilitates were destroyed. At the end of the war, the federal government anticipated a real explosion in the numbers of qualified candidates seeking university education, which, according to Gowon, called "for expansion of existing institutions either in size or in numbers and, possibly, both."[4] Gowon believed that such expansion was necessary in order to supply the skilled personnel required to champion economic development.[5] The statistics of student population in the existing universities in Ibadan, Nsukka, Lagos, Zaria, and Ife were marked by a dearth of university places, domination by southerners, and low enrolment in the sciences. In 1970, only 14,468 students were studying in all the universities. When compared to Nigeria's population, estimated at about 51 million, the number was statistically insignificant. The facilities at the existing universities were grossly inadequate to accommodate increasing demand for places. For instance, out of the 7,000 applicants in the 1969/70 session, only 1,500 secured admissions.[6] In addition, students from the South, who constituted more than 75.6 per cent of the total student population, dominated the universities; and less than 46 percent were in the science courses.[7] These numbers fell below government expectations. In fact, the inadequate access and the need to satisfy the educational needs of its indigenes compelled the Midwestern State to found the Institute of Technology in Benin. The planning of this institute began in 1967 but was suspended due to the civil war. It eventually opened on 23 November 1970 with 108 students, only to be become the University of Benin when the National Universities Commission granted it the status of a university on 1 July 1971.[8]

The primary factor that determined and limited student admission was the lack of facilities (classes and hostels) to accommodate demand and the increasing incidence of multiple admissions. The supply of university places was insufficient even when the number of potential entrants based on passes in the Advanced Level examination increased from 6,739 in 1970 to 15,363 in 1975.[9] For example, in the 1970/71 session, out of 8,926 candidates that applied to the University of Ife, the university admitted only 1,179, even though 4,311 applicants were qualified. In the University of Ibadan, 10,036 candidates applied for admission in 1970/71, 4,682 were qualified, but 1,383 were offered admission.[10] In his welcome addresses to new students, the vice-chancellor of the University of Lagos, J.F. Ade Ajayi, noted that "the gap between the demand for and supply of university places [was a] widening gap, which makes it necessary to accord special congratulations to those who have succeeded against odds to secure admission to the university."[11] He further observed that

> the transition from school to University in this country is no longer smooth; it has become a stormy and capricious passage that gives would-be students and their parents far more worries than the transition from Elementary to Secondary School.[12]

It was due to its determination to expand access to university education for economic development and national unity that the federal government launched the Second National Development Plan (Second NDP) that emphasized education. The plan proclaimed to transform Nigeria, among others things, into "a land of bright and full opportunities for all citizens."[13] As the plan noted, the federal government faced a choice to either provide university education to all Nigerians "for its own sake, as a means of enriching an individual's knowledge and developing his full personality ... or to prepare people to undertake specific tasks and employment functions which are essential for the transformation of their environment."[14] However, as the Second NDP acknowledged, "Nigeria should in her stage of development, regard education as both."[15] The plan sought to restore facilities and services damaged or disrupted by the civil war but desired to develop and expand education at various levels in order to attain higher admission ratios while at the same time reducing the educational gap in the country. Owing to the civil war, the UNN in particular suffered from "severe deterioration of existing faculties, academic and public buildings, student hostels and staff houses; serious environmental degradation; and inadequate space for academic activities, recreational facilities."[16] Therefore, the Second NDP allocated large funds for the rehabilitation, reconstruction, and expansion of its facilities and those of other universities. It was a prelude to federal takeover of universities.

Federal Control of University Education

The three successive military governments in the 1970s upheld a centralized control of university education as a strategic tool to both facilitate access and forge greater national integration. This posture marked a radical departure from the early 1960s when the three regions controlled much of their fate with minimal federal interference. Despite regional control of education, the educational gap between the North and South, which began during the colonial period, remained a source of tension between the two areas. By the 1970s, that gap, as the federal commissioner of education, A.Y. Eke, revealed, was so wide that

> roughly speaking, for every child in a primary school in the northern states there are four in the southern states; for every boy or girl in a secondary school in the north there are five in the south. And for every student in a post-secondary institution in the north there are six in the south.[17]

Gowon had unsuccessfully called on all the universities to close this gap by assuming a national outlook in their admission policies. He stressed that the success of universities would be contingent on "the extent to which [they] can meet the needs and aspirations of the society which they are established to serve."[18]

The federal government's move towards centralization of university education effectively began in 1967. In that year, the creation of twelve states from the four regions created a new dimension to the university question. States without universities began to campaign for one. But in 1970, six states out of twelve had universities. Ahmadu Bello University was located in the North Central State; the University of Nsukka in the East-Central State; the University of Lagos in the federal capital city of Lagos; the universities in Ibadan and Ile-Ife in the Western State; and the University of Benin in the Mid-Western State. The six remaining states – North-Eastern State, North-Western State, Kano State, Benue/Plateau State, South-Eastern State, and Rivers State – had none. Of the six states without universities, four were located in the former Northern Region, an area marked by low enrolment in university education and considered educationally disadvantaged. These states embarked on vigorous plans to establish their own universities. Ownership of a university was considered a symbol of state pride. Given the level of ethnic rivalry, an unregulated establishment of universities carried the potential of exacerbating the existing tensions and straining local resources. As noted in the *Ibadan* editorial of July 1970:

> The real danger [lies] in the creation of State institutions which will be inward-looking and inbreeding.... [The] isolation of the youth of each state of the Federation into their State Universities will not make for the much needed unity of the country. There exists the fearful danger that both students and their teachers will remain within their States and that a new type of "tribalism" will develop.[19]

Resisting the proliferation of state universities while consolidating and expanding the facilities in the existing universities seemed the right course of action. In its delegation to Nigeria in 1970, the Inter-University Council (IUC) condemned plans by some Nigerian states to establish their own universities. IUC urged the federal government through the CVC to strengthen the existing universities to enable them meet the demands for admission as well as to provide quality education rather than spending limited resources to fund new universities.[20] The federal government was also worried about the negative impact of an uncoordinated establishment of universities on both the academic standards and government finances. Given the shift in the nature of the country towards a unitary system of government, Gowon felt that the central control of universities was vital in the process of nation-building. The Dina Committee had recommended to the federal government in 1969 to take custody of all the revenue in the country as well as the universities that were hitherto controlled by the regions. Although the four regions protested, Gowon went ahead to implement most of the recommendations of the committee. In the biography of Gowon, Eliagwu notes, "The Dina Report was rejected by the states essentially because of its political assumptions.... Gowon did not raise dust over the issue, but quietly implemented most aspects of this report through the back door."[21] Given the fact that it had assumed full responsibility for financing prisons, public safety, and scientific and industrial research, the federal government control of higher education seemed unstoppable.

Gowon's determination to remake Nigeria into a unitary state was reflected in two successive decrees that stripped the states of their financial autonomy. Before the military took over in 1966, as many studies have shown, the regions played a dominant role in their respective areas, especially in finances and education.[22] Decree No. 13 of 1970 allocated majority of federally collected revenue to the federal government which in turn allocated to states based on need, often measured by population. The derivation principle that characterized revenue-sharing in Nigeria since the 1950s was suspended. In 1971, the federal government further promulgated Decree No. 9, which transferred rents and royalties of offshore petroleum mines from the states to the federal government.[23] The federal government now had massive resources at its disposal, resources that would enable it to play a much more decisive and influential role in the country's social and economic policies.

Quite notably, the increase in the number of states to twelve weakened the powers of the states relative to the federal government. Many of the states became increasingly dependent on grants from the federal government for such basic needs as administration, a situation that continued when Murtala Mohammed regime created seven more states in 1976.[24] The states were in no strong financial position to resist the federal government's encroachment. Cash-strapped, some states often sought federal takeover of some of their responsibilities, as demonstrated in 1973 when the East Central State and Mid-West State requested the federal government to take over their universities.[25] Gowon's march to centralization was on course. In a speech in 1972, he declared his support for

> a planned and conscientious national plan for university development ... since the states are not financially strong enough to finance their universities, and since the ability of the federal government, itself, to finance them is not always taken into account in planning new universities.[26]

Gowon took his first major step towards federal control of university education in 1972 when he suspended the constitutional provision with respect to higher education. He announced the decision of the Supreme Military Council to assume "full responsibility for higher education throughout the country," further stating that "education, other than higher education, should become the concurrent responsibility of both the Federal and the State Governments, and be transferred to the concurrent legislative list."[27] This change placed higher education on the Exclusive Legislative List. It was a significant amendment of the 1963 Constitution. The 1963 constitution had placed higher education on the Concurrent Legislative List, which granted power to both the federal and regional governments to legislate on higher education matters. It also placed primary and secondary education on the Residual List category, which meant that only the regional governments could legislate on them. The 1972 declaration reversed this. By implication, the federal government arrogated to itself the sole right to establish universities and to legislate on all matters concerning their further expansion. This step, dictated by regional bickering that led to the civil war, paved the way for the future centralization and nationalization of the university system in line with the federal government commitment to foster national unity. As Eke states, "instead of remaining the parochial or regional subject it had previously been, education is now a matter of immense national consequence to all the citizens of Nigeria."[28]

Nigeria's postwar national goals as outlined in the Second NDP was based on building national unity, a strong and self-reliant nation and democratic society with a dynamic economy and equal opportunity for all citizens.[29] Since the federal government acknowledged education as fundamental in realizing those objectives, there was therefore the need for a national philosophy and policy on education. *The Seminar on a National Policy on Education* (SNPE) provided that. On the directive of the federal government, and mainly based on the report of the proceedings of *National Curriculum Conference* (NCC) of 1969, the federal and state ministries of education drafted a new education policy in 1972.[30] The National Council on Education (NCE), a council of commissioners of education, considered the draft at its meeting in December 1972 and proposed a national seminar where Nigerian educators and other interested and knowledgeable persons would discuss it. NCE appointed the then head of the National Universities Commission (NUC) and a former Permanent Representative of Nigeria to the United Nations, S.O. Adebo, to chair the SNPE.[31] Gowon was the first Nigerian leader to involve Nigerians on a massive scale in the design of future educational programs, as shown in the number of people who participated in the 1969 Curriculum Conference as well as the 1973 SNPE. This contrasted sharply with the 1960 Ashby Commission, where only three Nigerians participated in its deliberations. The large section of the Nigerian population invited for these conferences was part of Gowon's public relations campaign to win popular acceptance of his regime while at the same time involving the end-users of university products in curriculum development as a means of meeting society's needs.

Addressing regional imbalance in education and using mass education to promote national unity was a compelling need for government for which the seminar must respond. As Adebo put it, "Imbalance in educational opportunities results in imbalance in economic opportunities which in turn adversely affects our national unity with the consequences that we all know. Surely, the time has come to deal firmly with this problem, and to give all it takes in financial and other terms to solve it."[32] Among the issues discussed at the seminar were university ownership and centralization, control and administration of educational institutions and democratization of education in order to correct imbalances. The report of the seminar provided the philosophy that guided educational development throughout the 1970s, and, in many instances, beyond. It defined Nigeria's national purpose in the context of the role of education in helping to build and nurture the nation and recommended the expansion, centralization, and democratization of access to university education in order to promote national unity and economic development. It suggested that the "goal of free university education must always be kept in view." The objectives of Nigerian higher education, as the seminar articulated, include the acquisition, development, and inculcation of the proper value-orientation for the survival of the individual and society, the development of the intellectual capacities of individuals to understand and appreciate their environment, the acquisition of both physical and intellectual skills which will enable individuals to develop into useful member of the community, and the acquisition of a detached view of the local and external environment.[33] The report restated and endorsed the five main ingredients of the Second NDP, which included, among others, the fostering of "a land of bright and full opportunities for its citizens." Addressing the issue of disunity and rivalry, and echoing the 1972 UNESCO report, the seminar declared that education should promote "learning to live, not simply learning to pass examinations," and to "develop in our youths a sense of unity, patriotism, and love of our country."[34] Above all, it advised the government to ensure a geographically equitable distribution of university facilities as a means of achieving national unity.[35]

The idea to employ university education to achieve national unity seemed cogent, especially after the experience of the civil war. If Nigerian youth – presumed to be future leaders – from various ethnicities received equal access to all Nigerian universities, every ethnic group would feel confident that it would have equal access to the national wealth. Besides, this would provide the youth a good opportunity to understand one another and build up friendships. Furthermore, if students learned about one another's culture and lived in areas outside their home states, they would most likely become broad-minded and tolerant. This reasoning motivated the federal government to establish Unity Schools (federally owned high schools) and introduce the National Youth Service Corps (NYSC) in 1973. The Unity Schools were designed to bring young adolescents of diverse ethnicity together to interact and grow up together in order to create a solid foundation for national unity. For the first time in Nigerian educational history, the government used the quota system of admission into these federal schools. The aim was to correct the educational imbalance between the South and the North by generating enough candidates for university admission, especially from the disadvantaged states. Similarly, the introduction of the NYSC compelled Nigerian university graduates under the age of thirty years to provide a twelve-month period of continuous service outside their home state. No Nigerian graduate was offered a job in the public sector without completing this national service. The government planned the program to expose graduates to the modes of living of the people in different parts of the country with a view of removing prejudices, eliminating ignorance, and confirming at first hand the many similarities among Nigerians of all ethnic groups.

Realigning the country's universities as an agent of nation-building, as SNPE outlined, became the slogan of the administration. After what Gowon described as "the widest consultations" with various governmental and non-governmental institutions on the SNPE's report, the federal government accepted the recommendations in November 1973 while it finalized discussions on the ambitious projects that would be included in the next plan: the Third National Development Plan (Third NDP).[36] Luckily, however, the country's unexpected economic boom of 1973–74, occasioned by the Yom Kippur War, which began on 6 October 1973 in the Middle East, boosted the government's ability to engage in far-reaching university expansion. Although Nigeria had made appreciable income from oil since 1970 when it joined the Organization of Petroleum Exporting Countries (OPEC), oil only became the country's major foreign exchange earner and contributor to Gross Domestic Product (GDP) with the 1973 war.[37]

With enormous financial resources from oil revenue at its disposal, the federal government launched the Third NDP in 1975, which outlined grand plans to expand agriculture, industry, transport, housing, water supplies, health facilities, education, rural electrification, community development, and state programs. The impact of oil wealth was clear. While the First NDP and the Second NDP allocated a capital expenditure of ₦2.2 billion and ₦3.0 billion respectively, the Third NDP earmarked an expenditure of ₦30 billion.[38] The potential expansion of the productive base of the economy required skilled labour to staff the expanding economy, placing university education at the centre of accomplishing government objectives. The objectives of the university educational program for the Third NDP period were "to expand facilities for education aimed at equalizing individual access to education throughout the country … to consolidate and develop the nation's system of education in response to the economy's manpower needs [and] … to make an impact in the area of technological education."[39] In pursuit of these objectives, the plan expressed its resolve to expand facilities in the existing universities, establish four new universities, and increase student enrolment from its current level of 23,000 to 53,000 by 1980. To that end, it allocated a total capital expenditure of ₦251.856 million to education.[40]

The Third NDP was a bold step in the government effort to accelerate the pace of economic and social change in Nigeria. It represents, as Gowon argued, "a major milestone in the evolution of economic planning in this country. It is undoubtedly the most ambitious development effort ever attempted in Nigeria."[41] Gowon was optimistic that the "full implementation of the plan should ensure a radical transformation of the Nigerian society."⁴² Economic development and nation-building were at the centre of Gowon's plan to revitalize the universities. This vision of universities, as Gowon stressed, "reflect not only the considerably increased resources now available to us but also the government's determination to translate the country's vast potential into a permanent improvement in the living condition of all Nigerians."⁴³ Since the oil wealth coincided with domestic pressure for university expansion, the federal government seized the moment to engage in unprecedented expansion of access, designed not only to provide a workforce to manage the expanding economy, but also to assuage regional, state, and ethnic demands.

Following Gowon's centralization posture and empowered by the country's oil wealth, the federal government took over all the state universities (Benin, Ife, and Zaria) in August 1975. Though the Third NDP approved the establishment of four universities, the federal government established seven in 1975. The new universities were deliberately sited in the so-called disadvantaged states, five in the North (Jos, Ilorin, Sokoto, Kano, and Maiduguri) and two among the minorities in the South (Port Harcourt and Calabar).⁴⁴ With thirteen universities under federal control, financial allocations to universities increased, now administered by the newly reconstituted NUC. The federal government had recomposed the NUC by Decree No. 1 of 1974 and extended its powers to ensure ordered control and expansion. The NUC, as previously constituted, was unable to perform its role properly because higher education was a joint responsibility of both state and federal governments. Since the federal government assumed full responsibility for higher education, NUC became the government's instrument for executing its vision of a centrally coordinated university system. The new NUC was empowered to draw "periodic master plans for the balanced and coordinated development of universities in Nigeria ... [and the] establishment and location of new universities as and when considered necessary." More importantly, the NUC was required to advise the government on the "financial needs, both recurrent and capital, of university education in Nigeria" as well as to receive block grants from the government for allocation to the universities "in accordance with such formula as may be laid down by the Federal Executive Council."⁴⁵

In keeping with its expansionist policy, the total budget for universities, put at ₦39 million in 1970/71, increased to ₦320 million in 1976, leading to expansion of facilities and higher student enrolment. Student enrolment rose from 14,468 in the 1970/71 session to 40,552 in 1976.[46] This development, as Alex Gboyega and Yinka Atoyebi noted, "marked the decisive turning point when university education became available to the masses in Nigeria."[47] However, enrolment would have greatly increased if the federal government had redirected the capital grants meant for the new universities to expand facilities in the existing universities as IUC advised in 1970. Political considerations, more than sustainable expansion of access, dictated the founding of the new institutions. The federal control of universities and equitable geographical distribution aimed at appeasing the educationally disadvantaged states. As J.F. Ade Ayayi and others observed, "It was the oil revenues that incited the federal government to create not only a national system of higher education, but also education as a whole, under the federal control as a factor of reconciliation and unification after the civil war."[48] There was little consideration of the long-term maintenance of those institutions. Besides, despite Gowon's efforts to 'massify' university education, admission problems continued to slow down enrolment and expansion of university education.

Quota System and Admission Reform

The demand by northerners for a quota system that would guarantee access to university education for their indigenes was well known.[49] The question of quotas was not new in the 1970s. It originated in the 1950s when the North advocated for an admission policy that would promote increased admission of its residents in the University College, Ibadan. However, the IUC had firmly opposed it and insisted that academic merit was the sole criterion for university admission. The federal government's white paper on the Ashby Commission report reaffirmed IUC's position in 1961. Thus, throughout the 1960s, students secured admission to universities based on academic merit alone, which favoured the more educationally advanced South. In the early 1970s, the northern states intensified their call for some sort of quota system to reserve admission spots for their residents in the existing universities. For instance, the former military governors of the northern states under the platform of Interim Common Services

Agency (ICSA) wrote to Gowon in September 1971, drawing attention to the fact that students from the northern states constituted less than 2 per cent of the total student population in the federal universities of Ibadan and Lagos. They asked the federal government to expand the preliminary courses in these universities and to give preference to students from the North in university admissions.[50] Given the bitter experience of civil war, the government began to reconsider its thinking on the merits of a quota system, naturally provoking a great deal of discussion and debate.

Because employment opportunities in Nigeria were few and highly competitive, the South, with higher educational and professional attainment, occupied most of the available jobs. In a public address at Ahmadu Bello University, Zaria, in 1972 Gowon had expressed his administration's commitment to "tackle and settle, if possible, once and for all a number of vital and controversial issues among which are the question of educational imbalance and the quota system of admission."[51] Gowon noted, however, that a long-term sustainable approach to overcome the educational imbalance was not through a quota system of admission into universities but through strengthening primary and secondary school education in the affected states in the North. According to Gowon, if that approach were taken, the states would over time produce enough qualified candidates for university admissions and job opportunities.[52]

Equity was the key to national unity, and Gowon recognized this. Despite his disapproval of the quota system, he admitted that in the interest of national unity a short-term solution was crucial. He affirmed that the "fears and anxieties of these relatively educationally backward areas are genuine and it would be irrational to dismiss those fears and anxieties as unfounded."[53] Gowon was from the North and was sympathetic to the plight of the educationally disadvantaged northern states. Yet, given that the South would perceive a quota system as discriminatory and that it would create national tension, Gowon was cautious. Still for the affected states, as Gowon noted, "unless they are able to provide enough graduates of their ethnic or state origin now, they will be denied what they regard as an equitable share of employment opportunities in the country."[54] As far as those states were concerned, "they are not unduly interested in the long-term solution; they want immediate solution and answers."[55] Because individual universities controlled admissions, Gowon could not effect immediate changes but rather cautioned them "to do a lot more than they are doing at present to reflect the federal structure of this country in their student admission." He also warned that if they fail "we have to accept that the quota system would be the only method that will provide some opportunities for the educationally backward areas to be represented in the universities."[56]

The incidence of multiple admissions that plagued the university system in Nigeria not only further dimmed admission prospects of northerners but also undermined the federal government's goal of mass university education. Since 1948 when UCI was established, there was no central admission body in the country. Individual universities admitted students. The absence of admission coordination into Nigerian universities resulted in multiple admissions with many unfilled spaces in universities. Multiple admissions occurred when students received admission offers from many universities and/or departments in a university. This situation, which began in the 1960s, occurred because individual universities independently operated different admission criteria, advertised separately, and conducted separate admission exercises. To increase their chances of admission, many candidates applied to many universities or to multiple departments within the same university. Top candidates frequently received multiple admission offers from many universities and/or departments, resulting in a multiplicity of admissions. Ultimately, such candidates would accept one admission offer.

The ideal admission practice was that when candidates reject admission offers and inform the university early enough, the affected university would offer admissions to other equally qualified applicants who did not receive initial admission offers due to limited spaces. However, many candidates failed to inform the concerned institutions or did so too late. T.M. Yesufu, the vice-chancellor of the University of Benin, noted that "by the time the universities are aware that their original offers would not be honored it is too late to admit those who would otherwise have accepted and utilized the places available."[57] In fact, universities could only ascertain the total number of students who accepted admission after the matriculation exercise. At this point, it would be too late to admit new sets of qualified students. Even after matriculation, some students could still withdraw if they received late admission into faculties or universities of their choice. They would often accept the first offer because they were unsure of gaining admission to their first choice of university or course.[58] What deprived many qualified candidates of university admissions each year and prevented the universities from meeting their enrolment targets were incidences of multiple applications, multiple acceptances, uncertainty as to whether a candidate would accept admission offers, and uncertainty as to whether those who accepted admission offers would actually register.

The vice-chancellor of the University of Lagos, Ade Ajayi, drew attention to the incidence of multiple admissions when he highlighted the inability of his university to meet its enrolment target. He revealed that the student enrolment targets for science, engineering, and environmental design in 1976 session were 130, 175, and 70, respectively. In the science, 241 students were offered admission but 78 registered; in engineering, 130 were offered admission but 54 registered; in environmental design, 54 were offered admission but 44 registered.[59] The deficit was not peculiar to the University of Lagos; it affected all the universities in the country. Altogether, the deficit at Ibadan, Nsukka, Zaria, Ife, Lagos, and Benin was 9.8 per cent in 1970–71; 11.2 per cent in 1971–72; 13.8 per cent in 1972–73; 11.8 per cent in 1973–74; 8.0 per cent in 1974–75; and 6.9 per cent in 1975–76.[60]

Applicants from the South benefited and at the same time suffered from the incidence of multiple admissions. Because they were often the most qualified, they secured placement in many universities but at the same time obstructed others who were on the margin of admission. An analysis of the distribution of candidates admitted into two or more universities in the 1974/75 session revealed that, out of the 766 candidates offered two or more admissions, most (31%) came from the Western State, followed by the East-Central State(23.12%), and the Mid-Western State (16.71%), all in the South.[61] Thus, southern candidates, who had maintained a lead in university population, accounted for more than 70 per cent of multiple admissions. Any meaningful explanation of this, according to Aderinto, "will have to do with intense determination of the candidates from the southern states to obtain university education. To them, a university degree was an 'International meal ticket.'"[62]

To address the admissions problem, the Committee of Vice-Chancellors in 1974 set up a panel of two experts, comprised of L.R. Kay, Secretary,

Universities Central Council on Admissions of the United Kingdom, and W.H. Pettipiere of the Ontario Universities Applications Centre of Canada. The report submitted by the two experts on 31 May 1975 recommended the setting up of a central admission board to coordinate admission to all Nigerian universities.[63] However, the CVC did not implement this proposal. By asking the two experts to make recommendations "without prejudice to existing individual standards and traditions of the various universities," it was apparent that the CVC preferred to preserve the universities' power to admit their own students. Thus, according to B.A. Salim, when the experts recommended a central admission system, it "touched on a sore side [which universities] saw as a breach of that fundamental clause which sought to preserve the status quo (University Autonomy on Admissions)."[64] In addition, since the study and the recommendation of the expatriate committee was a non-governmental affair, the federal government was not compelled to order the CVC or, more appropriately, the NUC, to implement the proposal.

The federal government was displeased with the admission practices of universities. As expressed in the Third NDP, it blamed the universities for adhering "too rigidly to restrictive admission policies which in the light of current realities are overdue for a drastic revision."[65] In a speech at the formal inauguration of the newly reconstituted NUC on 10 July 1975, Gowon reinstated the government's intention to direct education admission to serve the mission of nation-building. According to him,

> The Government is determined to boost the educational opportunities of every Nigerian. Education will be made to respond to the needs and the aspirations of the nation and its people. In the field of Higher Education in particular, the tremendous increase in opportunities will have to be accompanied by a realistic reappraisal of entry qualifications into our Universities so as to render these increased opportunities for University education accessible to a greater number of aspiring Nigerians.[66]

As it prepared to address the admission issue, Murtala Mohammed, a northerner, overthrew Gowon's administration on 29 July 1975 in a military coup. Mohammed accused Gowon's administration of corruption and indefinite postponement of earlier plans to hand over government to a civilian regime in 1976. To justify his intervention, Murtala blamed past leadership that "either by design or default, had become too insensitive to the true feelings and yearnings of the people."[67] In order to satisfy what he perceived as the true yearnings of Nigerians, Murtala immediately set 1979 as the deadline to hand over control to a civilian government. In addition, he created seven states in February 1976, bringing the total number of states to nineteen.[68] Murtala was convinced that the creation of more states in Nigeria would enhance the country's future political stability. In a way, the politics of the state creation was analogous to the demand for more universities. Both were made often to maximize the opportunities of partaking in sharing the country's wealth controlled by the federal government. One way to guarantee this was for states to train their own high-level workforce at the university level. Since universities existed in twelve out of the nineteen states, the seven remaining states were bound to demand their own universities, for, as the Inter-University Council observed, "The cohesion of the Nigerian State depends on Lagos [the seat of power] listening to these voices."[69]

As anticipated, Mohammed's regime took up the admission issue that Gowon initiated. For instance, during the 1974/75 academic year, the northern states with more than 50 per cent of the country's total population, accounted for only 5,764 or just fewer than 22 per cent of the national total university residents of 26,448.[70] This unequal access to university education made the northerners uncomfortable because university education was perceived to confer greater benefits on the recipients and greater access to national resources or 'cake' by Nigerian ethnic groups. According to T.M. Yesufu, "A federal or confederal country, in which some sections feel inferior and dominated because of educational imbalances, tends to be inherently unstable. Equal educational opportunity tends to ensure equal employment opportunities."[71] The advantage of equal educational opportunity was that

> it develops and diffuses unifying cultural and social traits, a sense of intellectual camaraderie and mutual complementarity; it promotes identity of perspectives and interests with regard to national issues; promotes mutual personal and group

understanding, a sense of equality and justice; and creates [a] bond of national unity.[72]

Once in power, Mohammed quickly set up the Committee on University Entrance (CUE), headed by M.S. Angulu in December 1975.[73] He charged the committee to study the problems of admission and make recommendations on how to remove "all the bottlenecks limiting entry," promote the "liberalization of admissions," and to review the entry requirements of the various universities in order to ensure uniformity.[74] This was the first time that the federal government had backed a reform of university admission since 1960. The terms of reference of the CUE reflected the urgency and seriousness of the problem of multiple admissions. Besides, it highlighted the federal government's willingness to liberalize admissions for the sake of regional equality and mass access. Although Mohammed's regime ended on 13 February 1976 when Lt. Col. B.S. Dimka assassinated him in an abortive coup, Olusegun Obasanjo, a southerner who replaced him, promised to continue with his programs amid concerns from northerners.

Uncertain about the step the new southern head of state would take to close the educational gap between the North and the South, northern states increased their pressure on the federal government to take action in reforming the admission process. One of the most ardent lobbyists was Jubril Aminu, a northerner, who was the executive secretary of National Universities Commission and a member of the CUE. Aminu used his influential position to agitate vigorously for equal representation of all ethnic groups in the existing universities. In a fifty-three-page paper that he addressed to the federal government, Aminu lamented:

> The four old states of East Central, Lagos, Midwest and West exercise an alarming monopoly of enrolment into the University system. These four states, with a combined population of about one third of the whole country, have for long had a disproportionate advantage in higher education. Even recently, in the 6 old Universities the four states had 75.6 per cent, 71.4 per cent, 72.9 per cent, 68.3 per cent and 69.4 per cent of the enrolments in the academic years 1970/71, 72/72, 72/73, 73/74, 74/75, respectively.[75]

Southern states, as Aminu noted, also dominated student population in science courses. He showed that the four old states located in the South dominated 80 per cent of the enrolment in medicine and pharmacy, 77 per cent in engineering and technology, 75 per cent in pure science and agriculture and forestry, as well as 75 per cent in education, 60 per cent in law, and 56 per cent in public administration in the year 1974/75 session. Based on these statistics, Aminu declared that, in relation to their population, the northern states suffered most. He warned that the future of Nigeria rested in the hands of southern states "since they have enjoyed a long monopoly of highly skilled manpower development in all disciplines, and since the situation is not improving."[76] Aminu insisted that the criteria for university admission "must only be uniformly applied if they are fair and just from first principles; namely, if all started the competition from the same line."[77] Even though Gowon established all the seven new universities in the educationally disadvantaged states, Aminu noted that "this action by itself would never solve the problem of imbalance without concomitant changes in the admission policies."[78]

To increase the opportunities and the eligibility of the students from the underprivileged areas, Aminu suggested, among other things, that the federal government should introduce "the system of quota admission." In addition, he insisted on "a sixty per cent quota admission for the twelve states, on population basis into the new universities; and fifty per cent quota admission for the twelve states, on population basis, into the existing universities."[79] Additionally, he requested that the government establish the urgently needed remedial centres in all the ten disadvantaged states of the former North, as well as Rivers and Cross Rivers states. While he urged the federal government to take responsibility for the entire financial burden of establishing these centres, he stressed that the centres should be under the complete control of the state governments, including the admission policies. The federal government, Aminu advised, should approve these proposals in order to lay a solid foundation "for unity and for contentment" among Nigerians by removing "all sources of strife – imminent or potential."[80] In carrying out this task, Aminu stated that the federal government "needs to offer no apologies, and the Committee on University Entrance needs to have no hesitations in recommending."[81]

Aminu was an influential advocate of admission reform. In 1976, following some of the recommendations contained his letter, the federal government announced the establishment of schools of Basic Studies in each of the ten states in the North (with the exception of Kwara), and the two states in the South considered educationally disadvantaged. The federal government financed each school, but states controlled them, including the admission policy. Each school, affiliated to the six older universities, was to prepare its students for admission to the universities. Although the federal government did not approve a quota system, it directed each of the six older universities to guarantee admission to the successful graduates of each school of Basic Studies affiliated with it. By implication, candidates from the remaining states would be considered on merit for whatever vacancies might exist thereafter. The federal government further directed each of the seven new universities to establish a remedial course within its system for students from the same disadvantaged states who might be deficient in some of the general or special university entry requirements. It insisted that students admitted to such courses would matriculate into the university straight away and any vacancies left after admission should go to candidates from the remaining states.[82]

Presumably influenced by Aminu's campaign, the head of state, Obasanjo, summoned a special meeting with the Committee of Vice Chancellors and officials of the NUC on 18 September 1976.[83] At the meeting, the head of state addressed, among others, the issues of admission into Nigerian universities, especially as it affected candidates from the educationally disadvantaged areas of the country and low enrolments in science disciplines.[84] Obasanjo bluntly blamed Nigerian universities for maintaining aristocratic seclusion and remoteness from the society they were meant to serve, a fact he considered "a big constraint in the expansion programme of all our universities because all other universities tended to follow the example of the University of Ibadan."[85] He cautioned that, since the federal government had committed large sums of money to the universities, it expected them to "reflect the true Nigerian character both in their intake, the content of the courses offered, and their physical environment."[86]

Comments such as these fuelled the fear that the federal government desired to impose a quota system in university admission. The federal commissioner for education denied it. As he stressed, instead of introducing a quota system, it was the desire of the federal government to see "a more pragmatic formula for admission into our universities that will reflect the federal nature of this country and that will redress the chronic imbalance without necessarily reducing standards. I must say categorically that no quota system is envisaged."[87] The commissioner also pointed out that the government had established schools of basic studies to remedy the imbalance in the availability of qualified students for admissions. Apparently, the commissioner was diplomatic in his appraisal of the situation. It was, in a sense, unlikely for the universities to produce a "more pragmatic formula" to admit students without fundamentally changing the prevailing admission system based on merit. Yet, because southerners who had resisted quota policy controlled administrative positions in most universities, and because individual universities controlled admission, they were prepared to sabotage the implementation of a quota system. Aminu recognized this factor when he stated that "Senates [responsible for admission] are very conservative bodies which jealously guard what they call university autonomy and academic freedom. But neither of these can over-ride national unity and harmony."[88] Tactically, the government favoured the setting up of a central examination body as a prelude to the eventual imposition of a quota system. Under this arrangement, the power of universities to admit would be constrained by the new body controlled by the federal government. Concerned that the establishment of a central admission body would strip them of their power to select their students, the CVC requested the government to give them the opportunity to comment on the awaited report of the University Entrance Committee before approving it.[89]

While awaiting the report on admission reform, Obasanjo's administration announced some radical university education policies that aimed at not only closing the educational gap between the North and the South but also facilitating mass university education. In his speech at the convocation ceremony of the University of Ibadan on 17 November 1976, Gowon announced his government's decision to make university education, including technical secondary school and post-secondary school, tuition-free and boarding-free; subsiding students' cost of food by 50 per cent. Obasanjo had launched the Universal Primary Education Scheme (UPE) on 2 September 1976, which made primary education free and compulsory in the country. Extending free education to post-primary and post-secondary education was revolutionary and unprecedented. With the increase in the number of universities as well as free tuition, Obasanjo believed that

> more Nigerians will continue to have the benefit of higher education until a stage was reached where no section of this country would find itself on the defensive in the quest for and attainment of knowledge.[90]

Following the recommendation of the Committee on University Entrance (CUE), which submitted its report in 1977, the federal government moved swiftly to establish a central admission body.[91] Since the deliberations of the CUE were spiced with a lot of rancour caused by the contentious issue of using a quota system, the committee avoided making a recommendation on that subject. Instead, it recommended the introduction of remedial programs for the educationally less-developed states. In February 1977, the commissioner of education summoned a meeting of the CVC and NUC during which he announced the setting up of a single body to embrace the functions of the two bodies that CUE had proposed. It was named the Joint Admissions and Matriculation Board (JAMB), and Professor O.O. Akinkugbe and M.S. Angulu were appointed chairperson and registrar of the board, respectively.[92]

With the creation of JAMB, admission to the universities became centralized and nationalized. Henceforth, students were to gain admission through either the University Matriculation Examination (UME) or Direct Entry. UME was open to those who possessed a School Certificate/WASC with five credits obtained at not more than two sittings, including English language for arts subject students and mathematics for science subject students. It was also open to teachers with grade II certificates with a minimum of five credits, and candidates who did not possess these requirements but had registered for the November/December 1977 GCE 'O' Level or June 1978 SC/GCE. Such candidates, who would have to await the outcome of their performance on these exams, would be eligible for university admission if they ultimately fulfilled the conditions stated above. For direct entry admission, candidates were expected to possess a General Certificate of Education (GCE) 'A' Level in at least two subjects relevant to the intended course of study; National Certificate of Education (NCE) for courses in education; International Baccalaureate; and the Interim Joint Matriculation (IJMB) conducted by Ahmadu Bello University.[93]

JAMB was founded to ease access to university education, but soon it became a source of tension between the North and the South. Empowered by Decree No. 2 of 1978 to "control of the conduct of matriculation examinations for admissions into all Universities in Nigeria [and determine] matriculation requirements and conducting examinations," JAMB conducted its first UME in 1978.[94] Although the heads of each university were members of the board, they resisted it. The CVC at the special meeting with the head of state in September 1976 had requested to have the opportunity to make an input on the recommendations of the CUE before government's approval. On the contrary, the federal government went ahead to announce the establishment of JAMB in 1977. Feeling slighted, and given that the CVC had rejected the recommendations for a central admission body in 1974 by two experts, the university vice-chancellors, dominated by southerners, opposed JAMB. "To the universities," according to Salim, "the Board was government's tool for reduction of the universities autonomy and bringing in the quota system through the back door."[95]

Opposition to JAMB intensified when it released the first UME results in April 1978. In the conduct of its first exams, JAMB recorded many administrative difficulties. The UME was conducted in one day, and many candidates missed the exam due to poor organization and communication. Under the caption "Thousands did not sit for JAMB," the *Nigerian Tribune* noted that a good number of candidates missed the examinations because of the late arrival of the examinations papers, noting that most of the centres marked for the examinations were non-existent.[96] As it was a yearly exam, candidates who missed or failed the exam would have to wait for one year before retaking it. These administrative lapses rendered the exam 'chaotic,' as the first JAMB Registrar, Angulu, later admitted, and prevented many students from gaining admissions in the 1978/79 session.[97] This raised questions about the ability of the new board to handle entrance exams successfully. The *New Nigerian* editorials consistently called for a review of the JAMB decree to transform it into a clearinghouse to avoid multiple admissions.[98] Blaming the problem on the haste with which the board was established, Adeyemo Aderinto argued: "If there is any lesson to be learnt from the JAMB episode, it is the fact that setting up ill-prepared, ill-designed super-structures, however well intentioned, would not achieve the perceived objectives."[99]

Worse still was the fact that the educationally disadvantaged states realized to their dismay that the board did not make much difference to their admission prospects. Of the 113,162 candidates who applied for admission in the 1978/79 session, fewer than 20,000 candidates came from the ten northern states.[100] In spite of the population of the North, this number was small when compared with the total number of applications received. While only 2,776 students from the North gained admission, 11,641 students from the South were successful.[101] The affected states blamed the board for admitting fewer students from their region. But according to JAMB registrar, the operation of JAMB in its first year did not affect the "disadvantaged states more adversely than in the past as has been alleged." In fact, he showed that the number of candidates who gained admission during this period was an improvement from the past.[102]

The JAMB-generated tension continued to affect ethnic relations. Students in the northern universities who had hoped to secure automatic admissions to universities after their preliminary studies were disappointed because universities followed JAMB guidelines (merit) in offering admission. An admission crisis in the University of Jos highlights this issue. In the university, Professor G.O. Onuaguluchi, a southerner and the vice-chancellor of the university failed to carry out the decision of the university council that required him to admit students from the educationally disadvantaged states who satisfy minimum requirement and fill the remaining vacancies on merit.[103] A commission of enquiry on the 1977/78 admissions exercise condemned the admission committee for using a higher pass mark in JAMB to eliminate candidates from the disadvantaged states. Although the federal government meant well when it initiated this discriminatory policy in 1976, it lost sight of the legitimate claims and aspirations of students from other states.[104]

Disappointed with JAMB, students from the North blamed southerners, embarked on violent protest, and demanded the abolition of the board in February 1979. This resulted in the closure of all the universities in the North. As reported by *West Africa*, the JAMB debate divided Nigerian students along ethnic lines, with southerners favouring JAMB and northerners determined to wipe it out. According to the paper, the southern press soon attacked "the demonstrating students, and [supported] the principle that university admissions be based only on exam-proven academic achievement (which they still dub 'merit') – a principle that will obviously favor the better resourced South."[105] The controversy that marked JAMB's first exam threatened to undermine the nation-building agenda for which the body was established.

Recession of 1978

The federal government had attempted to address the issues affecting the expansion of university education by establishing more institutions, spreading the institutions evenly in the country, providing free university education, and establishing a central admission body. With the drastic decline in oil revenue in 1978, the government could not fulfill its liberal education policies. Since oil revenue accounted for over 93 per cent of Nigeria's revenue and over 95 per cent of its foreign exchange, the decline affected the country's GDP, which declined by 5.7 per cent.[106] In his 1978 budget speech, Obasanjo noted that "although petroleum remained the greatest contributor to the economy, its share in the national income declined slightly. [Therefore] … the 1977/78 Budget had to be a strict one both in terms of government having to cut down its programmes and also in terms of sacrifices which were being demanded from all Nigerians."[107]

While the oil boom had fuelled university expansion policies, the 1977 decline in oil revenue led to policy reversal. Consequently, the federal government introduced austerity measures while it borrowed Nigeria's first huge loan of US$1 billion from the international capital market.[108] The impact of the government's belt-tightening measures on financing social services, including the universities, was immediate; government reduced subventions to universities and reintroduced some fees to enable universities to generate revenue. It revised hostel accommodation charges upwards at ₦90.00 per session of thirty-six weeks or ₦30.00 in a session of three terms and the feeding fees upwards from 50 Kobo per day to ₦1.50 per student per day (for three meals).[109] Although the federal government introduced these fees in order to ease its financial burden in funding university education, it was not clear that student fees were really the problem. A

Daily Times editorial noted that fee changes did not address the root of the universities' financial problems, stating that it "did not amount to a clear, consistent, and coherent policy statement on the financing of higher education."[110] It further cautioned that, instead of assuming the responsibility of student housing and accommodation, which saddled the government and university authorities with avoidable non-academic problems, they

> ought to put some bite into their off-campus policy, so that they become non-residential in the shortest time possible. They need to achieve that objective in order to be able to address themselves to the more important question of how to offer university education to a maximum number of students.[111]

The unintended consequence of proliferation of universities in the 1970s was that these universities constituted a heavy burden on the government's dwindling resources. According to Eniola Adeyeye, the existing thirteen universities involved separate and financially demanding administrative structures and personnel. He wondered why the federal government had not established fewer universities "with expanded facilities including scattered colleges all over the country such that a single university, like the University of Cairo could graduate annually tens of thousands of much needed graduates to man key posts in all the sectors of the economy."[112] Conversely, Jubril Aminu, the executive secretary of the NUC, defended the government's position on expansion. For him, "those who criticize the establishment of more universities will do well to find out the views of the large, usually silent, majority in the country. If the people want more universities, they are entitled to more universities and they deserve what they get."[113] This thinking is deficient in long-term strategic thinking and reflected, quite disappointingly, the mindset of those who advised the government on university expansion. Even with the establishment of thirteen universities, the total number of students they absorbed remained very low. For instance, in 1977, out of more than 90,000 applicants, only 47,499 secured admissions. Universities, accustomed to receiving massive grants from the federal government, responded to the economic downturn by devising cost-saving measures to survive. For instance, the university authority at UNN stopped the feeding of students during the 1977/1978 session and introduced a policy of "Pay-As-You-Eat."[114]

The NUC even intervened by setting up the Committee on University Finances (CUF) in 1977 to propose restructuring measures for the universities.[115] The terms of reference of the CUF recognized the country's current economic meltdown and the need for the universities to make adjustments. The CUF's report, submitted in May 1978, showed, among other things, that the rate of growth in student population and the expansion in academic activities out-stripped the rate of development of teaching facilities. It addition, it noted the prevalence of overcrowding in student hostels due to inadequate living accommodations for students; inadequate staff housing forcing the universities to spend too much money on rented accommodation; and inadequate meal subsidies provided for students.[116] In a way, these problems affected student enrolment as well as the quality of education obtained in these universities.[117] While the committee urged the government to raise the amount of grants to universities, it also warned university administrators not to embark on new capital projects without prior approval from the NUC, cautioning them to build a simpler structure "with greater emphasis on maximum utility at minimum cost."[118] However, the government did not increase subventions to the university, and the hopes of expanding access to universities seemed truncated.

Obasanjo's abolition of tuition fees and reduction in boarding and lodging charges in 1977 led to sharp increases in student enrolment from 40,552 in 1976 to 47,499 in 1977, and increases in government's financial commitments to the universities. However, it also led to a huge drop in local revenue in fees generated by the universities from ₦10.4 million to ₦4.7million.[119] Faced with a decline in oil revenue, financial grants to the universities declined, and the deficit in NUC recommendations and actual grants to universities in 1977/78 session was over ₦24 million.[120] As a result the "physical facilities [were not] developed at a sufficiently rapid rate to meet the demands for university places."[121] Due to inadequate accommodations, congestion and squalor worsened in Nigerian universities with the accompanying social problems.

Unable to provide adequate funds for universities and aggravated by the poor living conditions of university students, the Obasanjo government attempted to reintroduce tuition fees and hike boarding and lodging fees. These policies were unpopular, forcing universities to emerge "as centers of vigorous protest and often violent confrontation against the authorities."[122] In May 1978, the National Union of Nigerian Students (NUNS) embarked on a violent, massive protest. The federal government immediately closed down all the universities, banned NUNS, and expelled its president, Segun Okeowo, together with other student leaders.[123] Two vice-chancellors of the most affected universities, Professor Iya Abubakar of ABU and Professor J.F. Ade Ajayi of the University of Lagos, were relieved of their positions. The stage was now set for a showdown between the military and university intelligentsias. More notably, the Nigerian Association of University Teachers (NAUT), a hitherto conservative association that emerged in 1965, metamorphosed into a formidable opposition group, renamed Academic Staff Union of Universities (ASUU) in 1978. Henceforth, ASUU assumed a leadership position in the struggle against Obasanjo's harsh social policies and those of future regimes.[124] ASUU appearance seemed timely because it was

> the period of the beginning of the decline in the oil boom, when the country faced the consequences of the failure by its rulers to use the oil wealth to generate production and a social welfare system. Military dictatorship had eroded deeply the basic freedoms in the society. Academic freedom and university autonomy were casualties of military dictatorship. The funding of education, and so of universities, became poorer. The factors required a changed orientation of the union of academics, from 1980.[125]

Conclusion

The military administrations of Gowon, Mohammed, and Obasanjo adopted a federal system of higher education in the 1970s primarily due to the centralized organization of the military, the strong financial strength of the federal government, and the need for forge national unity and development. Using education to foster a united nation was tricky in Nigeria, as it was in other pluralistic African societies. Remi Clignet's study of educational development in postcolonial Cameroons, Ghana, and the Ivory Coast shows that although education acted as an important agent of social change it did not eradicate traditional ethnic tensions.[126] Studies on Nigeria have shown that education could exacerbate existing tensions by producing disproportionate rewards among groups.[127] In a sense, such an experiment was "a two-edged sword cutting either for or against national integration."[128] For Nigeria, the goal of nation-building through federal university control and management seemed unsustainable, as mounting criticism continued. This is because, according to Nwuzor, the federal government policy was an "ad hoc measure necessitated by circumstances and military action."[129]

Federal agencies such as JAMB and NUC naturally came under attack from the universities, not only as symbols of federal government inefficiency, but also as agents of discrimination and suppression. NUC was perceived as a body that arrogated authority over universities.[130] In fact, in the wake of the Mohammed Commission following university students' unrest in May 1978, a number of university officials assaulted NUC staff for encroaching on their autonomy. Despite the unprecedented expansion of access to university education in the 1970s, the goal of nation-building and economic development remained farfetched, as policies were often viewed from ethnic/regional lenses. According to Nwuzor,

> It is obvious that uniformity, even for balanced development and nation unity, is a very difficult problem in a pluralistic society like Nigeria. Such a policy carries the possibility, as already the case in Nigeria, of being interpreted by some as 'leveling down' where the declared intension is to 'level up.' Public monopoly of management and control of education without the means to meet demand and a policy of equality for all is another contradiction.[131]

While the goal of uniting Nigeria's pluralistic societies in a collective conscience proved elusive, remarkable achievements were recorded in university expansion. While the number of universities grew from six in 1970 to thirteen in 1979, enrolment surged from 14,468 in the 1970/71 session to 57,742 in the 1979/80 session.[132] Nonetheless, given Nigeria's population, estimated at 68 million in 1979, this number was statistically insignificant.

Its significance, however, lay in the fact that while enrolment grew from 1,360 in 1960 to 9,695 in 1969, it jumped to 57,742 in 1979.

Another major turning point in the country's educational development was in 1979 when Obasanjo handed over power to a democratically elected government. The new constitution that came into force removed legislation on higher education from the exclusive legislative list and placed it on the concurrent list. Accordingly, both the federal government and the nineteen states now had equal powers to control higher education. The federal government's monopoly on university education ended. This significant shift in the country's educational experiment had great consequence for the third push for mass university education policies, 1979–83.

5

The Second Republic and the Burden of Expansion, 1979–83: Free Education, Science and Technology, and the Quota System

Introduction

The 1979 constitution ushered in a new civilian administration called the Second Republic. The constitution introduced a United States-style presidential system to replace of the parliamentary system adopted during the First Republic (1960–66). It also ended the exclusive federal control of university education since 1970. Both federal and state assemblies were now empowered by the constitution to make laws "with respect to the establishment of an institution for purposes of university, professional or technological education."[1] To facilitate nation-building, the constitution enshrined the principle of federal character based on a quota system in the federal civil service appointments, a system that was later introduced in university admission.[2] The intention was to prevent domination by one or more states, ethnic groups, or sections at the federal level. Chapter 2, Section 3 of the 1979 constitution adopted quota system (affirmative action) in employment as a principle of state policy. It declared that the composition of the government of the federation and its agencies and operations would be carried out in a manner as to "reflect the federal character of Nigeria and the need to promote national unity."[3] The overall strategy was to use the system "to command national loyalty thereby ensuring that there shall be no predominance of persons from a few states or from a few ethnic or other sectional groups in that government or in any of its agencies."[4] Most significantly, the constitution enshrined the doctrine of free education as state policy by undertaking to provide, among other things, free university education "as and when practicable."[5]

Inspired by the constitutional changes and emboldened by the increased oil revenue of 1979, politicians made free education and educational expansion a crucial point in their campaigns. The five political parties that were registered when the Obasanjo's military government lifted the ban on political activities in 1978 prioritized education.[6] Even though the political parties were divided along regional and ethnic lines, they shared a similar commitment to free education. The UPN, led by Awolowo, proposed free education at all levels. It promised to cancel all loans granted to students, abolish all lodging fees for student hostels, and increase the national subsidy for student feeding.[7] Similarly, the NPN, under Makaman Bida, pledged to eradicate illiteracy throughout Nigeria and promote the learning of science, culture, and qualitative education. Waziri Ibrahim's GNPP vowed to work towards free and high quality education at all levels. The NPP under Nnamdi Azikiwe made similar declarations on education.[8] However, none of the parties articulated strategies for financing their ambitious and expensive educational promises. They trusted in the 'endless flow' of oil revenue.

On 1 October 1979, Shagari and the nineteen state governors assumed the positions of first executive president of Nigeria and executive governors respectively, marking a new beginning for Nigeria after thirteen years of military dictatorship. Given his party's emphasis on free and high quality education as well as the country's desire for social change, Shagari used his first nation-wide broadcast to make a commitment to educational expansion and economic development. Shagari declared that Nigeria needed "more schools, more playing-fields and numerous other supplies and equipment, all of which are involved with the increase in enrolment."[9] He noted, however, that the main problem was "how to make education accessible to all, given the … inadequacy of teachers and educational facilities."[10] Of course, much money was required to conduct Shagari's educational agenda. Oil revenue had been unstable since 1975, but, by 1979, the Gulf War between Iran and Iraq led to an increase in Nigeria's revenue. This increase gave Shagari's administration the confidence to pursue its ambitious campaign promises, the most prominent of which included educational expansion and free education.

In keeping with the country's vision of economic development and nation-building, Shagari's administration established seven universities of science and technology, introduced affirmative action policy, initiated the National Open University scheme, and involved the states in educational expansion. This chapter shows that the early 1980s were marked by an accelerated push for mass university education. It argues that central to understanding university education policies in the mid-1980s are the uncertainties of the country's oil revenue, the unrealistic and unsustainable expectations of the masses for free and equal access to higher education, the recklessness with which educational expansion was pursued, and the sudden economic downturn due partly to corruption of governmental officials.

National Open University and Universities of Technology

Since 1960, enrolment in Nigerian universities had been hampered by a combination of factors, including limited facilities to accommodate demand and exclusion of mature students, homemakers, and the handicapped. Following his promise of mass education, President Shagari introduced a bill on National Open University (NOU). The government intended NOU to address these problems. The concept of NOU was, unmistakably, at the centre of massification of university education. It derived from the objectives of making higher education accessible to those denied the opportunity at earlier stages of their lives. The objectives of the NOU, as envisioned by the federal government, were to provide programs, which would be flexible and responsive to changing circumstances. Such a university would

> run at the degree and post-graduate levels as well as for diploma, certificate, enrichment and refresher courses to meet the needs

of university students who will include working adults willing to combine work with learning, housewives, handicapped persons, and also young men and women who must have minimum qualifications for admissions as determined by the Senate of the University.[11]

On 1 May 1980, Shagari set up a Presidential Planning Committee on NOU and appointed Professor G.J. Afolabi Ojo to head it. The committee had the task of coming up with proposals on the nature of the university in the "context of Nigerian higher education, the administrative and academic structure of the University, the technical support services, staff establishments, relationships with other universities and related bodies within and outside the country, and also relationships with the mass media."[12] In its report, the committee suggested that the teaching methodology would be a combination of correspondence materials, radio and television, sound and videotapes suitable for use in transistorized equipment, face-to-face teaching at local study centres, and written assignments.[13] This approach was intended to reach a much wider audience than the existing traditional universities. However, given the unreliable and poor state of Nigeria's communication infrastructures, the provision of university education through this medium, particularly when the services were outside the control of the university, was challenging. Ojo hoped that in view of the wide range of teaching techniques to be used by the university, plans would be made to ensure that the university's dependence on some technical support services was "reasonable, feasible and reliable. Such essential technical support services include printing, radio, television, post and telegraphs, and computer facilities."[14]

Similarly, the unavailability of modern communication equipment in many rural areas was another problem that would affect the coverage of NOU. The vast majority of Nigerians, especially in rural areas, lacked easy access to radios and television sets. The Planning Committee stressed that finding a way to reach those Nigerians was necessary for the success of NOU. The committee therefore recommended that "such media resources should be provided at local study centers where they can be operated with the assistance of technicians and where generators can be used to supply power if and when the supply from the National Electric Power Authority is unavailable."¹⁵ The absence of communication infrastructures and steady power supply in most of the rural areas and their unreliability in the urban areas presented serious challenges to the NOU project. One way of overcoming these challenges, which would have been within the powers of NOU, was through the postal system. To deal with the slow or non-delivery of letters and parcels to students of the NOU, the Planning Committee suggested that the NOU should rely on an independent courier system to be managed by the university itself, which would relay learning materials to students. However, this strategy would have inevitably increased the cost of study at the NOU, making it inaccessible to many people. Given these uncertainties, it was not surprising that the Senate turned down the Open University Bill at the second reading on 16 September 1981, even though the House of Representatives had passed it on 16 July 1981.

Although the Senate had vetoed the National Open University Bill, Nigerians continued to mount pressure on the senators to pass it. For instance, a *Daily Times* editorial of 13 December 1982, strongly called on the Senate to pass the Open University Bill to help thousands of young Nigerians who desired opportunities for university education. The paper declared that "Senators as elected representatives of the people cannot afford to kill a bill which will be beneficial to thousands of the electorate."¹⁶ Although the senate eventually passed the bill, the university did not become operational because in 1984 the new military government suspended it, citing lack of adequate facilities as their major reason.

The infrastructural problems that raised doubts over the wisdom of establishing a NOU highlighted the poor state of science and technology in the country even after years the government pronounced commitment on the subject. Because of the critical role of science and technology in the smooth functioning of the proposed NOU as well as facilitating economic development, Shagari administration moved quickly to pursue his plans to establish seven universities of technology. These universities, he stated, would be located in states without universities. The thirteen existing universities operated in twelve out of the nineteen states, so the federal government proposed to situate the new universities in the seven states without university facilities, i.e., Bauchi, Gongola, Niger, Imo, Ogun, Benue, and Ondo.¹⁷ The idea of locating the proposed universities of technology in these states was designed to foster national unity through fair geographical spread of university amenities. It was also meant to help champion the drive to scientific and technological advancement of Nigeria's economy. The vice president, Alex Ekwueme, stated that this decision, "while placing prime focus on the development of technologies for the country, will also ensure proper distribution of university institutions and location of a federally operated university in each geo-political state of the country."[18]

The government's determination to privilege science and technology was based on the need to train relevant personnel to execute the technologically oriented programs it had embarked upon. Of high priority were projects such as the modernization of agricultural development (dubbed the Green Revolution), steel development, petro-chemical technology, urban and rural electrification, and the development of a new federal capital in Abuja. The workforce required to execute the programs were as follows: engineers, construction and allied trades, 36,820; agriculturalists, scientists, engineers and veterinary surgeons, 12,790; medical and paramedical personnel, 82,366; accountants, 58,185; and legal practitioners, 5,185.[19] To meet the technological human resource needs of the country, the government strongly believed that more specialized universities were needed.

The previous military administrations had made a series of pronouncements supporting science and technology without backing them with relevant policies. Shagari wanted to be different. Following the advice of the acting executive secretary of NUC, Abel Guobadia, the federal government decided to phase the founding of seven universities within a four-year period. The first phase was between 1980 and 1981, when it would set up universities of technology in Bauchi, Benue, and Imo states. While universities in Gongola and Ondo states were planned to emerge during the second phase, 1981/82, the remaining universities would be established in Niger and Ogun states during the third phase, 1982/83.[20] To facilitate the immediate opening of these universities, the federal government not only appointed vice-chancellors for the first-phase universities but also requested the NUC to organize a national conference of experts.[21] Held in December 1980, the conference focused on how to realize the government's vision of producing highly skilled workers in science and technology. In his opening address at the seminar, the vice president noted that the proposed universities were not just "an expansion of university opportunity: they were different from the traditional universities which we [Nigeria] inherited from our colonial past."²² Echoing the long-standing government commitment to decolonize higher education by moving away from dependency to real independence, he asked: "How much can ... [Nigeria] afford to depend on the importation of technological goods and expatriate personnel for our building and construction, transportation and communication and other services?"²³ The vice president implied that the new universities of technology would answer that question and besides provide "leadership to industrial and technological development in the country."²⁴

The report issued at the end of the seminar emphasized the need for the proposed universities to offer academic and professional programs leading to the award of diplomas, first degrees, postgraduate and higher degrees in planning, adaptive, technical, maintenance, developmental and productive skills in the engineering, scientific, agricultural, medical, and allied professional disciplines.²⁵ In addition, the report favoured the introduction of the following major academic programs: Management Sciences, Science Education, Environmental Science and Fine Arts, Earth, Mineral and Natural Sciences, Agriculture and Agricultural Technology, Engineering and Engineering Technology, Health Sciences and Technology, Pure and Applied Sciences, including Biotechnology. The report also recommended the maintenance of admission through JAMB and the retention of entry qualifications as obtainable in the existing universities. However, given the specialized and demanding nature of courses in the universities and the importance government attached to quality, the report stipulated that candidates with 'O' Level certificates should spend five years instead of four while those with 'A' Level certificates should spend four.

Unfortunately, the report failed to address adequately the more critical issue of how to fund and improve science education at the secondary school level in order to ensure a steady supply of students for the proposed specialized universities. This problem had been largely responsible for low enrolment in science subjects since the 1960s. The seminar report merely noted that since there were many potential students who would be interested in these universities "if adequate facilities are made available, each university should aim at initial intake of about 250 students and thereafter increase as facilities permit."²⁶ The huge cost of establishing seven new universities of technology aimed at admitting only 250 students seemed odd, especially when the faculties of applied science and technology in the regular universities remained underfunded.

Given the underfunding of the existing universities since 1978 and the uncertainties of oil revenue, the quality of training expected at the proposed universities caused some considerable concern to stakeholders. The concern was that these universities would end up producing amateur scientists. Professor G.O. Olusanya, the director of studies at the National Institute of Strategic Studies, Kuru, articulated this when he praised the government for emphasizing science and technology but warned against establishing universities of technology for political popularity. According to him,

> what we need today are men who can match theory competently with practice and a great deal of money would to be expended to achieve this. It must be remembered that the constant and genuine complaints about the products of our Engineering and other professional faculties and schools is that most of their product are mere textbook engineers and professionals. Unless these problems are clearly articulated and properly resolved, all we shall be doing is engaging in wishful thinking.[27]

Responding to increased doubt over its commitment to provide adequate funds for science education and educational expansion, the federal government reaffirmed its commitment in a budget speech delivered by Shagari at the joint session of the National Assembly on 24 November 1980. In that speech the president expressed the hope that the improved revenue from oil sales would help his government meet its obligations to the education sector. According to him, "The prospects for the economy in 1981 are good. The 1980 success will, I believe, constitute a launching pad for further achievement."[28] Based on the mistaken hopes of steady revenue from oil, and in order to meet its long-term objective of human resource development, the federal government launched the Fourth National Development Plan (Fourth NDP) in 1981. The plan, which covered the period between 1981 and 1985, had a program of ₦82 billion, the largest since planning began in 1960. It also projected student enrolment of over 103,000 in the federal universities by the 1984/85 session.[29] In addition, the plan envisaged a capital expenditure of ₦2.2 billion on education, representing about 5.5 per cent of projected total federal government capital investment during the period. The planned expenditure for universities was ₦1.25 billion, representing 56.6 per cent of the total investment in the sector. This allocation disproportionately favoured universities, but the plan observed that unlike other levels of education, the development in the universities was constrained due to budgetary stringencies since the third plan period. It stressed that this situation "did not augur well for the growth of the universities especially in areas concerned with academic programmes and research. Moreover, the level of demand for university places has increased beyond proportions."[30]

The large financial allocation to university education under the Fourth NDP sought to consolidate and expand the existing university facilities.[31] However, the plan had hardly taken off before the parameters on which the federal government based its revenue expectations changed dramatically following the collapse of the international oil market, beginning in 1981.[32] Although the plan operated amidst a grave threat to the economy, the federal government still maintained its commitment to university education. Eager to keep campaign promises and retain his popularity, the Shagari government went ahead to establish three new universities of technology in Bauchi, Benue, and Imo states in October 1981 (and four others later) largely through external borrowing.

Quota System and the Challenges of Nationhood

In line with the federal principle enunciated in the 1979 constitution and eager to close the educational gap between the North and the South, Shagari reopened the contentious quota system in university admissions. In spite of introducing of free education, the enrolment of students from the educationally disadvantaged regions remained low. Admission statistics for 1980 revealed that, out of 17,729 students offered admission, only 4,068 were from the North. To achieve the objective of ensuring geographical balance among the various geopolitical components, the federal ministry of education issued guidelines on the implementation of a quota system for university admission to JAMB in September 1981.[33] The quota system, like affirmative action in the United States of America, aimed at 'democratizing' access to university by easing admission competition for underrepresented groups in Nigerian universities.

The new admission guidelines, which would be implemented by the Joint Admission and Matriculation Board (a central admission body created in 1978), stipulated four criteria for securing admissions. First, it reserved 40 per cent of yearly admissions for Academic Merit. Universities would determine this criterion by ranking candidates based on their scores in the University Matriculation Examinations (UME). In other words, 40 per cent of the entire applicants in a year who scored highest were selected for various courses. The second criteria, Educationally Disadvantaged States, reserved 20 per cent of yearly admission for candidates from states such as Bauchi, Benue, Borno, Cross River, Gongola, Kaduna, Kano, Lagos, Niger, Plateau, Rivers, and Sokoto.[34] Twenty per cent of students from those states who scored a minimal average pass mark prescribed by the JAMB would secure admission.

The third criterion, called Catchment Area, reserved 30 per cent of admission for students from the immediate vicinity of an educational facility, which, in most cases, were the geographical or socio-cultural areas near to the institution. As with the second criterion, 30 per cent of students from a university's catchment areas with minimum pass marks received admission offers. This criterion was designed to help such students from surrounding states enjoy preferential treatment in admission.[35] The fourth criterion was Discretion, which reserved 10 per cent of admission to be based on the circumstances of the applicant. Benefiting students must meet JAMB's minimum pass mark, but individual universities admitted students under this category using different yardsticks without necessarily ranking the candidates. The new guidelines, however, did not change the basic qualifying requirements for university admissions, which included minimum passes in some prescribed 'O' Level subjects.

As an illustration, if the JAMB pass mark in a given year was 200 points, candidates who scored 200 or more were likely to secure admission. If 300 candidates whose scores ranged from 200 to 330 points sought 100 available places in history, only forty students with the highest points would be admitted under academic merit. Although students who scored below 280 passed the entry exam, they could still lose admission under merit. However, such candidates could still secure admission if they met any other quota criteria. Since candidates from educationally disadvantaged states received 20 per cent of the allocation, history would fill the admission quota by ranking relevant candidates by their scores and selecting twenty students. Similarly, thirty students from the catchment area of the university would be selected after ranking them by their scores. Finally, the university administrators would select the remaining 10 per cent of the students without necessarily following a ranking format, bringing the total number of students to 100 – though all the selected students must score above 200 points. The quota system, which had been resisted for so many years, was finally incorporated into the admission requirements of Nigeria.

It was easy for Shagari to introduce the quota system because the federal government controlled all the universities in the country as well as the central admission body, JAMB. Shagari's approach was quite democratic although quite diplomatic as well. Wary that the south would reject it, other criteria such as Academic Merit, Educationally Disadvantaged States, Catchment Area, and Discretion were included to blunt the impact of a quota system. Northerners, who had detested JAMB since its establishment in 1978 because it offered admissions to students solely on academic merit, welcomed this change because it accommodated their interests. The government was both sensitive to the North's peculiar interest without discriminating against the South or well-qualified students. In reality, a well-qualified student had a better chance. If not admitted on Academic Merit, such students could still gain admission through Catchment Area and Discretion admission criteria since selection would be based on ranking. In comparison, a less qualified student had fewer chances.

In reality, however, it was possible that qualified students from the South, who applied to a university in North, could to be denied admission. For instance, following the example above, if a student from the South scored 259 points, he would not secure admission under merit because the cut-off point was 280. In addition, since he was not from one of the educationally disadvantaged states as well as catchment areas, he would still be denied admission. Unless the student could influence the university authority to grant a discretionary admission, which was usually tricky, he might end up losing admission that year.[36] At the same time, a less qualified candidate with lower points (for example, 201) from one of the educationally disadvantaged states could secure admission. A notable example was T. Fagbulu, a candidate from Edo state who, despite scoring high in the exam, was denied admission because he came from an educationally advantaged state. Fagbulu unsuccessfully protested through a legal action, thus highlighting citizens' engagement with government policies. As the *National Concord* newspaper wrote: "An ambitious 16-year old fearing for his future, has taken on [the government] ... over the quota system of admission into universities."[37] The counsel for the complainant begged the court "to declare as unconstitutional, null and void, the policy of admission as practiced by JAMB."[38] Similar cases existed but the federal government maintained its position.

Like the establishment of JAMB, the introduction of the quota system under Shagari, a northern, generated misgivings. Many southerners perceived it as a strategy to help the northerners while halting the educational advancement of the South. According to J.M. Kosemani, an educationist, the quota system was an "aggravated parody and a fraud on the nation, designed to kill initiative in some areas and encourage mediocrity in other areas."[39] Similarly, T. Megaforce, a political commentator, suspected that the new admission policy was a deliberate attempt to stem the tide of educational advancement in the South so that the North could catch up.[40] More striking was the criticism from Michael Angulu, the first registrar of JAMB, who stated that the quota system was anchored on cheating, the cheating of states in the south. In an interview with *Newswatch*, he pointed out that he came from one of the most educationally backward states in Nigeria [Benue], but he, together with three other candidates from the same region, had gained admission into University of Ibadan in 1957. He revealed that the number of candidates of northern origin who demanded higher education before and after independence had remained comparatively low, which partly inspired the introduction of a quota system in 1981.[41] Nevertheless, he stressed that it would have been much better if the federal government went out of its way to strengthen the lower levels of education in the North over a period.

> [For] that would be cheating the rest of the country but in the end; I think it is a fairer cheating than the quota system. I think it will be better for the federal government to spend extra money

over and above the allocation to states to strengthen education in those places so that after a period, they will be in a position to compete with everybody else. Now, this is likely to cause less resentment than what is now generally called the quota system.[42]

The idea of a Nigeria divided into the educationally advantaged and disadvantaged states constituted the main source of controversy in the new admission policy. The federal government seemed to ignore the factors that disadvantaged the northerners in the first place. One of the main foundations rested with the political will of state governors in the South to commit large resources to education. The trend began during the colonial period when southern politicians embarked on universal education schemes while their northern counterparts dragged their feet. Compared to their northern counterparts, the southern governors allocated huge amounts to fund all levels of education.[43] Given this pattern of expenditure, increased numbers of southerners were in primary and secondary schools and later sought university admissions in greater numbers.

The federal government's desire to use the quota system to forge national unity seemed counterproductive. It did not enjoy the support of all Nigerians, mostly southern states. They believed that students of northern origin were given unfair advantage by exclusively granting them automatic admission since they came from educationally disadvantaged states – a privilege their counterparts from the South did not enjoy. Thus, the application of education policy aimed at uniting Nigerians had a negative impact on the notion of unity and patriotism. According to T.M. Yesefu, a former vice-chancellor of the University of Benin, a Nigerian who was deprived of an educational opportunity after meeting the qualifications for entrance because he came from the so-called educationally advantaged state, "has had the tenets and principles of a united Nigeria, demonstrably transformed into a mockery, if not totally and irrevocably destroyed within him."[44] As he further noted, "no amount of singing the national Anthem, nor voluble recitation of the Pledge, would ever again make him a complete Nigerian. Henceforth, he is native of his state first, and being a Nigerian becomes secondary."[45] To the beneficiary of the quota system, the effects, though unintended, would be the same. According to Yesefu, "the practice would have the same resultant effect on the student who, because he came from the disadvantaged state benefited from the admission exercise."[46] Having enjoyed special benefits because of state of origin, "his first loyalty would be to the state which apparently gave him the rare opportunity, not the Federal Government."[47] Given this scenario, the goal of national unity, which the policy aimed to achieve, seemed undermined. It was not surprising, therefore, that states, especially those in the South began a push to own their own universities.

State Participation in Higher Education

For bright students from the South to increase their chances of securing admissions, they were better off applying to neighbouring universities where they were at least certain to secure admission either on merit or catchment area criteria. Many states and students in the South felt alienated. Reactions were immediate. The affected states moved swiftly toward founding their own universities. Indeed, one of the consequences of federalization of university education since 1975 and of placing higher education on the concurrent legislative list in 1979 was the agitation by the nineteen states to own universities. One of the major projects prominent on the minds of every state governor when they came to power in 1979 was to establish a university. This action always enhanced the reputation of the governor as an effective leader. Under the 1979 constitutional arrangement, both the state and federal government were granted the power to legislate on the establishment of institutions of higher learning. With prompt exercise of this power, Anambra and Bendel states had established state universities Anambra State University of Science and Technology and Bendel State University, Ekpoma respectively in 1980.

Perhaps determined to overcome the limited opportunities for state residents evident in the quota system and eager to fulfill campaign promises of free education for all, other southern states pressed ahead with their university dreams, often with limited resources. In Imo State, which had recorded the highest number of university applicants, the gap between demand and supply was wide. In response to his electoral promise, the Imo State Governor, Sam Mbakwe, made a strong case for the establishment of a university to provide opportunities for qualified residents, hitherto denied opportunities in the federal universities. According to him, out of the 113,162 candidates who took the entrance exam in the 1978/79 session, "Imo State had 19,702 candidates, but only 2,126 or about 10% of them was offered admission. Therefore, we need our own University."[48] In addition, during the 1979/80 session, the number of applicants from Imo State increased to 20,485, but again, only 2,334 candidates successfully secured admission.[49] Before Mbakwe, other prominent Imo residents had made a similar case. For instance, earlier in 1978, Jaja Wachukwu, a former minister of foreign affairs, speaking at a press conference, noted that the federal government's decision to centralize the establishment of universities had stifled Imo State. He stated that Imo State had the greatest number of post-primary school products yearning for university education yearly. As he stressed, "no state has a better case for a new university than Imo State because it produces more students ripe for university education than any of the newly created states."[50]

Criticism from states without universities had continued to grow since the early years of Shagari administration. The senate debated the rising demand for state universities, even contemplating to transfer the control of all the universities to the state governments. Professor Akintoye proposed that the federal government should grant money to the seven states – Ondo, Niger, Gongola, Ogun, Imo, Bauchi, and Benue.[51] "A university was needed," Abubakar Barde, governor of Gongola State, told the local College of Preliminary Studies in Yola "due to the hardship [indigenes] encountered in seeking admission to the country's universities."[52] Such sentiments were common in Nigeria during the early 1980s.

In view of the limitation imposed on the students from the educationally advantaged states in the federal universities and the desire for state governors to fulfill electoral promises in order to remain relevant politically and to exercise their constitutional power, which permitted states to establish their universities, the following state universities emerged in 1981: Imo State University, Etiti (now Abia State University, Uturu), and Rivers State University of Science and Technology, Port Harcourt. Two more following state universities, Ondo State University, Ado Ekiti, and Ogun State University, Ago-Iwoye, emerged in 1982, followed in 1983 with the establishment of Lagos State University and Cross River University. By 1983, there were twenty-eight universities in the country.

The movement to establish universities at the state and federal levels, according to Adamolekun, "appears to be inexorably in the direction of university education for the masses."[53] However, these universities emerged in an atmosphere of severe economic constraints, which shows that politics dominated educational considerations. In their desire to score political advantages, governors of these states committed more of their increasingly scarce resources to university education. Given the fact that revenue from oil began to decline in 1981, state universities became financial burdens to the states' meagre resources.

Economic Meltdown of 1983

The proliferation of federal and state universities was bound to weigh heavily on government finances. As early as 1981, the federal government, worried about the heavy cost of supporting free education in the face of dwindling national income, set up the Onabamiro Commission on Alternative Sources of Funding.[54] Focusing on higher education, the commission recommended the sharing of education funding among the three branches of the government – local, state, and federal – with education taxes to be levied on all. It urged the government to abandon its free education policy and to re-introduce fees at all education levels. The recommendation was echoed in the report of the Presidential Commission on Salary and Conditions of Service of University Staff (otherwise called the Cookey Commission), which condemned the proliferation of universities in Nigeria and advised the government to build fewer centres of excellence.

The recommendation of the Onabamiro Commission seemed economically sound, but, given the country's mood, it was politically unrealistic. Implementing it would have been political suicide for the Shagari regime largely because Nigerians had been made to believe that access to education could be free. As Jubril Aminu noted: "It is doubtful if any civilian government would wish to entertain the commotion that would follow any attempt to reintroduce tuition fees or to increase charges in our educational institutions."[55] In fact, many Nigerians rejected the proposals of the Onabamiro and Cookey's commissions, believing that it "tilted the balance somewhat in favor of university education for an elite."[56] Despite the efforts

Table 5.1: Students' Applications and Admissions.

Period	Applied	Admitted	Percentage
1980/81	145,837	20, 429	14
1981/82	180, 685	22, 460	12.4
1982/83	191, 583	19, 897	10.07

Source: *The Guardian*, 8 September 1984, 8.

of both states and federal government to expand access to university, university education remained essentially elitist. Although student population rose to 116,822 in 1983, demand continued to outstrip supply, as shown in Table 5.1.[57]

Although the government intended the quota system to facilitate and equalize access to universities, the South still dominated educational opportunities between 1979 and 1983. In the 1979/80 session, the number of applicants from the former Northern Region was 15,449 and 23.1 per cent were offered admission. During the same period, 97,989 students from the South applied for admission and 75.7 per cent gained admission. The statistics remained the same during the 1982/83 session when out of 26,747 northern students who applied for admission, 22.7 per cent received admission offers; 177,618 students in the south applied and 76 per cent gained admission.[58]

In the area of science and technology, universities did not make significant progress. For instance, between 1975 and 1979, the combined average output of agriculturalists and technologists in all the Nigerian universities accounted for only 14 per cent of the yearly total of graduates. During this period, the percentage of students in the faculties of Agriculture, Engineering, Architecture, Medical and Natural Sciences were few compared to those in the Humanities, Social Sciences, Law, and Education. 55 per cent of students were in Nigerian universities in 1980 to study in the Arts and Humanities, Social Sciences and Law, a trend that continued up to 1983.[59] As a result, up to 1983, Nigerian universities trained a yearly average of only thirty scientists and engineers. This number did not meet the government target of training sufficient personnel to execute the technologically oriented programs it had embarked upon.

In spite of the federal government's desire to train more scientists and engineers, the demand for science courses was low because science education at the secondary-school level was not given a high priority. Thus, most universities relied on remedial programs to train candidates to fill up the admission quota in the sciences. This practice, however, did not address the root of the problem. As Professor M.J.C. Echeruo, the first Vice-Chancellor of Imo State University remarked,

> if I was given a million naira today to admit one hundred remedial students into Imo State University, I would immediately donate the money to ten good secondary schools in this state and I can assure you that they will produce more than enough sound and qualified university applicants for this country at a fraction of what it would cost the university.[60]

The logic of Echeruo's position as he noted was: "Good education is best established early in life. It costs less to do so anyway."[61] Similarly, displeased with the low enrolment and output of science-oriented students in the University of Lagos, the vice-chancellor, Professor Akin Adesola, stated in his 1983 convocation address that Nigeria "cannot build [its] technological pyramid from the top without due regard to the nature, structure and strength of the base – the Primary and Secondary Education systems."[62] It is surprising that a government that committed itself to science and technology by building federal universities of technology and allocating huge amounts to university education under the Fourth NDP, failed to pay equal attention to science education at the secondary school levels.

Any hopes of addressing the problems in the education sector dimmed with the economic recession that became severe in 1983. The over-reliance of government on oil revenue and the instability of the international market took a toll on government social programs, including university education. The price of oil, which was at its peak in 1980, slumped in 1982.[63] Consequently, the federal government revenue declined considerably. The level of oil production averaged 1.75 million barrels per day by 1981 while an average of 2.3 million barrels per day was used in the projections for the

Fourth National Development Plan. The combined effect of falling prices and production levels was to drop export earnings from oil from ₦4.199.7 million in 1980 to ₦10.529.5 million in 1981.⁶⁴ The resultant economic crisis of the 1980s worsened and dramatically affected the external sector. For example, between 1981 and 1983, the average monthly import bill was US$2.0 billion while exports averaged US$1.5 billion. Nigeria's foreign debt increased from ₦3.3 billion in 1978 to ₦14.7 billion in 1983. By 1983, the nineteen state governments had run up a combined debt of ₦13.3 billion. The ratio of debt service to exports climbed from 9.0 per cent in 1981 to 18.5 per cent in 1982 and 23.6 per cent in 1983. Arrears on letters of credit accumulated, and in 1983, some US$2.1 billion of such debts had to be refinanced over a thirty-month period.⁶⁵ The existing universities suffered from underfunding arising from the economic meltdown. National newspapers in Nigeria confirmed the financial strain of Nigerian universities when it reported increases in hostel fees and cancellation of bursary awards, among other things.⁶⁶

The seriousness of the economic crisis became unmistakable when the Committee of Vice-Chancellors convened a seminar to discuss the apt and relevant subject of "Nigeria: The Universities, the Nation, and the Economic Recession." In his keynote address, the vice president, Alex Ekwueme, compared the recession of the 1980s with world economic slumps of the early 1930s. He argued that the recession was not peculiar to Nigeria; it was a worldwide phenomenon, affecting mostly African countries.⁶⁷ Furthermore, Ekwueme argued that the Nigerian governments during the era of oil boom in the 1970s were unmindful of the trap set by the industrialized countries, which lured them into indiscriminate and heavy borrowing which brought the country's external debt to $15 billion in 1983.⁶⁸

Ekwueme, however, neglected to mention that just as the military government in the 1970s undertook ambitious projects based on unrealistic revenue expectation, the civilian government in the early 1980s suffered from a similar mentality. The 1983 economic recession revealed the peculiar extravagance that characterized civilian administrations at both federal and state government levels. The Fourth NDP stated as its policy objective "the building of new [universities]," but it was apparent even to a layman that it would be cheaper and more cost-effective in the long run to expand facilities in the existing universities to cope with increased demand than to build new ones. Instead of taking that route to expanding access, the civilian regime established seven new federal universities and eight state universities and upgraded five advanced colleges of education to university degree-awarding institutions.[69]

Why would the federal and state governments found fifteen new universities within a short period of four years when the existing ones were inadequately funded? The probable answer was politics, for education easily became vulnerable to mass politics and pressure. "Politics," as Dan Agabese noted, "remains a strong determinant in the development of Nigeria's social institutions – health, education, transportation."[70] Since the 1979 Constitution empowered states to own universities, governors "saw universities as amenities and so opted for mushrooming them."[71] The politicians had failed to read the economic signs of the time. Instead of operating the political system with the economic discretion of statesmanship, "they thrived in personal aggrandizement."[72] Official corruption and mismanagement of resources may account partly for the low funding of universities as well as the economic downturn. Corruption was a dominant issue in the execution of social and economic policies of the civilian regime, laying the foundation for future economic difficulties. As Ray Ekpu noted, since "the leadership was patently unpatriotic, mentally and morally bankrupt, the system was used and misused in building a concrete grave for the burial of Nigeria."[73] Politicians were more interested in the kickbacks they would receive from contracts awards than the actual execution of projects, including university projects.[74]

Instead of expanding facilities in the existing universities to accommodate more students, they expended resources to build new universities, each with its own jumbo bureaucracy without significant increase in school population. As Achike Okafo argued: "if we are inclined to proliferate the country with universities, we must be prepared to provide what it takes to make them proper universities. That is the inescapable truth."[75] There was no evidence of a long-term plan for the future sustainability of the government's massification policies. In a paper presented at the National Conference on Education Since Independence, N.A. Nwagwu, a professor at the University of Benin, noted that what passed as policy-making in education in Nigeria was "often a mere attempt to rationalize political decisions and actions hastily and expediently conceived and executed."[76]

The federal government pursued politically attractive projects such as establishing a federal university in every state, commissioning iron and steel plants, and indiscriminately awarding contracts to build the new federal capital at Abuja. Faced with the fall in oil revenue, the federal and state governments secured foreign loans to carry out their ambitious social spending, anticipating an oil-price recovery that never came. The collapse of crude oil prices in the world market and the government's inclination to external borrowing in order to prosecute its programs demonstrated that politicians of the Second Republic failed to learn useful lessons from the educational policies and programs of their military predecessors. They could hardly claim that "Nigeria's economic recession, obvious to vigilant observers since 1976, would not materially affect their calculations and over-generous promises in the manifestoes for the 1979 elections."[77] By first abolishing fees and then fixing boarding and lodging charges in most of the educational institutions, governments lost enormous sources of revenue for education. More importantly, they lost the participatory spirit of Nigerians in education. In 1978, the attempt to increase boarding charges from 15 kobo to 50 kobo per meal cost Nigerians countless lives from student riots. Similarly, in 1981, effort to remove rice from the menu of one university claimed the lives of two students. Thus, the federal government avoided potential social upheavals, as Jubril Aminu had noted.[78]

The civilian governments failed to realize that there were limits to expansion and that it was impossible to expand indefinitely without a sustainable means of funding. They ignored the wide gap between policy and implementation, between wishes and realities. The free education policy under the military in the 1970s led to unrealistic expectations from Nigerians who hoped to obtain education without making sacrifices. This mindset was heightened under the civilian government of Shagari when the pursuit of massification was accelerated without adequate long-term strategic planning. Nigerians, for political reasons, were "encouraged to believe that Government can do anything and everything for them.... Therefore, everyone wants education and, of course, see no reason why they have to pay for it."[79] With the large number of secondary school graduates, salary structure and qualifications for work, which placed emphasis on university education as the gateway to the upper social and economic strata, the increased provision of public and private grants, and government doctrine of free education and the need for trained workforce, the demand for university education remained phenomenal during the Second Republic. Unfortunately, in 1983 Nigeria was "caught in the web of recession just when [it was] ... still at the threshold of mass university education."[80]

Given the reality of Nigeria's ailing economy in 1983, the question was whether Nigeria would meet its financial obligation to satisfy demands for "free mass university education."[81] Shagari, who was inaugurated on 1 October 1983, for a second term in office, thought otherwise. He declared that Nigeria's "economy can simply not survive if we insist on living the styles we had been living in 1981 and part of 1982" and he cautioned that the government "cannot go on with a spending spree which is beyond the absorptive capacity of the economy."[82] The gloomy picture of the economy became apparent when the president acknowledged in his 1984 budget speech, delivered on 29 December 1983, that the country is going through an economic recession. Among the measures to revive the economy, as the president enumerated, were "reduction of public expenditures, diversification of revenues sources, privatization of government parastatals and companies, generation of more revenue through imposition of new or higher fees for public services, securing a World Bank structural adjustment loan as well as an IMF balance of payment loan, and payment of re-scheduled short-term debts."[83]

Conclusion

What makes the history of university education between 1979 and 1983 significant is the manner in which the federal and state governments seized the opportunity provided by the 1979 Constitution to expand the university system. The federal government was committed to accelerated decolonization of the British elitist system of higher education when it provided free university education to all Nigerians and unsuccessfully attempted to open a National Open University. It also engaged university education in the service of rapid economic development when it established seven universities of technology. In addition, when it introduced the quota system of admission in 1981 and located the new universities to satisfy regional interests, the federal government expressly identified itself with the notion that equal opportunities for university access was vital in promoting greater national unity and closing the educational gap between the South and the North. However, since state governments, particularly those in the South, felt that the quota system deprived many of their indigenes access to federal universities, they established eight universities. Yet, the demand for university places continued to outrun its supply. Economic depression, occasioned by the decline in oil revenues and aggravated by official corruption and mismanagement of public funds, set in in 1983. In response, the federal government decided to suspend its massive spending on social services, including university education. Before Shagari could carry out his vision, he was overthrown in a military coup on 31 December 1983. The struggling economy that the new military government inherited dictated their attitudes to social spending, including in university expansion, during fourth attempt at massification, 1984–90.

6

Rationalization Policy: The IMF/World Bank and Structural Adjustment Program, 1984–90

> To speak of the expansion of the university system in any way now, is to ignore [Nigeria's] economic indicators. The choice must be in favour of the consolidation of means and of excellence as against mindless growth and dissipation of resources.
> – Yahaya Aliyu, 1985

Introduction

The push for mass university education under President Shehu Shagari coincided with Nigeria's economic decline of the early 1980s, which constrained further expansion of universities. Funding of existing institutions constituted a heavy burden on the country's lean resources. As the economic situation worsened, the Shagari administration approached the International Monetary Fund (IMF) for a loan, but before concluding the deal, a coup – led by General Muhammadu Buhari – overthrew the civilian government on 31 December 1983.[1] Among other things, the coup plotters bemoaned the poor state of the economy as well as the educational system. According to their spokesperson, Brigadier Sani Abacha (who later became president in 1993), Nigeria's "economy has been hopelessly mismanaged; we have become a debtor and beggar nation.... Our educational system is deteriorating at alarming rate."[2] The urgent task as the new administration saw it was to restructure the economy by reconsidering expenditure of social services, including on the universities.

Having inherited both an expanded university system and an ailing economy, the successive administrations of Buhari (1983–85) and Ibrahim Babangida (1985–90) faced a choice either to continue with the ambitious social programs of previous administrations in response to social demand or to check expansion. They chose the latter. Further establishment of universities ceased. Repositioning Nigerian universities to facilitate economic recovery and development became a more crucial element of the government's agenda. Rationalization policy, aimed at reducing subsidies on social amenities, sharing the cost of education with the public through tuition fees, and streamlining university courses to avoid duplication, was embraced. This chapter examines university development in the context of an economic downturn. It shows how the country's economic difficulties and the involvement of the IMF/World Bank gave rise to the structural adjustment dimensions of university policies in Nigeria and resulted in the period of restricted expansion of university education, 1984–90. As efforts at economic recovery assumed centre stage in the governments' national programs, the goal of using mass university education to foster national unity increasingly diminished. Instead, restructuring universities to address the country's economic problems, often neglected by previous regimes (in spite of their official pronouncements), gained prominence.

Buhari and the Search for Cost-Saving Measures

Rather than seek IMF and World Bank assistance, as Shagari had attempted in 1983, Buhari sought indigenous, self-directed economic belt-tightening measures. In carrying out this rationalization policy, the federal government squeezed financial spending on social programs, exchange rate, trade, and administration. Increases in taxes and drastic cuts in public spending were accompanied by losses of jobs in the public sector. In fact, more than one million public sector workers lost their jobs within twelve months of the regime.[3] For Nigeria, it marked a remarkable departure from the extravagant spending that had characterized the preceding governments, particularly since the 1970s.

Universities were not spared. Since independence, the government had been the sole funding source for university education. Therefore, it was not surprising that the economic recession would have far-reaching implications for the proper functioning of universities. It meant that the amount the government was prepared to allocate to education in a given year determined exclusively what they received. When the government could not meet the financial requirements of the university system, allocations declined. The impact of reduced funding in 1984 was immediate. For instance, the senate of the University of Ibadan resolved to postpone indefinitely the resumption date for the 1983/84 session because of what it described as a "very serious financial situation facing the university and its consequent inability to effectively perform its duties."[4] This scenario, as the *Daily Times* reported, applied to many Nigerian universities in the early months of 1984. It was a direct consequence of the vigorous funding of university expansion since the 1970s based largely on unreliable oil revenue. The decline in oil revenue and the resultant economic recession in the early 1980s, worsened by official corruption as well as the often-neglected mismanagement and misapplication of funds by university authorities, led to a drastic reduction in university funding.[5]

Rationalization was an attractive option in Buhari's efforts to control the process and rate of expansion based on its own criteria. Between December 1983 and August 1985, the Buhari administration took steps to manage university expansion while getting the public to share the burden of university education. Eager to avert expenses on social programs, the federal government revisited the National Open University (NOU) that had started operations in February 1984 amid mounting complaints of students over poor reception due to poor communication infrastructures.[6] Lacking funds to rectify this problem due to the economic meltdown, the federal government suspended NOU on 7 May 1984. The compelling reason was economic: the desire to avoid additional burden on the declining financial revenue of the government. As Buhari confirmed in the 1984 budget speech:

> The administration has given serious consideration to the National Open University Programme. Because the infrastructure to make the programme succeed is either not available or inadequate, the government has decided that in the present financial situation, Nigeria could not afford the Open University Programme.[7]

Buhari's crusade to rationalize universities and consolidate them for sustained growth manifested eloquently in its decision to restructure the existing federal universities of technology. According to a release issued in May 1984 by the Cabinet Office, Lagos, the federal government expressed its intention to merge four federal universities of technology with some conventional universities. The release questioned the rationale behind the continued maintenance of seven universities of technology in Nigeria "taking into account the need to provide a good quality technological education [and] the stark realities and socio-political circumstance of the country."[8] It noted, in addition, that the merging of the existing universities of technology was necessary since they operated at their "temporary sites, ill-equipped and lack[ed] basic facilities in terms of human and materials resources for achieving the objectives for which they were set up."[9] Accordingly, the federal government directed the Federal Ministry of Education in collaboration with the NUC and the affected universities to work out modalities for effecting the merger as well as for rationalizing university programs and courses to "create centers of excellence" and make them cost-effective and efficient.[10] The decision to merge four universities reflects the sober disposition of the new administration towards reducing government's financial burden.

In response to the government's directive, officials of the federal ministry of education, the NUC, and the federal university of technology met and agreed on 1 October 1984 as the effective date of the merger. They also prescribed the merger of four federal universities of technology in Abeokuta, Bauchi, Makurdi, and Yola with some conventional universities while retaining the ones in Akure, Minna, and Owerri.[11] The merged universities henceforth were to function as campuses of their foster universities, served by one council, one senate, and one chief executive vice-chancellor. By this decision, the number of federal universities in Nigeria went down from twenty to sixteen, and, together with state universities, there were now twenty-four universities in the country. Although the federal government justified its decisions on the need to provide good, quality technological education as well as the socio-economic circumstances of the country, given the declining revenue of oil, it was clear that economic justification was the most compelling.

Why the federal government chose to merge universities of technology instead of conventional universities seemed odd. This is especially so when the same federal government had proclaimed its desire to promote economic development, which would be attained through science and technology. The heavy cost of running universities of technology seemed to be a factor. However, if reducing the number of universities was the decisive consideration, there was no reason why the government would not administer all the Nigerian universities from one campus, just like the California State University that had more students scattered in various campuses than all the Nigerian universities.[12] By merging some universities, the government thought it would save money. Ironically, this arrangement did not change the status quo as NUC allocated funds directly to the affected universities without reducing cost for the government.[13]

Maintaining a free university education policy, which began in 1978, seemed unsustainable in the context of the declining economy. Reacting to the heavy cost associated with funding education, the minister of education, Ibrahim Abdullahi, complained that free education at the primary and secondary school levels throughout the country cost the government about ₦6 billion a year, excluding an estimated ₦674 million to fund one conventional university with 10,000 students.[14] The *Daily Times* editorial of 7 March 1984 urged the government to debunk the concept of government as a free education provider, stating that "the unrealistic idea of getting something for nothing has always been sold by politicians as a calculated ploy for winning votes, but has remained suspect nonetheless."[15] The benefits of a free education policy to any nation are incontestable, but the central issue in 1984 lay in the practical ability of the government to carry it through. For the first time, the public began to consider the concept of free education on its merits rather than as a political ploy.

In line with it rationalization agenda, the federal government issued a directive to the NUC in March 1984 to withdraw its subsidies on student feeding in order to save the government the cost of catering staff, cafeteria facilities, and food. The directive mandated federal universities to re-introduce accommodation fees to help defray the cost of hostel services.[16] Though state universities from their inception had charged minimal tuition fees ranging from ₦250 to ₦400, it had taken the federal government five years to implement the decision that President Obasanjo made in 1978 to re-introduce fees in the federal universities. Due to unrest in the universities, that decision was not implemented. The Shagari administration, motivated by the desire to fulfill election promises, complicated the funding problem by establishing more universities and continuing with a free university policy amid declining national revenue. Although Buhari introduced feeding and accommodation fees, tuition remained free, an issue his administration was eager to confront.

The federal government set up two study groups in 1984: one on funding of education and the other on curricula and development. The study group on funding advised government on a realistic funding of education based on the notion that education "should be the responsibility of the federal, state, and local government and parents, each contributing its share and conscious of the prevailing economic situation."[17] The government requested that the group specifically review, among other things, the existing arrangements for funding education at all levels and ascertain the extent of the financial involvement of the federal, state, and local government, and in light of the prevailing economic realities "propose an arrangement for funding education which would involve voluntary organizations, communities, individuals, and parents."[18]

In its report, the group acknowledged that universities had enjoyed a high priority in government spending compared to other levels of education during the preceding civilian era. For instance, in 1981, higher education alone claimed 65 per cent of the entire federal government recurrent expenditure on education, broken into 1.1 per cent for colleges of education and schools of basic studies, 6 per cent for polytechnics, and 57.9 per cent for the universities. Similarly, during the same year, federal government capital expenditure on education showed that higher education consumed 81.9 per cent. Universities claimed the lion's share of nearly 90 per cent of the allocated amount.[19] Identifying with the economic realities of the country and responsive to the mindset of the federal government that set it up, the group declared that "the beneficiaries of higher education in Nigeria should be partners with government in funding education."[20] It recommended payment of fees in all institutions of higher learning, award of scholarships to about 10 per cent of new entrants on academic merit, especially for students in courses designed for national emergency (e.g., tertiary science teachers' education).[21]

The curricula committee that Buhari set up reviewed university curricula with the view of addressing the high level of graduate unemployment in the country.[22] Members for this study were drawn from the Ministry of Education, Science and Technology; Employment, Labour and Productivity; Manpower Board; and the National Universities Commission.[23] In its report, the committee called for changes in university curriculum that would privilege the funding of science courses. The thinking was that since Nigeria lived in an era of global economic recession and limited financial resources, one option open to graduate job seekers was self-employment. It suggested the overhauling of university curricula to reflect the need for self-employment by graduates based on the "changing structure of the society."[24] In addition, it called for a limitation on the number of students in the arts and humanities. The idea was to hold up the rate of expansion of university education in those disciplines because it far outstripped the rate of employment of graduates. This recommendation was based on the assumption that graduate unemployment was the result of the over-production of graduates in the arts and humanities, which explained why it demanded that

> government should through the instrumentality of the National Universities Commission (NUC) considerably slow down the rate of increase in university student enrolment in the Arts and Humanities to not more than 10% per annum in contrast to slightly over 20% annual increase recorded during the 1978/79–1980/81 period.[25]

The committee stipulated a 60:40 admission ratio in favour of science-based disciplines. To control expansion, the committee advised the government to ban the establishment of new universities (whether federal or state) during the next five years. In addition, the committee called for the phasing out of the following courses from university curricula: classical and African religious studies in the universities of Ibadan and Ife; language (German, Portuguese, French, and Russian), Arabic, and Islamic studies in all the universities offering them; and the newly established law faculties in the universities of Ibadan and Ilorin. It insisted that that graduate output in law, library studies, geology, geophysics, and pharmacy should be kept at the 1983 level, and no other university should start courses leading to the award of degrees in law.[26] To underscore its bias in favour of science courses, the committee urged the government to tie financial allocation to the universities to specific courses and projects, particularly in the sciences.[27] Finally, it emphasized that the universities should intensify their efforts at internal revenue-generating activities such as corporate consultancy services and investments to reduce their financial dependence on the government.[28] Except for Mrs. O.F. Okusami, who represented the NUC, the university community was absent. This was odd, given the fact that the committee's resolutions would not just have a potential effect on university education but would be implemented ultimately by the university community.

The driving force behind the attempt to reorganize the university curriculum was the mistaken perception that Nigeria's higher educational system was lopsided in favour of liberal courses that were scarcely needed by a developing country like Nigeria. The Academic Staff Union of Universities (ASUU) faulted this thinking when it asserted that government's move was a "very transparent attempt to cover up the obvious failure of the neo-colonial economy that Nigeria is operating."[29] This claim on the part of authorities, according to ASUU, would only hold water if graduate unemployment was limited to graduates of arts disciplines and spared graduates of science disciplines. As ASUU revealed, graduates of all disciplines roamed Nigerian streets "wearing the soles of their shoes out in search of jobs that are unavailable because of the bankruptcy of the economic system which the imperialists imposed on us and which, rather unintelligently, are maintained."[30] That unemployment existed among graduates in those disciplines most needed for economic development meant that the curriculum review was a misplaced exercise intended to shift the blame onto the educational sub-system. As ASUU warned, "enough of these diversionary tactics, this movement in circles, this running after shadows, this avoidance of the heart of the matter."[31]

Likewise, the Committee of Vice-Chancellors (CVC) rejected parts of the report dealing with phasing out selected courses in some universities. Since French-speaking countries surrounded Nigeria, CVC reasoned that it was in the long-term interest of the country to emphasize the French language. The CVC also noted that many of the recommendations of the group were short-sighted, stressing that they were "induced by panic and solely on considerations of the present economic situation."[32] In spite of criticisms of the proposed curriculum reform, and to underscore its resolve to carry on with the rationalization policy, Buhari promulgated Decree No. 16 of 1985 on Education (National Minimum Standards and Establishment of Institutions). The decree empowered the NUC to set minimum standards for all academic programs currently taught in Nigerian universities, mandating the NUC to undertake periodic accreditation visits to universities to determine the viability of programs run in all Nigerian universities, not only to ensure maintenance of minimum standards, but also to guide government in allocating funds.

The recommendations made by the committees on funding education and curricula understandably followed Buhari's austerity and stabilization measures. The objective was to curtail government expenditures on social services, save money to service external debts, and ultimately avoid external assistance from world bodies such as the IMF and the World Bank. Without entering into agreement with the IMF, however, the federal government did not reschedule its debt service payments; it partially serviced the debt. With unpaid interest, arrears on external debt built up and the stock of debt grew fivefold. Nigeria's economy, including universities, suffered under the weight of the austerity program.[33] High inflation became a common economic outcome of Buhari's economic program while government subvention to federal universities declined. With sustained decline in the capital and recurrent subvention to federal universities between 1984 and 1985, universities were compelled to search for alternative sources of funding.[34] Under the caption "Varsities in Search for Funds," the *Daily Times* commended the efforts of the universities of Nigeria, Nsukka, and Ilorin for embarking on profitable commercial ventures such as university bookshops and printing presses, guest houses, pilot bakery projects, commercial farms, gas stations, and consultancy services.[35] In 1985, the University of Maiduguri launched its consultancy services centre.[36]

Buhari's austerity and stabilization measures brought untold hardships, not only to the university system, but also to Nigerians, as inflation, hunger, and unemployment continued to rise. His administration failed to either restructure the economy or cushion the effects of the government's severe 'belt-tightening' programs. Worse still was that he operated a command economy with an extensive system of direct controls that suppressed meaningful market activities, discouraging private sector involvement. Import shortages and scarcity of food items led to rising social and political discontent. Nigerians groaned under Buhari's regime, giving an incentive to some discontented and ambiguous military officers, led by Ibrahim Babangida, to stage a coup that ousted the Buhari regime on 27 August 1985. The justification for the coup was obvious: "The present state of uncertainty and stagnation cannot be permitted to degenerate into suppression and retrogression."[37]

Babangida, IMF, and Universities

The economy that Babangida inherited was characterized by huge foreign and domestic debts, a rapidly declining per capita income, a high rate of unemployment, severe shortages of raw materials and spare parts for industries, and a high rate of inflation.[38] In his first address to the nation, Babangida stressed the need to depart from the limited economic policy of the ousted regime. As he noted: "It is the view of this government that austerity without structural adjustment is not the solution to our economic predicament. The present situation whereby 44 per cent of our revenue earning is utilized to service debts is not realistic."[39] He therefore promised to take steps "to ensure comprehensive strategy of economic reforms."[40] To continue to fund university education adequately, as well as other social programs, Babangida faced three policy options: (1) maintain the status quo (which meant a continuation of the austerity measures without structural adjustment reforms); (2) accept IMF Structural Adjustment Facility, including its conditions; (3) adopt a modified variant of the traditional structural adjustment package, designed and implemented by Nigerians.[41]

Weighing its options carefully, the new government still faced the reality that it's "survival hinged on the availability of revenues, which in turn depended upon its ability to negotiate a rescheduling of debt service payments."[42]

Very early in his regime, Babangida opened a public debate on IMF, focusing on whether the government should accept the IMF loan or not. Public mood, as expressed in news media reports, called on the government to reject the IMF loan. Overwhelming support seemed to be directed toward adopting 'homegrown' adjustment measures aimed at economic recovery. Pretending to acquiesce to public pressure, Babangida declared a fifteen-month national economic emergency.[43] As he later elaborated in his 1985 budget speech, such a move would allow the country time to reflect on the social and economic problems facing the country and to seek solution through indigenous efforts. Such efforts, he noted, would be "at our own pace and our volition, consistent with our own voluntary national interest."[44] In his search for homegrown efforts at national development, Babangida found the doctrine of rationalization an attractive policy in educational planning and thus revisited the recommendations of the committee on curriculum reform that the Buhari administration had not implemented before it was overthrown. In an address to members of the university community in November 1985, Babangida endorsed rationalization policy and emphasized the historic role of the universities in not only championing economic development but aiding economic recovery. He therefore called on universities not to remain a burden to the state but "to examine and reconsider aspects of the administration and financing of university education."[45]

Contrary to its earlier promises of exploring homegrown economic policy, Babangida introduced the Structural Adjustment Program (SAP) in June 1986. Even though SAP was a core part of the IMF reform package, official rhetoric, however, insisted that it was homegrown. In launching the program, Babangida praised Nigeria's "international creditors" for appreciating the country's "commitments in the path of agro-structural adjustment which we have started for ourselves."[46] He added that the IMF recognized and agreed with his "position not to take the IMF loan, and not to devalue the naira overnight."[47] Unlike the economic measures adopted by the preceding administration, SAP aimed to promote "restructuring and diversifying the productive base of the economy in order to reduce its dependence on the oil sector and on imports and achieving in the short to medium term fiscal and balance of payments viability."[48] Other objectives of SAP were to lay "the basis for a sustainable non-inflationary growth; and reducing the dominance of unproductive investments in the public sector, and improving that sector's efficiency and enhancing the potential of the Private Sector."[49]

Notwithstanding official pronouncements, the SAP was far from being an indigenous initiative. The major reason for its adoption was to open the door to official debt rescheduling, a topmost priority of the government. It was not surprising that the federal government soon entered into three standby arrangements with the IMF under a five-year plan (1986–91). Under the arrangement, agreement was reached on three debt rescheduling agreements with the Paris Club of creditor countries: (a) a 1986 agreement that rescheduled/refinanced debt worth about US$4.6 billion; (b) a 1989 agreement that rescheduled about US$5.2 billion; and (c) a 1991 agreement that rescheduled about US$3.3 billion.[50] Ultimately, the World Bank also supported the adjustment program through a US$450 million trade policy and export diversification loan.[51] One of the major implications of introducing SAP was that the federal government cut its funding of university education since the program required government to reduce spending on social services, including education.

The Fifth National Development Plan (Fifth NDP), launched in 1986, reflected the character of SAP by requiring governments to avoid further establishment of institutions of higher learning, stressing that the existing institutions would undergo internal structural reforms intended to improve their operational efficiency and effectiveness.[52] The Fifth NDP echoed the prevailing official government's mindset; it was austere and less grandiose than its immediate predecessor was. This ideological shift had a profound impact on all sectors of the economy, especially higher educational institutions that had until then run on a non-competitive and non-profit basis. Rationalization, consolidation, and effectiveness – supported by the IMF – were the key words of the Fifth NDP, dictating subsequent steps taken by the federal government on university expansion.

It must be stressed that the IMF and the World Bank had pushed for rationalization of African universities since the late 1970s when many

African countries suffered severe economic decline. At the meeting of African vice-chancellors in Harare in 1986, for instance, the World Bank representatives argued that higher education in Africa was a luxury and that African countries were better off closing universities at home and training graduates overseas. Since the World Bank understood this call to be politically untenable, it instead urged African leaders to trim and restructure their universities to produce only those skills that the "market" required.[53] Given that the Nigerian economy needed more science graduates to help facilitate economic development and recovery, Babangida found the World Bank advice attractive. During the Silver Jubilee Celebration and Twenty-first Convocation of the UNN on December 6, 1986, Babangida stressed his government's preference for science courses because of their crucial role in national development. According to him,

> while numbers are still important, in this era of science and technology, quality has now assumed greater significance [and] emphasis would henceforth have to be shifted to science and technology, and to quality.[54]

With SAP in place, the rationalization program seemed unstoppable and universities prepared for it. Following a federal government directive on the review of the curricula report, the federal ministry of education had formed a ministerial committee in February 1986 under the leadership of Professor Akin O. Adesola, the vice-chancellor of the University of Lagos. The committee was charged with the responsibility of converting into a White Paper the recommendations of the study group on curricula for the consideration of the minister of education and the federal executive council.[55] As part of the review of university curricula, and in anticipation of rationalization of university programs, the executive secretary of the NUC and the chair of the CVC travelled to the UK between 30 March and 5 April 1987 to "gain a first hand knowledge of the British Universities scene and in particular to find out how the universities have responded to rationalization and continuous shortage of funds for their operations."[56] Under the program in the UK, the Thatcher government had cut financial allocations to the universities in 1979, almost forcing them to close down. However, the universities came back strong through commercialization of their entire operations.⁵⁷ Managers of university education in Nigeria believed that they would gain useful insights from the British experience, which would help them to handle Nigeria's impending rationalization policy.

The trip involved a series of meetings, which revealed the potential steps Nigerian universities would take to respond proactively to rationalization. For instance, at the meeting with the University Grants Committee (UGC) on March 30, N.T. Hardyman, the Secretary of the Committee, informed the visitors that the initial cuts in the financial allocations to British universities were a reduction in the 'value' of the grants.⁵⁸ According to him, the British government justified the cuts based on the philosophy of making the universities 'leaner and fitter.'⁵⁹ As he further recounted, the negative result of rationalization was that for the first time since the Middle Ages student numbers were cut in British universities. In order to allow the universities to survive, the UGC in 1984 came up with a strategy of saving universities from further financial cuts by recommending the closure of one or two of them.⁶⁰ At the meeting with Dr. J.B. Lowe, the secretary and registrar of St. Andrews University, it was stated that the commercial projects embarked on by the university could serve as a model for Nigeria.⁶¹ Similarly, Professor Ashford, vice-chancellor, University of Salford, stressed the need for vigorous fund-raising through a strong managerial ethos.⁶² This visit showed that, under rationalization, universities would not survive unless they became innovative and less dependent on the government for financial support.

The World Bank and the White Paper on University Reform

The federal government had invited the World Bank study group to carry out a study on how to salvage the deteriorating conditions in Nigerian universities and advise it on the most cost-effective way of running federal universities.⁶³ The group conducted its fieldwork in early 1987 and submitted its report to the government in October 1987. The report observed that, despite the tremendous expansion of the university system since 1960, higher education in Nigeria faced a crisis largely due to the unplanned, ad-hoc expansion of enrolments, universities, and faculties during periods of peak oil revenues, resulting in higher overall costs and unit costs. The report revealed two areas of excessive costs: the proportion of expenditures devoted to administration, and the high costs of running postgraduate programs in all subjects at all universities, even when there were few students in each course.[64] The study found that Nigerian universities spent about 46–57 per cent of their allocations on administration and much less on teaching.[65]

The World Bank report endorsed the doctrine of rationalization. Largely echoing the spirit behind SAP, it recommended the freezing of a number of departments and faculties in all federal universities. It also urged the closure of all postgraduate programs where enrolments failed to reach a cost-effective level; an increase in the number of courses for which an economically feasible level of fees can be charged, and the gradual introduction of tuition fees to cover 15 to 20 per cent of the unit recurrent cost. To encourage the study of science, it asked the government to charge a lower percentage of total costs for students in priority science fields and a higher percentage for those in non-priority arts fields as well as 100 per cent of direct teaching costs for all postgraduate students. It also requested government to charge user fees for housing, schools, water, health services, and so forth. Finally, it called for frequent workshops to be conducted on how the university system and its functions could be rationalized so as to become less of a burden on federal and state budgets, while maintaining or even improving quality and effectiveness.[66] The report, above all, indicated the World Bank's readiness to grant Nigeria a loan to help it consolidate the quality and effectiveness of university education.

Rationalization of universities, as endorsed by the World Bank, was a highly discussed issue in 1987. It dominated the proceedings of the international seminar sponsored by the NUC, the CVC, and the British Council titled, "Management of University Resources." In his address at the seminar, the federal minister for education, Jibril Aminu, highlighted the government's resolve to pursue the policy, indicating that the anticipated government white paper on curriculum reform would reflect that.[67] Additionally, all universities, as the communiqué issued at the end of the CVC meeting indicated, would be required to draw up plans of rationalization of academic programs that would remove duplication of similar courses within and between universities and provide modalities for phasing out, where necessary, programs that were neither attractive to students nor relevant to the economy.⁶⁸ It also subscribed to the government's vision of the university as contained in Aminu's speech and emphasized the need for universities to explore alternative sources of funding as well as the need for industries to support the rehabilitation of university education.⁶⁹

After due consultation, the federal government released the White Paper on higher education curriculum and development in December 1987. The paper reflected both the objectives of SAP and the observations and recommendations of the World Bank study group. It expressed the federal government's acceptance of the principle of rationalization as a blueprint in developing Nigerian universities "in view of the present economic recession and the scarcity of funds."⁷⁰ The paper endorsed the vigorous pursuit and implementation of the 60:40 admission ratio in favour of sciences by both federal and state universities because of the importance of sciences in technological development. It therefore required universities to submit a schedule for achieving that ratio by the year 1990. Despite government's stringent measure, it still wanted the expansion of university education in response to public demand. But this time, expansion must be controlled. To that end, the white paper approved 2.5 per cent and 10 per cent overall growth for older universities and younger universities respectively. In addition, it approved 15 per cent overall growth for the federal universities of technology (FUT), including four campuses/colleges resulting from merger of four former FUT.⁷¹ For state universities, it directed the NUC to ensure that they adopt the same principles in their development.

Directing the universities to draw up a plan of rationalization, the federal government empowered the NUC through Decree No. 16 to regulate the establishment of courses and standards in all universities.⁷² The NUC was to determine that by having a "complete inventory of facilities available in various faculties and departments of universities ... and draw proposals for broad areas of concentration [forming] the nucleus of the concept of centers of excellence."⁷³ These directives were inspired by economic considerations occasioned by SAP. It provided the federal government the opportunity to slow down the rate of growth in Nigerian universities, especially in the arts. In his address at the 11th Annual Seminar of the Committee of Vice-Chancellors on the theme *Mobilizing Nigeria's Education Towards Technological Self-Reliance*, the president charged the universities to help champion economic development and economic recovery.[74] He insisted that universities would do that by supporting the government's policy on science and technology and by being mindful of the need for Nigeria to take its rightful place in science and technology among advanced countries in the twenty-first century. As Babangida stated:

> [Nigeria] cannot continue to depend indefinitely on the advanced countries for our technological needs. In our attempt to achieve self-reliance, we have taken a number of measures, one of which is to encourage our universities to restructure their programmes to make them more relevant to the needs of the nation. This need to be self-reliant is very pressing now – perhaps more so now than it has been at any other time. The economy is in a bad shape, occasioned by the international economic crisis, and, yet, as a nation, we cannot afford to be left behind in the march towards technological advancement.[75]

The vision of expanding access to science students seemed unrealistic unless facilities in the existing university could accommodate them. The aggregates data for the entire 1978/79–1984/85 period revealed that, out of 1,151,018 who sought university admission, less than 12 per cent secured admission.[76] Percentages of admissions spread across disciplines reveal shortages of university places in all areas. Education ranked highest (18.0%); Arts (17.0%), Science (15.3%), and Social Sciences (14.5%) followed it. Engineering and Technology achieved an 11.8 per cent admission rate while the corresponding figure for Medicine was 11.0 per cent. The admission rate for the discipline of Law, which ranked second in the level of applications, was only 5.6 per cent or eight out of nine in terms of ranking.[77] These numbers show that the demand for university places in all the disciplines was higher than its supply, and so there was need for more places as well as more courses to satisfy demand. In that sense, rationalization threatened access to university education. As Festus Iyayi puts it, the solutions are far from "programme closures, mergers or concentration with their attendant and apparent implications for reduced student enrolment in the universities, but the expansion of existing programmes and opening of new ones to ensure that a greater level of demand is satisfied."[78] Moreover, government's insistence on 60:40 for science and arts courses seemed doomed to be unsuccessful without addressing the root of the problem – funding science education in primary and secondary schools. Since the 1960s, the governments had failed to make an adequate effort to invest in science subjects at the primary and secondary schools, thus accounting for the continued low demand for science courses at the university level. The existing secondary schools were ill-equipped to produce scientifically minded candidates for university education. As a professor B.I.C. Ijeomah noted,

> Even with the best legislation, unless the primary and secondary schools are science oriented, unless technocratic consciousness permeates the home, primary and secondary levels, unless the teachers themselves *ab initio*, think and teach scientifically the 60–40 ratio will remain a twentieth century mirage.[79]

Although the development of universities in the late 1980s was sensitive to the needs of the economy, the emphasis on sciences generated constant debate because of the feeling that discrimination in favour of science and technology courses was not a guarantee to economic development. Indeed, government's efforts to train more technocrats to the neglect of the bureaucrats, as Ijeomah noted, "would breed incompetence in the management of human resources."[80] Moreover, the emphasis on science and technology, he insisted, "is the tragedy of modem trend in university education."[81] The White Paper, however, believed otherwise, insisting that the lopsided university enrolment in favour of arts-related disciplines was laying the foundation to development. In line with the new attitude of the administration, Babangida revisited the federal universities of technology that were merged by his predecessor. The six-man committee he appointed under the leadership of Professor Nurudeen Adedipe, had the responsibility of making recommendations on demerging the campuses at Yola, Bauchi, Makurdi, and Abeokuta from the conventional universities, as well as considering the possibility of converting two into specialized universities of agriculture mindful of its financial, physical, and academic implications.[82]

After conducting a study of all the federal universities of technology, the Adedipe-led committee discovered that nothing had really changed for the better after the merger of the four universities. On the contrary, the committee noted that the merger promoted "high administrative cost and the risk to life and property occasioned by physical separation by long distances involving frequent commuting of staff between them and foster Universities."[83] According to the committee, despite the merger, the NUC had continued to fund the merged universities thus ensuring that they retained their financial autonomy while bearing the names of their parent universities.[84] Acting on the committee's report, the federal government restored the former federal universities of technology at Bauchi and Yola to their autonomous status in 1988 and re-established those in Abeokuta and Makurdi as specialized universities of Agriculture.[85] With the demerging of four former universities in Yola, Bauchi, Makurdi, and Abeokuta and the establishment of the University of Abuja (UA) in 1988, the number of universities in Nigeria returned to thirty-one.

The federal government had established UA based on the recognition that Abuja, the new federal capital of Nigeria, required an institution of higher learning that would cater to the educational needs of the inhabitants of the territory in particular and the nation in general. Given the poor state of the economy, the founding of UA was not immediate. In fact, it took the federal government two years to establish the minimum necessary facilities for the university to open for academic activities in 1990 at its temporary campus located in Gwagwalada. This was even as Babangida created two additional states in the country, which shortly began to push for a university.[86]

The Impact of IMF/World Bank Policies on Universities

Since the introduction of SAP in 1986, allocation to universities declined even as inflation continued to rise. In 1986 the federal universities requested the sum of ₦720,922,533 but received only ₦347,940,519. In 1987 and 1988, while the universities requested ₦731,077,751 and ₦805,284,664, the federal government allocated ₦270,356,000 and ₦434, 356, 000 respectively.[87] Shortfalls in allocations led to the suspension of further expansion of facilities and the gradual decay of existing facilities due to lack of maintenance. Concerned that the universities could not properly function let alone fulfill the responsibilities outlined by the president, given the crippling effects of under-funding, the Vice-Chancellors of Nigerian universities sent a delegation to the president in 1988 to demand more funds. Adamu Nayaya Mohammed, chairperson of the CVC and the leader of the delegation, notified the president of the dilemma facing Nigerian universities. He asked,

> Given the increasing number of potential University students, the shortage of financial resources and the necessity for re-definition of the contents, distribution and method of delivery of academic programmes, what should we do in the universities in order to survive and ensure that the system is sustained?[88]

Though the president seemed sympathetic, he did not make a commitment to increase funding but lent his support for a World Bank loan for the education sector.[89] The loan aimed to make foreign exchange available for the provision of facilities such as library books, journals, provision and maintenance of science-related equipment, and completion of abandoned academic facilities.[90] This loan satisfied government's notion of quality education as opposed to mass education. It aimed at equipping the federal universities with quality laboratories and research facilities, especially to champion the country's scientific and technological development.[91] As a condition for the extension of the loan (called eligibility criteria), the World Bank demanded that universities implement the recommendations outlined in the government white paper on curricular reform by reducing all the uneconomical and unviable faculties and departments and remove some support and administrative staff. In addition, they were required to raise postgraduate fees, make hostels self-financing, and increase revenues from non-governmental sources.[92] The World Bank extended a credit of $120 million, dubbed the Federal Universities Development Sector Adjustment Credit.[93] The credit was the Bank's first attempt to assist major university reform in sub-Saharan Africa, targeting Nigeria, the country with the largest university system in Africa.[94] It came at a time of low supply of university places and declining government financing caused by the sharp fall in petroleum prices.

By pushing a structural adjustment of universities as a condition for the $120 million loan, the World Bank reaffirmed its faulty and questionable position on limited investment in higher education. Since the 1970s, the World Bank had advised African governments to redirect funds from their "incompetent, inefficient, and inequitable" higher education to basic education, and allow privatization to fill the gap.[95] Drawing on social rates of return analyses to emphasize the importance of basic education, it insisted that it was more productive for African countries to invest their meagre resources in primary and basic education. Nigeria rightly resisted the pressure to give in to World Bank prescriptions in the 1970s and early 1980s because resources were available to fund educational expansion at all levels. The federal and state governments sought to provide as many young people as possible access to primary, secondary, and higher education. However, in 1986, when the government of Babangida was in dire need of World Bank/IMF assistance to resolve its balance of payment deficits, it accepted their conditions, which stipulated diverting resources from higher education. This thinking consequently guided post-1986 higher education policies as state support for higher education declined. University education became one of its casualties "for it was said to be an expensive luxury."[96] In his study, Sadique revealed that the World Bank influenced the federal government in reallocating resources in order to shift emphasis from arts and humanities to science, engineering, and accountancy. He further reported that the bank even insisted on choosing the contractors who were to supply the needed materials such as books, journals, and laboratory consumables, and that all of these contractors were foreign companies.[97] World Bank's selfish neo-colonial interest is quite evident here.

The drastic reduction in university funding had negative consequences on the university system. Expansion of facilities halted while enrolment grew faster than the absorptive capacity of the universities. The result was overcrowding, infrastructural decay, and an unfriendly learning environment for both students and faculty. Besides, irregular payment of faculty salaries created related problems as faculty either took on part-time jobs or accepted bribes from students. The quality of education received by the students declined considerably, compromising the relevance of higher education to societal needs. In its 1989 annual conference on the theme "The Role of Universities in National Recovery," the CVC blamed the SAP for the fate of universities.⁹⁸ Proper funding of universities was essential to their smooth development. Denying them funds badly disorganized the universities' central operation and consequently produced an agitated academic climate. As Ray Ekpu confirmed,

> This cash crisis has resulted in jammed classrooms, suffocating hostel accommodation, congested laboratories and empty libraries.... These pressures on facilities are not merely physical, they are psychological as well. They raise the blood pressure of teachers and the taught and render them easily irritable, frustrated, angry, and the cumulative effect of these pressures is that if a little match is struck they catch fire.⁹⁹

Many university teachers left for the private sector due to their frustration with government's inability to address problems in the universities. Others went overseas for higher salaries and better conditions of service, a phenomenon called 'brain drain.' The presidential committee on brain drain, set up in February 1989 to examine the problem, defined it as "the departure of highly trained professionals, intellectuals, talents and specialists in any field of endeavor ... as a result of frustration from poor or inadequate remuneration, or from not having opportunities to fulfill professional aspirations in the given social context."¹⁰⁰ The committee's report revealed a sustained exodus of intellectuals from Nigerian universities from 1987 to 1990. For instance, data from seven universities indicate that 45 left from the sciences while 37 left from the arts in 1987/88 session. In 1988/89 session, 82 left from the sciences while 43 left from the arts. In 1989/90, 46 left from the sciences and 90 from the arts.¹⁰¹ As the *Report of the Study Group Submitted to The World Bank Project Implementation Unit* noted, the departing faculty were dissatisfied with the "ghetto-like work environment characterized by inadequate facilities (offices, lecture and seminar rooms, lecture theatres, laboratories, water, electricity) and short supplies in equipment, reagents, current books and journals, teaching/learning resources and basic furniture."¹⁰²

An *African Concord* editorial of 25 September 1989 reported that in Obafemi Awolowo University (former University of Ife) many academic departments were in danger of being closed down because of the mass departure of lecturers and the devaluation of the naira.[103] Though the annual student population increase in the universities was low, faculty increase was far lower. While student enrolment in universities grew at an annual rate of 7 per cent, the academic staff numbers increased by only 2 per cent. Academic staff strength increased as follows: 8770 in 1984/85; 9014 in 1985/86; 9103 in 1986/87; 9216 in 1987/88; 9547 in 1988/89; and 9621 in 1989/90.[104]

The impact of rationalization of policies of the Babangida regime was largely felt in university admissions. Annual enrolment rate between 1986 and 1990 dropped significantly. It was 10.9 in 1986, but later dropped as follows: 6.7 in 1987/88; 7.2 in 1988/89; and 4.9 in 1989/90.[105] Although the number of students rose from 116,822 in 1983 to 180,871 in 1990, that number was still insignificant, given the huge population of Nigerians within the eligible university age group between fifteen and twenty-five years.[106] That age group, according to Sam Aluko, a top Nigerian economist, constituted about 25 per cent of the total population of Nigeria.[107] This means that only 0.8 per cent of them were in school in 1990. Compared to other countries, Nigeria fell below Kenya's 2 per cent; Ghana, Liberia, Zambia, and Ivory Coast's 4 per cent; Morocco's 8 per cent; and Egypt's 15 per cent. It was 18 per cent in the Philippines, as well as in most Latin American countries such as Brazil, Colombia, Nicaragua, Ecuador, and Guatemala.[108] However, in keeping with government science policy, enrolments in science courses slightly surged between 1984 and 1990. Students in the sciences and related courses were more than those in the arts. While the number of students in arts-related courses increased from 60,818 in 1984/85 to 81,339 in 1989/1990, enrolment in science-related courses increased from 52,920 to 91,736 during the same period.[109] While these statistics suggest that government's efforts at promoting science courses yielded dividends, ironically, there was more graduate output in the arts than in the sciences. Graduate output in science-related courses increased from 11,403 in 1984/85 to 16,080 in 1989/90 while the number in arts-related courses jumped from 15,269 to 21,410 during the same period.[110]

Although the total student enrolment in the universities was low, the demand for admission slots was high. For instance, in 1990, JAMB received 290,296 applications for placement in universities, out of which only 48,504 gained admissions. This represented only 16 per cent of applicants.

More than 80 per cent of candidates denied admissions were from the South. Consequently, a high-pressure bottleneck developed for new candidates with each passing year. Besides, the incidence of exam cancellation due to massive malpractices prevented many potential candidates from securing university admission. This situation has continued annually since the establishment of JAMB in 1977.[111]

Reaffirming its emphasis on technological and science-based education, in January 1990, the federal government launched the First National Rolling Plan (FNRP), 1990–92, which restated that the doctrine of rationalization, consolidation, and cost-effectiveness to be the "guiding principle in the overall strategy to use the available resources to maintain and improve existing infrastructures and the internal efficiency of the entire educational system."[112] The FNRP also maintained that the various cost-reduction and cost-recovery measures started during the preceding plan period, such as removal of the subsidy on student feeding and movement towards off-campus accommodation for students would remain. Given the limited resources available and the scarcity of paid employment in the organized labour market, the FNRP aimed

> at consolidation and maintenance of existing facilities. For this reason no new universities will be established during the rolling plan period 1990–1992 and any state government wishing to do so will receive no assistance whatsoever from the federal government.[113]

The FNRP allocated a total amount of ₦285 million to all the federal universities. This accounted for about 35 per cent of the total allocation for the education sector, showing a reduction in the previous pattern whereby universities received a predominantly higher amount. This reduction was explained by the federal government's new emphasis on training a middle-level technical workforce from the polytechnics and technical colleges.[114] However, the FNRP underscored the government's determination to reduce poverty and hunger when it stated that the newly established universities of agriculture at Makurdi and Abeokuta would be "sufficiently funded in order to make the desired impact on the nation's food production programme."[115] By converting two universities of technology to that of agriculture and making huge financial allocations to these universities, it was clear that the federal government aimed to produce agriculturalists to help in alleviating hunger. This did not constitute massification because only a few segments of university-eligible candidates desired to study agriculture.

At the thirteenth annual seminar of the CVC in 1990, the president reaffirmed his commitment to implement the provision of the FNRP and cautioned the academic community, except the universities of agriculture, against excessive optimism. He informed the vice-chancellors that the problems facing the universities were the direct consequence of government's "shrinking financial resources."[116] According to the president, "the insatiable demand for university education" had combined with the "economic difficulties facing the country" to affect the proper funding of universities. He maintained that "the universities should always bear in mind that they constitute only a part of the national education system [and] in spite of the competing demands from other sectors of our public life, the Federal Government remains resolutely committed to ensure that the universities survive."[117] By using the word "survive," it was apparent that the president was not prepared to embark on further establishment or expansion of university facilities but instead sought to cope with the consequences of past experiments with massification as well as to control the process.

Conclusion

What is remarkable about the period between 1983 and 1990 was the negative impact of the rationalization policies of the Buhari and Babangida governments on university expansion. By suspending further proliferation of universities due to the ailing economy, the federal government unsuccessfully sought to consolidate and re-position the existing universities to make effective contributions to national economic recovery. Owing to the drastic reduction in government financial grants, the universities lacked sufficient funds to build new facilities, let alone maintain the existing ones. Consequently, the existing facilities in virtually all universities deteriorated. Massification suffered. Nevertheless, another increase in oil revenue in August 1990 due to the first Gulf War compelled Babangida to re-think his university policy in favour of expansion, resulting in the fifth push for massification, 1990–2000.

7

Crisis of Nationhood: Funding Issues, Socio-Political Instability, and Private University Education, 1990–2000

> If you ask any Vice Chancellor of a Nigerian university what keeps him awake in the night, the response is likely student problems: accommodation, electricity, water and classrooms. Note that these are basically municipal services. The other core responsibilities of the university such as research, innovation, and publications are not on their radar not because they do not care but it reflects the reality of the day-to-day existence in campuses.
> – Kole Ahmed Shettima, 2006

Introduction

The pursuit of rationalization policies by the regimes of presidents Mahammed Buhari and Ibrahim Babangida checked university expansion between 1983 and 1990. Funding decreased as university facilities consequently deteriorated, leading to a decline in annual percentage of student enrolment. In its 2 April 1990 cover story, "The Crash of Education," *Newswatch* articulated the gradual decay of the physical and instructional facilities in all universities.[1] As the problems in the universities persisted, the country's economic, political, and social crisis deepened, motivating an unsuccessful coup attempt to topple the Babangida administration in

1990. This chapter examines university education at a time of ongoing political and economic crisis in the Nigerian nation-state. It shows how the attempted military coup in 1990 and the renewed debate over a quota system highlighted the lingering divisions and conflicts that continue to threaten the nation-building project of postcolonial Nigerian governments. It also demonstrates how economic and political instability affected adequate funding and expansion of universities, making the establishment of satellite campuses inevitable and the emergence of private universities a welcome initiative. As this chapter demonstrates, the impact of political instability on the universities, the politicization of university expansion, and the radicalization of the Academic Staff Union of Universities (ASUU) are essential in understanding the problems confronting universities during the period of incessant socio-economic and political crisis in Nigeria, 1990–2000.

Nigeria, Still a Divided Nation

The successive postcolonial governments in Nigeria had sought to engage, among other things, mass university education in promoting both economic development and nation-building. The country's domestic scene in the 1990s showed that the goal was improbable. As in many developing countries, the implementation of the IMF-Structural Adjustment Program since 1986 led to increased poverty, inflation, unemployment, crime, and unrest in Nigeria.[2] Ethnic/religious conflicts, largely involving northerners and southerners, continued to generate bad blood in national politics.[3] In spite of its abundant human and materials resources, Nigeria seemed, as many analysts have acknowledged, a dream unfulfilled. Thomas-Ogboji captures Nigeria's situation fittingly when he states,

> Nigeria, the comatose giant of Africa, may go down in history as the biggest country ever to go directly from colonial subjugation to complete collapse, without an intervening period of successful rule. So much promise, so much waste; such a disappointment. Such a shame. Makes you sick.[4]

Faced with increasing economic hardship, many southerners easily blamed northern political elite for mismanaging the country's resources and for holding on to power endlessly. Beside President Olusegun Obasanjo, whose regime was brief, only lasting from 1976 to 1979, all past Nigerian presidents since independence were northerners. Babangida had, beginning in 1986, started an endless process of transfer of power to civilian regime, frequently reneging on his promises. Major Gideon Okar, a military officer from a minority ethnic group in the Middle Belt region of Nigeria, captured the frustrations of many Nigerians with the country's political leadership in a coup he led in April 1990. This coup highlighted the instability in Nigeria and the fear of domination and deprivation that had dominated the relations between the North and the South since the amalgamation of the two areas in 1914.[5] Emphasizing southern misgivings, Gideon Orkar declared that the coup was different from others as it was "a well conceived, planned and executed revolution for the marginalized, oppressed and enslaved peoples of the Middle Belt and the south with a view to freeing ourselves and children yet unborn from eternal slavery and colonization by a clique of this country."[6]

The coup plotters viewed Babangida's transition program with suspicion, believing that he wanted to remain in power in order to protect the privilege the North had enjoyed since Nigeria's independence.[7] They saw Babangida's delays in handing over power as an attempt to "install himself as Nigeria's life president at all cost," and an example of "repressive intrigues by those who think it is their birthright to dominate till eternity the political and economic privileges of this great country to the exclusion of the people of the Middle Belt and the south."[8] The coup plotters demonstrated their seriousness when Orkar announced "a temporary decision to excise the following states namely, Sokoto, Borno, Katsina, Kano and Bauchi states from the Federal Republic of Nigeria."[9] These states are located in the far North and had produced most of the presidents from the North who dictated major policies in the country. Orkar summed up the obstacle to Nigeria's development when he blamed the leadership controlled by northerners:

> This clique has an unabated penchant for domination and unrivalled fostering of mediocrity and outright detest for

accountability, all put together have been our undoing as a nation. This will ever remain our threat if not checked immediately. It is strongly believed that without the intrigues perpetrated by this clique and misrule, Nigeria will have in all ways achieved developmental virtues comparable to those in Korea, Taiwan, Brazil, India, and even Japan.[10]

With reference to quota system, which many southerners criticized, Orkar blamed the leaders for the "deliberate disruption of the educational culture and retarding its place to suit the favoured class to the detriment of other educational minded parts of this country."[11] Although Babangida's administration eventually apprehended and executed the coup plotters, the coup continued to resonate in different circles in the country, including in university education. For instance when Babangida set up the commission on *Higher Education in the 90s and Beyond* chaired by Gray Longe to mainly "review the development of Post-Secondary and Higher Education in Nigeria since the last comprehensive report of the 1960 commission," the issue of a quota system resurfaced.[12] Most of the submissions to the Gray Longe Commission from South questioned the quota system of admission that continued to mandate 20 per cent of intakes from the educationally disadvantaged states. Particularly infuriating for many southerners was the wisdom of basing significant percentage of university admission on the "disadvantaged status" and "catchment area" formula. Many of the submissions argued that the quota system was morally defenceless and contrary to the spirit of the constitution. The argument was that if the system was justified two decades ago because of imbalance in educational opportunity, the creation of thousands of primary and hundreds of secondary schools in the North ought to have given the so-called disadvantaged states the opportunity to catch up.[13]

As some Nigerians argued, the quota system failed to close the gap between the two regions due to northerner's negative attitude towards Western education. According to Emman Shehu, a northerner and the publisher of *Envoy*, a weekly newspaper, "the feudal order has made it difficult for parents to allow their children to stay in school. You want to bridge the gap, yet you tell people that Western education is evil."[14] However, Shehu perceived the quota system as an insult to the North because it cast the region as inherently inferior to the South. As he said, "I write the same examination with somebody from another state. Then you say because I am from Sokoto, my cut-off is 20 percent while the other man's cut-off is 60 percent. This is an insult."[15] Although the northern states had been classified as disadvantaged since independence, the status was not meant to confer on them a permanent advantage. In fact, the underlying philosophy of the quota system was to place the North ultimately on equal footing with the South. But the most sustainable approach to closing the educational gap was to set a timeframe when the implementation of the quota system would stop while at the same time addressing the root causes of the North's disadvantaged status. Chimere Ikoku, the vice-chancellor of UNN, affirmed that the idea of a quota system is

> that someday in the future, the policy will dissolve. And we should ask the question, how have these states fared? Yes, state X is disadvantaged today. If we really want to remove the disadvantage, we must time the process. When will that state stop being disadvantaged? ... What is responsible for the disadvantaged status? Is it classrooms, books, or teachers?"[16]

Although the introduction of a quota system represents government's efforts to guarantee equal representations of all Nigerians in order to foster national unity, ironically it became a source of disunity itself. It seemed to be an easy way out for the disadvantaged status of the North, but after what the Longe commission described as a "considerable soul-searching" and "careful weighting of the pros and cons," it proposed a quota formula to correct many deep-seated prejudices and mollify "justified indignation" toward a quota system. As shown in Table 7.1, the commission wanted the percentage of admission allocated to merit to increase while those for disadvantaged states and catchment area were to decrease. It also wanted the criteria for discretionary admission to remain at 10 per cent from 1990 to 2000.[17]

Table 7.1: Percentage of Admission Allocated to: Merit, Catchment Area, Disadvantaged States, and Discretion.

	1990	1992	1994	1996	1998	2000
Merit	40	50	55	60	65	70
Catchment Area	30	25	25	25	20	20
Disadvantaged States	20	15	10	5	5	0
Discretion	10	10	10	10	10	10

Source: Federal Republic of Nigeria, *Higher Education in the 90s and Beyond: Report of the Commission on the Review of Higher Education in Nigeria* (Lagos: Government Printing Office, 1991), 153.

Not all the members of the commission accepted the gradual phasing out of the quota system. For instance, Rex F.O. Akpofure argued that the majority report did not go far enough. In a minority report, Akpofure stressed that the quota system had continued to harm the minds of Nigerian youth precisely because its implementation contradicted the spirit of social justice. According to him, "the system should be ended quickly, before it does more harm to our ethos as one people."[18] Akpofure affirmed that since a quota system was first introduced in 1976 in admissions to federal government secondary schools, "it should substantially have solved or reduced the gap between advantaged and disadvantaged States. That it is said not to have done so, is in my honest view because those it was intended to assist, no longer see the need for that special effort to close the gap."[19] The debate on the quota system meant that the Nigerian state still carried with it the burden of history. It shows that the desire to forge a united nation through quota in a pluralistic society where educational attainments and opportunities were unequal presents a risk of compromising the unity that the policy originally intended to affirm.

The federal government rejected the recommendation of the commission with respect to quota. In a white paper on the recommendations of the Longe's Commission, the federal government insisted that inequality was an inescapable 'fact of life' and the government's duty was to "recognize and address the problem pragmatically," noting, however, that it will "continue to review the admissions formula from time to time within the context of our development."[20] This decision only confirmed southern suspicion of northern domination and further added to their frustration. That the government discarded the phasing out of the quota system is not surprising. The quota system was introduced to enhance equal representations of northerners and southerners in all universities. The educationally 'backward' North hoped that the system would help the region catch up with the educationally advanced South. The phasing out of the quota system would affect northerners, who, of course, dominated the apex of the federal government. Therefore, it was only natural (though not excusable) for the federal government to resist this aspect of the commission's recommendations. Since the federal government was conscious of closing the educational gap between the North and the South, regional and ethnic considerations, not academic quality, overshadowed government's decision.

The continuing tension in the country affected university education. Given the instability in the country, education assumed less importance in the scheme of things, as keeping the country together became an overriding concern of the government. Unrest in the country relegated university education to the background as maintaining the integrity of the state through dictatorial powers became crucial. The Orkar coup, which was popular in the South and the Middle Belt, showed how vulnerable the state was; it made the federal government desperate to protect it at all cost. Thus, during the 1990s, according to *The Economist*, "Defense and police budgets enjoy the largest slice of the national cake (and even so the figures are underestimated, since the military imports are paid for with dollars bought cheaply at the government exchange rates)."[21] As funding for universities shrank in spite of government's rhetoric regarding its commitment to the expansion of university education, facilities deteriorated and learning suffered. Thus, the Academic Staff Union of Universities (ASUU) was compelled to embark on a difficult crusade to rescue the life of universities.

Poor Funding, ASUU, and Military Dictatorship

The Orkar's coup terrified Babangida, but he was relieved that the country's economic fortunes changed dramatically following the U.S.-led war against Iraq (Gulf War) in 1990/91. Oil prices suddenly rose with a positive effect on Nigerian finances. The World Bank estimated that the total oil export revenue in 1990 was US$14 billion, a 49 per cent increase over the 1989 level.[22] Having successfully rescheduled Nigerian debts, there was far less fiscal pressure on the federal government. One would have thought that addressing social and economic issues would take centre stage in government's policies. In fact, in a memorandum to the Longe Commission, the Committee of Vice-Chancellors advised that the oil "windfall should be institutionalized and made at not less than ₦20 million for at least 5 years from 1990, specifically for the provision and maintenance of [university] projects of a capital nature."[23] The CVC knew that oil sales had brought increased revenue to the government and called on the government to apply the money to maintain and expand university facilities. Judging by previous experience where the federal government went on a spending spree in similar circumstances, the CVC had good reasons to demand the institutionalization of grants over a five-year period.

In its report, the Longe commission blamed the funding crisis facing Nigerian universities on the military and civilian regime of the 1970s and 1980 for pursuing an extravagant and unrestrained proliferation of universities because of a mistaken faith in the continuity of oil revenue. It noted that Nigeria's "higher educational institutions have grown far more rapidly in numbers than the Ashby commission could possibly have projected."[24] Although many factors accounted for this expansion, the commission located "political considerations" as the "predominant single factor."[25] It stated that for the next ten to twenty years, Nigeria would not be able to afford the luxury of indiscriminate establishment of institutions because of the "far reaching and often irrevocable consequences of inadequate planning for such institutions."[26] Such consequences, as the World Bank noted, include the incidence of "extravagance in physical development of the universities, with many grandiose projects started without the fund needed to complete them."[27] The commission revealed that the cost of unfinished projects in 1988 was ₦1.2 billion, and at 1991 rates, "the cost of completion could be up to ₦3.0 billion."[28] The commission cautioned government to avoid haphazard establishment of institutions and embarking on extravagant physical projects. The *Guardian* special report on the "Sorry State of the Universities" uncovered many abandoned projects in most universities, which limited student enrolment as well as tied university funds.[29] What the commission implied in its recommendation was that adequate financial and physical planning ought to precede the establishment of universities in order to guarantee sustainable expansion of university education.

Notwithstanding the recommendation of the Longe Commission, political considerations still drove the founding of new universities that emerged in the 1990s. Although the federal government retained the states' right to own universities since 1979, the creation of states, which were mostly economically unviable, reinforced their dependency on the federal government.[30] In 1991, the federal government created ten states, bringing the total number of states to thirty-one. Due to the centralized nature of military governments, the federal government did not perceive state creation as a tool for decentralization, yet the beneficiaries saw them as federal handouts or their fair share of the national wealth. While political in its motivation, the creation of states had implications for university expansion. Some of the newly created states were fortunate to inherit existing universities within their territories, leaving the parent states without either a state or federal university. For instance, Imo State forfeited Imo State University located in Okigwe to the newly created Abia State. Consequently, Imo State commenced plans to set up a university, since they had no control over the federal university of technology located within it. Because Akwa Ibom State, created in 1987, had secured a federal university, the newly created states demanded the same, including the location of federal universities in their states. By 1992, five state universities emerged to satisfy political interests. The federal government set up the Nnamdi Azikiwe University, Awka, in Anambra State, in addition to establishing the University of Agriculture, Umudike, to balance the location of the federal universities of agriculture in the former northern and western regions.[31] Similarly, four state universities were also established: Imo State University, Owerri; Benue State University; Bagauda University of Science and Technology, Kano; and Delta State University, Abraka. These new universities had one thing in common: they followed the creation of new states. For instance, the creation of Abia State from former Imo State and subsequent forfeiture of former Imo State University (established in 1981) to Abia State, compelled Imo to establish its own university. The same applied to all other universities. The politics of state creation were, therefore, an essential part of the politics of founding universities.

Members of the Longe Commission were aware of the 1990 oil boom and the improved financial strength of the federal government and as such requested the federal government to provide "80 percent of the annual recurrent expenditure of each of the Federal Universities and those institutions should find the balance of 20 percent from internal revenue generation efforts and other sources."[32] Implementation of this recommendation would have halted the decay in the universities but the federal government issued a response in 1992 that flatly rejected it. Instead, it insisted that the government would "continue to make its contributions towards higher education within its budgetary constraint [while] ... each institution should work towards self-sufficiency."[33] It was odd that a government that asked JAMB in 1991 to increase student intake by 20 per cent would at the same time refuse to make a financial commitment to universities mindful of the potential pressure the increase would put on the existing facilities. Nigerians aspiring for university education hoped that the directive would boost the supply of university education by reducing the pressure mounted on JAMB each year. A very high number of candidates sat for UME exams yearly owing to the cumulative carry-over of unsuccessful candidates from previous years. Due to insufficient facilitates, many students who passed the exam still failed to secure admission.[34] In any case, increasing student intake without an urgent and corresponding expansion of facilities was certainly not in the interest of universities. If anything, it threatened to strain already overstretched facilities.

While Babangida acknowledged in his 1991 budget speech that the universities "are the apex of our educational system and a veritable lever for national cohesion and development," his subsequent actions contradicted his words.[35] Consolidation of political power through patronage of members of the armed forces became a top priority for the government. While the government did not favour the idea of providing 80 per cent of the financial needs of the universities, it was willing to spend lavishly to retain power. Motivated by the oil wealth and determined to sustain the loyalty of the armed forces, the Babangida regime launched a huge, irresponsible spending program aimed at rehabilitating the police and military barracks, thus increasing spending on security. A World Bank report completed in early 1991 noted that "there was a breakdown in fiscal and monetary discipline in 1990 ... not only characterized by additional spending and monetary expansion but also by a major surge in expenditures bypassing budgetary mechanisms for expenditure authorization and control."[36] In 1992, Babangida offered new Peugeot cars to nearly 3,000 of his loyal military officers, which cost the equivalent of $21,000 each. This amount was five times the yearly salary of a senior university professor, who earned about $4,000 a year.[37]

Equal attention was not paid to other sectors of the economy, including university education where limited vacancies denied admission to a "large number of eligible candidates aspiring to study in these institutions."[38] This apparent disregard of the plight of universities irked the Academic Staff Union of Universities (ASUU). It was largely due to the neglect of university education that ASUU emerged as a strong voice for the university system. Since the introduction of SAP in 1986, ASUU had made unsuccessful demands on the government to provide adequate funds for the universities, often citing the decay of infrastructural facilities. The government rejection of the Longe Commission recommendation to increase its financial allocation for universities while it continued to spend on security, as well as mismanaging the oil revenue, compelled ASUU to embark on a strike on May 1992, forcing all the universities to close down.[39]

The reasons for the ASUU strike and their demands echoed the main proposal of Longe's report. The union proposed three ways the government could fund the universities, namely: (1) Stabilization (or Restoration) Grant of at least 5 per cent of total government revenue to be earmarked for universities and phased in over five years; (2) Endowment Fund of ₦1billion, administered by NUC, under an appropriate Trust Deed to finance research, which would insulate the universities against "variability in grants and assure them of the funds needed to pursue their objectives vigorously"; and (3) a three year Rolling Plan for recurrent grant allocations to the universities.[40] With the universities closed down, the federal government was compelled to commence negotiation with ASUU in June. As the ASUU/federal government negotiation commenced, the minister for education inaugurated the National Implementation Committee on the Report of the Review of Higher Education in Nigeria (NICRHEN) on 19 June 1992. Part of the role of NICRHEN was to advise the federal government, among other things, on all financial, material, and other implications of Longe's recommendations.[41] ASUU strike, which paralyzed university activities, delayed the work of the committee. However, due to intense pressure from the civil society between 25 May and 3 September 1992, Babangida accepted ASUU proposal and signed the agreement that met their demands. Universities reopened.

To guarantee sustainable financing of public universities, and in line with its agreement with ASUU, the federal government promulgated Decree No. 7 of 1993, which established the Education Tax Fund (ETF). Among other things, the objective of ETF was to provide funding for educational facilities and infrastructural development in all universities, polytechnics, and colleges of education, both federal and state. This included the construction and renovation of lecture theatres, auditoriums, administrative blocks, and hostels.[42] The decree required companies registered in Nigeria to pay 2 per cent of yearly profit to the ETF fund as an education tax. In addition, it stipulated that 50 per cent of the total collectable revenue would go to higher education, shared in the ratio of 2:1:1 for universities, polytechnics, and colleges of education, respectively.[43] When the government imposed the education tax, many foreign oil companies demanded exemption, arguing that the policy ran contrary to the Petroleum Profit Tax (PPT) Act of 1959, which precluded oil companies from paying any other tax after paying the PPT. The oil companies subsequently petitioned the finance minister, Anthony Ani. After a series of meetings, the federal government exempted the foreign companies from paying the education tax for 1993 but demanded that they still pay it to the tune of ₦2 billion in 1994 and 1995.[44] However, since the federal government did not appoint an ETF board until 1998, there was no assessment for the education tax for all companies in 1993 or collections. However, collections were made subsequently as follows: ₦4.5 billion in 1994–95; ₦6.6 billion in 1996–97; ₦6.4 billion in 1998–99. Nevertheless, it was not until 1999 that the money was allocated to different levels of the educational system.[45]

Following ASUU's agreement with the federal government, the federal government increased the capital and recurrent grants to the federal universities from ₦3,055,864,940 in 1992 to ₦3,905,915,278 in 1993.[46] However, this increase did not have a significant impact on the universities partly because the value of the national currency had gone down such that the huge budgetary allocations amounted to little in real terms. According to the executive secretary of NUC, "the rate at which the Naira value has been deteriorating has been faster than the rate at which we have been able to utilize the new funds that have been allocated to the universities for both recurrent and capital needs."[47] Besides, given the widespread corruption in the Babangida administration, there was a gap between what the government budgeted and what it eventually disbursed.[48] Therefore, the ASUU accused the government of non-implementation and violation of the 1992 agreement and embarked on another four-month strike from May through September 1993.

Worse still was that due to the financial irresponsibility of the federal government in implementing the Structural Adjustment Program, the IMF withdrew its adjustment support, which led to the termination of the program. The attendant large fiscal deficits and economic stagnation heated the body politic, worsened the plight of universities, and showed that Nigeria's economic problems were not necessarily fiscal, as the World Bank/IMF had dubiously suggested – and as Nigerian leaders had naively believed. Fiscal adjustment is not a panacea for the country's fiscal-related ills unless it is "supported by measures to strengthen the quality of spending, addressing corruption and transparency issues."[49] Therefore, as Alexander Bamiloye commented, "The structural adjustment … is academic. The real adjustment is that of the mind as a people and as a nation."[50] Clearly, the real problem was human, not fiscal, and any solution that failed to address the human problem was bound to fail, as SAP's failure demonstrated. The major human problem was leadership. As Chinua Achebe aptly stated,

> There is nothing wrong with the Nigerian land or climate or water or air or anything else. The Nigerian problem is the unwillingness or inability of its leaders to rise to the responsibility, to the challenges of personal example which are the hallmarks of true leadership.[51]

This is not, of course, a simple task, given the pluralistic nature of Nigerian society and the historic regional conflict.

The fear of continued northern domination of the country crystallized in 1993 when Babangida annulled the 12 June 1993 presidential election in which a southerner, Moshood Abiola, emerged as the winner. The violence that followed the annulment threatened the corporate existence of the

Nigerian state, forcing Babangida to resign in August 1993.[52] In an apparent ploy to appease the South, Babangida handed over power to an interim government headed by a southerner, Ernest Shonekan. Three months into the new government, another military coup swept Shonekan out of power; Sani Abacha, a northerner, emerged as the new president. Increased violent pressure on Abacha to honour the June 12 election was met with brutal force, even as Abiola was thrown in prison, where he later died in 1998.

The fate of universities was sealed when Abacha became the president in November 1993. Taking over power in the wake of violence generated by the cancellation of the 12 June presidential elections, Abacha's government was in no mood to negotiate with ASUU, much less implement the 1992 ASUU/FGN agreement. Consequently, ASUU embarked on another strike in order to secure a commitment by government to respect the 1992 agreement, thereby paralyzing academic activities for five months from August 1994 to January 1995. In his 1995 budget speech, Abacha promised, as many of his predecessors had done, to devote a huge amount of funds to rehabilitate facilities in the existing universities in line with ASUU's agreement with government in September 1992.[53] Aware that no social and economic program would be executed successfully without addressing the root causes of Nigerian economic problems, Abacha launched the Economic Recovery Programme, 1996–98. He argued that under SAP, debt rescheduling imposed a burden by bunching up payments later as well as attracting an extra annual sum of $2.5 billion in interest payments.[54] Despite Abacha's economic recovery policies, the conditions of universities did not get better; his government ignored ASSU's consistent demand for improved condition of service and better funding of universities. Consequently, the union embarked on a seven-month strike in 1996. Incensed by the frequent suspension of academic activities in the universities due to ASUU strikes, Abacha banned ASUU, including other university staff unions. He also dissolved their executives and asked them to forfeit their assets to the government.[55] ASUU went underground and became ineffective. This ban remained in force until 1999.

Partly in search of a solution to social, economic, and political problems, and mostly to divert Nigerian attention from the dictatorship and corruption of his administration, Abacha promised to set up a committee to review the current situation of higher education, particularly to explain why it had failed "to meet the nation's developmental aspirations."[56] In his address, Abacha expressed concern about the sad situation of universities, emphasizing the need for immediate action "to address the issues so as to lay a solid foundation for the emergence of a befitting educational system that will help propel the nation into the 21st Century."[57] On 1 October 1996, Abacha set up the Committee on the Future of Higher Education (COFHE), comprised of twenty-five Nigerians and chaired by a traditional ruler, Alhaji Umaru Sanda Ndayako. Abacha's decision to include five traditional rulers in COFHE was remarkable. In Nigeria, successive military governments since 1983 had relied on the support of traditional rulers to further legitimize their regimes. Abacha's regime went further to grant the traditional rulers throughout Nigeria 5 per cent of local government's monthly allocations. The traditional rulers visited the government house, often wining and dining with the dictator. Among those who supported Abacha's continued stay in power were the traditional rulers who unequivocally said that Abacha was the only viable candidate to lead Nigeria.[58] Thus, by involving traditional rulers in the COFHE, the government hoped to receive recommendations that would reflect its preferences.

The terms of reference of the COFHE were largely similar to those of the Longe Commission. It was odd that Abacha had not fully implemented the recommendations of the Longe Commission before setting up the COFHE. In fact, the setting up of higher education committees, especially since 1983, had become a favourite pastime of the military rulers whose motives were anything but sheer love of higher education and who used them as tools for political distraction and diversion. This often produced discontinuity and public ruse in policy formulation and implementation. The COFHE's conscious desire to please the government informed its recommendations to reduce the number of universities, reduce grants to universities, and thus save Abacha the financial nightmare of financial demands by the universities. However, until Abacha's regime ended in 1998, these recommendations were not implemented.

Low financial allocations to the universities since 1994 affected the maintenance and expansion of facilities to accommodate increasing demand. Admission statistics revealed that demand for university places continued to outstrip its supply. In 1996/97, for instance, 472,362 applied for admission into all Nigerian universities but 76,430 secured admissions (16%). In 1997/98, 419,807 applied but only 72,791 were admitted (17.3%).[59] The major reason for low intake was inadequate facilities arising from low funding and mismanagement of resources. A 1997 special report titled "The Sorry State of the Universities," published by one of Nigeria's leading newspapers (*The Guardian*), revealed how the infrastructural decay in all Nigerian universities not only affected the quality of learning but also limited the intake of students. It noted, for instance, that since the establishment of the Lagos State University in 1984 with 300 students, the population of the institution had increased to 15,000 without any meaningful improvement in the initial infrastructures with the consequence that "the classrooms, laboratories (where they exist), offices, and equipment have become overstretched."[60] At the Rivers State University of Science and Technology, the story of lack of facilities was the same. The head of the petroleum and chemical engineering department bemoaned the sorry state of the university thus: "the system is dead and buried. No other comment."[61] In the University of Jos, the report noted: "There are no seats to accommodate [students]."[62] The report also observed that, due to insufficient classrooms in Imo State University, many lecturers fought literally over classrooms located at C and D blocks.[63]

Since universities lacked funds to expand facilities, many universities that were designed to accommodate 10,000 students ended up admitting many more. Data from the planning office of the University of Ibadan shows that "whereas student enrolment was 9,176 in the 1982/83 session, it had risen to 18,228 (about 100%) by 1998/99 session without any corresponding expansion in facilities."[64] These problems, common in all Nigerian universities, significantly affected enrolment. Faced with tight financial constraints as well as rising public demand for university opportunities, universities, especially the state-owned, were left with no choice but to establish satellite campuses around the country, aimed at generating enough revenue to meet their financial obligations while expanding access.

Satellite Campuses

The phenomenon of satellite campuses was not new in the 1990s. In fact, many universities had begun as satellite campuses of older universities.

Notable among them was the Jos campus of the University of Ibadan, which later became University of Jos in 1975. However, the satellite campuses that emerged in the 1990s were different. The government did not establish them, rather the respective universities did. Lectures were often conducted in primary or secondary school buildings – sometimes in business centres. While the original intent of establishing satellite campuses was to turn them eventually into full-fledged universities, the universities that established these campuses had no such plan since they mostly intended to use them as revenue-generating outlets. Most satellite campuses were located in major cities, notably Lagos, and were established without NUC approval. Institutions with campuses in Lagos include, among others, Enugu State University of Science and Technology, Delta State University, Ogun State University, University of Calabar, Nnamdi Azikiwe University, and Obafemi Awolowo University.[65]

Financial gains largely motivated the proliferation of satellite campuses. This phenomenon followed increasing demand for part-time university training by full-time-employed Nigerians. According to Sola Dixon and Victor Onyeka-Ben, "Because of the resources at the disposal of such working candidates, the universities in no time began to see in them opportunities to boost their revenue and thus supplement their lean purses."[66] Thus, due to the government's insufficient funding of universities and their bid to look for alternative sources of revenue, universities rushed to establish many learning centres in major cities. Maduabuchi Dukor, a senior lecturer in Lagos State University, stated that "the proliferation of satellite campuses, certificates and Diplomas has a primitive capitalist underpinning. It is symptom of the overall greed and avarice in the Nigerian society."[67]

On the other hand, the explosion of satellite campuses was motivated by the desire of universities to satisfy the yearning of a large number of citizens to further their education. O. Eruvbetine and Bamidele Folarin of the University of Lagos argued that the situation was "necessitated by the law of demand and supply in the face of the inability of government and the conventional university system to cope."[68] For instance, at the matriculation of the Lagos satellite students of Delta State University, the vice-chancellor, Pius Sada, affirmed that the popularity of the program was manifest in the number of applicants for the program. According to him, out of the 6,000 qualified applicants, only 2,736 secured admission.[69]

He further noted that, in due time when facilities of the campus located at Ikorodu Road expanded, more students would secure places.[70]

Although the increase of these campuses under questionable circumstances and learning environments had the potential effect of expanding access, it threatened the quality of university education. Facing mounting complaints, the NUC whose responsibility it was to advise government on the establishment of universities, ordered all satellite campuses to close down in January 1998. A letter signed by Professor I.I. Uvah, director of academic planning for NUC, alleged that the satellite campuses were established without due clearance from government. He further insisted that such a development was contrary to the requirements that all degree courses be domiciled in academic departments. As Uvah warned, "It is illegal for any university to set up a satellite campus or study center outside the location approved at its inception by the federal government for its academic activity towards the award of degree of whatever nature without fresh clearance."[71] The federal minister for education, Dauda Birma, later endorsed this decision.[72] Since over 90 per cent of the satellite campuses were located in the South and were largely dominated by southerners, critics from the South dismissed the decision as anti-southern and largely inspired by political considerations. However, the reduction of the issue here to regional politics seemed misplaced. Although satellite campuses were banned, many universities established institute of continuing education programs within their campuses to cater for the interests of non-traditional students.

Private Universities

From 1948 (when Nigeria's first university was established) to 1998, state and federal governments monopolized the provision of university education. In 1983 twenty-six private universities were founded or proposed in Nigeria. These universities were still in the process of securing facilities to admit students when the Buhari government closed them down by promulgating Decree No. 19 of February, called the "Private Universities (Abolition and Prohibition) Decree 1984."[73] By criminalizing the establishment of private universities in Nigeria, the military government chose to ignore other options and seemed to offer a misleading impression that the emergence of these private universities had contributed to the financial difficulties that confronted the university system in particular and the country in general. If anything, the existence of private universities was supposed to spare the government the headache of being the sole provider of university education. It was difficult to understand Buhari's justification in abolishing private universities when the government had the option of restructuring their operations with stiff guidelines stipulated by the NUC to ensure quality and standards. Pursuing this option would have gone a long way towards meeting the increasing demand for university places. Perhaps the idea of commercially run universities was strange to an average Nigerian in 1984 because the government had monopolized the sector since independence and was unprepared to shift its position notwithstanding the economic situation.

Buhari's swift closure of private universities after barely two months in office and without plans to fund the public universities adequately seemed short-sighted. In addition, Babangida's inability to reopen the issue until 1993 in the midst of poor funding of universities reveals the contradictions and confusions of government policy. However, the point of how people could afford private education in a period of negative economic climate must have probably weighed heavily on the minds of policy-makers. Yet, private universities had the potential of discouraging many wealthy Nigerians from sending their children abroad for university training. In spite of the country's economic recession, government's inability to maintain and expand facilities in the existing universities and the short supply of university places, successive Nigerian governments prohibited the private sector from supplying university education until 1998 when General Abdulsalami Abubakar issued licences to three private universities. The shift in the conservative attitude of policy-makers toward private ownership of universities was primarily born out of rising unmet demand for university admission, bred by the steady deterioration of facilities in public universities, and ultimately nourished by World Bank/IMF's intervention in Nigeria's domestic economic policies.

Motivated by the Structural Adjustment Program, which endorsed both privatization and reduction in government spending, Babangida asked the Longe Commission to consider the possibility of engaging the private sector in the provision of university education. It was the first time in the country's educational history that a commission seriously considered the issue of private university education. While recognizing the right of the federal and state governments to own universities, the commission proposed similar rights to private individuals and corporations.[74] This recommendation superseded the ban on private universities by the Buhari regime in 1984, and it was based on the recognition that private universities would complement public universities in providing more opportunities for university training. However, the commission required evidence of adequate and diverse sources of capital and recurrent funding by the sponsoring body, public or private, before the government would approve the establishment of a new university.[75]

Although the federal government declined to make fundamental changes in university funding and quota as the Longe Commission had recommended, it nonetheless endorsed the commission's recommendation to lift the ban on private ownership of universities. Clearly, the federal government knew that the establishment of private universities would further expand opportunities for university education as well as ease its burden of financing university expansion. Thus, it whole-heartedly accepted the idea and added that "individuals that satisfy the eligibility criteria can establish higher institutions."[76] The federal government knew that the rationalization policies of the IMF/World Bank would make adequate funding of universities difficult. The emergence of private universities would thus be a welcome relief for the government.

In 1993, the federal government promulgated the National Minimum Standards and Establishment of Institutions (Amendment) Decree No. 9 of 1993. This decree, among other things, repealed the Decree No. 19 of 1984 called "The Private University (Abolition and Prohibition) Decree 1984." Decree No. 9 granted the right to establish universities to local governments, companies incorporated in Nigeria, and even individuals or associations of individuals who were citizens and who meet the criteria for founding new universities. It legitimized the involvement of the private sector in the provision of higher education. Unlike the emergence of private universities in 1983 without prescribed regulatory guidelines, Decree No. 9 stipulated rigid criteria for the establishment of private universities. The main criteria were evidence of concrete and guaranteed sources of financial support to the tune of ₦200 million and a minimum land area of 100 hectares.[77] These conditions recognized that lack of sustainable funding of public universities affected the maintenance and expansion of facilities. Buhari had faced a similar choice in 1984, but he chose to abolish the private universities. But after nine years of banning private universities, the federal government decided to permit their operation. It was inadequate funding of universities as well as the rising demand for university places in the face of deteriorating facilities between the late 1980s and the 1990s that Nigeria, like many other African countries, welcomed private-sector involvement in the provision of university education.[78]

Public response to Decree No. 9 was cautious. Twelve private individuals and organizations collected application forms from NUC in 1993 for their proposed universities.[79] Yet no private university was established until 1998. The delay reflects the problem associated with private firms in Nigeria as well as the country's unstable polity. According to the COFHE, private firms in the country experienced many problems that also affected private universities. They relied too largely on a single individual, and such firms survive only in the lifetime of the individual, even where the firms are incorporated. In addition, the firms were over-dependent on patronage by the governments as the main financier of the economy, thus making their fortunes unstable with each change in government. This factor, including the stringent requirement established by the NUC, may have accounted for why many persons who obtained application forms in 1991 for private universities were reluctant to submit them. Of the twenty-nine applications forms collected from 1993 to 1996, only six were completed and duly returned to the NUC.[80] One other reason was the scepticism of the public, who saw what happened to private universities in 1984, coupled with the uncertainties of the country's political arena. However, by the end of 1998 when the country's political situation quieted, more Nigerians submitted applications to establish private universities.

Under Abubakar, the military leader who replaced Abacha at his death in 1998, the process was accelerated in that by April 1999 he approved licences to three private universities: Igbinedion University, Okada; Babcock University, Ilishan Remo; and Madonna University, Okija.[81] The philosophies of these universities demonstrated awareness of the unstable and decaying atmosphere under which students studied in the public universities, the limited intake of students, and the need to make a difference. Madonna University sought to "provide higher education and well balanced training in an atmosphere of peace without discrimination."[82] The philosophy of Igbinedion University was to "provide opportunity for young men and women to learn under the most conducive atmosphere, imbibe the highest moral and ethical values and to develop their entrepreneurial instincts."[83] Babcock University's mission was "to offer high quality professional, pre-professional, general and vocational education to prepare men and women for responsible, dedicated and committed service to God and humanity."[84]

Many Nigerians found private universities very attractive because of the prospect of uninterrupted academic activities. Also, some of these private universities, such as Babcock and Madonna, were founded by religious organizations, and parents expected them to have an impact on their children in both academic knowledge and high morals. Moreover, many parents whose children were denied admissions in the public universities due to limited and inadequate facilities hoped that the private universities would provide an alternative route. As a *Punch* editorial noted, since only about 14.73 per cent of applicants secured admission into the few Nigerian universities, the establishment of private universities became "a normal and commendable supply response to a huge and growing demand for university education."[85]

With the establishment of three private universities, the total number of universities in Nigeria climbed to forty-five in 2000 with a total student enrolment of about 526,780. This number was huge but the pressure for expansion remained. For instance, out of the 550,399 candidates that applied for admission to all the universities in 1999/2000, only 60,718 secured admission (11.0%).[86] States from the South accounted for the highest number of applicants and admission while those in the North accounted for the lowest.[87] That the South maintained its lead in university enrolment in spite of their bigger population showed that the quota system had failed to address the educational disparity. Besides, the fact that the demand for university training remained high despite graduate unemployment occasioned by economic downturn demonstrated the importance Nigerians attached to university education both as a means to an end and as an end in itself. According to Y. Lebeau,

> Even if the university as a direct passport to becoming an elite in the country is no longer a reality ... higher education as a pre-requisite to social climbing is an ideology that is still widely supported in Nigeria.[88]

This was (and is) the most formidable driving force behind the demand for university education.

Towards a Renewed Commitment to Educational Expansion

The late 1990s were a remarkable period in the country's history as well as university education. World Bank's rethinking on investment in university education coincided with Nigeria's return to democracy to open up a new chapter in university expansion. The reduction in university funding since 1986 was largely due to the IMF condition for SAP and the World Bank reports that had encouraged Africans to reduce funding for higher education. This advice was driven by the conviction that public investment in universities brought meagre returns compared to investment in primary and secondary schools. This advice influenced the federal government's drastic reduction of grants to universities. However, the bank eventually realized that this economic analysis was both narrow and misleading. In its 2000 report, the bank affirmed that the prevailing "traditional economic arguments are based on a limited understanding of what higher education institutions contribute."[89] It emphasized the importance of educated people as "economic and social entrepreneurs" who are needed in "creating an environment in which economic development is possible."[90] That need was acute in developing countries, especially in Africa because

> Demographic change, income growth, urbanization, and the growing economic importance of knowledge and skills have combined to ensure that, in most developing countries, higher education is no longer a small cultural enterprise for the elite. Rather, it has become vital to nearly every nation's plans for development.[91]

Having accorded high priority to higher education, the World Bank encouraged governments around the world to invest in higher education. This is because, as Malcolm Gills, president of Rice University, affirmed, "Today, more than ever before in human history, the wealth – or poverty – of nations depends on the quality of higher education. Those with a larger repertoire of skills and a greater capacity for learning can look forward to lifetimes of unprecedented economic fulfillment."[92] Gills further stressed that the poorly educated would face hard times in the coming decades.[93] In support of renewed attention to higher education, the bank's president, James D. Wolfensohn declared that "it is impossible to have a complete education system without appropriate and strong higher education system." For him,

> You have to have centers of excellence and learning and training if you are going to advance the issue of poverty and development in developing countries … the key is … higher education, not just on the technological side, but to create people with enough wisdom to be able to use it.[94]

Training people with "enough wisdom" to champion economic development had been one of the major goals of Nigeria's massification program since 1960. Poor policy formulation and execution, coupled with geo-ethnic politics and economic meltdown compromised that goal, as university facilities failed to accommodate rising demand. The World Bank's recognition of the critical importance of higher education and call for expansion thus became a renewed slogan for the revitalization of Nigeria's university education. It was a slogan that gathered momentum as Nigeria returned to a democratic form of government in 1999 after seven years of military dictatorship.

The sudden death of Abacha on 8 June 1998 and his replacement by Abubakar marked a turning point in the history of the country and university education. Abubakar successfully calmed the heated North/South tension by lifting the ban on political activities and successfully returning the country to democratic governance in 1999, led by a southerner and former military head of state, Obasanjo. Also, Abubakar lifted the ban on ASUU in 1998. Until its ban in 1996 by Abacha regime, ASUU was in the forefront of the call for better funding of universities to ensure high standards and provide adequate facilities to accommodate increasing demand. Shortly after lifting the ban on ASUU, it commenced negotiations with the new civilian government for better "salaries, wages and other conditions of service in the university system."[95] Though the government and ASUU signed an agreement on these three issues on 25 May 1999, the government's negotiating team promised to negotiate other aspects of university problems. The agreement was "intended to be an interim palliative measure to enhance the income of academics, without prejudice to a comprehensive negotiation at a future date."[96] It only adjusted allowances without covering other aspects of university funding.

A comprehensive negotiation between ASUU and the federal government took place in 2000. The agenda for negotiation was arranged in order of importance with the funding of universities at the top, followed by basic salary, university autonomy, academic freedom, and other matters.[97] Negotiation between government and ASUU teams began on 28 August 2000, and by 11 September 2000 they reached an agreement.[98] The agreement was comprehensive. It addressed the contentious issues of funding, basic salary, university autonomy, and academic freedom. It provided specific funds for recurrent and capital expenditure, as well as restoration and stabilization funds. It also included a clause providing for the subvention of state universities by the federal government. It contained a provision whereby the federal and state governments would allocate to education a minimum of 26 per cent of their annual budgets, subject to an upward review beginning in 2003. In addition, it agreed that half of the 26 per cent annual budget allocation would be allocated to the universities. Finally, it provided for the restructuring of NUC and JAMB with additional admission requirements to be stipulated by the senate of each university.[99]

The 2000 ASUU agreement with the federal government aimed at reversing "the decay in the universities, in order to reposition them for greater responsibilities in national development ... the restoration of Nigerian universities through immediate massive and sustained financial intervention [and] a vast improvement in the living and learning conditions of university students."[100] It aimed to stabilize and restore universities, enhance opportunities for university education, halt brain drain, and promote high standards. In his speech at the CVC annual seminar in 2000, President

Obasanjo reiterated the federal government's commitment to honour the August agreement and expand university education when he declared, "If we must join the league of developed nations, we must expand access to twelve times the present [university] size in the next decade."[101] By implication, the president envisaged the enrolment of about 5 million students in the universities by 2010. To make that possible, the communiqué at the end of the seminar declared: "Open access based on the principle of social demand for university places, remains the best option for providing entry to university education."[102]

These pronouncements reflect the country's' postcolonial pursuit of expansion, democratization, and liberalization of opportunities for university education not only to train high-level personnel for economic and technological development but also to promote national unity and cohesion. In addition, they demonstrate the awareness of government and other education stakeholders of the place of highly educated Nigerians in the twenty-first century knowledge-driven world. Fulfilling these promises in the midst of economic decline, ethnic clashes, official corruption, and regional tension constituted the major challenge of university education between 2000 and 2008. It is a challenge that must be met in order to achieve the country's postcolonial goal of using university education to promote economic development and nation-building. As Julius A. Okojie, executive secretary National Universities Commission puts it,

> To realize the vision of becoming one of the top 20 economies in the world by 2020AD, Nigeria must produce world class manpower, possible only through world class tertiary institutions, with world class physical infrastructure, world class instructional facilities and, above all, world class human capacity to impart knowledge, conduct research, publish the outcomes and administer/run the institutions properly.[103]

Conclusion

Colonial Origins

Overwhelming demand for university education and limited opportunities typified the higher educational scene in twentieth-century Nigeria. The British colonial educational policy did not aim to promote nation-building or socio-economic development of Nigeria. From 1948 when the first degree-awarding institution in Nigeria, the University College of Ibadan (UCI), was established, until 1960, the British upheld an elitist admission policy at the college. Many qualified Nigerians thereby lost the chance to receive higher education training at the college. Only very few who had the means travelled to Europe, North America and Australia to obtain university degrees. As an ivory tower devoted to educating the country's future leaders, UCI fulfilled the British educational vision for Nigeria; colonial authorities were thus consistently reluctant to expand higher education facilities and opportunities.

Nationalist struggle for educational expansion began in the 1950s. Then, dissatisfied with the elitist British educational practices, some highly educated Nigerians led a campaign against UCI and demanded changes in its enrolment and curriculum policies to satisfy high demand and lay the foundation for nation-building after independence. The exclusive control of all levels of education by either the missionaries or colonial government ended when two constitutional changes empowered Nigerians to legislate on education. The Macpherson Constitution (created in 1951) granted regional legislatures the power to legislate on primary and secondary school education. In prompt exercise of its new legislative power, the two regions in the South, the Western and Eastern Regions, declared universal primary free education in 1952 and 1953 respectively. These steps underscored the importance that the South attached to the expansion of educational opportunities, an importance depicted by S.O. Awokoya as "a national emergency, second only to war."[1] The predominantly Muslim North, a region educationally disadvantaged due to religious, geographical, and political factors, was rather slow in pushing for expansion. Consequently, the educational gap between the North and South widened, and, as the country moved towards independence, it became a source of disunity. As this work has demonstrated, it was largely due to their desire to promote nation-building that successive postcolonial governments embraced policies aimed at equal opportunity, educational expansion, and the controversial quota system (affirmative action).

Educational development in Nigeria took a remarkable turn in 1954 when the Lyttleton Constitution granted the regions legislative power over higher education matters, prompting the three regions to contemplate establishing universities. Although the regions independently pursued their education policies without central coordination, the scheduled independence of Nigeria, agreed upon at the 1957 London Constitutional Conference, meant that the three regions would be merged into one country. Educational concerns immediately assumed a national dimension. With the dire shortages of high-level personnel and the regional disparity in educational attainment, the need for higher education reforms became compelling. However, while nationalists called for educational reform, no study had been conducted to assess the country's educational needs. When the Carnegie Corporation of New York, which had previously advocated the expansion of education in British colonies, particularly in Nigeria, offered to sponsor a study on Nigeria's higher education needs, the national and regional governments enthusiastically accepted the proposal. Driven by the politics of the Cold War and decolonization, the Carnegie Corporation hoped that pushing for a reform of the British higher education system was vital, not only in winning the Cold War, but also in America's future involvement in the emerging African nations, beginning with Nigeria.

This book has demonstrated that the mutual understanding of higher educational reforms reached by the departing colonial officials, the Carnegie Corporation, and emerging Nigerian leaders led to the setting up of the Commission on Post-Secondary and Higher Education in Nigeria (the Ashby Commission) in 1959. The timing was significant. The Ashby Commission was appointed on the eve of independence when the role of university graduates in the process of national development had become imperative. In addition, the commission was set up when the North had realized the importance of Western education largely due to an uncomfortable prospect of southern domination of the country's top policy-making positions. Thus, Nigeria's new leaders reformed the university system to help fulfill a new mission. As Okojie, the executive secretary of the NUC stated,

> It is through education that the human resource capacity of a nation is developed, harnessed and deployed for nation building. Simply put, without education, we have no society or future as a nation.[2]

The 1960s

Following the report of the Ashby Commission that called for 'massive' expansion of university education, the federal and regional governments realigned university education policies to build a modern nation at independence in 1960. This study has revealed that the implementation of the Ashby recommendations marked a turning point in the development of higher education, particularly in the 1960s. During that period, the federal and regional governments expanded the opportunities for university education in order to train the human resources for economic development and engaged university education in a conscious attempt to integrate Nigeria's pluralistic society. Consequently, the federal government approved the establishment of four universities, at Nsukka, Zaria, Ife, and Lagos, between 1960 and 1962, and expanded the university curriculum to include courses in African studies, commerce and business administration, teaching, engineering, medicine and veterinary science, agriculture, law, and extension services.

The federal government underscored the importance of enhanced access to universities, particularly in science and technology courses, when it increased the Ashby Commission's projection of 7,500 students to 10,000 students.[3] It also insisted that "7,580 should be taking courses in pure and applied sciences in view of the shortage of qualified Nigerians in those fields of study."[4] By establishing more universities and projecting higher enrolment in sciences, the federal government demonstrated its belief that training the work force in the universities was a vital component of national development. The emphasis on science courses reflects the trend of thinking in the 1960s, when many political elites and scholars believed that the wonders of the Western world derived from the sciences. Therefore, to sustain independence as well as to justify itself to Nigerians, the government sought to train Nigerians in diverse fields to help in transforming the economy. The emphasis on science subjects was a radical departure from the British concept of university education, which the Ashby report described as "too inflexible and too academic to meet national needs."[5] Thus, the pursuit of diversity, modeled after the American land-grant colleges, coupled with the federal and regional awarding of scholarships and external financial support, greatly increased student enrolment from 939 in 1959 (excluding about 1,000 who were studying overseas) to 9,695 in 1969 (excluding enrolment in UNN).[6]

Even though top government officials, policy-makers, and other proponents of change emphasized applied sciences and vocational subjects as in America's land-grant colleges, the actual implementation of the project, with the exception of the University of Nigeria, Nsukka, did not reflect this emphasis. Unlike UNN, which admitted candidates with GCE Ordinary Level certificates, other universities still followed the British pattern, insisting on Advanced Level. Only a few sixth form schools were available to prepare candidates for 'A' Level examinations. Because the cost of expanding these schools to prepare enough candidates for university education was enormous, there were shortages of candidates, especially for science courses, including those in applied sciences. Besides, fewer candidates demanded courses in the sciences, compared to those in the humanities, law, and liberal arts. The retention of the sixth form was largely responsible for this. In fact, six years after the publication of the Ashby Commission report, its chair, Eric Ashby, regretted the decision to retain the sixth form. According to Ashby, "The consequences are already unfortunate: a valuable opportunity to provide flexibility in the educational system has been lost, and one university [UNN] has found it advisable to circumvent the rigidities of the British pattern of schooling by admitting students at O level."[7]

By upholding even geographical location of universities to all the regions, the federal government sought to promote national unity through the provision of equal educational opportunity to all Nigerians. Yet, rivalries between the North and the South undermined government's efforts. A notable example was the call by the vice-chancellor of Ahmadu Bello University, Ishaya Audu, and other lecturers in the institution in 1969 to scrap the inter-regional scholarships awarded to poor students under the *Indigent Students Scheme*. Their opposition was simply because the scheme benefited candidates from the South, who maintained higher enrolment in all Nigerian universities.[8] Instead of helping to unite the country, regional universities became the axis of bitter inter-regional rivalries. Animosities intensified when the Eastern Region decided to separate from the rest of the country, resulting in the Nigerian Civil War (1967–70). The war exemplified the lack of national unity in Nigeria. After the war, the president, Yakubu Gowon, adopted a centralized approach to governance in his administration's determination to promote national unity and reconciliation, a posture largely shaped by the recommendations of the Dina Committee and the Curriculum Conference in 1968 and 1969 respectively. Federal management of university expansion likewise characterized the postwar government's social policies.

Post-Civil War Nation-Building

Official attempts to increase access to university education regardless of class, ethnicity, gender, or creed manifest themselves in the 1970s and 1980s with the award of regional and federal scholarships to indigent students, the equitable geographical location and expansion of university facilities, the introduction of free education and the quota system, and the establishment of federal regulatory and admission agencies such as the National Universities Commission (NUC) and the Joint Admission and Matriculation Board. Some of these policies were either ill-conceived or poorly implemented. They, in fact, mirrored larger problems in Nigeria's pluralistic society. More consequential were the efforts by military regimes of 1966–79 and 1983–99 at pursuing centralization of university education policies aimed at fostering a sense of national unity and promoting socio-economic development. The implementation of these policies had unintended consequences. Not only did they compromise the sustainable expansion of universities but they also threatened to diminish, if not wipe out, the collective consciousness of Nigerians that mass university education originally sought to affirm.

It was in search of greater national unity after the bitter experience of the Nigerian civil war that Gowon embraced the notion of "fairer spread of higher education facilities" by locating five new universities (established in 1975) in the educationally disadvantaged states, mostly in the north. This policy sought to promote the understanding that "there can only be true unity where educational opportunities and resultant facilities, amenities and benefits are evenly distributed."[9] The sudden oil wealth of 1973, occasioned by the Yom Kippur War, swayed the Gowon's regime to pursue university expansion confidently. In 1970, Gowon's regime committed itself to building "a land of bright and full opportunities for all its citizens" by providing education not only for its own sake as a means of developing an individual's full potentials but also to prepare Nigerians for specific tasks and skills needed to transform the country. Oil became a major contributor to the Gross Domestic Product (GDP) beginning in 1973. The country's buoyant oil revenue provided the basis for huge increases in government expenditures intended to expand infrastructure and non-oil productive capacity.

Amid the euphoria of the oil price boom, Gowon outlined grand plans to expand virtually all sectors of the economy in order to facilitate economic development. The expansion of the productive base of the economy simultaneously required the production of skilled labour to manage the expanding economy. Educating Nigerians, especially in the sciences, became central to fulfilling Gowon's plans and greatly influenced the federal government's deliberate pursuit of a 60:40 science/humanities ratio in university admission. Nevertheless, despite the government's determination to promote science education, students in the arts and social sciences predominated in all the universities, largely because the government failed to pay attention to the teaching and funding of science education at the secondary-school level.

Gowon's search for a common inter-regional educational policy led him to grant statutory powers to the NUC and to convene a seminar on national educational policy in 1973. While the NUC became an instrument in maintaining central control of universities, the national seminar provided the blueprint for the implementation of an ambitious educational program such as free education, the geographical distribution of educational facilities, the abolition of the British sixth form, and the introduction of the American-style 6-3-3-4 system of education. What influenced these changes were recommendations of the Curriculum Conference of 1969, the UNESCO report of 1972, and increased Nigerian interest in the American system of education. Furthermore, to remove the bottlenecks that impeded access to the universities as well as to promote national unity, the Obasanjo regime (1976–79) further centralized university admission by setting up the Joint Admission and Matriculation Board (JAMB) in 1978, introduced a free university education policy, and adopted 'O' Level certificates as the minimum entry requirements to all universities. Due to the federal government's policies during the second attempt at expansion, the university education system witnessed an accelerated growth. Student population increased from 9,695 in 1969 to 57,742 in 1979, while the number of universities increased from five to thirteen.

After thirteen years of military dictatorship in Nigeria, a civilian government headed by Shehu Shagari came to power in 1979. Aided by the 1979/81 oil windfall, Shagari continued the expansion of universities in response to public demand. Notwithstanding the collapse of crude oil prices in the world market in 1981/82, the federal government borrowed from external financial institutions in order to finance its ambitious social programs, including free education and university expansion. It established seven universities of science and technology between 1981 and 1983. The location of the new federal universities in Bauchi, Gongola, Niger, Imo, Ogun, Benue, and Ondo states reflected the federal government's sensitivity to states without universities, an attempt to 'democratize' university facilities in the country. These universities were designed as specialized institutions meant to meet Nigeria's growing needs for scientific and technological developments. Yet, the massive corruption among government officials and the mismanagement of the economy affected not just the economy but also sustainable expansion of university education.

Eager to close the educational gap between the North and the South, the Shagari regime introduced the quota system (affirmative action) in university admissions in 1981. From the 1950s to the 1970s, both the British and the southerners had objected to implementing a quota system in university admission. While the British rejected it because of their insistence on merit and high academic standards, the southerners feared that it would halt their educational advancement. However, by 1981 Shagari believed that the policy was vital in facilitating national unity. Of the four criteria for securing university admission under the new quota system, the Educational Disadvantaged criterion, which allocated 20 per cent of admissions into the federal universities to students from the twelve educationally disadvantaged states (ten from the North), was the most contentious. By all accounts, the introduction of the quota system represented a flawed solution to closing the educational gap between the South and the North. As the data on university enrolment reveal, enrolment of northerners in universities remained significantly low in comparison with southerners. Although the policy sought to reduce tension that educational disparities generated between the two areas, it achieved the opposite effect. Perceiving the policy as a form of discrimination favouring the under-represented states, the 'advantaged' states, mostly in the South, were exasperated. Faced with the increasing number of their qualified indigenes who were denied admission into federal universities partly due to the new quota policy, state governors in the South moved swiftly to establish their own institutions. Backed, of course, by the 1979 constitution that empowered states to own universities, eight states established universities between 1981 and 1983, even when their financial capabilities declined sharply due to the fall in oil revenue.

The short period of civilian rule from 1979 to 1983 witnessed rapid expansion of university education. The number of universities increased from thirteen to fifty-three; and student enrolment rose from 57,742 to 116,822. Yet, the economic depression of 1982/83, occasioned by the decline in oil revenue and aggravated by official corruption and mismanagement of the economy, forced the Shagari regime to reduce the government's social expenditure and attempted to impose higher fees for public services, including university education. Although the Shagari regime ended in a military coup in December 1983, the military administrations that ruled Nigeria between 1983 and 1990 implemented the policy initiated by Shagari in 1983. This study has shown that official reaction to the economic meltdown of 1983 shaped the rationalization policy instituted by the Buhari and Babangida administrations from 1983 to 1999. During this period, economic recovery overshadowed the goal of national integration and development through liberal social policies.

Setbacks in Expansion

One of the most potentially significant steps in the push for mass university education was the creation of the National Open University (NOU) in 1983. NOU conceptually was at the heart of education for all. It sought to put university education within the reach of all Nigerians, regardless of age or location. Poor communication infrastructure, however, delayed the successful commencement of studies. Lacking the financial resources to address the problems, the Buhari regime disbanded NOU in 1984, just a few months after he came to office. In this same year, Buhari also abolished the twenty-six private universities that had emerged under questionable circumstances in 1983. The swiftness with which the federal government promulgated the decrees that shut down these universities underscores how policy decisions were often rooted not in thoughtful considerations but in hysteria. It provides a window into the problems of Nigeria itself that made Chinua Achebe to liken the country as "a child. Gifted, enormously talented, prodigiously endowed and incredibly wayward."[10] Engaging the private sector in providing higher education would have afforded the country a viable option to expand educational opportunities. The idea of private ownership of universities that Buhari overlooked in 1984 ultimately became a welcome initiative in 1998 when the Abubakar government issued licenses to three private universities. Along with NOU, which was resuscitated in 2001, private university education has remained a common feature of the country's educational scene since 2000.

Buhari's austerity measure gave way to the IMF-sponsored Structural Adjustment Program introduced by Ibrahim Babangida (1985–93) to revamp the economy. SAP implied a reduction in the government's social expenditures. The federal government reintroduced fees in universities; reduced the grants allocated to universities, and required them to generate income to supplement government grants. This was the thrust of the rationalization policy. Expansion contracted. Although student population increased from 116,822 in 1983 to 180,871 in 1990, the annual percentage increase dropped from 10.9 per cent in 1986 to 4.9 per cent in 1989/90. Worse still, as this study has demonstrated, the population increase without improvement in funding or the establishment of more universities or the maintenance of existing facilities resulted in overcrowding and deterioration in university facilities, a decline in academic quality, a brain drain, and the radicalization of the Academic Staff Union of Universities (ASUU) in the 1980s and 1990s.

Nigeria's sudden increases in oil revenue following the Gulf War in 1990/91 seemed to have inspired Babangida to set up the Gray Longe Commission, aimed at articulating a proposal to guide the federal government's long-term sustainable support of universities. The commission, among other things, recommended that government should phase out the 20 per cent admission quota allocated to candidates from the disadvantaged states and provide 80 per cent of the capital and recurrent financial needs of the universities. Babangida rejected these proposals. Notwithstanding the failure of the quota system to close the educational gap between the North and the South, the federal government's refusal to phase it out shows its stubborn refusal to acknowledge reality. It also demonstrates that the quota system performed a political rather than an educational purpose for the ruling northern elite.

Rejecting the funding proposal even as the administration carried on with its corrupt practices and wasteful spending caused great disaffection within the university community. Demand by ASUU for adequate funding of universities and the resultant showdown with successive governments in Nigeria came to dominate the higher education scene throughout the 1990s. Frequent boycotts of classes by ASUU to press for their demands disrupted academic activities in all universities, compelling Abacha's government to proscribe the union in 1996. Deprived of funds to expand their facilities, many universities set up satellite campuses around the country to expand access and generate revenue to meet their financial obligations. By all standards, the satellite campuses made a mockery of higher education since they operated under questionable circumstances with inadequate learning facilities. The total student population of 526,780 in the year 2000 was a remarkable increase in access to university education, yet only less than 20 per cent of the qualified and aspiring candidates secured admission each year due to the lack of available spaces.[11] The expansion of university facilities did not keep pace with increase in student population. As universities admitted students beyond their capacity to absorb them, the result was overcrowding. Data from the University of Ibadan show that "whereas student enrolment was 9,176 in the 1982/83 session, it had risen by about 100% to 18,228 by the 1998/99 session without any corresponding expansion in facilities."[12]

Recent Trends

By 1999, "Nigeria emerged from the more than three decades of political instability and military dictatorship with its once-proud university in tatters."[13] The new civilian government under President Obasanjo believed that "in the knowledge economy of the twenty-first century, human capital contributes up to 60% of the wealth of nations," and therefore insisted that "The key instrument for our development lies … in education, especially tertiary education."[14] Renewed emphasis on university expansion led to major developments in the education system since 1999. Not only is it outside the parameters of this study to attempt a historical account of these events, but it is also imprudent for historical studies to focus on current issues. Yet no history text on Nigeria that ignores the accelerated and astonishing changes in the country's higher educational scene since 2000 can claim completeness.

The proliferation of universities, the struggle for funding, and the resultant instability in universities are some of the conspicuous trends in the country's higher educational scene during the first decade of the twenty-first century. By 2008, the number of universities stood at 93. While the federal and state governments respectively owned 27 and 32 of these universities, 34 were private institutions. Only 9 out of 34 private universities were located in North, meaning that 11 out of the 19 states in the North had no private universities.[15] This, no doubt, has the potential of widening the educational gap between the North and the South. Even with a total student population of 1,096,312, only 150,000 out of over a million candidates who apply annually for admission into universities secured spots.[16] Taking advantage of candidates who are desperate to obtain higher education, many profit-motivated and criminally minded persons have established universities without approval. Since 2000, universities of questionable legal status "have mushroomed across Nigeria."[17] Although the NUC embarked on a crusade to identify and close these universities, their existence underscored the limited opportunities that characterized university education since 1948.

If Nigeria hopes to realize its ambition to become one of the top twenty world economies by 2020, it has to provide adequate higher education facilities and opportunities for training a workforce capable of meeting the challenges of global competition. Given the inadequate facilities in Nigerian universities, that prospect seem "entirely delusional," as Dan Agbese of *Newswatch* affirmed.[18] Harnessing its abundant human capital as other industrialized countries do stands between Nigeria and economic development. During his visit to some Nigerian universities in 2001, MacArthur Foundation president, Jonathan Fanton, came away with two distinct impressions of Nigeria:

> the people I met with ... were truly inspiring. The deep reservoir of human talent is there. But the conditions are clearly not equal to the potential of the people: under-maintained buildings, empty library shelves, over-crowded classrooms, science labs without modern equipment.[19]

Nothing much has changed since Fanton made his assessment in 2001. ASUU's insistence on better funding of universities led to frequent strikes for most of the subsequent years, disrupting academic activities in universities. ASUU's four-month strike (June–October 2009) ended when the federal government made a commitment to progressively attain "UNESCO's prescription that a minimum of 26 per cent of the annual budget should be allocated to education" by 2020.[20] That remains to be seen. Troubled by the incidence of malpractices and irregularities in the conduct of JAMB's annual conduct of the University Entrance Examination (UME), most universities have instituted post-UMEs, which threaten the legitimacy of JAMB. Since JAMB has failed to accomplish what it was establish to do, i.e., ease access to university education, its abrogation is only a matter of time.

While public universities enroll 96.6 per cent of university students, the 34 private universities contributes only 3.4 per cent.[21] Private universities can only make significant contributions to educational expansion and human capital development if they address what Okebukola, the former executive secretary of the NUC, called their "high fee regime" and "aristocratic network."[22] Even so, Okebukola, like other stakeholders, must recognize that, unless government plays an active role in university education, as many advanced countries did at various periods in their history, crushing demand and limited opportunities will continue to defer the country's dream of becoming an industrial power. Blind obedience to the IMF/World Bank's one-size-fits-all prescription of both reducing subsidizes to education and pursuing privatization is a recipe for failure. Although the involvement of the private sector is a welcome development, they alone cannot meet the demand for university education. Unless government takes investment in higher education as a high order political business and holds university administrators accountable for the funds allocated to improve the quantity and quality of education, Nigeria may lose the critical human capital needed to maximize its developmental potentials in the twenty-first century.

Holding the university managers accountable is as critical as allocating adequate funds. In that regard, efforts by Ikedi Ohakim, the governor of Imo State, to investigate top university administrators at Imo State University is a refreshing development in the search for the soul of university education. Ohakim constituted a panel in 2008, headed by Nnamdi Asika, to investigate, among other things, the award of contracts in the university. In its report, released in 2009, the panel indicted, among other persons, the vice-chancellor, I.C. Okonkwo for various offences.[23] Okonkwo appeared before the panel in November 2008 and claimed that he was receiving only ₦57.5 million as a monthly subvention, whereas the actual sum, according to the panel, was ₦113 million. The panel found him liable of corruption, gross mismanagement of funds, and questionable practices. Okonkwo was immediately retired and was asked to refund ₦55 million to the university.[24] Adequate funding of universities while instilling financial discipline, as Okonkwo's case illustrates, may be a model (if done without political considerations) in overhauling the battered university system. This is crucial because, as Ray Ekpu cautioned, "If we don't rescue education, we can't rescue anything, not the economy, not democracy, not development, not our values."[25]

Notes

Introduction

1. Wood to Halliday, 24 July 1854, *Wood Papers, India Board: Letter Book*, vol. 4 (Wood Papers at the India Office Library, London), cited in Suresh Chandra Ghosh, "The Genesis of Curzon's University Reform: 1899–1905," *Minerva* 26, no.4 (December 1988): 463–92.

2. Eric Ashby, *Universities: British, Indian, African: A Study in the Ecology of Higher Education* (Cambridge, MA: Harvard University Press, 1966), 224.

3. H.A. Oluwasanmi, "The Preservation of Intellectual Freedom and Cultural Integrity" (paper presented at a symposium on *The Role of the University in a Post-Colonial World*, Duke University, Durham, North Carolina, 11–13 April 1975), 5.

4. Great Britain, Committee on Higher Education, *Higher Education: Report of the Committee Appointed by the Prime Minister under the Chairmanship of Lord Robbins, 1961–63* (London: HMSO, 1963), para. 31. See also H.R. Bowen, *Investing in Learning: The Individual and Social Value of American Higher Education* (San Francisco: Jossey-Bass, 1977).

5. Martin Trow, *Problems in the Transition from Elite to Mass Higher Education* (Berkeley, CA: Carnegie Commission on Higher Education, 1973). See also Earl J. MacGrath, ed., *Universal Higher Education* (New York: McGraw-Hill, 1966).

6. Ernest Renan, "Qu'est-ce qu'une nation?" In *Nationalism*, ed. John Hutchinson and Anthony Smith (Oxford: Oxford University Press, 1994), 17.

7. Emile Durkheim, *The Evolution of Educational Thought: Lectures on the Formation and Development of Secondary Education in France*, trans. P. Collins (London: Routledge and Kegan Paul, 1977), 167.

8. *The Development of Higher Education in Africa: Report of the Conference on Development of Higher Education in Africa*, Tananarive, 3–12 September 1962 (Paris: UNESCO, 1963), 12.

9. Richard Sklar, "Political Science and National Integration – A Radical

Approach," *Journal of Modern African Studies* 5, no. 1 (1967): 2.

10 James S. Coleman and Carl G. Roseberg, *Political Parties and National Integration in Tropical Africa* (Berkeley: University of California Press, 1964), 8–9.

11 E.E. Osaghae, *Structural Adjustment and Ethnicity in Nigeria* (Uppsala: Nordic African Institute, 1995), 11. See also O. Nnoli, *Ethnic Politics in Nigeria* (Enugu: Forth Dimension, 1978).

12 Sklar, "Political Science and National Integration," 6.

13 Emile Durkheim, *Education and Sociology*, trans. Sherwood D. Fox (New York: Free Press, 1956), 65.

14 Ibid., 70.

15 Ibid.

16 J.T. Saunders, *University College Ibadan* (Cambridge: Cambridge University Press, 1960), 194.

17 Inter-University Commission, *Report of Visitation to University College Ibadan* (Ibadan: Ibadan University Press, 1952), 4.

18 Editorial, *Gaskiya Ta Fi Kwabo*, Kaduna, 18 February 1950, cited in *Report on the Kano Disturbances of May 1953* (Kaduna: Northern Regional Government, 1953), 43.

19 B.A. Fafunwa, *A History of Nigerian Higher Education* (Lagos: Macmillan, 1971); Vincent Ike, *University Development in Africa: The Nigerian Experience* (Ibadan: Oxford University Press, 1976); Nduka Otonti, *Western Education and the Nigerian Cultural Background* (Ibadan: Oxford University Press, 1964); Nduka Okafor, *The Development of Universities in Nigeria: A Study of the Influence of Political and Other Factors on University Development in Nigeria, 1868–1967* (London: Longman, 1971).

20 See "The Dawn of National Reconciliation," Gowon's Victory Message to the Nation, Broadcast from Lagos, 15 January 1970, http://dawodu.com/gowon3.htm (accessed 19 May 2006), 3.

21 Frederick Harbison and C.A. Myers, *Education, Manpower and Economic Growth* (New York: McGraw-Hill, 1964); Frederick Harbison, "The African University and Human Resource Development," *Journal of Modern African Studies* 3, no. 1 (1965): 53–62.

22 Harbison, "The African University," 53.

23 Harbison, "The African University"; T.W. Schultz, *Investment in Human Capital* (New York: Free Press, 1971); A. Sakamota and P.A. Powers, "Education and the Dual Labour Market for Japanese Men," *American Sociological Review* 60, no. 22 (1995): 222–46; G. Psacharopoulos and M. Woodhall, *Education for Development: An Analysis of Investment Choice* (New York: Oxford University Press, 1997).

24 A. Fagerlind and L.J. Saha, *Education and National Developments* (New Delhi: Reed, 1997).

25 Psacharopoulos and Woodhall, *Education for Development*, 102. For more information, see D.A Olaniyan and T. Okemakinde, "Human Capital Theory: Implications for Educational Development," *Pakistan Journal of Social Sciences* 5, no. 5 (2008): 479–83.

26 For detailed information on European system of education, see Florian Znaniecki, *The Social Role of the Man of Knowledge* (New York: Columbia University Press, 1940) and José Ortega Y Gasset, *Mission of the University* (Princeton: Princeton University Press, 1944).

27 K.A. Busia, *Purposeful Education for Africa* (The Hague: Mouton, 1968).

28 Eric Ashby, *African Universities and Western Tradition* (Cambridge, MA: Harvard University Press, 1964), 31.

29 J.F. Ajayi and T.N. Tamuno, eds., *The University of Ibadan, 1948-1973* (Ibadan: Ibadan University Press, 1973), 293–97.

30 See Aliu Babatunde Fafunwa, *A History of Nigerian Higher Education* (Lagos: Macmillan, 1971), 19–20.

31 World Bank, *The African Capacity Building Initiative: Towards Improved Policy Analysis and Development* (Washington, D.C.: World Bank, 1991).

32 T.O. Eisemon, *The Science Profession in the Third World: Studies from India and Kenya* (New York: Praeger, 1982).

33 *Development of Higher Education in Africa*, 11.

34 The conference urged African countries to uphold the university's traditional role of "giving a broad liberal education" in addition to reflecting "the needs of the African world by providing African society with men and women equipped with skills that will enable them to participate fully and usefully in the economic and social development of their continent." Ibid., 12.

35 Michael O. Afolayan, ed., *Higher Education in Postcolonial Africa: Paradigms of Development, Decline and Dilemmas* (Trenton, NJ: Africa World Press, 2007), 1. See also H.F. Makulu, *Education, Development and Nation-building in Independent Africa* (London: SCM, 1971).

36 Eric Ashby, *Adapting Universities to a Technological Society* (San Francisco: Jossey-Bass, 1974), 7.

37 J.F. Ade Ajayi, "The American Factor in the Development of Higher Education in Africa" (*James Smoot Coleman Memorial Papers Series*, African Studies Center, University of California at Los Angeles, 1988), 3.

38 Chinweizu, *The West and the Rest of Us* (New York: Random House, 1974), 322.

39 "Message from the Hon. Aja Nwachuku, Minister of Education, Federal Government of Nigeria," *West African Journal of Education* 1, no. 1 (February 1959): 1.

40 Sudan, a British colony, regained independence in 1956 and refused to join the British Commonwealth of Nations. Britain did not want Nigeria to take similar action.

41 Carnegie Corporation of New York, I.D, 1, "Carnegie Corporation and the World Scene," Policy and Program, 1947–1955, n.d. The Carnegie Corporation's files used in this book are located in the Rare Book and Manuscript Library in Columbia University. They are hereinafter cited as CCNY.

42 Ibid.

43 Under the BDC program, established in the 1920s, Carnegie earmarked $10 million to provide educational assistance to British colonies around the world. Pifer joined Carnegie in 1953 with greater knowledge of Africa having worked in the Fulbright Program for four years. He had already forged a close relationship with top colonial officials in London, and through his trips to Africa, he had not only made friends with colonial officials but also garnered greater understanding of both colonial politics and nationalist aspirations. For more information, see Ogechi Anyanwu, *"Pointing the Way Forward:* Alan Pifer and Higher Education in Colonial Nigeria" (paper presented at the Southern Interdisciplinary Roundtable on African Studies (SIRAS) held at Kentucky State University, Frankfort, April 3–5, 2009).

44 CCNY, I.D, 5.4, Alan Pifer, "Some Notes on Carnegie Corporation Grants in Africa," 1954, 4.

45 Federal Republic of Nigeria, *Investment in Education: The Report of the Commission on Post-School Certificate and Higher Education* (Lagos, Nigeria: Federal Ministry of Education, 1960).

46 J.F. Ade Ajayi, Lameck K.H. Goma, and G. Ampah Johnson, *The African Experience with Higher Education* (Athens, OH: Ohio University Press, 1996); Eric Ashby, *African Universities*; Eric Ashby, *Universities: British, Indian, African*; Apollos Nwauwa, *Imperialism, Academe and Nationalism: British and University Education for Africans, 1860–1960* (London: Frank Cass, 1996).

47 For detailed information, see *Damtew Teferra and Philip. G. Altbach, eds., African Higher Education: An International Reference Handbook* (Bloomington: Indiana University Press, 2003).

48 Task Force on Higher Education and Society, *Higher Education in Developing Countries: Peril and Promise* (Washington, D.C.: World Bank, 2000).

49 Nigerian figures represent the total number of students in all tertiary institutions in the country. There were more than 200 institutions in Nigeria in 1998. The country's 63 colleges of education had a total enrolment of 105,817 students. There were 216,782 students in the country's 45 polytechnics, 411,347 students in 36 universities, and 120,000 students enrolled in 87 monotechnics and 100 schools of nursing and midwifery, and other professional training institutions. This book, however, focuses on university education. See *Damtew Teferra and Philip. G. Altbach, African Higher Education, 4*; and Jibril Munzali, "Nigeria," in ibid., 492–99.

50 World Bank, *Accelerating Catch-up: Tertiary Education for Growth in Sub-Saharan Africa* (Washington, D.C.: World Bank, 2009),46.

51 *Jibril Munzali in Teferra and Altbach, African Higher Education, 493.*

52 *Teferra and Altbach, African Higher Education, 4–5.*

53 "Address by His Excellency Major-General Yakubu Gowon, Head of the Federal Military Government and Visitor of the University, during the 21st Anniversary of the University of Ibadan," *Ibadan* no. 28 (July 1970): 17. Kwame Nkrumah, the president of Ghana, 1957–67, posed similar challenge to the University of Ghana. According to him, "A very heavy responsibility is being entrusted to you. The whole future of Ghana depends to a very considerable extent on the success of our programme for higher education and research." See Wilton S. Dillon, "Universities and Nation Building in Africa," *Journal of Modern African Studies* 1, no. 1 (1963): 75.

54 See Eghosa Osaghae, *The Crippled Giant: Nigeria since Independence* (Bloomington: Indiana University Press, 1998).

55 Federal Republic of Nigeria, *Higher Education in the 90s and Beyond: Report of the Commission on the Review of Higher Education in Nigeria* (Lagos: Government Printing Office, 1991), 34.

56 Editorial, *Punch*, 28 June 2006, 2.

1: The Politics of Colonial Education

1 ADEA Working Group on Educational Statistics, *Assessment of Basic Education in Sub-Saharan Africa 1990–2000* (Harare: NESIS Regional Center, 2000), 10.

2 Paul Desalmand, *Histoire de l'éducation en Côte d'Ivoire – Des Origines la Conérence de Brazzaville* (Abidjan: CEDA, 1983), 456.

3. UNESCO, Report of *International Commission on Education for the Twenty-First Century, Learning: The Treasure Within* (Paris: UNESCO, 1996), 86.

4. Thomas Birch Freeman, the first Christian missionary to work in Nigeria, was born at Twyford, Hampshire, England. He was a son of an English mother and a freed African slave. His pioneering work in founding many mission stations and chapels in the area underpinned the later development of mission schools and the Methodist success in Ghana, Western Nigeria, Benin, and Dahomey.

5. L.J. Lewis, *Society, Schools and Progress in Nigeria* (London: Pergamon, 1965), 23.

6. Thomas Fowell Buxton, *The African Slave Trade and Its Remedy* (London: Frank Cass, 1840), 282.

7. Some of the missionary bodies include the Church Missionary Society (CMS), the Wesleyan Methodist Missionary Society (WMMS), the Presbyterian Church of Scotland, the (American) Southern Baptist Convention, the Catholic Church's Society of African Missions, the Jesuits, the Basel Missionaries, and the Lutherans.

8. Cited in David Abernethy, *The Political Dilemma of Popular Education: An African Case* (Stanford, CA: Stanford University Press, 1969), 39.

9. Cited in H. Debrunner, *A History of Christianity in Ghana* (Accra: Waterville Publishing, 1967), 145.

10. K.O. Dike, "Development of Modern Education in Nigeria," in *The One and the Many: Individual in the Modern World*, ed. J.N. Brookes (New York: Harper & Row, 1962), 236.

11. L.J. Lewis, ed., *Phelps-Stocks Report on Education in Africa* (London: Oxford University Press, 1962), 9.

12. J.F.A. Ajayi, *Christian Missions in Nigeria, 1841–1891: The Making of a New Elite* (Evanston, IL: Northwestern University Press, 1965). See also Magnus O. Bassey, *Western Education and Political Domination: A Study in Critical and Dialogical Pedagogy* (Westport, CT: Bergin & Garvey, 1999).

13. Ibid., xv.

14. O. Osadolor, "The Development of the Federal Idea and the Federal Framework," in *Federalism and Political Restructuring in Nigeria*, ed. K. Amuwo, A. Agbaje, R. Suberu, and G. Herault (Ibadan: Spectrum Books, 1998), 35.

15. Education Sector Analysis, *Historical Background on the Development of Education in Nigeria* (Abuja: Education Sector Analysis, 2003), 14.

16. Ahmadu Bello, *My Life* (Cambridge: Cambridge University Press, 1962), 160.

17. Obafemi Awolowo, *Path to Nigerian Freedom* (London: Faber, 1947), 47–48.

18. For the 1882 Education Ordinance, see National Archives Ibadan (NAI) CSO/26: "A Special List of Records on the subject of Education."

19. H.S. Scott, "The Development of the Education of the Africans in Relation to Western Contact," *The Year Book of Education, 1938* (London: Evans Brothers, 1938), 737.

20. See Emmanuel Ayandele, *Nigerian Historical Studies* (London: Frank Cass, 1979), 178.

21. Apollos Nwauwa, "After Tragedies: New Hopes for Nigeria," *Providence Journal*, 8 October 1999, 3.

22. See Dike, "Development of Modern Education in Nigeria," 237.

23. This system requires women to cover their body, stay in seclusion, keep silent when men are talking, etc. These requirements were expected to make women appear pure and modest.

24 See Dike, "Development of Modern Education in Nigeria," 237.

25 Ibid.

26 James Coleman, *Nigeria: Background to Nationalism* (Berkeley: University of California Press), 113.

27 A.V. Murray, *The School in the Bush*, New Impression of the 2nd. ed (New York: Barnes and Noble, INC, 1967), 65.

28 R.O.A. Aluede, "Regional Demands and Contemporary Educational Disparities in Nigeria," *Journal of Social Science* 13, no. 3 (2006): 187.

29 Jubril Aminu, "Educational Imbalance: Its Extent, History, Dangers and Correction in Nigeria," *Isokan Yoruba Magazine* 3, no. 3 (Summer 1997): 26. http://www.yoruba.org/Magazine/Summer97/File5.htm (accessed 21 May 2005).

30 Dike, "Development of Modern Education in Nigeria," 238.

31 Public Records Office (PRO), CO 583, 35, *Report on Education Department, Northern Nigeria*, 1915.

32 *Daily Service* (Lagos), 17 October 1944, 2.

33 Minutes of the first inaugural conference of the Egbe Omo Oduduwa, June 1948, cited in Coleman, *Nigeria*, 346.

34 *West African Pilot*, 6 July 1949.

35 *Legislative Council Debates*, Nigeria, 4 March 1948, 227, cited in Coleman, *Nigeria*, 361.

36 Editorial, *Gaskiya Ta Fi Kwabo*, 18 February 1950, cited in *Report on the Kano Disturbances of May 1953* (Kaduna: Northern Regional Government, 1953), 43.

37 See Apollos Nwauwa, *Imperialism, Academe and Nationalism: British and University Education for Africans, 1860–1960* (London: Frank Cass, 1996); J.F. Ade Ajayi, Lameck K.H. Goma, and G. Ampah Johnson, *The African Experience with Higher Education* (Athens, OH: Ohio University Press, 1996); Eric Ashby, *African Universities and Western Tradition* (Cambridge, MA: Harvard University Press, 1964).

38 Fourah Bay College was also established to provide its pupils, the liberated Africans and their children, with opportunities to obtain training in the basic skills needed to survive in their new environment. It was also designed to train those pupils who displayed the requisite aptitude as teachers and priests. In 1876, the CMS succeeded in getting the college affiliated with Durham University, which meant that the students could sit for Durham's matriculation examinations and take Durham University degree examinations, although Durham had no control over the appointment of lecturers and lecturing. The affiliation led to a revision of the courses to include Latin and Greek. Fourah Bay College eventually moved towards university status in January 1965 and offered courses such as Hebrew, Arabic, history, natural science, French, and German.

39 Dike, "Development of Modern Education in Nigeria," 235.

40 Kenneth Mellanby, "Establishing a New University in Africa," *Minerva* 1 (Winter 1963): 151.

41 Lord Hailey, *An African Survey* (Oxford: Oxford University Press, 1938), 1288.

42 Wood to Halliday, 24 July 1854, *Wood Papers, India Board: Letter Book*, vol. 4 (Wood Papers at the India Office Library, London), cited in Suresh Chandra Ghosh, "The Genesis of Curzon's University Reform: 1899–1905," *Minerva* 26, no. 4 (December 1988): 463–92.

43 *African Mail*, 13 December 1912, as cited in Coleman, *Nigeria*, 145.

44 Ibid., 146.

8   K.O. Dike, "Development of Modern Education in Nigeria," in *The One and the Many: Individual in the Modern World*, ed. J.N. Brookes (New York: Harper & Row, 1962), 234.

9   NAI, *Annual Report of the Development of Education, 1/4/51–31/3/52* (Lagos: Government Printer, 1952), 30. The policy further noted that "the present policy while recognizing the desirability of universal primary education wisely refrains from attempting any estimate as to when it can be achieved, but wisely proceeds on the assumption that the first step towards its consummation is to increase, within the resources available, provision for secondary education and teacher training so as to increase the flow of teachers."

10 Dike, "Development of Modern Education in Nigeria," 234.

11 Gray Cowan, James O'Connell, David Scanlon Cowan, eds., *Education and Nation Building in Africa* (New York: Frederick A. Praeger, 1965), v.

12 S.O. Awokoya, *Sessional Paper on an Education Policy Presented to the Western House of Assembly*, July 1952, 5.

13 Ibid.

14 The program required the local governments in the region to pay 45 per cent of the cost of providing free education. The policy also proposed an increase in teachers from 1,300 to 2,500 annually as well as the establishment of secondary schools in all the divisions.

15 International Bank for Reconstruction and Development, *The Economic Development of Nigeria* (Baltimore: Johns Hopkins Press, 1955), 573.

16 Ibid., 3.

17 Ibid., 69.

18 With time, however, some of the emirs and chiefs did send their children to school to obtain training for administrative roles.

19 Inter-University Commission, *Report of Visitation to University College Ibadan* (Ibadan: Ibadan University Press, 1952), 4.

20 International Bank for Reconstruction and Development, *The Economic Development of Nigeria*, 72.

21 Ibid., 72–3.

22 Colonial Office, *Report of the Commission on Higher Education in West Africa*, Cmd 6655 (London: HM Stationary Office, 1945), 23. Hereinafter cited as Elliot Commission report.

23 Legislative lists are the designated subjects on which the constitution empowers each level of government to enact laws.

24 The Western Region led the way when it enacted Education Law No. 6 of 1954, which officially endorsed free education at the primary and secondary levels. Likewise, the Eastern Region promulgated Education Law No. 28 of 1956 and the federal government enacted the Education (Lagos) Act, 1957. The Northern Region enacted Education Law No. 17 of 1956, which emphasized teacher training as the first step toward the introduction of free education. See C.O. Taiwo, *The Nigerian Education System: Past, Present and Future* (Lagos: Nelson Pitman, 1980), 194.

25 *Eastern House of Assembly Debates* (Enugu: Government Printer, 18 May 1955), 150–55.

26 Ibid.

27 Nnamdi Azikiwe, "Hope to a Frustrated People" (paper presented at the Inaugural Meeting of the Provincial Council of the University of Nigeria, Enugu, 3 March 1960). Azikiwe added the following: "Its sources of income will in addition to the regular practice in the United Kingdom include earnings from its agricultural and commercial estates. Its curriculum will be prepared not only

to measure up to the highest standards of the older universities of Europe and America, but efforts will be made to emphasize the problems created in the environments of Nigeria and Africa, e.g., Nigerian History, Nigerian Geography, Nigerian Literature, Economic History of Nigeria, African Ethnography, etc."

28 See Apollos Nwauwa, "The British Establishment of Universities in Tropical Africa, 1920–1948: A Reaction against the Spread of American 'Radical' Influence," *Cahiers d'Études Africaines* 33, no. 130 (1993): 247–74.

29 *The Proposed University of Nigeria* (Enugu: Eastern Information Service, 1954).

30 Coleman, *Nigeria*, 243. However, the advocacy of the American-trained Nigerians bore fruit during the 1969 curriculum conference: the recommendations of this conference for educational reforms reflected American influence.

31 NAE, *Eastern Nigeria House of Assembly, Debates*, 18 May 1955, 150–55.

32 Okechukwu Ikejiani, ed., *Nigerian Education* (New York: Praeger, 1965), 157.

33 See Fred Marte, *Political Cycles in International Relations: The Cold War and Africa, 1945–1990* (Amsterdam: VU University Press, 1994).

34 Roger Fieldhouse, "Cold War and Colonial Conflicts in British West African Adult Education, 1947–1953," *History of Education Quarterly* 24, no. 3 (Autumn 1984): 359–60.

35 See Singh Narasingha, "Nigerian Intellectuals and Socialism: Retrospect and Prospect," *Journal of Modern African Studies* 31, no. 3 (September 1993): 361–85; and Tajudeen Abdulraheem and Adebayo Olukoshi, "The Left in Nigerian Politics and the Struggle for Socialism: 1945–1985," *Review of African Political Economy* 13, no. 37 (1986): 64–80.

36 Hakeem Ibikunle Tijani, *Britain, Leftist Nationalists and the Transfer of Power in Nigeria, 1945–1965* (London: Routledge, 2005).

37 Ibid. See Hakeem Ibikunle Tijani, "Britain and the Foundation of Anti-Communist Policies in Nigeria, 1945–1960," *African and Asian Studies* 8, nos. 1–2 (2009): 54–55.

38 Ibid., 60.

39 Hakeem I. Tijani, "McCarthyism in Colonial Nigeria: The Ban on the Employment of Communists," in *The Foundations of Nigeria: Essays in Honor of Toyin Falola*, ed. Adebayo Oyebade (Trenton: Africa World Press, 2004), 651–53.

40 E.H. Berman, "Foundations, United States Foreign Policy, and African Education, 1945–1975," *Harvard Educational Review* 49, no. 2 (May 1979): 146.

41 Carnegie Corporation of New York, 111 A, 634.2, "Walter Adams, Visit by the Secretary to the United States of America (11 May–1June 1954)," June 17, 1954. Inter-University Council for Higher Education. Hereinafter cited as CCNY.

42 Ogechi Anyanwu, "Pointing the Way Forward: Alan Pifer and Higher Education in Colonial Nigeria" (paper presented at the Southern Interdisciplinary Roundtable on African Studies [SIRAS] held at Frankfort, on April 3–5, 2009).

43 Alan Pifer, *Forecasts of the Fulbright Program in British Africa* (London: United States Educational Commission in the United Kingdom, 1953), 21.

44 CCNY, 111 A, 634, "Rough Notes of Talks between SHS, AP, Walter Adams and Mrs. E.M. Chilver," May 11, 1954:

Inter-University Council for Higher Education.

45 CCNY, 111 A, 746.2, "Memo from Alan Pifer to Staff," 29 September 1958, Nigeria, Federal Government Post-Secondary Requirements.

46 CCNY, 111 A, 746.2, "Letter from Pifer to Stackpole," 28 October 1958: Nigeria, Federal Government Post-Secondary Requirements.

47 Ibid.

48 CCNY, 111 A, 634.2, "Walter Adam, Suggestion for a Review of Higher Education in the Colonies," 4 July 1955: Anglo-American Conference.

49 CCNY, 111 A, 634.2, "Letter from I.C.M. Maxwell to Alan Pifer," 19 October 1955: Anglo-American Conference.

50 Cited in O. Albert, "Federalism, Inter-ethnic Conflicts and the Northernisation Policy of the 1950s and 1960s," in *Federalism and Political Restructuring in Nigeria*, eds. K. Amuwo, A. Agbaje, R. Suberu, and G. Herault (Ibadan: Spectrum Books, 1998), 54.

51 Federation of Nigeria, *Annual Report of the Nigerianization Officer for the Year 1957* (Lagos: Government Printer, 1958).

52 *Final Report of the Parliamentary Committee on the Nigerianization of the Federal Public Service* (Lagos, Government Printer, 1959).

53 NAI, Nigerianization Policy – Higher Training of Nigerians, Senior Service Staff, CFEO, 638/S. 4, 1957: See also NAI, PSO. 4/3.3/C 130, 1960. Total regional and federal government expenditure on scholarships increased from £235.8 thousand during the 1952/53 fiscal year to £820.9 thousand during the 1959/60 fiscal year.

54 *White Paper on the Establishment of a University in Western Nigeria, Western Nigeria Legislature Sessional Paper No. 12 of 1960* (Ibadan: Government Printer, 1960), 7.

55 Ministry of Education, *Annual Report 1960* (Enugu: Government Printer, 1963), 24–25.

56 Dike, "The Ashby Commission and its Report," 8.

57 See *Annual Report of the Nigerianization Officer, 1957* (Lagos: Government Printer, 1958), 7.

58 Arewa House, Kaduna Northern Region of Nigeria, Public Service Commission, *Report of the Public Service Commission for the Period 1 November 1954 to 31 December 1957* (Kaduna, 1958), 7.

59 See *Daily Service*, 17 February 1960, 2.

60 Robin Hallett, "Unity, Double-Think and the University," *Ibadan* 6 (1959): 4.

61 Alan Burns, "The Movement toward Self-Government in British Colonial territories," *Optima* 4 (June 1954): 9.

62 Lord Milverton, "Thoughts on Nationalism in Africa," *Corona* 7 (December 1955): 447. Awolowo echoed this statement throughout the 1950s and early 1960s.

63 Martin Kilson, "The Rise of Nationalist Organization and Parties in British West Africa," in *Africa Seen by American Negroes*, ed. John A Davis (Paris: Présence Africaine, 1958), 62–63.

64 CCNY, 111 A, 746.2, "Letter from Pifer to Stackpole," 28 November 1958: Nigeria, Federal Government Post-Secondary Requirements.

65 Ibid.

66 Ibid.

67 For details on the role of the United States in decolonization in Africa, see Ebere Nwaubani, *The United States and Decolonization in West Africa, 1950–1960* (Rochester, NY: University of Rochester Press, 2000).

68 CCNY, 111 A, 849.7, "Report on the Greenbrier Meeting, White Sulphur Springs, West Virginia," 21–25 May 1958, Conference on Tropical African Countries.

69 Ibid.

70 CCNY, 111 A, 746.2, "Letter from Christopher Cox to Alan Pifer," 1 July 1958: Nigeria, Federal Government Post-Secondary Requirements.

71 CCNY, 111 A, 746, "Report of the Meeting at Colonial Office, London," 20 October 1958: Nigeria, Federal Government Post-Secondary Requirements.

72 CCNY, 111 A, 746.2, "Letter from Pifer to Stackpole," 28 November 1958: Nigeria, Federal Government Post-Secondary Requirements.

73 Alan Pifer, "American Interest in Africa" (paper presented to the Philosophical Society, University College, Ibadan, 16 November 1958), 1. The other five great periods of African discovery, as he mentioned, were those of the Egyptians, Greeks, Romans, and Portuguese (and others from the fifteenth to the seventeenth centuries), and the period of political exploration ending with the partition of Africa by the European powers.

74 Ibid., 3–4.

75 Ibid., 4–5.

76 Ibid., 9.

77 Ibid.

78 Ibid., 10.

79 Ibid.

80 Anyanwu, "Pointing the Way Forward," 3.

81 *Western Region of Nigeria: Triennial Report on Education 1/4/55–31/3/58, Sessional Paper No. 11 of 1959* (Ibadan, Government Printer, 1959), 10.

82 *Report on the Educational System in Eastern Nigeria, No. 19* (Enugu Government Printer, 1962).

83 D.H. Williams, *A Short Survey of Education in Northern Nigeria* (Kaduna: Ministry of Education, 1960), 45–47.

84 Education Sector Analysis, *Historical Background on the Development of Education in Nigeria* (Abuja: Education Sector Analysis, 2003), 88.

85 See B.O. Ukeje, *Education for Social Reconstruction* (Lagos: Macmillan Nigeria, 1966), 65. See also Federal Ministry of Education, *Digest of Statistics 1959* (Lagos: Federal Ministry of Information, 1959).

86 Aliu Babatunde Fafunwa "The Growth and Development of Nigerian Universities," Overseas Liaison Commission, *American Council on Education*, no. 4 (April 1974): 7–8.

87 J.T. Saunders, *University College Ibadan* (Cambridge: Cambridge University Press, 1960), 194.

88 Ashby began his career at Bristol University and later served the colonial administration in Australia. He returned to teach at Manchester University and then went to Belfast. He was a member of the Ibadan Visitation Committee in 1957 and made extensive tours of American universities for the Commonwealth Fund in 1958.

89 CCNY, 111 A, 746, "Memo from Alan Pifer to V.H.K. Littlehood," 5 January 1959, Nigeria, Federal Government Post-Secondary Requirements. See also CCNY, 111 A, 746, "Memorandum of Meeting Held April 4 at Birkbeck College, London, on the Nigerian Higher Educational Survey," 9 April 1959, Nigeria, Federal Government Post-Secondary Requirement.

90 CCNY, 111 A, 746.2, "Letter from Eric Ashby to Alan Pifer," 15 January 1959, Nigeria, Federal Government Post-Secondary Requirement.

91 CCNY, 111 A, 745.9, "Letter from Alan Pifer to J.F. Lockwood," 17 February 1959, Nigeria, Federal Government Post-Secondary Requirement.

92 F.H. Harbison and C.A. Myers, *Education, Manpower, and Economic Growth; Strategies of Human Resource Development* (New York: McGraw-Hill, 1964).

93 "Memorandum from Alan Pifer to Sir Ralph Gray," 30 March 1959, in Lockwood Papers (Files on Higher Education), Birkbeck College Archives, University of London.

94 Memorandum from Alan Pifer to Eric Ashby, 10 April 1959, Lockwood Papers.

95 Cox to Sir John Lockwood, 17 February 1959, Lockwood Papers.

96 *West African Journal of Education* 3, no. 1 (February 1959): 4.

97 PRO, CO 554/2029, James Wilson Robertson, Federation of Nigeria Dispatch no. 423, 10 March 1959.

98 Ibid. By 'these sources,' Robertson was referring to Nigerians trained at University College, Ibadan, and institutions in the United Kingdom and United States of America.

99 PRO: CO 554/2029, Announcement on Survey of Nigerian Education, Colonial Office Information Department, 27 April 1959.

100 The Nigerian members of the commission were Professor K.O. Dike (East), Senator Shettima Kashim (North), and Dr. S.D. Onabamiro (West). Sir Eric Ashby, Master of Clare College, Cambridge University, and formerly president and vice-chancellor of Queen's University, Belfast, chaired it. Other British members were Sir J.F. Lockwood and Mr. G.E. Watts. The American members were President Eric Walker, Professor H.W. Hannah, and Dean F. Keppel.

101 Professor F. Harbison of the Industrial Relations Section, Princeton University, prepared a report on high-level manpower for Nigeria's future; V.L. Griffiths of the Department of Education, Oxford University, prepared a paper on teacher training; and M.W. Pritchard, one of Her Majesty's Inspectors of Schools, prepared a report on secondary schools. Professor R.B. Sergeant and Professor J.N.D. Anderson, both of the School of Oriental and African Studies, University of London, submitted reports on Islamic education and Islamic legal studies respectively.

102 *Daily Times*, 4 May 1959.

103 Ajayi, J.F. Ade, Lameck K.H. Goma, and G. Ampah Johnson, *The African Experience with Higher Education* (Athens, OH: Ohio University Press, 1996), 163.

104 John Lockwood, "Nature of the Nigerian College," Ashby Commission Background Papers, 1960, Lockwood Papers, as reproduced in Ajuji Ahmed, "The Asquith Tradition, the Ashby reform, and the Development of Higher Education in Nigeria," *Minerva* 27 no. 1 (1989): 1–20.

105 Ibid.

106 Memo from Francis Keppel to H.W Hannah, 24 February 1960, Lockwood Papers, as reproduced in Ahmed.

107 "Summary of the Views of Mr. G.E. Watts," Ashby Commission Background Papers, Lockwood Papers, as reproduced in Ahmed.

108 Ibid.

109 Eric Ashby, *Universities: British, Indian, African: A Study in the Ecology of Higher Education* (Cambridge, MA: Harvard University Press, 1966), 274.

110 Ibid., 269–70.

111 K.O. Dike, "Summary of Professor K.O. Dike's Views," Ashby Commission

Background Papers, as reproduced in Ahmed.

112 Ibid.

113 See J. Fergusson, "Ibadan Arts and Classics," *University Quarterly* 9 (September 1965), 399–405.

114 S. Onabamiro, Ashby Commission Background Papers, as reproduced in Ahmed.

115 Minutes of Meeting with the Senate of the University College, Ibadan, 11 January 1960, Ashby Commission Background Papers, as reproduced in Ahmed.

116 NAK, Minutes of Meetings of the JCC, 1960–1961, CDN C. 16. Formed in 1955, the JCC was an independent body representing major organizations involved in educational activities in the country (the universities, the regional education ministries, and the Union of Teachers). It acted in an advisory capacity to both the federal and state ministries of education, the universities, the institutes of education, the West African Examinations Council, and all other education agencies.

117 Geoffrey D. Sime, "Higher Education for All in Today's Society," in *Higher Education for All*, ed. Gordon Roderick and Michael Stephens (London: Falmer Press, 1979), 44.

118 Minutes of Meetings of the Ashby Commission, January 1960, Ashby Commission Background Papers, as reproduced in Ahmed.

119 See Western Region of Nigeria, *Policy on the Establishment of a University in Western Nigeria* (Ibadan: Government Printer, 1960).

120 Minutes of the Meeting with J.O. Udoji, Chief Secretary to the Premier of Eastern Nigeria, 18 January 1960, Ashby Commission Background Papers, as reproduced in Ahmed.

121 Sir Ronald Gould undertook the tour at the request of the British Council; the tour was organized by British Council officials in London, aided by the E.E. Eaus, the general secretary of the Nigerian Union of Teachers. See *Daily Times*, 30 April 1960, 5.

122 See *Daily Times*, 15 December 1960, 5.

123 Frank Bowls, *Access to Higher Education* (Paris: UNESCO, 1963).

124 Olalekan Are, "Suggestions for UCI," *Daily Times*, 23 May 1960, 5. Similar ideas featured in the *Daily Times* appear on the following dates: 6 March, 28 March, 19 April, and 9 September 1960.

125 Ibid.

126 S.D. Onabamiro, "There is Chance for Every Student," *Daily Times*, 3 May 1960, 9.

127 Ibid.

128 Orotayo Kitchie, "Expand Educational Facilities," *Daily Times*, 7 June 1960, 13. See also *Daily Times*, 6 August, 28 January, 10 April, and 20 February 1960.

129 J.A.O. Odupitan, "The Defects in our Education Policy," *Daily Times*, 27 April 1960, 17. See also Elizabeth Pryse, "Education policy must fit our needs," *Daily Times*, 22 January 1960, 5; *Daily Times*, 16 March 1960, 5; 28 June 1960, 5; 31 July 1960, 5; 1 September 1960, 5; 31 March 1960, 5.

130 See CCNY, I.E. 17, "Memo from Alan Pifer to Carnegie Staff on Follow up of the Ashby Commission," February 10, 1961, Alan Pifer.

## 3: The Ashby Commission, Regionalism, and University Education in the 1960s

1. Gray Cowan, James O'Connell, and David Scanlon Cowan, eds., *Education and Nation Building in Africa* (New York: Praeger, 1965), v.

2. *West African Journal of Education* (February 1964): 9.

3. *Fraternité* (Abidjan), 15 February 1963, 6.

4. *Voice of Ethiopia*, 18 December 1961, 1.

5. Martin Carnoy and Joel Samoff, *Education and Social Transition in the Third World* (Princeton, NJ: Princeton University Press, 1990), 7.

6. Abubakar Tafawa Balewa, "Inaugural Address Delivered on the Occasion of His Installation as the First Chancellor of the University of Ibadan," *Ibadan* 18 (February 1964): 14.

7. Federal Republic of Nigeria, *Investment in Education: The Report of the Commission on Post-School Certificate and Higher Education* (Lagos, Nigeria: Federal Ministry of Education, 1960), 3. Hereinafter cited as the *Ashby Commission Report*.

8. Ibid.

9. Ibid., 7.

10. In addition to 30,000 Nigerians with university degrees, the Ashby Commission report estimated 50,000 people with intermediate qualification (which meant people with two or three years of full-time study in technical institutes or agricultural colleges after School Certificate).

11. *Ashby Commission Report*, 7.

12. Ibid., 50.

13. Ibid., 26–29.

14. Ibid., 25.

15. Ibid., 26.

16. Ibid., 28.

17. Ibid.

18. Ibid., 48.

19. Ibid., 10.

20. Ibid., 41.

21. Ibid., 12.

22. Ibid., 22.

23. Ibid.

24. Ibid.

25. Ibid.

26. Kenneth Dike, "Address at the 12th Anniversary of UCI," *Daily Times*, 19 November 1960, 16.

27. *Ashby Commission Report*, 46.

28. Ibid., 25.

29. Ibid.

30. Ibid., 3

31. Ibid., 41.

32. The University of Nigeria, Nsukka, offered a wide range of courses such as accountancy, agricultural economics, agricultural engineering, agricultural mechanization, animal science, anthropology, architecture, botany, business administration, chemistry, economics, education, and engineering (civil, electrical, and mechanical), among others.

33. George M. Johnson, "Aims of the University of Nigeria," *Daily Times*, 30 November 1960, 5. Some of those critical of UNN were a few highly educated Nigerians who were brainwashed to believe that the British system is the best and were therefore blind to other systems.

34. The Western Region's idea of a university was in agreement with the reasons why the University of Nigeria, Nsukka, was established, which

included, among others, curriculum diversity and liberalization of access.

35 *White Paper on the Establishment of a University in Western Nigeria, Western Nigeria Legislature Sessional Paper No. 12 of 1960* (Ibadan: Government Printer, 1960), 1–2.

36 Ibid.

37 Federation of Nigeria, *Educational Development, 1961–1970, Sessional Paper No. 3 of 1961* (Lagos: Federal Government Press, 1961), 4.

38 Ibid., 9

39 Ibid.

40 Ibid., 7.

41 Ibid.

42 Federal Republic of Nigeria, *First National Development Plan* (Lagos: Federal Ministry of Education, 1962), 21.

43 Ibid., 1.

44 See W.F. Stolpher, "The Main Features of the 1962–1968 National Plan," *Nigerian Journal of Economic and Social Studies* 4, no. 2 (July 1962): 90.

45 See B.A. Fafunwa, *A History of Nigerian Higher Education* (Lagos: Macmillan, 1971), 227.

46 *Educational Development, 1961–1970*, 9.

47 *Federal Republic of Nigeria, Annual Report of National Manpower Board*, 1 December 1962–31 March 1964 (Lagos: Federal Ministry of Information, 1965), 21.

48 Address by the Hon. Minister of Economic Development to the Third Meeting of the National Manpower Board, 4 July 1963, in *Annual Report of National Manpower Board*, 24.

49 Federal Republic of Nigeria, *University Development in Nigeria: Report of the National Universities Commission* (Apapa, Lagos: Federal Ministry of Information, 1963), i.

50 Bello A. Salim, "Admission Crisis in the Nigerian University System: The Way Forward" (paper presented at the 22nd Convocation Ceremony of the University of Ilorin, Ilorin, Nigeria, 22 April 2004), 10.

51 University of Northern Nigeria, *Report of the Inter-University Council Delegation* (London: London University Press, 1961).

52 *Report of the UNESCO Advisory Commission for the Establishment of the University of Lagos* (Paris: UNESCO, 1961).

53 See *Annual Review of Nigerian Universities, 1964–65* (Lagos: Federal Ministry of Information, 1966), 3.

54 Ibid.

55 See UNESCO, *The Development of Higher Education in Africa: Report of the Conference on the Development of Higher Education in Africa, Tananarive, 3–12 September 1962* (Paris: UNESCO, 1963), 114. An additional 3,050 students were in other forms of higher education.

56 Jubril Aminu, *Quality and Stress in Nigerian Education* (Maiduguri: Northern Nigerian Publishing, 1986), 36–38.

57 Federal Republic of Nigeria, *University Development in Nigeria: Report of the National Universities Commission* (Apapa, Lagos: Federal Ministry of Information, 1963).

58 Ibid., 21.

59 Ibid., 13.

60 Ibid., 19.

61 Ibid.

62 Federation of Nigeria, *Decision of the Government of the Federal Republic of Nigeria on the Report of the National Universities Commission Educational Development, Seasonal Paper No. 4 of 1964* (Lagos: Federal Ministry of Information, 1964), 7.

63 Ibid.
64 Ibid., 5.
65 Manpower Study, *A Study of Nigeria's Professional manpower in Selected Occupation 1964, no. 3* (Lagos: Nigerian National Press Limited, 1964), 2.
66 S.O. Biobaku, "The Purpose of University Education" (paper presented at the National Curriculum Conference, Lagos, 8–12 September 1969). See also A. Adaralegbe, ed., *A Philosophy for Nigerian Education: Proceedings of the Nigeria National Curriculum Conference* (Ibadan: Heinemann, 1972), 69.
67 *Daily Times*, 18 November 1960, 14.
68 Abubakar Tafawa Balewa, "Inaugural Address," 15.
69 Ibid.
70 "Memo by the Committee of Vice-Chancellors of Nigerian Universities to the Public Service Review Commission," 1973.
71 Adaralegbe, *Philosophy for Nigerian Education*, 82.
72 K.O. Dike, "Address by the Vice-Chancellor to Congregation on Foundation Day, 19 November 1964," 7. See University of Ibadan, Nigeria, *Annual Report, 1963–1964*. The reasons why the federal government gave little attention to science education at the primary and secondary school levels deserve more study than this book could undertake.
73 World University Service, *Economic Factors Affecting Access to the University: Studies on the University Scene in 35 Countries* (Geneva, Switzerland: World University Service, 1961).
74 Fafunwa, *History of Nigerian Higher Education*, 243.
75 Eric Ashby, *Universities: British, Indian, African: A Study in the Ecology of Higher Education* (Cambridge, MA: Harvard University Press, 1966), 275–76.
76 O. Arikpo, "The Sixth Form," in *Report of the Commission on the Sixth Form and University Entry* (Lagos: National Universities Commission, 1967), 16
77 Editorial, "The Sixth Form and After," *West African Journal of Education* 9, no. 1 (February 1965): 3.
78 Ibid.
79 *The Committee of Vice Chancellors of Nigerian Universities, Sessional Report*, 1967/68 and 1968/69, 2.
80 Ibid.
81 *Report of the Commission on the Sixth Form and University Entry*, 8.
82 Ibid.
83 Ibid.
84 *Annual Review of Nigerian Universities Year, 1964–65*, 7.
85 "Dr. Kenneth Dike's Address at the 12th Anniversary of UCI," *Daily Times*, 19 November 1960, 16.
86 *An Address by the Principal, Dr. K.O. Dike, to Congregation in Trenchard Hall on Foundation Day, 17 November* (Ibadan: Ibadan University Press, 1962), 9. Similar problems existed in other universities. For instance, the *Daily Times* of 10 January 1969 reported that more than 261 students of the University of Ife failed to register for classes due to non-payment of fees.
87 See Eghosa Osaghae, *The Crippled Giant: Nigeria since Independence* (Bloomington: Indiana University Press, 1998).
88 Federal Republic of Nigeria, *Decree No. 1*, 1966; *Daily Times*, 29 January 1966.
89 Claude E. Welch and Arthur K. Smith, *Military Role and Rule: Perspectives on Civil-Military Relations* (Belmont, CA: Wadsworth, 1974), 128.
90 See Osaghae, *Crippled Giant*.
91 *Nigerian National Petroleum Corporation (NNPC), Annual Statistical Bulletin*, 1994.

92 W. Ehwarieme, "The Military, Oil and Development: The Political Economy of Fiscal Federalism in Nigeria," in *Fiscal Federalism and Nigeria's Economic Development*, ed. E. Aigbokhan (Ibadan: Nigerian Economic Society, 1999), 57.

93 Indeed, after independence the demand for state creation especially from the minority groups, which began in 1939, continued and was intensified following the overthrow of Aguyi-Ironsi in July 1966. See N. Azikiwe, "Essentials for Nigerian Survival," *Foreign Affairs* 43 (1964/65): 445--61; O. Awolowo, *Thoughts on Nigerian Constitution* (Ibadan: Oxford University Press, 1966). Gowon set up an ad hoc committee to examine the possibility of state creation. The committee submitted its recommendation on 30 September. It considered that the Federal Constitution had certain defects. Among the most important of these were the disparity in sizes of the constituent regions of the federation and the small number of the federating units. See Nigeria, Federal Republic, *Memoranda Submitted by the Delegation to the Ad-Hoc Conference on Constitutional Proposals for Nigeria* (Lagos: National Nigerian Press, 1966), 61.

94 Federal Republic of Nigeria, *Decree No. 14 of 1967*.

95 See Eghosa E Osaghae, Ebere Onwudiwe, and Rotimi T Suberu, *The Nigerian Civil War and its Aftermath* (Ibadan, Nigeria: John Archers, 2002); A. Adejoh, *The Nigerian Civil War: Forty Years After, What Lessons* (Ibadan, Nigeria: Aboki Publishers, 2008).

96 Federal Republic of Nigeria, *Blue Print for Post-War Reconstruction* (Lagos: Federal Ministry of Information, 1967), 5.

97 Ibid., 5–6.

98 *Daily Times*, 10 January 1969, 5. The ethnic group Tahir was referring to were the Yorubas, not the Igbos who were still cut off from the rest of the country due to the civil war.

99 *Daily Times*, 16 January 1969, front page.

100 *Daily Times*, 15 January 1969, 3.

101 Ibid.

102 *Daily Times*, 16 January 1969, front page.

103 Federal Republic of Nigeria, *Higher Education in the 90s and Beyond: Report of the Commission on the Review of Higher Education in Nigeria* (Lagos: Government Printing Office, 1991), 34.

104 See Vincent Ike, *University Development in Africa: The Nigerian Experience* (Ibadan: Oxford University Press, 1976), 122.

105 See Folayan Ojo, *Nigerian Universities and High Level Manpower Development* (Lagos: Lagos University Press, 1983), 42–43.

106 Adaralegbe, *Philosophy for Nigerian Education*, xiii.

107 Federal Government of Nigeria, *Dina Committee Report* (Lagos: Federal Ministry of Information Printing Division, 1969), 29. All revenues accruing from offshore operations should be shared along the following lines: Federal Government, 60%; States Joint Account (SJA), 30%; and a Special Grants Account (SGA), 10%. Royalties from onshore operations was to be assigned on the following basis: Federal Government, 15%; State of derivation, 10%; States Joint Account, 70% and SGA, 5%. Revenue from Excise Duty was to be allocated on the following basis: Federal Government, 60%; SJA, 30%; and SGA, 10% while that from Import Duty was to be shared on the following basis: Federal Government, 50% and SJA, 50%. Finally, revenue from Export Duty was to be shared as follows: Federal Government, 15%; State of Derivation, 10%; SJA, 70%; and SGA, 5%. See Dina Committee Report, 1969, 103–107 and Chibuike

U. Uche and Ogbonnaya C. Uche, "Oil and the Politics of Revenue Allocation in Nigeria," ASC Working Paper 54/2004, African Studies Centre, The Netherlands.

108 Ibid.

109 See O. Oyediran and O. Olagunju, "The Military and the Politics of Revenue Allocation," in *Nigerian Government and Politics Under Military Rule*, ed. O. Oyediran (London: Macmillan, 1979), 200.

110 NERC was an organization under the federal ministry of education devoted to the development of specialized aspects of education and actively involved in curricular review and renewal.

111 The federal government voted special funds for the conference. In addition, USAID paid for the expenses of non-governmental Nigerian participants who wished to take part in the conference, while the Ford Foundation, UNESCO, and CREDO provided financial assistance to service the conference.

112 Adaralegbe, *Philosophy for Nigerian Education*, ix.

113 Ibid.

114 Ibid.

115 Ibid.

116 Ibid., xix.

117 Ibid., xviii.

118 Ibid., xxviii.

119 The 6-3-3-4 system was different from the prevailing 6-5-2-3 system, which involved six years of primary school, five years of secondary school, two years of sixth form, and three years of university education. See Abdalla Uba Adamu, "Educational Reforms in Nigeria," http://www.kanoonline.com/publications/educational_reform_in_nigeria.htm#_ftnref1 (accessed 12 November 2007).

120 Adaralegbe, *Philosophy for Nigerian Education*, 69 and 78.

121 Ibid., 75.

122 Ibid., 76.

123 E.O. Fagbamiye, "Curricular Implications of a Science and Technology Oriented Education," in *Mobilizing Nigeria's Education Towards Technological Self-Reliance: Proceedings of the 11th Annual Seminar of the Committee of Vice-Chancellors, Federal University of Technology, Akure, 10–11 March, 1988*, eds. T.I. Francis, A. Akinyotu, and L.B. Kolawole (Akure: Hope Printers, 1988), 46.

4: Centralization of Universities and National Integration, 1970–79: The Legacy of the Nigerian Civil War

1 Emile Durkheim, *Education and Sociology*, trans. Sherwood D. Fox (New York: Free Press, 1956), 70.

2 See Stanley Diamond, *Nigeria: Model of a Colonial Failure* (New York: American Committee on Africa 1967), 44–46; Aluko Sam, "How Many Nigerians?" *Journal of Modern African Studies* 3 (October 1965): 371–92; Thomas M. Franck, "Clan and Superclan: Loyalty, Identity and Community in Law and Practice," *American Journal of International Law* 90 (July 1996): 359–83.

3 Yakubu Gowon, "The Dawn of National Reconciliation" (victory speech to the nation, broadcast from Lagos, 15 January 1970), http://dawodu.com/gowon3.htm (accessed 19 May 2006), 3.

4 Address by his Excellency, Major-General Yakubu Gowon, Head of the Federal Military Government and Visitor of the University during the 21st

Anniversary of the University of Ibadan, Ibadan no. 28 (July 1970): 16.

5 Ibid.

6 Ibid.

7 See Total Enrollment in Nigerian Universities 1968/69, National Universities Commission, Lagos, July 1969, 2.

8 UNIBEN, *First Congregation, November 23, 1974*, (Benin: Uniben Press, 1974), 5.

9 See Federal Ministry of Education, *Statistics of Education in Nigeria*, various years, 1975.

10 See Folayan Ojo, *Nigerian Universities and High Level Manpower Development* (Lagos: Lagos University Press, 1983), 42–43.

11 J.F. Ade Ajayi, "Matriculation Address," *Mimeo*, University of Lagos, 1973, 1.

12 J.F. Ade Ajayi, "Matriculation Address" *Mimeo*, University of Lagos, 1974, 2.

13 Federal Republic of Nigeria: *Second National Development Plan 1970–1974: Programme of Post-War Reconstruction and Development* (Lagos: Ministry of Information, 1970), 12.

14 Ibid., 235.

15 Ibid.

16 *University of Nigeria Nsukka at 40: 40th Anniversary Celebrations* (Enugu: University of Nigeria Press, 2001), 4.

17 *West Africa*, 16 October 1978, 2027.

18 Address by his Excellency, Major-General Yakubu Gowon, 15–16.

19 "State Universities and National Disunity," *Ibadan*, 28 July 1970, 1.

20 Inter-University Council, "Report of a Visit to Nigerian Universities," 1970, 1.

21 J. Eliagwu, *Gowon* (Ibadan: West Book Publishers, 1986), 177.

22 See David Abernethy, *The Political Dilemma of Popular Education: An African Case Study* (Stanford, CA, Stanford University Press, 1969), 129–39; A. Callaway and A. Musone, *Financial Education in Nigeria* (Paris: UNESCO; International Institute for Educational Planning, 1968), 93.

23 Ehtisham Ahmad and Raju Singh, "Political Economy of Oil-Revenue Sharing in a Developing Country: Illustrations from Nigeria," IMF Working Paper, No. 03/16 (Washington, D.C.: IMF, 2003), 10.

24 C. Ashwe, *Fiscal Federalism in Nigeria* (Canberra: Centre for Research on Federal Financial Relations, Australian National University, 1986), 34.

25 See Anene Nwuzor, "The Military and Education in Nigeria: An Experiment in Centralization in a Federal Context," *Journal of Educational Administration and History* 15, no. 1 (1983): 50–55.

26 *Daily Times*, 21 August 1972, 17.

27 Ibid. Supreme Military Council was the highest law-making body comprised of all the military service chiefs and the state governors.

28 See Federal Republic of Nigeria, *Report of the Seminar on a National Policy on Education*, held in Lagos, 4–8 June 1973, 38.

29 *Second National Development Plan, 1970–1974*.

30 See *Report of the Seminar on a National Policy on Education*, 5.

31 The SNPE was held between 4 and 8 June 1973 at the Nigerian Institute of International Affairs, Victoria Island, Lagos. Participants at the SNPE included representatives of the federal and state ministries of education, educational institutions, representatives of various interest groups, and organizations including UNESCO. Observers included representatives of the British Council, Ford Foundation, USAID, and

UNICEF – a truly international group. The SNPE worked with the twenty-one memoranda sent by the public in addition to four important documents. The documents that guided the SNPE's deliberations include: "A National Policy on Education" – working paper produced by the federal and the state ministries of education; "A Philosophy for Nigerian Education" – a report of the Nigerian Curriculum Conference, 8–12 September 1969; "Learning to Be: The World of Education Today and Tomorrow," UNESCO, 1972; and the opening address "Charting Nigeria's National Aspirations," by the Federal Commissioner for Education, Chief A.Y. Eke

32 Ibid.

33 Ibid, 18.

34 The chairman of the seminar acknowledged the report of UNESCO's Commission on the Development of Education, which advocated 'Learning to be' and 'Learning to live' as fundamental components of a good educational system. See S.O. Adebo, "Seminar Chairman's Address," 42.

35 Report of the Seminar on a National Policy on Education, 14–19. The report also reiterated the 1969 recommendations of the curriculum conference on the need to abolish sixth form and its replacement with 6-3-3-4 system of education, as obtainable in the United States (which means six years of primary school, three years of junior secondary school, three years of senior secondary school, and four years of university education). It replaced the 6-5-2-3 system (six years of primary school, five years at the secondary, two years of Higher School [sixth form], and three years of university education).

36 Federal Republic of Nigeria, *Third National Development Plan 1975–1980* (Lagos: Nigeria, Federal Ministry of Economic Development and Reconstruction, Central Planning Office, 1975), foreword. The government white paper was ready to be published when a military coup led by Murtala Mohammed toppled Gowon's administration in 1975. Although this disruption deferred the publication of the document, it was eventually released in 1977. See Federal Republic of Nigeria, *National Policy on Education* (Lagos: Government Press 1977), 2.

37 The war was fought between Israel, on one side, and Egypt and Syria, on the other, backed by Iraq and Jordan, and supported economically by Saudi Arabia. The war led to oil shock when Arab members of the OPEC stopped shipping petroleum to nations that supported Israel in its conflict with Egypt – that is, the United States and its allies in Western Europe. The demand for Nigerian oil rose. Oil prices quadrupled. Revenue from Nigerian crude oil exports increased from ₦1.4 billion in 1971 to ₦5.6 billion in 1973. Nigeria's GDP also rose from ₦9.442 billion in 1970/71 to ₦14.410 billion in 1973. G.O. Nwankwo, *Nigeria and OPEC: To Be or Not to Be* (Ibadan: African University Press, 1983), 11. See also the *Third National Development Plan, 1975–80*, 11.

38 *Third National Development Plan 1975–1980*, 237.

39 Ibid., 245.

40 Ibid.

41 Ibid., Foreword.

42 Ibid.

43 Ibid.

44 See Jubril Aminu, "The Factor of Centralization in Two Decades of Nigerian University Development," in *Twenty Years of University Education in Nigeria*, ed. Chinelo Amaka Chizea (Lagos: National Universities Commission, 1983), 37.

45 Federal Military Government, *Decree No. 1*, 15 January 1974. Universities, hitherto accustomed to having direct contact with the federal government, now had to pass through the NUC. This change generated bitter controversy that has endured until the present. A further study is needed to account for how the power tussles between the NUC officials and universities authorities affected the smooth expansion of universities.

46 National Universities Commission, *Report of the Academic Planning Group* (Lagos: NUC, 1976), 200. See also *Higher Education in the 90s and Beyond*, 34.

47 Alex Gboyega and Yinka Atoyebi, "The Role of Universities in the Transformation of Societies: The Nigerian Case Study," www.open.ac.uk/cheri/TRnigeriafinal.pdf (accessed 10 October 2005).

48 J.F. Ade Ajayi, Lameck K.H. Goma, and G. Ampah Johnson, *The African Experience with Higher Education* (Athens, OH: Ohio University Press, 1996), 140.

49 These states include North Central State, North Eastern State, North Western State, Kano State, Kwara State, and Benue-Plateau State.

50 See Jubril Aminu, "Educational Imbalance: Its Extent, History, Dangers and Correction in Nigeria," *Isokan Yoruba Magazine* 3 no. 3 (Summer 1997): 26; http://www.yoruba.org/Magazine/Summer97/File5.htm (accessed 21 May 2005). The ICSA was designed to oversee assets held in common by northern states at the time they were created from the former Northern Region in 1967. Many southerners perceived ICSA as a sign of perpetuation of the former allegedly monolithic "North."

51 Address by his Excellency General Yakubu Gowon, on the Occasion of the Tenth Anniversary of Ahmadu Bello University, Zaria on Saturday, 2 December 1972, 6.

52 Ibid., 8.

53 Ibid., 9.

54 Ibid.

55 Ibid.

56 Ibid., 10.

57 See address delivered at the Congregation for the conferment of degrees by the vice-chancellor, Professor T.M. Yesufu, 26 February 1977, 6.

58 Adeyemo Aderinto, "Multiple Admissions in Nigerian Universities," *Research Bulletin No. 79/02*, Human Resources Research, University of Lagos, 1979, 392.

59 J.F. Ade Ajayi, Vice Chancellor's Matriculation Address, Mimeo, University of Lagos, 13 November 1976.

60 National Universities Commission, *Report of the Academic Planning Group* (Lagos: NUC, 1976), 205.

61 Aderinto, "Multiple Admissions in Nigerian Universities," 395.

62 Ibid. The report of the Public Service Review Commission (the Udoji Report), set up to review the need for senior administrative staff at the Nigerian civil service, confirmed the southern educational lead. It drew government's attention to the regional imbalance in the high-level administrative positions in the federal service, positions that university graduates occupied. The report also revealed that the Northern region, with a population of a little more than half the entire country, had only 54 senior administrators or 4.3 per cent of the national total. The Western region had 39.5 per cent (499); the Midwest 12.8 per cent (162), the Eastern region, 37 per cent (468); and the federal district 6.3 per cent (79). These figures corresponded closely to university enrolments over the previous decade.

Cited in P. Beckett and J. O'Connell, *Education and Power in Nigeria* (London: Hodder and Stoughton, 1977), 47.

63 Report by Mr. L.R. Kay and Mr. W.H. Pettipiere on Central Admissions Procedure in Nigerian Universities, P& D.C. Paper NO. 74/74, Com./FO/van, 31/5/75.

64 Prof. B.A. Salim, "Problems of Assessment and Selection into Tertiary Institutions in Nigeria" (paper presented by the Registrar/Chief Executive Joint Admissions and Matriculation Board (JAMB), Nigeria, at the 21st Annual Conference of AEAA held at Cape Town, South Africa from 25–29 August 2003). AEAA stands for the Association for Educational Assessment in Africa.

65 *Third National Development Plan 1975–1980*, 245.

66 Speech delivered at the Inauguration of the National Universities Commission, 10 July 1975.

67 Murtala Mohammed, televised broadcast in the evening of 30 July 1975. He noted that with the intervention of his regime Nigeria would have another opportunity of rebuilding the nation.

68 The nineteen states were Benue, Kaduna, Borno, Sokoto, Plateau, Kano, Kwara, Oyo, Lagos, Bendel, Cross River, Rivers, Anambra, Imo, Gongola, Niger, Bauchi, Ondo, and Ogun.

69 Inter-University Council, "Visit to New Nigerian Universities by D.P. Saville," report no. 13 of 1977, December 1977, para. 1.4.

70 National Universities Commission, Annual Report, July 1975–June 1977 (Lagos: NUC, 1977).

71 T.M. Yesufu, "Nigerian Education in the 1990s: Some Fundamental Issues," in *Nigerian Universities and the Challenges of the Decade: 1990–1999*, Proceedings of the Thirteenth Annual Seminar of the Committee of Vice-Chancellors of Nigerian Universities, University of Ilorin, 12–13 March 1990, ed. H.O. Danmole (Ilorin: University of Illorin Press, 1990), 22.

72 Ibid.

73 M.S. Angulu was the permanent secretary of the Ministry of Agriculture and Natural Resources, Minna.

74 *Report of the National Committee on University Entrance* (Lagos: Federal Ministry of Education, February 1977), ii–iii.

75 Jubril Aminu, "Educational Imbalance," 3. Aminu was referring to the four states out of the twelve created by Gowon in 1967. Murtala Mohammed created more in 1975 and the former East Central State became Anambra and Imo; former Western State became Oyo, Ondo, and Ogun; former Mid-West became Bendel, and Lagos State was retained. These seven new states are located in the South. Out of the remaining twelve states described as disadvantaged, ten (Benue, Kaduna, Borno, Sokoto, Plateau, Kano, Kwara, Gongola, Niger, and Bauchi) are located in the North and two (Cross-River, Rivers) are located in the South.

76 Ibid., 3.

77 Ibid., 9. Aminu's argument was similar to the one made by President Lyndon Johnson to justify the introduction of affirmative action in the United States. Speaking of the historically disadvantaged blacks in the United States, Johnson stated: "You do not take a person who for years has been hobbled by chains and liberate him, bring him up to the starting line of a race and then say, 'you're free to compete with all the others,' and still justly believe that you have been completely fair." See President Lyndon B. Johnson's Commencement Address at Howard: To Fulfil These Rights, 4 June 1965, http://www.lbjlib.utexas.edu/johnson/archives.hom/

speeches.hom/650604.asp (accessed 12 May 2007).

78 Ibid., 12.
79 Ibid., 25.
80 Ibid., 10.
81 Ibid.
82 *Report of the National Committee on University Entrance*, 57–59.
83 In attendance at the meeting were Professor J.F. Ade Ajayi, chairman of the Committee of Vice-Chancellors, and Vice-Chancellors of all universities in Nigeria.
84 Minutes of Special Meeting of the Committee of Vice-Chancellors with the Head of State at Dodan Barracks on Saturday, 18 September 1976, 1.
85 Ibid., 3.
86 Ibid., Annexure 'A' 2.
87 Ibid., Annexure 'B' 2.
88 Aminu, "Educational Imbalance," 20.
89 *Report of the National Committee on University Entrance*, 5.
90 Olusegun Obasanjo, "Our Educational Legacy" (speech delivered on the convocation ceremony of the University of Ibadan, 17 November 1976), 13.
91 Report of the National Committee on University Entrance, 68.
92 See M.S. Angulu, "The Early Years," unpublished manuscript, 1987, and M.S. Angulu, "The New Examination Board," 4 October 1999, as reproduced in Prof. B.A. Salim "Problems of Assessment and Selection into Tertiary Institutions in Nigeria" (a paper presented by the Registrar/Chief Executive Joint Admissions and Matriculation Board [JAMB], Nigeria, at the 21st Annual Conference of AEAA held at Cape Town, South Africa, from 25 to 29 August, 2003). AEAA stands for the Association for Educational Assessment in Africa.
93 *Daily Times*, Monday 23 January 1978, 17.
94 Federal Republic of Nigeria, *Decree No. 2*, 13 February 1978, A28. A quota system was not mentioned because of its volatile nature. It was merely deferred.
95 B.A. Salim, "Problems of Assessment and Selection into Tertiary Institutions in Nigeria" (paper presented by the Registrar/Chief Executive Joint Admissions and Matriculation Board [JAMB], Nigeria, at the 21st Annual Conference of AEAA, Cape Town, South Africa, 25–29 August 2003).
96 *Nigerian Tribune*, 4 May 1978, 1.
97 See Mike Angulu, "Jamb – Were the Critics Right," in *25 Years of Centralized University Education in Nigeria*, ed. A.U. Kadiri (Lagos: National Universities Commission, 1988), 113.
98 See *New Nigerian*, 7–8 February, 14 December 1978; 15 January, 16 March 1979.
99 Aderinto, "Multiple Admissions in Nigerian Universities," 20.
100 M.S. Angulu, *Press Release*, Joint Admission and Matriculation Board: Admission into Universities 1978/79 Session, March 1979, 5.
101 Joint Admission and Matriculation Board, Lagos, 1978/79 and 1979/80, as reproduced in *Higher Education and Development in the Context of the Nigerian Constitution*, The Proceedings of the Fifth Annual Seminar of the Committee of Vice-Chancellor of Nigerian Universities, University of Benin, Benin City, 26–27 February 1982, ed. Adamu Baikie (Benin: Office of the Vice-Chancellor, 1982), 68.
102 M.S. Angulu, *Press Release*, 5.
103 "Report of the Commission of Enquiry into Certain Matters in the University of Jos," *Sunday Tribune*, 30 April 1978, 8.

104 See Chukuwemeka Ike, "Nigerian Universities and National Integration," in *Higher Education and Development in the Context of the Nigerian Constitution*, Proceedings of the Fifth Annual Seminar of the Committee of Vice-Chancellor of Nigerian Universities, University of Benin, Benin City, 26–27 February 1982, ed. Adamu Baikie (Benin: Office of the Vice-Chancellor, 1982),152.

105 *West Africa*, 9 April 1979, 626.

106 Oil Boom Era (1971–77), http://www.onlinenigeria.com/economics/?blurb=490 (accessed 20 May 2006).

107 *The Punch*, Monday, 3 April 1978, 13.

108 See Jeffrey Herbst and Charles C. Soludo, "Nigeria," in *Aid and Reform in Africa: Lessons from Ten Case Studies* ed. Shantayanan Devarajan, David R. Dollar, Torgny Holmgren, 661–65 (Washington, DC: World Bank, 2001).

109 National Universities Commission, *Annual Report, July 1977–June 1978* (Lagos: NUC, 1978), 21.

110 "Going Beyond Palliatives," *Daily Times*, 11 April 1978, 3.

111 Ibid.

112 See Eniola Adeyeye, *Sunday Times*, 16 April 1978, 5. See also *Daily Times*, 15 March 1978, 3.

113 National Universities Commission, *Bulletin of the National Universities Commission* 1, no. 3 (Lagos: NUC, July–September, 1977), 51.

114 See National Universities Commission, *Bulletin of the National Universities Commission*, no. 7 (Lagos: NUC, July–September, 1978), 21.

115 National Universities Commission, *Report on University Finances*, 1978, 2. National Universities Commission, *Bulletin of the National Universities Commission*, no. 8 (Lagos: NUC, October–December, 1978), 2.

116 *Report on University Finances*.

117 Dennis Austin observed that the turbulent inter-state rivalries that produced the expansion of university education and affected by the financial difficulties of 1977 led to the future fall in academic standards. After his visit to Nigeria, he noted with shock that he "could not find much that suggested 'the gold standard' or any recognition of high excellence once ascribed to Ibadan and its successors." See Dennis Austin, "Universities and the Academic Gold Standard in Nigeria," *Minerva* 18, no. 2 (June 1980): 242.

118 National Universities Commission, *Bulletin of the National Universities Commission*, no. 8 (Lagos: NUC, October–December 1978), 3, 18.

119 National Universities Commission, *Annual Report, July 1977–June 1978*, 27.

120 Ibid.

121 Ibid.

122 See A. Kirk-Green and D. Rimmer, *Nigeria Since 1970: A Political and Economic Outline* (London: Hodder and Stoughton, 1981), 53.

123 *Annual Report, July 1977–June 1978*, 28–29.

124 See Attahiru Jega, "Nigerian Universities and Academic Staff under Military Rule," in *A Thousand Flowers: Social Struggles Against Structural Adjustment in African Universities*, ed. Silvia Federici et al. (Trenton, NJ: Africa World Press, 2000), 176. For more information on the relationship between the intellectuals and government in Africa, see Thandika Mkandawire, *African Intellectuals: Rethinking Politics, Language, Gender and Development* (London: Zed Books, 2006) and *Intellectuals and African Development: Pretension and Resistance in*

African Politics, ed. Bjorn Beckman and Gbemisola Remi Adeoti (London: Zed Books, 2006).

125 "History and Struggles of ASUU," http://www.asuunigeria.org/index.php/about-us (accessed 26 July 2009), 1.

126 R. Clignet and P. Foster, *Fortunate Few: A Study of Secondary Schools and Students in the Ivory Coast* (Evanston, IL: Northwestern University Press, 1966); R. Clignet, *Liberty and Equality in the Educational Process: A Comparative Sociology of Education* (New York: Wiley, 1974); R. Clignet, *The Africanization of the Labor Market: Educational and Occupational Segmentations in the Camerouns* (Berkeley: University of California Press, 1976). See also Philip J. Foster, "Ethnicity and the Schools in Ghana," *Comparative Education Review* 6 (October 1962): 127–34.

127 See James S. Coleman, *Education and Political Development* (Princeton, NJ: Princeton University Press, 1965) and N. Konyeaso Onuoha, "The Role of Education in Nation-Building: A Case Study of Nigeria," *West African Journal of Education* 6 (1976): 435–50.

128 Thomas J. Davis and Azubike Kalu-Nwiwu, "Education, Ethnicity and National Integration in the History of Nigeria: Continuing Problems of Africa's Colonial Legacy," *Journal of Negro History* 86, no. 1 (Winter 2001): 1–11.

129 See Nwuzor, "The Military and Education in Nigeria," 54.

130 *West Africa*, no. 3171, 1 May 1978, 883.

131 Nwuzor, "The Military and Education in Nigeria," 54.

132 Academic Planning Division, "Twenty Years of Academic Development in the Nigerian Federal University System," in *Twenty Years of University Education*, ed. Chinelo Amaka Chizea, 86.

5: The Second Republic and the Burden of Expansion, 1979–83: Free Education, Science and Technology, and Quota System

1 Federal Republic of Nigeria, *The Constitution of the Federal Republic of Nigeria* (Lagos: Department of Information, 1979), 103.

2 Ibid.

3 Ibid., 7.

4 Ibid.

5 Ibid.

6 They included the National Party of Nigeria (NPN), representing chiefly the North; the Nigerian People's Party (NPP), strong among the Ibos; and the United Party of Nigeria (UPN), a Yoruba-led socialist-oriented party. Other parties were the Great Nigeria People's Party (GNPP) and the People's Redemption Party (PRP).

7 See Segun Adesina, *The Development of Modern Education in Nigeria* (Ibadan: Heinemann Educational Books (Nigeria), 1988), 235–36.

8 Ibid.

9 *Text of the First Nation-Wide Broadcast by the President, Alhaji Shehu Shagari, 1 October 1979* (Lagos: Federal Ministry of Information, 1979), 11.

10 Ibid., 12–13.

11 G.J.A. Ojo, "Laying the Foundations of the Open University of Nigeria" (lecture delivered during an International Conference on West African University Outreach at the University of Ibadan, 3–7 October 1982), and reproduced in Ojo, *Planning for Distance Education at Tertiary Level in Nigeria* (Lagos: Government Printer, 1982), 15.

12 Ibid., 13.

13 Ibid.

14 Ibid., 15.
15 Ibid., 17.
16 *Daily Times*, 13 December 1982, 3.
17 National Universities Commission, *Bulletin of the National Universities Commission* 11, no. 2 (Lagos: NUC, July–September 1980), 29.
18 National Universities Commission, *Seminar on the Establishment of New University of Technology 8–11 December 1980 Preliminary Report* (Lagos: National Universities Commission, 1981), iv–v.
19 Yahaya Aliyu, "University Expansion during Recession: Demand versus Available Resources," in *Nigeria: The Universities, the Nation and the Economic Recession*, Proceedings of the 1983 Annual Seminar of the Committee of Vice-Chancellors of Nigerian Universities, the University of Maiduguri, 24–26 February 1983, ed. Akinjide Osuntokun (Ibadan: Ibadan University Press, 1987), 1–2.
20 *Bulletin of the National Universities Commission*, 29.
21 The newly appointed vice-chancellors were Professors A.O. Adekola (FUT, Bauchi), G. Igboechi (FUT, Makurdi), and U.D. Gomwalk (FUT, Owerri).
22 *Seminar on the Establishment of New University of Technology*, vi.
23 Ibid.
24 Ibid.
25 Ibid., 1.
26 Ibid., 6.
27 G.O. Olusanya, "If Wishes Were Horses…" (lecture delivered at University of Ilorin, Nigeria, 6 November 1980), 8.
28 Address by President Shehu Shagari on Budget Proposals to a Joint session of the National Assembly on Monday, 24 November 1980. See also *Nigeria Year Book 1981: A Record of Events and Developments* (Lagos: Times Press, 1981), 110.
29 *West Africa*, "Nigeria's Fourth National Development Plan," March 1981.
30 Ibid.
31 *Nigeria Year Book 1981*.
32 For more information, see Federal Republic of Nigeria, *First National Rolling Plan 1990–92*, vol. 1 (Lagos: Federal Ministry of Budget and Planning, 1990), 3.
33 FME/S/518/Vol.1/99 of 2 September 1981, as reproduced in M.S. Abdulrahman, "Admission Policy and Procedures" (paper presented at the University of Lagos during the Seminar on the Challenges of Higher Education in the 1990s, 30 November 1989), 5.
34 The criteria for selecting these states, especially the inclusion of three southern states (Rivers, Cross River, Lagos), were not mentioned in the guidelines, but they were perhaps related to low enrolments of these states at the secondary-school level and the concomitant low demand for university education.
35 For instance, the catchment states for the University of Nigeria, Nsukka, were the neighbouring states like Imo, Cross River, Rivers, Bendel, Benue, and Anambra. The catchment states for the University of Sokoto were Sokoto, Niger, and Kano. Similar patterns existed for the remaining universities.
36 Many university administrators abused the Discretion admission criterion by extending favours to their friends in top government positions as well as their relations. Oftentimes, offers of admission under this criterion were commercialized.
37 "Youth takes JAMB to Court," *National Concord*, 20 March 1984, back page.
38 Ibid.

39 J.M. Kosemani, "Democratic Values and University Admissions in Nigeria," *Nigerian Journal of Professional Studies in Education* 3 (1995): 78–83.

40 T. Megaforce, "Federal Government, Teachers, Students," *Nigerian Tribune*, 6 September 1999.

41 *Newswatch*, 18 January 1988, 15.

42 Ibid.

43 For detailed information on state allocation to education, see Federal Ministry of Education: *Statistics of Education in Nigeria, 1980–1984* (Lagos: Federal Ministry of Information, 1984), 25.

44 T.M. Yesufu, "Nigerian Education in the 1990s: Some Fundamental Issues," in *Nigerian Universities and the Challenges of the Decade: 1990–1999*, Proceedings of the Thirteenth Annual Seminar of the Committee of Vice-Chancellors of Nigerian Universities, University of Ilorin, 12–13 March 1990, ed. H.O. Danmole (Ilorin: University of Ilorin Press, 1990), 24.

45 Ibid.

46 Ibid.

47 Ibid.

48 *New Nigerian*, 2 November 1979, 3.

49 See Joint Admission and Matriculation Board, Lagos, as reproduced in *Higher Education and Development in the Context of the Nigerian Constitution*, Proceedings of the 5th Annual Seminar of the Committee of Vice-Chancellors of Nigerian Universities, the University of Benin, 26–27 February 1982, ed. Adamu Baike (Benin City: Office of the Vice-Chancellor, 1982), 68.

50 *Daily Times*, 28 January 1978, 11.

51 *Daily Times*, 18 January 1980.

52 *Daily Times*, 30 September 1979.

53 Ladipo Adamolekun, "Education at the Crossroads," *West Africa*, 20 September 1982, 2433.

54 Federal Ministry of Education, *Report of the Panel on Alternative Sources of Funding Education* (Lagos: Federal Ministry of Information, 1981), chap. 5, 102–18. A similar commission, Eke Commission, which focused on primary education and submitted its report on 6 December 1983, came out with the conclusion that "modern education cannot be free." See Federal Ministry of Education, *Report of the Presidential Commission on Funding Primary Education* (Lagos: Federal Ministry of Information, 1983), 52.

55 Jubril Aminu, "University Funding," *The University Demonstrator* 1, no. 2 (April 1986): 6.

56 Adamolekun, "Education at the Crossroads," 2433.

57 See Federal Republic of Nigeria, *Higher Education in the 90s and Beyond: Report of the Commission on the Review of Higher Education in Nigeria* (Lagos: Government Printing Office, 1991), 34.

58 Federal Government of Nigeria, *Statistics of Education in Nigeria* (Lagos: Ministry of Education, 1992).

59 Ajuji Ahmed, "The Asquith Tradition, the Ashby Reform, and the Development of Higher Education in Nigeria," *Minerva* 27, no. 1 (1989): 1–20.

60 Address by Professor M.J.C. Echeruo, Vice-Chancellor, Imo State University, on the Third Matriculation Ceremony of Imo State University, Etiti, 11 February 1984, 4.

61 Ibid.

62 See *Daily Times*, 29 March 1984, 7.

63 P.C. Asiodu, "Nigerian and Oil Technology," *in Nigeria: The Universities, the Nation and the Economic Recession*, Proceedings of the 1983 Annual Seminar of the Committee of Vice-

Chancellors of Nigerian Universities, the University of Maiduguri, 24–26 February 1983, ed. Akinjide Osuntokun (Ibadan: Ibadan University Press, 1987), 49.

64 The 1982 figures fell further to an estimated level of ₦8.000 million; and in 1983, the estimated total federal government revenue was only ₦5, 561 billion. When matched against an estimated total expenditure of ₦12.095 billion, made up of ₦3.435 billion recurrent expenditure, ₦1.44 billion consolidated revenue fund charges, and ₦7.22 billion for capital expenditure, it became clear that the picture was gloomy. See Alex Ekwueme, "Universities, The Nation and Economic Recession," in *Nigeria: The Universities, the Nation and the Economic Recession*, Proceedings of the 1983 Annual Seminar of the Committee of Vice-Chancellors of Nigerian Universities, the University of Maiduguri, 24–26 February 1983, ed. Akinjide Osuntokun (Ibadan: Ibadan University Press, 1987),197. See also *First National Rolling Plan 1990–92*, vol. 1, 3–4.

65 Ekwueme, "Universities," 200.

66 *See National Champion*, 11 March 1983, 13; 14 July 1983, 3; 13 March 1984; and 14 February 1983, 3.

67 Ekwueme, "Universities," 197.

68 Ibid. Other oil exporting countries equally suffered during the same period. For instance, Mexico, the fourth world oil exporter, was burdened with a debt of $83 billion; Argentina, $39 billion; Brazil, $89 billion; and Chile, $17 billion.

69 They include the following: Adeyemi College of Education, Ondo (attached to Ife); Advanced Teachers College, Kano (attached to Zaria); Alvan Ikoku College of Education, Owerri (attached to Nsukka); College of Education Port-Harcourt (attached to Ibadan), and Advanced Teachers College, Zaria (Zaria).

70 Dan Agbese, "The Albatross," *Newswatch*, 6 October 1986, 45.

71 Ray Ekpu, "Gone to the Dogs," *Newswatch*, 3 May 2004, 10.

72 Adamu Baike and Osaren S.B. Omoregie, "University Education: Perspectives of an Educationist and Planners," in *Nigerian since Independence: The First 25 Years*, ed. Tekena N. Tamuno and J.A. Atanda, vol. 11 (Ibadan: Heinemann, 1989), 285.

73 See Ray Ekpu, "The End Justifies the Means," *Newswatch*, 6 October 1986, 25.

74 For more information on corruption associated with contracts awarded during the Second Republic, see Ogechi Anyanwu, "Indigenous Contractors and Nigeria's Economic Development (1970–1992): A Case Study of Chief T.I. Ozoemenam's Construction Company" (BA thesis, Abia State University, Uturu, Nigeria, 1994).

75 Achike Okafo, "Are the university people listening," *Daily Times*, 24 November 1982, 7.

76 See *Newswatch*, 6 October 1986, 49.

77 Tekena N. Tamuno, "Introduction: A New Nation and the Learning Process," in *Nigeria since Independence: The First 25 Years*, vol. 11, ed. Tekena N. Tamuno and J.A. Atanda (Ibadan: Heinemann, 1989), 4.

78 Jubril Aminu, "Better Career in the Nigerian University System," Memorandum Submitted to the Presidential Commission on Salaries and Conditions of Service of University, Maiduguri, 21 February 1981.

79 Ibid., 29.

80 See E.U. Emevon, "An Address by the Chairman of the Committee of Vice-Chancellors of Nigerian Universities," in *Nigeria: The Universities, the Nation*

and the Economic Recession, Proceedings of the 1983 Annual Seminar of the Committee of Vice-Chancellors of Nigerian Universities, the University of Maiduguri, 24–26 February 1983, ed. Akinjide Osuntokun (Ibadan: Ibadan University Press, 1987), 191.

81 Ibid.

82 See T.A. Akinyele, *Budgeting under Structural Adjustment Programme in Nigeria* (Ibadan: Bolayele Commercial Press Limited, 1988), 1–2.

83 *New Nigerian*, 30 December 1984, 3.

6: Rationalization Policy: The IMF/World Bank and Structural Adjustment Program, 1984–90

1 *Financial Times* (London), 16 August 1983, 14.

2 "The 1983 Military Coup – 31 December 1983," http://dawodu.com/abacha2.htm (accessed 20 May 2006).

3 *Financial Times* (London), 25 and 26 February 1985 and *International Herald Tribune*, 12 March 1985.

4 *Daily Times*, 24 January 1984, 7.

5 More research is needed to determine how the recklessness of university administrators negatively affected the expansion of facilities during the Second Republic and beyond.

6 See *Daily Times*, 7, 9, 23, 20 February 1984, and *Democrat Weekly*, 1 April 1984, Letters page.

7 *Daily Times*, 11 May 1984, 12. In addition, Buhari announced that the staff of the Open University would be suitably re-deployed and that the existing universities with schemes for part-time students should be encouraged to expand their programs and take in more students.

8 *Release by the Cabinet Office, Lagos*, May 1984. See National Universities Commission, *Bulletin of the National Universities Commission* (Lagos: NUC, September 1984), 4.

9 Ibid.

10 Ibid., 6.

11 The Federal University of Technology (FUT) Abeokuta became University of Lagos Abeokuta Campus. FUT Bauchi became Tafawa Belewa campus; FUT Makurdi, University of Jos campus, and FUT Yola, Madibbo Adamu campus. See *Bulletin of the National Universities Commission*.

12 See *Daily Times*, 30 August 1984, 3. In 2005, the California State University system was comprised of 23 campuses with a population of 405,000 students. See http://www.calstate.edu/ (accessed 21 May 2006).

13 See National Universities Commission, *The Commission's Recommendations to the Federal Government on the Report of the Committee on Demerging of Federal Universities of Technology and the Creation of Universities of Agriculture* (Lagos: National Universities Commission: July 1987), 3.

14 *Daily Times*, 15 March 1984, 3.

15 "Editorial: Realistic Policy on Education," *Daily Times*, 7 March 1984, 3.

16 Akin Adesola, "The Nigerian University System: Meeting the Challenges of Growth in a Depressed Economy," *Higher Education* 21 (1991): 126.

17 Nigeria, *Report of the Study Group on Funding Education* (Lagos: Federal Government Press, 1984), 114–30. Professor A.B. Fafunwa chaired the Study Group. Other members included Prof. S.D. Onabamiro, Alhaji A. Koko, Dr. J.A.O. Sofolahan, Mrs. Theresa Bowyer, Alhaji Yahaya Hamza, Chief

J.U. Etukokwu, and Prof. Segun Adesina with Mr. N. Malo as Secretary.

18 See Segun Adesina, *The Development of Modern Education in Nigeria* (Ibadan: Heinemann, 1988), 264.

19 *Report of the Study Group on Funding Education*. See also See National Universities Commission, *Bulletin of the National Universities Commission* (Lagos: NUC, December 1985), 12.

20 See Adesina, *Development of Modern Education in Nigeria*, 266.

21 Ibid.

22 Federal Republic of Nigeria, *The Report on the Study of Higher Education Curricula and Development in Nigeria* (Lagos: NERC Press, 1984), 1. The finding of the committee revealed that as many as 55,000–60,000 graduates could be unemployed in Nigeria in 1984.

23 Ibid.

24 Ibid., 18.

25 Ibid., 24.

26 Ibid., 40.

27 Ibid., 81.

28 Ibid., 39.

29 Academic Staff Union of Universities, National Secretariat, "Press Release," *Sunday Tribune*, 16 February 1986, 14.

30 Ibid.

31 Ibid.

32 Committee of Vice-Chancellors, *Rationalization of Courses and Programs of the Universities* (n.d.).

33 For more information, see Jeffrey Herbst and Charles C. Soludo, "Nigeria," In *Aid and Reform in Africa: Lessons from Ten Case Studies*, eds. Shantayanan Devarajan, David R. Dollar, and Torgny Holmgren (Washington, DC: World Bank, 2001), 662.

34 Ibid.

35 *Daily Times*, 6 December 1984, front page.

36 Ibid., 23 January 1985. The extent to which these economic ventures solved the funding problems of Nigerian universities deserves more study than I can provide in the present study. That university financial difficulty continued afterwards perhaps revealed how either inadequate or poorly managed the revenue from such economic ventures were.

37 "Coup Announcement by Brigadier Dogonyaro, 27 August 1985," http://dawodu.com/dogony1.htm (accessed 12 July 2005).

38 Olatunde Ojo and Peter Koehn, "Nigeria's Foreign Exchange Controls: An Alternative to IMF Conditions and Dependency?" *Africa Today* 33, no. 4 (1986): 7–32.

39 "Major-General Babaginda Address to the Nation – August 27, 1985," http://dawodu.com/ibb4.htm (accessed 12 July 2005).

40 Ibid.

41 See M.I. Obadan, "Withered Structural Adjustment in Nigeria," *NCEMA Monograph Series No. 3* (Ibadan: The National Centre for Economic Management and Administration [NCEMA], 1993).

42 Herbst and Soludo, "Nigeria," 663.

43 See Ufot B. Inamete, "Nigeria's IMF Loan Arrangement Decision-Making (Shagari to Babangida Administrations) and Decision-Making Theories," *Australian Journal of Politics & History* 36, no. 1 (June 2008): 39 – 50.

44 Ibrahim Babangida, "Excerpts from broadcast of President Babangida's speech in Lagos on 31 December 1985," as cited in Herbst and Soludo "Nigeria."

45 Address delivered by the President, Ibrahim Babangida, to selected members of the academic community

on 16 November 1985. Meanwhile, in December 1985, the federal government elevated the Nigerian Defense Academy to the status of a military university, bringing the total number of universities to twenty-five.

46 Ibrahim Babangida, "Nigerian President's 27th June Address: Economic and Social Issues," British Broadcasting Corporation, Summary of World Broadcasts, 1 July 1986.

47 Ibid.

48 See Federal Republic of Nigeria, *First National Rolling Plan 1990–92* (Lagos: Federal Ministry of Budget and Planning, 1990), 4.

49 Ibid.

50 A.O. Ikem, "The Paris Club and Nigeria's Debt Rescheduling: The Way Forward," *Central Bank of Nigeria Debt Trends* 2, no. 1 (1996):1-3. See also Gary Moser, Scott Rogers, and Reinhold van Til, *Nigeria: Experience with Structural Adjustment* (Washington, DC: International Monetary Fund, 1997); Nigeria, *The Evolution and Management of Nigeria's External Debt: The Way Forward* (Lagos: Federal Ministry of Finance: 1997). The following countries are permanent Paris Club of creditor countries: Austria, Australia, Belgium, Canada, Denmark, Finland, France, Germany, Ireland, Italy, Japan, Netherlands, Norway, Russian Federation, Spain, Sweden, Switzerland, United Kingdom, and United States of America.

51 National Centre for Economic Management and Administration (NCEMA), "Understanding Structural Adjustment Programme in Nigeria," a draft report presented at the Workshop on Understanding Reform, New Delhi, India: 25–26 January 2004, 14.

52 Federal Republic of Nigeria: *Fifth National Development Plan 1986–1991* (Lagos, Ministry of Information, 1991), 2.

53 See M. Mamdani, "University Crisis and Reform: A Reflection on the African Experience," *Review of African Political Economy* 58 (1993): 7–19.

54 An Address by the President on the Occasion of the Silver Jubilee Celebration and Twenty-first Convocation of the University of Nigeria, at Nsukka on Saturday, 6 December 1986 (Enugu: University of Nigeria Press, 1987), 11.

55 Committee of Vice-Chancellors of Nigerian Universities, Office of the Secretary, *Letter to All Vice-Chancellors of Nigerian Universities*, 20 February 1986.

56 Minutes of the various meetings held by the Executive Secretary, NUC, and the Chairman of the Committee of Vice-Chancellors of the Nigerian Universities on the occasion of their Study-Visit to Britain from 30 March to 4 April 1987, 2.

57 See Idris A. Abdulkadir, Seminar Opening Remarks delivered at NUC/CVC/BC Seminar at Kongo Conference Hotel, ABU, Zaria, 9–10 November 1987.

58 The UGC was a body, similar to the NUC, which coordinated university development in Britain.

59 Minutes of the various meetings held by the Executive Secretary, NUC, 3.

60 Ibid., 3–4. Mr Hardyman talked about the criteria for financial allocation to British universities: number of students for each subject for each university; units of resources for each subject taking consideration for teaching and research elements; grants for Research Councils.

61 Ibid., 6.

62 Ibid., 11.

63 This sub-sector study was prepared by Nicholas Bennett, education planner and

mission leader, and Richard Johnson, special advisor – both World Bank staff, and Keith Hinchliffe, economist, and Christopher Modu, evaluator – both consultants. Although focused on federal universities alone, the report had implications for state universities.

64 *World Bank, Nigeria: Costs and Financing of Universities, Report No. 6920-UNI* (Washington, D.C.: The World Bank, 1988).

65 Ibid., vi.

66 Ibid., viii–x.

67 Jibril Aminu, "Resources for Higher Education, Number, Cost, and Common Sense" (address at the Opening Ceremony of the NUC/CVC/British Council Seminar on the Management of University Resources, held at the Congo Conference Hotel, Ahmadu Bello University, Zaria, 9 November 1987).

68 Communiqué of the NUC/CVC/British Council Seminar, 12 November 1987.

69 Ibid.

70 Federal Republic of Nigeria, *View and Comments of the Federal Military Government on the Report of the Study Group of Higher Education Curricula and Development in Nigeria* (Lagos: Federal Government Printer, 1987), 3.

71 Universities in Ibadan, Nsukka, Ife, ABU, Lagos and Benin were regarded as first generation universities. Universities in Jos, Maiduguri, Sokoto, Kano, Illorin, Calabar and Port Harcourt were regarded as second-generation universities.

72 *View and Comments of the Federal Military Government on the Report of the Study*, 3.

73 Ibid., 13.

74 Theodore Idibiye Francis, Adetunji Akinyotu, and L.B. Kolawole, eds., *Mobilizing Nigeria's Education towards Technological Self-Reliance*, Proceedings of the 11th Annual Seminar of the Committee of Vice-Chancellors, the Federal University of Technology, Akure, 10–11 March 1988 (Akure: Hope Printers, 1988), 11.

75 Ibid., 11–12.

76 JAMB Raw Data, "Satisfaction of Global Demand for University Places in Each Discipline, 1978/79–1984/85," as *University Education: Its Standard and Relevance to the Nigerian Community*, Proceedings of a Joint Seminar organized by the CVC and NUC held at the Usman Danfodiyo University, Sokoto, 17–19 March 1986, ed. Mahdi Adamu (Zaria: M.I.S. Press, 1989), 75.

77 Ibid.

78 Festus Iyayi, "The Dimensions of Programme Rationalization in Nigerian Universities," in *University Education: Its Standard and Relevance to the Nigerian Community*, Proceedings of a Joint Seminar organized by the CVC and NUC held at the Usman Danfodiyo University, Sokoto, 17–19 March 1986, ed. Mahdi Adamu (Zaria: M.I.S. Press, 1989), 62.

79 B.I.C. Ijeomah, "Manpower Development for Science and Technology: The Crisis of Bureaucracy and technocratic Consciousness," in *Mobilizing Nigeria's Education Towards Technological Self-Reliance*, Proceedings of the 11th Annual Seminar of the Committee of Vice-Chancellors, the Federal University of Technology, Akure, 10–11 March 1988, ed. Theodore Idibiye Francis, Adetunji Akinyotu, and L.B. Kolawole (Akure: Hope Printers, 1988), 69.

80 Ibid.

81 Ibid., 67.

82 *The Commission's Recommendations to the Federal Government on the Report of the Committee on Demerging of Federal Universities of Technology and the Creation of Universities of Agriculture*, 6–7.

83 Ibid., 3.

84 Ibid.

85 Ibid.

86 The two states Babangida created were Akwa Ibom and Katsina states, bringing the total number of states to 21. Other states were Anambra, Bauchi, Bendel, Benue, Borno, Cross River, Gongola, Imo, Kaduna, Kano, Kwara, Lagos, Niger, Ogun, Ondo, Oyo, Plateau, Rivers, Sokoto, Abuja, the Federal Territory. Shortly afterwards, Akwa Ibom began to demand a university, which materialized in 1991.

87 Stephen D. Akangbou, "Funding of Higher Education" (paper presented at the seminar on Challenges of Higher Education in the 1990s held at the University of Lagos from 28 November to 1 December 1989).

88 An Address presented by Professor Adamu Nayaya Mohammed, Chairman, Committee of Vice-Chancellors, to the President General Ibrahim B. Babangida, during a Courtesy Call on the President by the Vice-Chancellors of Nigerian Universities, 4 July 1988.

89 Committee of Vice-Chancellors, *Comment by the Committee of Vice-Chancellors on the World Bank Draft report on Nigeria: Cost and Financing of Universities*, CVC Secretariat, Lagos, 6 July 1988, 1.

90 Policy-Based Loan, sometimes called 'Sector Adjustment Loans,' provides flexible support for institutional and policy changes on the sector or sub-sector level, through fast-disbursing funds.

91 During this period, emphasis was on federal universities. State universities suffered more. More research is needed to determine the level of underfunding of state universities.

92 See Federal Republic of Nigeria, *Federal Universities Development Sector Adjustment Credit* (IDA Credit 2139-UNI) (Abuja: National University Commission, 1996), 1.

93 The fund was not granted until 1990.

94 Prior to this project, the bank had a limited role in Nigeria's educational development. Three education projects amounting to US$91.3 million were approved in 1965, 1972, and 1973. Shortly thereafter, persistent differences between the government and the bank over the country's macro-economic policies led to a cessation of lending. See World Bank, *Implementation Completion Report, Nigeria: Federal Universities Development Sector Adjustment Credit*, no. 16639 (Washington, D.C.: World Bank, 1997), 2.

95 See World Bank, *Education Sector Working Paper* (Washington, D.C., 1974); World Bank, *Education Sector Working Paper* (Washington, D.C., 1980); Memorandum of the President of the World Bank on "Proposed Bank/IDA Policies in the field of education," October 1963, quoted in World Bank, *Education Sector Working Paper* (Washington, D.C., 1971); William S. Saint, *Universities in Africa: Strategies for Stabilization and Revitalization* (Washington, DC: World Bank, 1992). World Bank, *Education in Sub-Saharan Africa, Strategies for Adjustment, Revitalization and Expansion* (Washington, DC: World Bank, 1988).

96 Ebrima Sall, "Academic Freedom and the African Community of Scholars: The Challenges," *News from the Nordic Africa Institute* (2001) <www.nai.uu.se/newsfromnai/arkiv/2001/sall.html> (accessed 10 June 2005).

97 See I. Sadique, "The Image of the World Bank within Nigerian Universities." In *States or Markets? Neo-liberal Solutions in the Educational Policies of Sub-Saharan Africa. Proceedings from a seminar*, ed. B. Brock Utne (Oslo: Institute for Educational Research, 1995), 108–35.

98 The Communiqué for the 12th Committee of Vice-Chancellors' Annual Seminar held at the Federal University of Technology Minna, on 2–3 March 1989.

99 Ray Ekpu, "An Excursion of the Mind," *Newswatch*, 2 April 1990, 10.

100 Federal Republic of Nigeria, *Report of Presidential Committee on Brain Drain*, February 1989, vol. 1, 3. The departing brains were dissatisfied with the state of the national economy and the consequent devaluation of the naira, which effectively reduced the purchasing power of university staff members.

101 Ibid. These statistics cover two first-generation federal universities, two second-generation federal universities, two federal universities of technology, and one state university.

102 National Universities Commission, "Brain Drain in Nigerian Universities (1982/83–1992/93)," *Report of the Study Group Submitted to the World Bank Project Implementation Unit*, September, 1994, iv.

103 *African Concord*, 25 September 1989 4, no. 22, 2.

104 "Brain Drain in Nigerian Universities," 49. The quality of university education obtained under this circumstance was clearly questionable.

105 Federal Republic of Nigeria, *Higher Education in the 90s and Beyond: Report of the Commission on the Review of Higher Education in Nigeria* (The Gray Longe Commission) (Lagos: Government Printing Office, 1991), 34.

106 Ibid., 34 and 148.

107 See Sam Aluko, "Do We Need More Universities in Nigeria" (lecture delivered at the 1st Convocation of the Federal University of Technology Akure, 7 November 1987), 48.

108 Ibid.

109 Compiled from various records available in National Manpower Board, as reproduced in John Adeboye Adeyemo, "The Demand for Higher Education and Employment Opportunities in Nigeria," in *The Dilemma of Post-Colonial Universities*, ed. Yann Lebeau and Mobolaji Ogunsanya (Ibadan: IFRA, African Book Builders, 2000), 250.

110 Ibid.

111 Federal Republic of Nigeria, *Higher Education in the 90s and Beyond: Report of the Commission on the Review of Higher Education in Nigeria* (Lagos: Government Printing Office, 1991), 115.

112 *First National Rolling Plan*, 1990–92, 214.

113 Ibid.

114 Ibid., 219.

115 Ibid., 216.

116 See H.O. Danmole, ed., *Nigerian Universities and the Challenges of the Decade: 1990–1999*, Proceedings of the Thirteenth Annual Seminar of the Committee of Vice-Chancellors of Nigerian Universities, University of Ilorin, 12–13 March 1990 (Ilorin: University of Ilorin Press, 1990), 12.

117 Ibid.

7: Crisis of Nationhood: Funding Issues, Socio-Political Instability, and Private University Education, 1990–2000

1 *Newswatch*, 2 April 1990.

2 Joan M. Nelson, *Economic Crisis and Policy Choice: The Politics of Adjustment in the Third World* (Princeton, NJ: Princeton University Press, 1990).

3 See Ogechi Anyanwu, "Religious Conflict and Integration in a

Democratic Nigeria: The Peril and the Promise," *Journal of Nigerian Languages and Culture* 3 (May 2002): 70–76; and Jonah I. Onuoha and Pat Uche Okpoko, *Ethnic Nationalism and Democratic Consolidation: Perspectives from Nigeria and the United States of America* (Nsukka: Great AP Express, 2004).

4   Linus U.J. Thomas-Ogboji, *African News Weekly*, 26 May 1995, 6.

5   Sowaribi Tolofar, *Exploitation and Instability in Nigeria: The Orkar Coup in Perspective* (Lagos: Press Alliance Network, 2004).

6   "April 1990 Coup d'état Speech," http://www.dawodu.com/orkar.htm (accessed 1 August 2007).

7   Larry Diamond, Anthony Kirk-Greene, and Oyeleye Oyediran, eds., *Transition without End: Nigerian Politics and Civil Society under Babangida* (Boulder, CO: Lynne Rienner, 1997).

8   "April 1990 Coup d'état Speech."

9   Ibid.

10 Ibid.

11 Ibid.

12 Federal Republic of Nigeria, *Higher Education in the 90s and Beyond: Report of the Commission on the review of Higher education in Nigeria* (Lagos: Government Printing Office, 1991), 15–16.

13 Ibid.

14 See *Newswatch*, 8 October 1990, 58.

15 Ibid.

16 *Quality*, 7 March 1991, 33.

17 *Higher Education in the 90s and Beyond*, 153.

18 Ibid., 189.

19 Ibid.

20 Federal Republic of Nigeria, *Views and Comments of the Federal Government on the Report of the Commission on the Review of Higher Education in Nigeria* (Lagos: Federal Director of Printing, 1992), 44.

21 *The Economist*, 25 January 1997, 41.

22 World Bank, *World Development Report* (New York: Oxford University Press, 1991), 404.

23 Draft Committee of Vice-Chancellors paper to the Longe Commission on the Review of Higher Education in Nigeria, CVC Secretariat Lagos, 3 May 1991, 5.

24 *Higher Education in the 90s and Beyond*, 178.

25 Ibid.

26 Ibid., 175.

27 World Bank report, as cited in *Higher Education in the 90s and Beyond*, 115–16.

28 *Higher Education in the 90s and Beyond*, 116.

29 *The Guardian*, 26 October 1997, 14–19.

30 The states include Taraba State, Yobe State, Osun State, Kebbi State, Kogi State, Jigawa State, Enugu State, Delta State, Adamawa State, and Abia State.

31 Hanza Abdullahi, University Management in Nigeria: A Study of the rate of expansion in relation to the level of funding of the Nigerian university system, 1985–1995 (Master's thesis, Ahmadu Bello University, Zaria, 2000), 121–22.

32 *Views and Comments of the Federal Government on the Report of the Commission on the Review of Higher Education in Nigeria*, 23.

33 Ibid.

34 Emmanuel Alabi, *African Guardian*, 13 May 1991, 53.

35 President 1991 Budget Speech, cited in *Higher Education in the 90s and Beyond*, 120.

36 John Holman, "Inconsistencies' in State Funds," *Financial Times*, 16 March 1992, 14.

37 *The New York Times*, 2 December 1993, A3.

38 Munzali Jibril, "Nigerian Higher Education: Agenda for Reform" (Keynote Address at the CVC Seminar 2002), 9.

39 Babangida's regime was alleged to be the most corrupt in Nigeria. He was instrumental to the culture of "settlement," a slogan for bribery and corruption in Nigeria. His administration embezzled over $12.5 billion during the Gulf War from the oil 'windfall' money. See Diamond et al., *Transition without End*.

40 Kunle Amuwo, "Confronting the Crisis of the University in Africa-Nigerian Academics and their Many Struggles," *Occasional Paper Series* 3, no. 2 (Zimbabwe: African Association of Political Science, 1999), 22.

41 Federal Republic of Nigeria, *Report of the National Implementation Committee on the Report on Review of Higher Education in Nigeria*, vol. 1, Main Report, December 1993. The committee was chaired by Professor O.O. Akinkugbe. Other members included Dr. (Mrs.) A.S. Afolabi, Professor C.O. Njoku, Chief B. Kotun, Dr. P.T. Mirchaulum, Professor A. Akindoyeni, Dr. (Mrs.) H. Ali, Chief M.S.N. Mbajiorgu, Dr. G.C. Ezimora, Dr. N.A. Yakubu and Alhaji T.A. Abdulkadir.

42 Okwudiba Nnoli, "Broadening Public/Private Sector Partnership for Educational Development, The Education tax Fund (ETF) Perspective," *Education Today* (June 2003): 8

43 *University System News*, 9.

44 Ibid.

45 See *The Guardian*, 2 July 2000, 29.

46 Peter Okebukola, *Issues In Funding University Education in Nigeria*, NUC Monograph Series Vol.1 No 7, 2003, 8.

47 Idris A. Abdulkadir, "The Nigerian University System at the receiving end of national socio-political economic instability" (paper delivered at the Distinguished Annual Lecture of the National Institute of Strategic Studies, Kuru, Plateau,1993). See also *University System News* (National Universities Commission, Abuja, Nigeria) 3, no. 4 (December 1993): 8.

48 Kunle Amuwo, "Confronting the Crisis," 3.

49 Thomas Baunsgard, "Fiscal Policy in Nigeria: Any Role for Rules?" *IMF Working Paper WP/03/155*, The IMF, Washington, D.C., 2003, 23.

50 See National Centre for Economic Management and Administration (NCEMA), "Understanding Structural adjustment Programme in Nigeria," A draft report presented at the Workshop on Understanding Reform, New Delhi, India: 25–26 January 2004, 39.

51 Chinua Achebe, *The Trouble with Nigeria* (Enugu, Nigeria: Fourth Dimension Publishing, 1985), 3.

52 Abraham Oshoko, *June 12: The Struggle for Power in Nigeria* (Lagos, Nigeria: Farafina, 2006).

53 *Guardian*, 28 December 1995, 25.

54 "Economic Recovery Programme, 1996–1998: An Alternative to the Medium-Term Programme of the World Bank/IMF," http://www.dawodu.com/neic2.htm (accessed 4 July 2006).

55 *New Nigerian*, 4 September 1996, front page. See also Academic Staff Union of Universities: University of Lagos Branch; http://www.asuulag.org/ (accessed 4 July 2006).

56 Federal Republic of Nigeria, *Committee on the Future of Higher Education in Nigeria*, vol. 1, Main Report, June 1997, 1.

57 Ibid.

58 *BBC News*, 13 February 1998; http://news.bbc.co.uk/1/hi/despatches/56419.stm (accessed 4 July 2006).

59 Peter Okebukola, *The State of University Education in Nigeria*, NUC Monograph, 2002, 6.

60 *The Guardian*, "The Sorry State of the Universities," 26 October 1997, 15.

61 Ibid., 15.

62 Ibid., 14.

63 Ibid, 15.

64 Olusegun Agagu, "The Nigerian Universities: Reviving" (lecture to mark the 30th anniversary of the University of Ibadan Alumni Association, at the auditorium of the federal polytechnic, Ado-Ekiti, on Tuesday 11 November 2000).

65 *The Guardian*, 23 January 1998, 13.

66 Ibid.

67 Ibid.

68 *The Guardian*, 25 February 1998, 15.

69 *The Guardian*, 23 January 1998, 13.

70 Ibid.

71 Ibid.

72 See *The Guardian*, 25 February 1998, 15

73 Federal Republic of Nigeria, *Decree No. 19*, 9 February 1984. See also *National Universities Commission, Bulletin of the National Universities Commission* (Lagos: NUC, September 1984), 1. This decree declared as unlawful any attempt by "any person or group of persons to establish any private university or similar institution of higher learning in any part of the country." It also provided a penalty of more than three years' imprisonment for defaulters. *Decree No. 19*, 9 February 1984.

74 *Higher Education in the 90s and Beyond*, 180.

75 Ibid. The commission urged institutions to set up income-generating enterprises to encourage the spirit of self-reliance from the earliest stage.

76 Ibid., 50.

77 National Universities Commission, *University System News* 4, no. 1 (March 1994): 9.

78 See Kingsley Banya, "Are Private Universities the Solution to the Higher Education Crisis in Sub-Saharan Africa," *Higher Education Policy* 14, no. 2 (2001): 161–74.

79 National Universities Commission Report, http://www.nuc.edu.ng/ (accessed 4 July 2006). The proposed universities were Madonna University, Anambra State; Institute of Christian Studies, Gboko, Benue State; Educational Co-operative Society of Nigeria, Lagos; Northern Institute of Management and Technology, Kano; Prof. T.M. Yesufu; Adventist University of West Africa; and African University of Technology, Akwa Ibom State. Other applicants were Pan-African Homoeo Medical College; Catholic Institute of West Africa; Bell University, Badagry, Lagos; Rev. Gains M. Musa, ECWA Headquarters; John D. Eimunjeze Esq. for Solomon Asemota & Co., Abuja.

80 *Committee on the Future of Higher Education in Nigeria*, 147.

81 National Universities Commission, *State of Private Universities in Nigeria, Report of the 2003 Annual Monitoring and Quality Assurance of Private Universities in Nigeria*, 2003.

82 National Universities Commission, State of Private Universities in Nigeria: Report of the 2004 Annual Monitoring and Quality Assurance of Private Universities in Nigeria, 111.

83 Ibid., vi.

84 Ibid.

85 Editorial, *Punch*, 28 June 2006, 2.

86 Peter Okebukola, *The State of University Education in Nigeria* (Abuja: NUC Monograph, 2002), 6.

87 See Joint Admission and Matriculation Board, *Application and Admissions Statistics, 1996–2000*; http://www.jambng.com/app_ume2000.php (accessed 4 July 2006).

88 Y. Lebeau, "Aspects of the Instrumentalization of the University in Nigeria: Student Experiences and Current Significance of the Certificate," in *The Dilemma of Postcolonial Universities*, ed. Y. Lebeau and M. Ogunsanya (Ibadan: IFRA/ABB, 2000).

89 Task Force on Higher Education and Society, *Higher Education in Developing Countries: Peril and Promise* (Washington, D.C.: World Bank, 2000), 39. See also Kingsley Banya, "Are Private Universities the Solution?"

90 Ibid.

91 *Higher Education in Developing Countries*, 34

92 Ibid.

93 Ibid.

94 World Bank, *Constructing Knowledge Societies: New Challenges for Tertiary Education* (Washington, DC: World Bank, 2002), 76.

95 See Emmanuel Edukugho, "ASUU Strike, Crisis without End," *Vanguard*, 4 May 2006; http://www.vanguardngr.com/section/education.html (4 May 2006).

96 Ibid.

97 Ibid.

98 The head of the Government Negotiating Team was Prof. Ayo Banjo, pro-chancellor of the University of Port Harcourt with fourteen others, the majority of whom were pro-chancellors and vice-chancellors of universities. There were ten advisers to the government team. Dr. Oladipo Fashina, ASUU's national president, led ASUU's negotiating team with twenty-three others drawn from the various universities across the country.

99 Academic Staff Union of Universities: University of Lagos Branch; http://www.asuulag.org/ (accessed 4 July 2006).

100 Edukugho, "ASUU Strike."

101 Olusegun Obasanjo, "Address by the President," in *University Education, Democracy and Development in Nigeria, The Proceedings of the 18th Annual Seminar of the Committee of Vice-Chancellors of Nigerian Universities, 13–17 November 2000*, ed. J.D. Okoh (Port Harcourt: Committee of Vice-Chancellors, 2000), 33.

102 "Coommunique," in *University Education, Democracy and Development in Nigeria, The Proceedings of the 18th Annual Seminar of the Committee of Vice-Chancellors of Nigerian Universities, 13–17 November 2000*, ed. J.D. Okoh (Port Harcourt: Committee of Vice-Chancellors, 2000), 184.

103 Julius A. Okojie, "Education and Human Capital Development in Nation Building" (paper delivered by Executive Secretary National Universities Commission at the Northern Nigeria Economic and Investment Summit, 7 October 2008).

Conclusion

1 *Sessional Paper on an Education Policy presented to the Western House of Assembly* (Lagos, Government Printer, July 1952), 5.

2 Julius A. Okojie, "Education and Human Capital Development in Nation Building" (paper Presented at

the Northern Nigeria Economic and Investment Summit, 7 October 2008), 1.

3   See Federation of Nigeria, *Educational Development, 1961–1970, Sessional Paper No. 3 of 1961* (Lagos: Federal Government Printer, 1961), 7.

4   Ibid.

5   Federal Republic of Nigeria, *Investment in Education: The Report of the Commission on Post-School Certificate and Higher Education* (Lagos: Federal Ministry of Education, 1960), 22.

6   Federal Republic of Nigeria, *Higher Education in the 90s and Beyond: Report of the Commission on the Review of Higher Education in Nigeria* (Lagos: Government Printing Office, 1991), 34.

7   Eric Ashby, *Universities: British, Indian, African: A Study in the Ecology of Higher Education* (Cambridge, MA: Harvard University Press, 1966), 275–76.

8   *Daily Times*, 16 January 1969, front page.

9   Minutes of Special Meeting of the Committee of Vice-Chancellors with the Head of State at Dodan Barracks on Saturday, 18 September 1976, 2–3.

10 Chinua Achebe, *The Education of a British-Protected Child: Essays* (New York: Alfred A. Knopf, 2009), 45.

11 Peter Okebukola, *The State of University Education in Nigeria* (Abuja: NUC Monograph, 2002), 6.

12 Olusegun Agagu, "The Nigerian Universities: Reviving" (lecture to mark the 30th anniversary of the university of Ibadan Alumni Association, Federal Polytechnic, Ado-Ekiti, 11 November 2000).

13 Megan Lindow, "As Degree Mills Proliferate, Nigeria Struggle to Fix a Tattered University System," *Chronicle of Higher Education*, 6 November 2009, A24.

14 Olusegun Obasanjo, "Address by the President," in *University Education, Democracy and Development in Nigeria, The Proceedings of the 18th Annual Seminar of the Committee of Vice-Chancellors of Nigerian Universities, 13–17 November 2000*, ed. J.D. Okoh (Port Harcourt: Committee of Vice-Chancellors, 2000), 33.

15 Okojie, "Education and Human Capital Development in Nation Building,"5.

16 Ibid.

17 Lindow, "As Degree Mills Proliferate," A24.

18 Dan Agbese, "My Naivety and I," *Newswatch*, 22 November 2009.

19 Jonathan Fanton, "Remarks about Strengthening Higher Education in Nigeria," May 1, 2001; http://www.macfound.org/site/c.lkLXJ8MQKrH/b.4293517/apps/s/content.asp?ct=1270225 (accessed 4 July 2006).

20 Editorial, *The Guardian*, 17 November 2009.

21 "Nigeria: Private Universities – Challenges of Qualitative Education," *Daily Champion*, 4 November 2009.

22 Peter Okebukola, "Partly Cloudy University Horizon: Promise of Sunshine by Private Providers" (speech delivered at the Foundation Day Lecture, Bells University of Technology, Ota, 19 November 2005), 14.

23 "Imo orders IMSU VC to refund N55m," *Vanguard*, 15 July 2009. There may be other 'Okonkwos' out there that need to be uncovered. More research is needed to assess the role university administrators played in (mis)managing funds allocated to their universities and thus compromising sustainable university expansion.

24 Ibid.

25 Ray Ekpu, "Gone to the Dogs," *Newswatch*, 3 May 2004.

Bibliography

Archival Manuscripts

Carnegie Corporation of New York Records in Columbia University Rare Book and Manuscript Library
CCNY, I.D. 1: Policy and Program, 1947–1955.
CCNY, 111 A, 849.7: Conference on Tropical African Countries.
CCNY, 111 A, 634: Inter-University Council for Higher Education.
CCNY, 111 A, 746.2: Nigeria, Federal Government Post-Secondary Requirements.
CCNY, 111 A, 634.2: Anglo-American Conference.
CCNY, I.E. 17: Alan Pifer.

National Archives, Ibadan
NAI: CSO/26: "A Special List of Records on the Subject of Education."
NAI: CFEO, 638/S. 4, 1957: Nigerianization Policy.
NAI: PSO, 4/3.3/C 130, 1960: Nigerianization Policy.

Public Records Office, London
PRO: CO 583, 35: *Report on Education Department, Northern Nigeria*, 1915.
PRO, CO 554/2029: Commission on Post-Secondary and Higher Education.

National Archives Kaduna (NAK)

NAK, CDN C. 16: Minutes of Meetings of the JCC, 1960–1961.

National Universities Commission

HQ FILE REF LA/2501/138: Minutes of Meetings.

Minutes of Meetings, 30 March to 4 April 1987.

Minutes of Special Meeting of the Committee of Vice-Chancellors with the Head of State at Dodan Barracks on Saturday, 18 September 1976.

Communiqué of the NUC/CVC/British Council Seminar, 12 November 1987.

Periodicals and Newspapers

African Concord, September 1989.
African Guardian, May 1991.
African News Weekly, 26 May 1995.
Chronicle of Higher Education, November 2009.
Daily Champion, 4 November 2009.
Daily Service, October 1944–February 17, 1960.
Daily Times, August 1954–August 1957, May 1959, January–November 1960, January 1969, August 1972, March 1975, January–April 1978, January 1980, November–December 1982, January–December 1984, January 1985.
Democrat Weekly, April 1984.
Economist, January 1997.
Financial Times (London), 16 August 1983, 25 and 26 February 1985, March 1992;
Fraternité (Abidjan), February 1963.
Guardian, December 1995–October 1997, January–February 1998, July 2000, November 2009.
International Herald Tribune, 12 March 1985.
National Champion, February–July 1983, March 1984.
National Concord, March 1983–March 1984.
New Nigerian, February 1978–November 1979, December 1984, September 1996.
Newswatch, October 1986, April 1987, January 1988, April–October 1990, May 2004, November 2009.
New York Times, December 1993.

Nigerian Tribune, May 1978–September 1999.
Post Express, March 2000.
Providence Journal, October 1999.
Punch, April 1978, June 2006.
Quality, March 1991.
Sunday Times, March 1975, April 1978, February 1986.
Sunday Tribune, February 1986.
Vanguard, May 2006, July 2009.
Voice of Ethiopia, December 1961.
West Africa, October 1960, October 1978–April 1979, March 1981–September 1982.
West African Pilot, July 1949–October 1953.

Published Official Sources

Ahmad, Ehtisham, and Raju Singh. "Political Economy of Oil-Revenue Sharing in a Developing Country: Illustrations from Nigeria." IMF Working Paper, No. 03/16. Washington, D.C.: IMF, 2003.

Baunsgard, Thomas. "Fiscal Policy in Nigeria: Any Role for Rules?" *IMF Working Paper, No 3/155*. Washington, D.C.: IMF, 2003.

Colonial Office. *Report of the Commission on Higher Education in West Africa*, Cmd 6655. London: HM Stationery Office, 1945.

———. *Report on Higher Education in the Colonies*, Cmd 6647. London: HMSO, 1945.

Committee of Vice Chancellors of Nigerian Universities. *Sessional Report, 1967/68 & 1968/69*. Lagos: Federal Ministry of Information, 1969.

Cook, J.W., John A. Hannah, and Glen L. Taggart. *University of Nigeria, Eastern Regional Official Document No. 4 of 1958*. Enugu: Government Printer, 1958.

The Development of Higher Education in Africa: Report of the Conference on the Development of Higher Education in Africa, Tananarive, 3–12 September 1962. Paris: UNESCO, 1963.

Eastern House of Assembly Debates. Enugu: Government Printer, 1955.

Education Sector Analysis. *Historical Background on the Development of Education in Nigeria*. Abuja: Education Sector Analysis, 2003.

Federal Government of Nigeria. *Statistics of Education in Nigeria*. Lagos: Ministry of Education, 1992.

Federal Ministry of Education. *Digest of Statistics 1959*. Lagos: Federal Ministry of Information, 1959.

———. *Report of the Panel on Alternative Sources of Funding Education*. Lagos: Federal Ministry of Information, 1981.

———. *Statistics of Education in Nigeria, 1980–1984*. Lagos: Federal Ministry of Information, 1984.

Federal Republic of Nigeria. *Annual Report of National Manpower Board 1ˢᵗ December 1962–31ˢᵗ March 1964*. Lagos: Federal Ministry of Information, 1965.

———. *Blue Print for Post –War Reconstruction*. Lagos: Federal Ministry of Information, 1967.

———. *Committee on the Future of Higher Education in Nigeria*, vol. 1, Main Report, June 1997.

———. *The Constitution of the Federal Republic of Nigeria*. Lagos: Department of Information, 1979.

———. *Decision of the Government of the Federal Republic of Nigeria on the Report of the National Universities Commission Educational Development*, Sessional Paper No. 4. Lagos: Federal Ministry of Information, 1964.

———. *Decree No. 1*, 1966.

———. *Decree No. 1*, 15 January 1974.

———. *Decree No. 2*, 13 February 1978.

———. *Decree No. 14*, 1967.

———. *Decree No. 19*, 9 February 1984.

———. *Dina Committee Report*. Lagos: Federal Ministry of Information, 1969.

———. *Federal Universities Development Sector Adjustment Credit*. IDA Credit 2139-UNI. Abuja: National University Commission, 1996.

———. *Fifth National Development Plan 1986–1991*. Lagos: Ministry of Information, 1991.

———. *First National Development Plan*. Lagos: Federal Ministry of Education, 1962.

———. *First National Rolling Plan, 1990–92*. Lagos: Federal Ministry of Budget and Planning, 1990.

———. *Fourth National Development Plan 1981–85*, vol. 1. Lagos: National Planning Office, Federal Ministry of National Planning, January 1981.

———. *Higher Education in the 90s and Beyond: Report of the Commission on the Review of Higher Education in Nigeria*. Lagos: Government Printing Office, 1991.

———. *Investment in Education: The Report of the Commission on Post-School Certificate and Higher Education*. [*Ashby Commission Report*]. Lagos: Federal Ministry of Education, 1960.

———. *Memoranda Submitted by the Delegation to the Ad-Hoc Conference on Constitutional Proposals for Nigeria*. Lagos: National Nigerian Press, 1966.

———. *National Policy on Education*. Lagos: Government Press, 1977.

———. *National Policy on Education. Revised*. Lagos: Federal Government Press, 1981.

———. *Report of Presidential Committee on Brain Drain*, vol. 1. February 1989.

———. *Report of the National Implementation Committee on the Report on Review of Higher Education in Nigeria*. vol. 1, Main Report, December 1993.

———. *Report of the Seminar on a National Policy on Education*. Lagos: Government Press, 1973.

———. *Report of the Study Group on Funding Education*. Lagos: Federal Government Press, 1984.

———. *Report on the Study of Higher Education Curricula and Development in Nigeria*. Lagos: NERC Press, 1984.

———. *Second National Development Plan 1970–1974: Programme of Post-War Reconstruction and Development*. Lagos: Ministry of Information, 1970.

———. *Third National Development Plan 1975–1980*. Lagos: Federal Ministry of Economic Development and Reconstruction, Central Planning Office, 1975.

———. *University Development in Nigeria: Report of the National Universities Commission*. Lagos: Federal Ministry of Information, 1963.

———. *View and Comments of the Federal Military Government on the Report of the Study Group of Higher Education Curricula and Development in Nigeria*. Lagos: Federal Government Printer, 1987.

———. *Views and Comments of the Federal Government on the Report of the Commission on the Review of Higher Education in Nigeria*. Lagos: Federal Director of Printing, 1992.

Federation of Nigeria. *Educational Development, 1961–1970, Sessional Paper No. 3 of 1961*. Lagos: Federal Government Printer, 1961.

Final Report of the Parliamentary Committee on the Nigerianization of the Federal Public Service, 1959.

Great Britain, Committee on Higher Education. *Higher Education: Report of the Committee Appointed by the Prime Minister under the Chairmanship of Lord Robbins, 1961–63*. London: HMSO, 1963.

Higher Education in Developing Countries: Perils and Promise: *The International Bank for Reconstruction and Development*. Washington, D.C.: World Bank, 2000.

International Bank for Reconstruction and Development. *The Economic Development of Nigeria*. Baltimore: Johns Hopkins University Press, 1955.

Inter-University Council. "Estimates Category B: West Africa 1973/74." IUC/WAWG 2/72. Inter-University Council files, mimeographed, 1974.

———. "Report of a Visit to Nigerian Universities." Inter-University Council files, mimeographed, 1970.

———. *Report of Visitation to University College Ibadan*. Ibadan: Ibadan University Press, 1952.

———. "Visit to New Nigerian Universities by D.P. Saville." Report no. 13 of 1977, Inter-University Council files, mimeographed, 1977.

Manpower Study No. 3: A Study of Nigeria's Professional Manpower in Selected Occupation 1964. Lagos: Nigerian National Press, 1964.

Ministry of Education. *Annual Report 1960*. Enugu: Government Printer, 1963.

National Universities Commission. *Annual Report, July 1975–June 1977*. Lagos: NUC, 1977.

———. *Annual Report, July 1977–June 1978*. Lagos: NUC, 1978.

———. *Annual Review of Nigerian Universities: Academic Year 1964–65*. Lagos: Federal Ministry of Information, 1966.

———. *Annual Review of Nigerian Universities: Academic Year 1967–68*. Lagos: Federal Ministry of Information, 1968.

———. "Brain Drain in Nigerian Universities (1982/83–1992/93)." *Report of the Study Group Submitted to the World Bank Project Implementation Unit*, September, 1994.

———. *Bulletin of the National Universities Commission* 1, no. 3. Lagos: NUC, July–September, 1977.

———. *Bulletin of the National Universities Commission*, 11, No. 2. Lagos: NUC, July–September, 1980.

———. *Bulletin of the National Universities Commission*, No. 7. Lagos: NUC, July–September, 1978.

———. *Bulletin of the National Universities Commission*, No. 8. Lagos: NUC, October–December, 1978.

———. *Bulletin of the National Universities Commission*, September Lagos: NUC, 1984.

———. *The Commission's Recommendations to the Federal Government on the Report of the Committee on Demerging of Federal Universities of Technology and the Creation of Universities of Agriculture*. Lagos: National Universities Commission, July 1987.

———. *Executive Perspectives of the Development of Nigerian Universities*. Speeches at the Commissioning of NUC Secretariat and Thirtieth Anniversary of the Commission, 17 November 1992. Abuja: National Universities Commission, 1992.

———. *Report of the Academic Planning Group*. Lagos: NUC, 1976.

———. *Seminar on the Establishment of New University of Technology December 8–11, 1980 Preliminary Report*. Lagos: National Universities Commission, 1981.

———. *State of Private Universities in Nigeria, Report of the 2003 Annual Monitoring and Quality Assurance of Private Universities in Nigeria*, 2003.

———. *State of Private Universities in Nigeria: Report of the 2004 Annual Monitoring and Quality Assurance of Private Universities in Nigeria*, 2004.

———. *Total Enrolment in Nigerian Universities 1968/69*. Lagos: National Universities Commission, July 1969.

———. *University System News* 6, No. 1, March 1996.

———. *University System News, A Quarterly Publication of the National Universities Commission*. Abuja, Nigeria, 4, No. 1, March 1994.

Nigeria. *Annual Report of the Development of Education*, 1/4/51–31/3/52. Lagos: Government Printer, 1952.

———. *Annual Reports of Education*, 1952–1955. Lagos: Government Printer, 1955.

———. *Annual Report of the Nigerianization Officer*, 1957. Lagos: Government Printer, 1958.

———. *The Evolution and Management of Nigeria's External Debt: The Way Forward*. Lagos: Federal Ministry of Finance, 1997.

———. *A Record of Events and Developments*. Lagos: Times Press, 1981.

Nigeria Year Book 1981.

Nigerian National Petroleum Corporation (NNPC). *Annual Statistical Bulletin*, 1994.

Northern Region of Nigeria: Public Service Commission. *Report of the Public Service Commission for the Period 1st November 1954 to 31 December 1957*. Kaduna, 1958.

Phillipson, Sydney, and S.O. Adebo. *The Nigerianization of the Civil Service, Review of Policy and Machinery*. Lagos, 1954.

Proposed University of Nigeria. Pamphlet published by the Eastern Information Service, Enugu, 1954.

Report by Mr. L.R. Kay & Mr. W.H. Pettipiere on Central Admissions Procedure in Nigerian Universities. P.&D.C. Paper No. 74/74, Com./FO/van, 31/5/75.

Report of the Commission on the Sixth Form and University Entry. Lagos: National Universities Commission, 1968.

Report of International Commission on Education for the Twenty-first Century, Learning: The Treasure Within. Paris: UNESCO, 1996.

Report of the National Committee on University Entrance. Lagos, Federal Ministry of Education, February 1977.

Report of the UNESCO Advisory Commission for the Establishment of the University of Lagos. Paris: UNESCO, 1961.

Report on the Educational System in Eastern Nigeria, No. 19. Enugu: Government Printer, 1962.

Report on University Finances. Lagos: National Universities Commission, 1978.

Sessional Paper on an Education Policy Presented to the Western House of Assembly. July 1952.

Statistics of Education in Nigeria for the Years 1961–1970. Lagos: Ministry of Information, 1973.

Task Force on Higher Education and Society. *Higher Education in Developing Countries: Peril and Promise*. Washington, D.C.: World Bank, 2000.

UNIBEN. *First Congregation, November 23, 1974*. Benin: Uniben Press, 1974.

University of Nigeria Calendar, 1961–62. Nsukka: Printed under the direction of Michigan State University, 1961.

University of Nigeria Nsukka at 40: 40th Anniversary Celebrations. Enugu: University of Nigeria Press, 2001

University of Northern Nigeria. *Report of the Inter-University Council Delegation*. London: London University Press, 1961.

Western Region of Nigeria: Triennial Report on Education 1/4/55–31/3/58. Sessional Paper No. 11. Ibadan: Government Printer, 1959.

———. *Policy on the Establishment of a University in Western Nigeria*. Ibadan: Government Printer, 1960.

White Paper on the Establishment of a University in Western Nigeria. Western Nigeria Legislature Sessional Paper No. 12 of 1960. Ibadan: Government Printer, 1960.

World University Service. *Economic Factors Affecting Access to the University: Studies on the University Scene in 35 Countries*. Geneva: World University Service, 1961.

World Bank. *Accelerating Catch-up: Tertiary Education for Growth in Sub-Saharan Africa*. Washington, D.C.: World Bank, 2009.

———. *The African Capacity Building Initiative: Towards Improved Policy Analysis and Development*. Washington, D.C.: World Bank, 1991.

———. *Constructing Knowledge Societies: New Challenges for Tertiary Education*. Washington, D.C.: World Bank, 2002.

———. *Education in Sub-Saharan Africa, Strategies for Adjustment, Revitalization and Expansion*. Washington, D.C.: World Bank, 1988.

———. *Education Sector Policy Paper*. Washington, D.C.: World Bank, 1985.

———. *Education Sector Working Paper*. Washington, D.C.: World Bank, 1974.

———. *Education Sector Working Paper*. Washington, D.C.: World Bank, 1980.

———. *Higher Education in Developing Countries: Peril and Promise*. Washington, D.C.: World Bank, 2000.

———. *Implementation Completion Report, Nigeria: Federal Universities Development Sector Adjustment Credit*, no. 16639. Washington, D.C.: World Bank, 1997.

———. *World Bank. Nigeria: Costs and Financing of Universities, Report No. 6920-UNI*. Washington, D.C.: The World Bank, 1988.

———. *World Development Report*. New York: Oxford University Press, 1991.

Conference Proceedings, Speeches, and Addresses

Abdulkadir, Idris A. "National Universities Crisis." Paper presented at the Post Graduate Institute of Medical Research and Training, Monthly Guest Lecture, College of Medicine, University of Ibadan, Ibadan 16 September 1987.

———. "The Nigerian University System at the Receiving End of National Socio-Political Economic Instability." Paper delivered at the Distinguished Annual Lecture of the National Institute of Strategic Studies, Kuru, Plateau, 1993.

———. Seminar Opening Remarks delivered at NUC/CVC/BC Seminar at Kongo Conference Hotel, ABU, Zaria, 9–10 November 1987.

Abdulrahman, M.S. "Admission Policy and Procedures." Paper presented at the University of Lagos at the Seminar on the Challenges of Higher Education in the 1990s, 30 November 1989.

Adamu, Mahdi, ed. *University Education: Its Standard and Relevance to the Nigerian Community*. Proceedings of a Joint Seminar organized by the CVC and NUC held at the Usman Danfodiyo University, Sokoto, 17–19 March 1986. Zaria: M.I.S. Press, 1989.

Address by his Excellency General Yakubu Gowon, on the Occasion of the Tenth Anniversary of Ahmadu Bello University, Zaria on Saturday, 2 December 1972.

Address by his Excellency Major-General Yakubu Gowon, Head of the Federal Military Government and Visitor of the University during the 21st Anniversary of the University of Ibadan, July 1970.

Address by President Babangida on the Occasion of the Silver Jubilee Celebration and Twenty-first Convocation of the University of Nigeria, at Nsukka on Saturday, 6 December 1986. Enugu: University of Nigeria Press, 1987.

Address by President Shehu Shagari on Budget Proposals to a Joint session of the National Assembly on Monday, 24 November 1980.

Address by President Shehu Shagari, on the launching of the Fourth National Development Plan 1981–1985, 12 January 1981.

Address by Professor M.J.C. Echeruo, Vice-Chancellor, Imo State University, on the Third Matriculation Ceremony, 11 February 1984.

Address by the Hon. Minister of Economic Development to the Third Meeting of the National Manpower Board, 4 July 1963 in *Annual Report of National Manpower Board*.

Address by the Principal, Dr. K.O. Dike, to Congregation in Trenchard Hall on Foundation Day of the University of Ibadan, 17 November 1962.

Address by the Vice-Chancellor to Congregation on Foundation Day of the University of Ibadan, 19 November 1964.

Address delivered at the Congregation for the conferment of degrees by the Vice-Chancellor, Professor T.M. Yesufu, 26 February 1977.

Address delivered by the President, Ibrahim Babangida, to selected members of the academic community on 16 November 1985.

Address presented by Professor Adamu Nayaya Mohammed, Chairman, Committee of Vice-Chancellors, to the President General Ibrahim B. Babangida, During a Courtesy Call on the President by the Vice-Chancellors of Nigerian Universities, 4 July 1988.

Agagu, Olusegun. "The Nigerian Universities: Reviving." Lecture to mark the 30th Anniversary of the University of Ibadan Alumni Association, at the auditorium of the federal polytechnic, Ado-Ekiti, on Saturday, 11 November 2000.

Ajayi, J.F. "The American Factor in the Development of Higher Education in Africa." *James Smoot Coleman Memorial Papers Series*, African Studies Center, University of California at Los Angeles, 1988.

Ajayi, J.F. Ade. "Matriculation Address." *Mimeo*. University of Lagos, 1973.

———. "Matriculation Address." *Mimeo*. University of Lagos, 1974.

———. "Vice Chancellor's Matriculation Address." *Mimeo*. University of Lagos, November 13, 1976.

Akangbou, Stephen D. "Funding of Higher Education." Paper presented at the seminar on Challenges of Higher Education in the 1990s, the University of Lagos, 28 November to 1 December 1989.

Aliyu, Yahaya. Keynote address at the opening session of the British Council/NUC Third Workshop for Senior University Administrators, University of Jos, 1985.

Aluko, Sam. "Better Career in the Nigerian University System." Memorandum submitted to the Presidential Commission on Salaries and Conditions of Service of the University, Maiduguri, 21 February 1981.

———. "Do We Need More Universities in Nigeria." Lecture delivered at the 1st Convocation of the Federal University of Technology Akure, 7 November 1987.

———. "Resources for Higher Education, Number, Cost, and Common Sense." Guest of Honour's Address at the Opening Ceremony of the NUC/CVC/British Council Seminar on the Management of University Resources, Ahmadu Bello University, Zaria, 9 November 1987.

Angulu, M.S. Press Release, Joint Admission and Matriculation Board: Admission into Universities 1978/79 Session. March 1979.

Anyanwu, Ogechi. "Pointing the Way Forward: Alan Pifer and Higher Education in Colonial Nigeria." Paper presented at the Southern Interdisciplinary Roundtable on African Studies (SIRAS), Kentucky State University, Frankfort, April 3–5, 2009.

Azikiwe, Nnamdi. "Hope to a Frustrated People." An address made by Dr. Nnamdi Azikiwe, Chairman of the Provincial Council of the University of Nigeria, at the Inaugural Meeting of the Council, 3 March 1960.

Baikie, Adamu, ed. *Higher Education and Development in the Context of the Nigerian Constitution*. Proceedings of the Fifth Annual Seminar of the Committee of Vice-Chancellors of Nigerian Universities, University of Benin, Benin City, 26–27 February 1982. Benin: Office of the Vice-Chancellor, 1982.

Balewa, Abubakar Tafawa. "Inaugural Address Delivered on the Occasion of His Installation as the First Chancellor of the University of Ibadan." February 1964.

Biobaku, S.O. Comment by the Committee of Vice-Chancellors on the World Bank Draft Report on Nigeria: Cost and Financing of Universities, CVC Secretariat, Lagos, 6 July 1988.

———. Communiqué of the NUC/CVC/British Council Seminar, 12 November 1987.

———. Confidential, Committee of Vice-Chancellors: Rationalization of Courses and Programs of the Universities (n.d.).

———. Draft Committee of Vice-Chancellors Paper to the Longe Commission on the Review of Higher Education in Nigeria, CVC Secretariat Lagos, 3 May 1991.

———. The Communiqué for the 12th Committee of Vice-Chancellors' Annual Seminar held at the Federal University of Technology, Minna, 2–3 March 1989.

———. "The Purpose of University Education." Paper presented at the National Curriculum Conference held in Lagos, 8–12 September 1969.

Committee of Vice-Chancellors. Office of the Secretary, Letter to All Vice-Chancellors of Nigerian Universities, 20 February 1986.

Danmole, H.O, ed. *Nigerian Universities and the Challenges of the Decade: 1990–1999*. Proceedings of the Thirteenth Annual Seminar of the Committee of Vice-Chancellors of Nigerian Universities, University of Ilorin, 12–13 March 1990. Ilorin: University of Illorin Press, 1990.

Francis, Theodore Idibiye, Adetunji Akinyotu, and L.B. Kolawole, eds. *Mobilizing Nigeria's Education towards Technological Self-Reliance*. Proceedings of the 11th Annual Seminar of the Committee of Vice-Chancellors, the Federal University of Technology, Akure, 10–11 March 1988. Akure: Hope Printers, 1988.

Munzali, Jibril. "Nigerian Higher Education: Agenda for Reform." Keynote Address at the CVC Seminar 2002.

National Centre for Economic Management and Administration (NCEMA). "Understanding Structural Adjustment Programme in Nigeria." A draft report presented at the Workshop on Understanding Reform, New Delhi, India: 25–26 January 2004.

Okoh, J.D. *University Education, Democracy and Development in Nigeria*. Proceedings of the 18th Annual Seminar of the Committee of Vice-Chancellors of Nigerian Universities, 13–17 November 2000. Port Harcourt: Committee of Vice-Chancellors, 2000.

Okojie, Julius A. "Education and Human Capital Development in Nation Building." Paper delivered by Executive Secretary National Universities Commission at the Northern Nigeria Economic and Investment Summit, 7 October 2008.

Olusanya, G.O. "If Wishes Were Horses …" Lecture delivered at University of Ilorin, Nigeria, 6 November 1980.

Oluwasanmi, H.A. "The Preservation of Intellectual Freedom and Cultural Integrity." Paper presented at a symposium on *The Role of the University in a Post-Colonial World*, Duke University, Durham, North Carolina, 11–13 April 1975.

Osuntokun, Akinjide, ed. *Nigeria: The Universities, the Nation and the Economic Recession*. Proceedings of the 1983 Annual Seminar of the Committee of Vice-Chancellors of Nigerian Universities, the University of Maiduguri, 24–26 February 1983. Ibadan: Ibadan University Press, 1987.

"Our Educational Legacy." Olusegun Obasanjo's Speech on the convocation ceremony of the University of Ibadan on 17 November 1976.

Federal Government of Nigeria, Proceedings of the General Conference on Review of the Constitution, January 1950. Lagos: Government Printer, 1950.

Pifer, Alan. "American Interest in Africa." Paper presented to the Philosophical Society, University College, Ibadan, 16 November 1958.

Salim, Bello A. "Admission Crisis in the Nigerian University System: The Way Forward." Convocation Lecture delivered on the occasion of the 22nd Convocation Ceremony of the University of Ilorin, Ilorin, Nigeria, Thursday, 22 April 2004.

———. "Problems of Assessment and Selection into Tertiary Institutions in Nigeria." Paper presented by the Registrar/Chief Executive Joint Admissions and Matriculation Board (JAMB), Nigeria, at the 21st Annual Conference of AEAA held at Cape Town, South Africa, 25–29 August 2003.

Shettima, Kole Ahmed. "Nigeria's University Education in the 21st Century." Paper delivered at the Distinguished Lecture of the University of Benin November 4, 2005.

Speech delivered by Yakubu Gowon at the Inauguration of the National Universities Commission, 10 July 1975.

Text of the First Nation-Wide Broadcast by the President, Alhaji Shehu Shagari, on Monday, 1 October 1979. Lagos: Federal Ministry of Information, 1979.

Uche, Chibuike U., and Ogbonnaya C. Uche. "Oil and the Politics of Revenue Allocation in Nigeria." ASC Working Paper 54, African Studies Centre, The Netherlands, 2004.

Theses and Monographs

Abdullahi, Hanza. "University Management in Nigeria: A Study of the Rate of Expansion in Relation to the Level of Funding of the Nigerian University System, 1985–1995." Master's thesis: Ahmadu Bello University, Zaria, 2000.

Ajayi, T., and Alani, R.A. *A Study on Cost Recovery in Nigerian University Education: Issues of Quality, Access and Equity.* Final Report. Accra: Association of African Universities, 1996.

Amuwo, Kunle. "Confronting the Crisis of the University in Africa-Nigerian Academics and their Many Struggles." *Occasional Paper Series*, 3, no. 2. Zimbabwe: African Association of Political Science, 1999.

Anyanwu, Ogechi. "Indigenous Contractors and Nigeria's Economic Development, 1970–1992: A Case Study of Chief T.I. Ozoemenam's Construction Company." BA thesis: Abia State University, Uturu, Nigeria, 1994.

Callaway, A. and A. Musone. *Financing of Education in Nigeria.* Paris: UNESCO, International Institute for Educational Planning, 1968.

Fafunwa, Aliu *Babatunde.* "The Growth and Development of Nigerian Universities." *Overseas Liaison Commission, American Council on Education* no. 4 (April 1974):1-41.

Godonoo, Prosper. "Educational Policy Making in Nigeria: A Case Study of the Impact of Foreign Funding on Nigerian Universities." PhD dissertation, University of California, Los Angeles, 1994.

Moser, Gary, Scott Rogers, and Reinhold van Til. *Nigeria: Experience with Structural Adjustment.* Washington, D.C.: IMF, 1997.

Obadan, M.I. "Withered Structural Adjustment in Nigeria." *NCEMA Monograph Series No. 3.* Ibadan: National Centre for Economic Management and Administration (NCEMA), 1993.

Obasogie, Aimufua Osa. "Universal Primary Education in Nigeria: Its Origin, Current Status and Prospect for Success." PhD dissertation, University of Cincinnati, 1980.

Okebukola, Peter. *Issues in Funding University Education in Nigeria*, NUC Monograph Series 1, no. 7, 2003.

———. "Partly Cloudy University Horizon: Promise of Sunshine by Private Providers." Speech delivered at the Foundation Day Lecture, Bells University of Technology, Ota, 19 November 2005.

———. *The State of University Education in Nigeria*. Abuja: NUC Monograph, 2002.

Rhodes, Barbara Anthony. "The Genesis of the 1959 Ashby Commission Report on Education in Nigeria." PhD dissertation, University of Southern California, 1973.

Saint, William S. *Universities in Africa: Strategies for Stabilization and Revitalization*. Washington, D.C.: World Bank, 1992.

Trow, Martin. *Problems in the Transition from Elite to Mass Higher Education*. Berkeley, CA: Carnegie Commission on Higher Education, 1973.

Books

Abdulla, Adamu. *Reform and Adaptation in Nigerian University Curricula. 1960–1992*. Lewiston, NY: Edwin Mellen Press, 1994.

Abernethy, David. *The Political Dilemma of Popular Education: An African Case*. Stanford, CA: Stanford University Press, 1969.

Achebe, Chinua. *The Education of a British-Protected Child: Essays*. New York: Alfred A. Knopf, 2009.

———. *The Trouble with Nigeria*. Enugu: Fourth Dimension, 1985.

Adaralegbe, Adeneji, ed. *A Philosophy for Nigerian Education*. Proceedings of the Nigeria National Curriculum Conference. Ibadan: Heinemann, 1972.

Adejoh, A. *The Nigerian Civil War: Forty Years After, What Lessons*. Ibadan: Aboki, 2008.

Adesina, Segun. *The Development of Modern Education in Nigeria*. Ibadan: Heinemann, 1988.

Afolayan, Michael O., ed. *Higher Education in Postcolonial Africa: Paradigms of Development, Decline and Dilemmas*. Trenton, NJ: Africa World Press, 2007.

African Education. London: Oxford University Press, 1953.

Aigbokhan, E. *Fiscal Federalism and Nigeria's Economic Development*. Ibadan: Nigerian Economic Society, 1999.

Ajayi, J.F.A. *Christian Missions in Nigeria, 1841–1891: The Making of a New Elite*. Evanston, IL: Northwestern University Press, 1965.

Ajayi, J.F., and N. Tekena, eds. *The University of Ibadan, 1948–1973: A History of the First Twenty-Five Years*. Ibadan: Ibadan University Press, 1973.

Ajayi, J.F. Ade, Lameck K.H. Goma, and G. Ampah Johnson. *The African Experience with Higher Education*. Athens, OH: Ohio University Press, 1996.

Akinyele, T.A. *Budgeting Under Structural Adjustment Programme in Nigeria*. Ibadan: Bolayele Commercial Press, 1988.

Aminu, Jubril. *Quality and Stress in Nigerian Education*. Maiduguri: Northern Nigerian Publishing, 1986.

Amuwo, K., A. Agbaje, R. Suberu, and G. Herault, eds. *Federalism and Political Restructuring in Nigeria*. Ibadan: Spectrum Books, 1998.

Ashby, Eric. *Adapting Universities to a Technological Society*. San Francisco: Jossey-Bass, 1974.

———. *African Universities and Western Tradition*. Cambridge, MA: Harvard University Press, 1964.

———. *Universities: British, Indian, African: A Study in the Ecology of Higher Education*. Cambridge, MA: Harvard University Press, 1966.

Ashwe, C. *Fiscal Federalism in Nigeria*. Canberra: Centre for Research on Federal Financial Relations, Australian National University, 1986.

Awolowo, Obafemi. *Path to Nigerian Freedom*. London: Faber, 1947.

———. *Thoughts on Nigerian Constitution*. Ibadan: Oxford University Press, 1966.

Ayandele, Emmanuel. *Nigerian Historical Studies*. London: Frank Cass, 1979.

Azikiwe, Nnamdi. *Zik: A Selection from the Speeches of Nnamdi Azikiwe*. Cambridge: Cambridge University Press, 1960.

Bassey, Magnus O. *Western Education and Political Domination: A Study in Critical and Dialogical Pedagogy*. Westport, CT: Bergin & Garvey, 1999.

Beckett, P., and J. O'Connell. *Education and Power in Nigeria*. London: Hodder and Stoughton, 1977.

Beckman, Bjorn, and Gbemisola Remi Adeoti, eds. *Intellectuals and African Development: Pretension and Resistance in African Politics*. London: Zed Books, 2006.

Bello, Ahmadu. *My Life*. Cambridge: Cambridge University Press, 1962.

Bowen, H.R. *Investing in Learning: The Individual and Social Value of American Higher Education*. San Francisco: Jossey Bass, 1977.

Brookes, J.N., ed. *The One and the Many: Individual in the Modern World*. New York: Harper & Row, 1962.

Busia, K.A. *Purposeful Education for Africa*. The Hague: Mouton, 1968.

Buxton, Thomas Fowell. *The African Slave Trade and Its Remedy*. London: Frank Cass, 1840.

Carnoy, Martin, and Joel Samoff. *Education and Social Transition in the Third World*. Princeton, NJ: Princeton University Press, 1990.

Chinweizu. *The West and the Rest of Us*. New York: Random House, 1974.

Chizea, Chinelo Amaka, ed. *Twenty Years of University Education in Nigeria*. Lagos: National Universities Commission, 1983.

Clignet, R. *The Africanization of the Labor Market: Educational and Occupational Segmentations in the Cameroons*. Berkeley: University of California Press, 1976.

———. *Liberty and Equality in the Educational Process: A Comparative Sociology of Education*. New York: Wiley, 1974.

Clignet, R., and P. Foster. *Fortunate Few: A Study of Secondary Schools and Students in the Ivory Coast*. Evanston, IL: Northwestern University Press, 1966.

Coleman, James S. *Nigeria: Background to Nationalism*. Berkeley: University of California Press, 1958.

———. *Education and Political Development*. Princeton, NJ: Princeton University Press, 1965.

Coleman, James S., and Carl G. Roseberg. *Political Parties and National Integration in Tropical Africa*. Berkeley: University of California Press, 1964.

Crocker, W.R. *Nigeria: A Critique of British Colonial Administration*. London: Allen & Unwin, 1936.

Debrunner, H. *A History of Christianity in Ghana*. Accra: Waterville Publishing, 1967.

Devarajan, Shantayanan, David R. Dollar, and Torgny Holmgren, eds. *Aid and Reform in Africa: Lessons from Ten Case Studies*. Washington, D.C.: World Bank, 2001.

Diamond, Larry, Anthony Kirk-Greene, and Oyeleye Oyediran, eds. *Transition without End: Nigerian Politics and Civil Society under Babangida*. Boulder, CO: Lynne Rienner, 1997.

Diamond, Stanley. *Nigeria: Model of a Colonial Failure*. New York: American Committee on Africa, 1967.

Durkheim, Emile. *Education and Sociology*, trans. Sherwood D. Fox. New York: Free Press, 1956.

———. *The Evolution of Educational Thought Lectures on the Formation and Development of Secondary Education in France*, trans. P. Collins. London: Routledge and Kegan Paul, 1977.

Eisemon, T.O. *The Science Profession in the Third World: Studies from India and Kenya*. New York: Praeger, 1982.

Ejiaga, Romanus. *Higher Education and the Labor Market: A Study of University Access and Graduate Employment Opportunities in Nigeria*. Stockholm: Institute of Internal Education Stockholm University, 1997.

Ekeh, Peter, and Eghosa Osaghae, eds. *Federal Character and Federalism in Nigeria.* Ibadan: Heinemann, 1989.

Eliagwu, J. *Gowon.* Ibadan: West Book, 1986.

Fafunwa, B.A. *A History of Nigerian Higher Education.* Lagos: Macmillan, 1971.

Fagbamiye, E.O, ed. *University of Lagos Series in Education.* Lagos: Nelson, 1987.

Fagerlind, A., and L.J. Saha. *Education and National Developments.* New Delhi: Reed, 1997.

Falola, Toyin, ed. *The Dark Webs: Perspectives on Colonialism in Nigeria.* Durham, NC: Carolina Academic Press, 2005.

Federici, Silvia, Constantine George Caffentzis, and Ousseina Alidou, eds. *A Thousand Flowers: Social Struggles against Structural Adjustment in African Universities.* Trenton, NJ: Africa World Press, 2000.

Hailey, Lord. *An African Survey.* Oxford: Oxford University Press, 1938.

Harbison, F.H., and C.A. Myers. *Education, Manpower, and Economic Growth: Strategies of Human Resource Development.* New York: McGraw-Hill, 1964.

Hutchinson, John, and Anthony Smith, eds. *Nationalism.* Oxford: Oxford University Press, 1994.

Ike, Vincent. *University Development in Africa: The Nigerian Experience.* Ibadan: Oxford University Press, 1976.

Ikejiani, Okechukuwu, ed. *Nigerian Education.* Ikeja, Nigeria: Longman, 1964.

Kadiri, A.U, ed. *25 Years of Centralized University Education in Nigeria.* Lagos: National Universities Commission, 1988.

Kirk-Green, A., and D. Rimmer. *Nigeria Since 1970: A Political and Economic Outline.* London: Hodder and Stoughton, 1981.

Lebeau, Yann, and Mobolaji Ogunsanya, eds. *The Dilemma of Post-Colonial Universities.* Ibadan: IFRA, African Book Builders, 2000.

Lewis, L.J. *Society, Schools and Progress in Nigeria.* London: Pergamon, 1965.

———, ed. *Phelps-Stocks Report on Education in Africa.* London: Oxford University Press, 1962.

MacGrath, Earl J., ed. *Universal Higher Education.* New York: McGraw-Hill, 1966.

Makulu, H.F. *Education, Development and Nation-building in Independent Africa.* London: SCM, 1971.

Marte, Fred. *Political Cycles in International Relations: The Cold War and Africa, 1945–1990.* Amsterdam: VU University Press, 1994.

Mkandawire, Thandika. *African Intellectuals: Rethinking Politics, Language, Gender and Development.* London: Zed Books, 2006.

Murray, A.V. *The School in the Bush*, 2nd ed. New York: Barnes & Noble, 1967.

Nelson, Joan M. *Economic Crisis and Policy Choice: The Politics of Adjustment in the Third World*. Princeton, NJ: Princeton University Press, 1990.

Nnoli, O. *Ethnic Politics in Nigeria*. Enugu: Fourth Dimension, 1978.

Nwankwo, G.O. *Nigeria and OPEC: To Be or Not to Be*. Ibadan: African University Press, 1983.

Nwaubani, Ebere. *The United States and Decolonization in West Africa, 1950–1960*. Rochester, NY: University of Rochester Press, 2000.

Nwauwa, Apollos. *Imperialism, Academe and Nationalism: British and University Education for Africans, 1860–1960*. London: Frank Cass, 1996.

Obiechina, Emmanuel, Chukwuemeka Ike, and John Anenechukwu Umeh. *The University of Nigeria, 1960–1985: An Experiment in Higher Education*. Nsukka: University of Nigeria Press, 1986.

Ojo, Folayan. *Nigerian Universities and High Level Manpower Development*. Lagos: Lagos University Press, 1983.

Ojo, G.J.A. *Planning for Distance Education at Tertiary Level in Nigeria*. Lagos: Government Printer, 1982.

Okafor, Nduka. *The Development of Universities in Nigeria: A Study of the Influence of Political and Other Factors on University Development in Nigeria, 1868–1967*. London: Longman, 1971.

Onuoha, Jonah I., and Pat Uche Okpoko. *Ethnic Nationalism and Democratic Consolidation : Perspectives from Nigeria and the United States of America*. Nsukka: Great AP Express, 2004.

Ortega y Gasset, José. *Mission of the University*. Princeton, NJ: Princeton University Press, 1944.

Osaghae, Eghosa. *The Crippled Giant: Nigeria since Independence*. Bloomington: Indiana University Press, 1998.

———. *Structural Adjustment and Ethnicity in Nigeria*. Uppsala: Nordic African Institute, 1995.

Osaghae, Eghosa E., Ebere Onwudiwe, and Rotimi T. Suberu. *The Nigerian Civil War and its Aftermath*. Ibadan: John Archers, 2002.

Oshoko, Abraham. *June 12: The Struggle for Power in Nigeria*. Lagos: Farafina, 2006.

Otonti, Nduka. *Western Education and the Nigerian Cultural Background*. Ibadan: Oxford University Press, 1964.

Oyebade, Adebayo, ed. *The Foundations of Nigeria: Essays in Honor of Toyin Falola*. Trenton, NJ: Africa World Press, 2004.

Oyediran, O. *Nigerian Government and Politics Under Military Rule*. London: Macmillan, 1979.

Pifer, Alan. *Forecasts of the Fulbright Program in British Africa.* London: United States Educational Commission in the United Kingdom, 1953.

Psacharopoulos, G., and M. Woodhall. *Education for Development: An Analysis of Investment Choice.* New York: Oxford University Press, 1997.

Roderick, Gordon, and Michael Stephens, eds. *Higher Education for All.* London: Falmer Press, 1979.

Saunders, J.T. *University College Ibadan.* Cambridge: Cambridge University Press, 1960.

Schultz, T.W. *Investment in Human Capital.* New York: Free Press, 1971.

Taiwo, C.O. *The Nigerian Education System: Past, Present and Future.* Lagos: Nelson Pitman, 1980.

Tamuno, Tekena N., and J.A. Atanda, eds. *Nigerian since Independence: the First 25 Years*, vol. 11. Ibadan: Heinemann, 1989.

Teferra, Damtew, and Philip. G. Altbach, eds. *African Higher Education: An International Reference Handbook.* Bloomington: Indiana University Press, 2003.

Tijani, Hakeem Ibikunle. *Britain, Leftist Nationalists and the Transfer of Power in Nigeria, 1945–1965.* London: Routledge, 2005.

Tolofar, Sowaribi. *Exploitation and Instability in Nigeria: The Orkar Coup in Perspective.* Lagos: Press Alliance Network, 2004.

Ukeje, B.O. *Education for Social Reconstruction.* Lagos: Macmillan, 1966.

Utne, B. Brock. *States or Markets? Neo-liberal Solutions in the Educational Policies of Sub-Saharan Africa.* Proceedings from a Seminar. Rapport Nr. 3. Oslo: Institute for Educational Research, 1995.

Welch, Claude E., and Arthur K. Smith. *Military Role and Rule: Perspectives on Civil-Military Relations.* Belmont, CA: Wadsworth, 1974.

Williams, D.H. *A Short Survey of Education in Northern Nigeria.* Kaduna: Ministry of Education, 1960.

Znaniecki, Florian. *The Social Role of the Man of Knowledge.* New York: Columbia University Press, 1940.

Articles

Abdulraheem, Tajudeen, and Adebayo Olukoshi. "The Left in Nigerian Politics and the Struggle for Socialism: 1945–1985." *Review of African Political Economy* 13, no. 37 (1986): 64–80.

Aderinto, Adeyemi. "Multiple Admissions in Nigerian Universities." *West African Journal of Education* 20, no. 3 (October 1976): 389–97.

Adesola, A.O. "The Nigerian University System: Meeting the Challenges of Growth in a Depressed Economy." *Higher Education* 21, no. 1 (1991): 121–33.

Adeyemi, K. "An Analysis of the Supplemental Sources of Financing Higher Education in a Developing Country: A Case of Nigerian Universities." *Educational Planner* 1, nos. 3/4 (1990): 44–53.

———. "Equality of Access and Catchment Area Factor in University Admissions in Nigeria." *Higher Education* 42, no. 3 (2001): 307–32.

Ahmed, Ajuji. "The Asquith Tradition, the Ashby Reform, and the Development of Higher Education in Nigeria." *Minerva* 27, no. 1 (1989): 1–20.

Ajayi, T. "An Analysis of Recurrent Unit Cost of Higher Education: Ogun State University." *Higher Education Policy* 1, no. 4 (1988): 11–15.

Akpan, P.A. "Inequality of Access to Higher Education in Nigeria." *Higher Education Review* 22 (1989): 21–33.

Aluede, R.O.A. "Regional Demands and Contemporary Educational Disparities in Nigeria." *Journal of Social Science* 13, no. 3 (2006): 183–89.

Amonoo-Neizer, Eugenen H. "Universities in Africa – Need for Adaptation, Transformation, Reformation and Revitalization." *Higher Education Policy* 11 (1998): 301–10.

Anyanwu, Ogechi. "Religious Conflict and Integration in a Democratic Nigeria: The Peril and the Promise." *Journal of Nigerian Languages and Culture* 3 (May 2002): 70–76.

Austin, Dennis. "The Role of Higher Education in National Integration in Nigeria." *Higher Education* 19, no. 3 (1990): 293–305.

———. "The Spatial Aspects of Higher Education in Nigeria." *Higher Education* 16, no. 5 (1987): 545–55.

———. "Universities and the Academic Gold Standard in Nigeria." *Minerva* 18, no. 2 (1980): 468–77.

Azikiwe, N. "Essentials for Nigerian Survival." *Foreign Affairs* 43 (1964/65): 447–61.

Babalola, J.B. "Cost and Financing of University Education in Nigeria." *Higher Education* 36, no. 1 (1998): 43–66.

———. "Education under Structural Adjustment in Nigeria and Zambia." *Journal of Education* 34, no. 1 (1999): 79–98.

Banya, Kingsley. "Are Private Universities the Solution to the Higher Education Crisis in Sub-Saharan Africa?" *Higher Education Policy* 14, no. 2 (2001): 161–74.

Berman, E.H. "Foundations, United States Foreign Policy, and African Education, 1945–1975." *Harvard Educational Review* 49, no. 2 (1979): 145–79.

Brock-Utne, Birgit. "Formulating Higher Education Policies in Africa: The Pressure from External Forces and the Neoliberal Agenda." *Journal of Higher Education in Africa* 1, no. 1 (2003): 24–56.

Chuta, E.J. "Student Loans in Nigeria." *Higher Education* 23, no. 4 (1992): 443–49.

Dabalen, A., B. Oni, and A. Adekola. "Labor Market Prospects of University Graduates in Nigeria." *Higher Education Policy* 14, no. 2 (2000): 149–59.

Davis, Thomas J., and Azubike Kalu-Nwiwu. "Education, Ethnicity and National Integration in the History of Nigeria: Continuing Problems of Africa's Colonial Legacy." *Journal of Negro History* 86, no. 1 (Winter, 2001): 1–11.

Dillon, Wilton S. "Universities and Nation Building in Africa." *Journal of Modern African Studies* 1, no. 1 (1963): 75–89.

Fergusson, J. "Ibadan Arts and Classics." *University Quarterly* 9 (September 1965):399-405.

Fieldhouse, Roger. "Cold War and Colonial Conflicts in British West African Adult Education, 1947–1953." *History of Education Quarterly* 24, no. 3 (Autumn 1984): 359–71.

Foster, Philip J. "Ethnicity and the Schools in Ghana." *Comparative Education Review* 6 (October 1962): 127–34.

Franck, Thomas M. "Clan and Superclan: Loyalty, Identity and Community in Law and Practice." *American Journal of International Law* 90 (July 1996): 359–383.

Hallett, Robin. "Unity, Double-Think and the University." *Ibadan* no. 6 (1959):1-6.

Harbison, Frederick. "The African University and Human Resource Development." *Journal of Modern African Studies* 3, no. 1 (1965): 53–62.

Inamete, Ufot B. "Nigeria's IMF Loan Arrangement Decision-Making (Shagari to Babangida Administrations) and Decision-Making Theories." *Australian Journal of Politics & History* 36, no. 1 (June 2008): 39 – 50.

Kolinsky, M. "The Growth of Nigerian Universities 1948–1980: The British Share." *Minerva* 23, no. 1 (1985): 29–61.

———. "Universities and the British Aid Program: The Case of Nigeria during the 1970s." *Higher Education* 16, no. 2 (1987): 199–219.

Kosemani, J.M. "Democratic Values and University Admissions in Nigeria." *Nigerian Journal of Professional Studies in Education* 3 (1995): 78–83.

Mamdani, M. "University Crisis and Reform: A Reflection on the African Experience." *Review of African Political Economy* no. 58 (1993): 7–19.

Mellanby, Kenneth. "Establishing a New University in Africa." *Minerva* 1 (Winter, 1963): 149-58.

Narasingha, Singh. "Nigerian Intellectuals and Socialism: Retrospect and Prospect." *Journal of Modern African Studies* 31, no. 3 (September 1993): 361–85.

Nwauwa, Apollos. "The British Establishment of Universities in Tropical Africa, 1920–1948: A Reaction against the Spread of American 'Radical' Influence." *Cahiers d'Études Africaines* 33, no. 130 (1993): 247–74.

Nwideeduh, S.B. "Ethnicity and the Nigerian University System." *Nigerian Journal of Professional Studies in Education* 3 (1995): 91–97.

Nwuzor, Anene. "The Military and Education in Nigeria: An Experiment in Centralization in a Federal Context." *Journal of Educational Administration and History* 15, no. 1 (1983): 50–55.

Oduleye, S.O. 1985. "Decline in Nigerian Universities." *Higher Education* 14, no. 1 (1985): 17–40.

Ojo, Olatunde, and Peter Koehn. "Nigeria's Foreign Exchange Controls: An Alternative to IMF Conditions and Dependency?" *Africa Today* 33, no. 4 (1986): 7–32.

Oketech, Moses. "Affording the Unaffordable: Cost Sharing in Higher Education in Sub-Saharan Africa." *Peabody Journal of Education* 78, no. 3 (2003): 88–106.

Olaniyan, D.A., and T. Okemakinde. "Human Capital Theory: Implications for Educational Development." *Pakistan Journal of Social Sciences* 5, no. 5 (2008): 479–83.

Onuoha, N. Konyeaso. "The Role of Education in Nation-Building: A Case Study of Nigeria." *West African Journal of Education* 6 (1976): 435–50.

Saint, William, Teresa Hartnett, and Erich Strassner. "Higher Education in Nigeria: A Status Report." *Higher Education Policy* 16, no. 3 (2003): 259–81.

Sakamota, A., and P.A. Powers. "Education and the Dual Labour Market for Japanese Men." *American Sociological Review* 60, no. 22 (1995): 222–46.

Sam, Aluko. "How Many Nigerians?" *Journal of Modem African Studies* 3 (October 1965): 371–92.

Sklar, Richard. "Political Science and National Integration – A Radical Approach." *Journal of Modern African Studies* 5, no. 1 (1967): 1–11.

Tawari, Osa, and Maureen Koko. "Student Enrolment and Educational Expenditure in University Education: An Examination of Trends in Nigeria, 1980–1990." *International Journal of Educational Development* 16 (1996): 79–87.

Tijani, Hakeem Ibikunle. "Britain and the Foundation of Anti-Communist Policies in Nigeria, 1945–1960." *African and Asian Studies* 8, nos. 1–2 (2009): 54–55.

Van den Berghe, P. L, and C.M, Nuttney. "Some Social Characteristics of University of Ibadan." *Nigerian Journal of Economic and Social Studies* 11, no. 3 (November 1969): 355–76.

Index

A

Abacha, Sani, 159, 198–99, 205, 208
Abdullahi, Ibrahim, 163
Abeokuta, 162, 176–77, 182
Abiola, Moshood, 197–98
A.B.U., 82, 85, 88, 95, 131
Abubakar, Abdulsalami, 131, 203, 205, 208
Abubakar, Iya, 131
Abuja, 140, 155, 177
academic merit, 144–45
Academic Staff Union of Universities, 131, 166, 186, 191, 195–98, 208
Achebe, Chinua, 197
Achimota College, 30
Action Group, 40–41, 77
Ad Hoc Constitutional Conference, 93
Adams, Walter, 49
Adaralegbe, Adeneji, 97, 99
Adebo, S.O., 110–11
Aderinto, Adeyemo, 118, 126
admission, 20, 28, 143, 199
Advanced Level, 87, 90–91, 105
Advisory Committee on Education in the Colonies, 30–31
Agbese, Dan, 154

agriculturalists, 140, 151
Aguiyi-Ironsi, J.T.U., 93
Ahmadu, Bello, 51
Ajayi, J.F. Ade, 12, 20, 63, 106, 115, 118, 131
Akinkugbe, O.O., 125
Akintoye, 149
Akpabio, I.U., 42
Akpofure, Rex F.O., 190
Aluko, Sam, 181
amalgamation, 21–22, 187
Aminu, Jubril, 26, 84, 121–24, 129, 150, 155, 173–74
Anglo-American collaboration, 14, 54–55, 58
Anglo-American–Nigerian collaboration, 47
Angulu, Michael, 121, 125–26, 146
Arikpo, Okoi, 82, 90
Ashby Commission, 59, 64
Ashby, Eric (Sir), 3, 9–10, 12, 33, 60–62, 64, 69, 71–72, 77–78, 80, 82, 90, 96, 100, 192
Assembly, House of, 41, 44, 46, 82
assimilation, 22

287

Audu, Ishaya, 95
austerity, 128, 167–68
autonomy, 30, 38–39, 53, 76, 84, 92–94, 98, 109, 124, 126, 131–32, 177
Awokoya, S.O., 33, 41
Awolowo, Obafemi, 3, 22, 40–41, 95–96, 136, 180, 201
Azikiwe, Nnamdi, 3, 27–28, 35, 40, 96
  advises students, 86
  American educational support, 59
  declaration on education, 136
  free education plan, 42
  regional universities, 44–45
  university, 193, 201

B

Babangida, Ibrahim, 15
  coup of 1985 that ousted Buhari, 168–69
  coup plotters' suspicion, 187–88
  diverted resources from higher education, 179
  establishment of universities ceased, 160
  policy contradiction on university education, 194–98, 203
  rationalization policies, 181–85
  universities to restructure their programmes, 175–77
  World Bank advice, 171
Balewa, Tafawa, 14, 21–22, 27, 51, 58, 68, 70, 86, 92
Bamiloye, Alexander, 197
Bauchi, 139–40, 143–44, 149, 162, 176–77, 187
Bello, Ahmadu, 40, 51, 78, 82, 87, 95, 107, 116, 126
Benin, 19, 105, 107, 114, 117–18, 147, 154
Benue, 94, 107, 139–40, 143–44, 146, 149
Biafra, 94
Bida, Makaman, 136

Biobaku, 86
blueprint, 12, 32, 47, 71, 77, 174
Blyden, Edward, 28
Board
  Manpower, 165
  Marketing, 46
  Matriculation, 125, 144
  Scholarship, 48
Bourdillon, Henry, 23
Boyd, Lennox, 62
Briggs, Wenike, 95, 99–100
Britain, Great, 23, 47. *See also* United Kingdom
British
  cabinet, 32
  colonies, 49
  Parliament, 31
budgets, 143, 194–96
Buhari, Mohammed, 15, 159–62, 164–65, 167–69, 183, 185, 202–5
Burns, Alan (Sir), 53
Buxton, Fowell, 19, 29

C

Calabar, 114, 201
Cameroon, 58
campaign
  for universities, 107
campuses, 162–63, 174, 176, 185–86, 200–202
Canada, 9, 90, 119
Carnegie Corporation, 11–12, 14, 37–38, 48–49, 54, 60–61, 81
Casely-Hayford, J.E., 28
casualties, 131, 179
Catchment Area, 144–45, 148, 188–90
census, 92
Central (state)
  East, 109, 121
  North, 94, 107
centralization, 93

of university education, 107
to foster national unity, 110–11
Gowon's, 114
chancellor, 70
Chilvers, Sally, 49
Chinweizu, 10
Christianity, 19–20, 25, 42
citizenship, 100
classrooms, 180, 185, 189, 200
Church Missionary Society, 19, 23, 30
Committee on the Future of Higher
    Education, 199, 205
Cold War, 12, 32, 36, 46–48, 55, 57
Coleman, James, 29
colonial, 1–7
    administration, 20
    advisor on education, 62
    authorities against the establishment of
        universities, 28–34
    British government, 19, 22, 60
    educational planning and
        development, 71–80
    legacy, 87
    Social and Science Research Council,
        49
colonialism, 22, 29
colonialists, 22, 29
colonies, 2–3, 9–12, 29–33, 43, 47–50,
    54–56, 59, 62, 71, 90
colony, 21, 28, 61
commerce, 19, 72, 74, 83
commercialization, 171
Commissions
    acceptance of its recommendation,
        79–83
    Ashby, 12, 14, 70
    Asquith, 3, 32–33, 50
    Cookey, 150
    Educational, 49
    Elliot, 3, 32–33, 43
    Longe, 192–95, 199, 203–4
    Mohammed, 132

Onabamiro, 150
Presidential, 150
Commissioner, 95, 99, 107, 123–25
commissioners, 98, 110
commitment
    to free education, 136
    to mass education, 12, 16
Committee
    Advisory, 30
    Dina, 98, 108
    Joint Consultative, 65, 88
    Planning, 138–39
    University Entrance on, 121–22,
        124–25
Committee on University Finances, 130
Committee of Vice-Chancellors, 84, 91,
    108, 119, 124–26, 167, 171, 173,
    178–79, 183, 192
Commonwealth, 57
communication, 22, 70, 80, 126, 138–39,
    141, 161
communiqué, 173
Communism, 12, 37, 46–48, 81
competition, 5–6, 27, 53, 65, 79, 95, 122,
    144
Concurrent Legislative List, 44, 77, 110
Conference, 5–6, 10, 38–39, 50–51, 55,
    89, 94, 99–100, 110, 140, 149, 179
    Berlin, 20
    Constitutional, 93
    Curriculum, 111
    Education since Independence on, 154
    Greenbrier, 55
    Jamaica, 50
confrontation, 47, 131
Congo, 9
Congress, 39–40
Constitution, 38
    amendment of, 1963, 110
    Lyttleton, 43–44
    Macpherson, 40–41, 57
    1979 (adoption of a Second Republic),
        135–36

Index   289

regional autonomy and ownership of higher institutions, 76–78
Richards, 38
convocation, 86, 124, 152, 171
Cookey, S.J., 99–100, 150
corruption, 13, 15, 92, 119, 137, 154, 157, 161, 197–98
Côte d'Ivoire, 70
Council
   British, 173
   National, 40, 110
   Provisional, 82
   Research, 99
   University, 33, 43, 49–50, 79, 82, 108, 120
coup, 92–94, 119, 121, 157, 159, 168, 185–88, 191, 198
Cox, Christopher (Sir), 54–56, 62
creation
   of Joint Admissions and Matriculation Board (JAMB), 125
   of states and impact on founding of universities, 193
Criminal Code, 47
crisis
   political, 13, 92
   economic, 16, 153, 186–93
Cross River, 122, 144, 149
cult, 29, 89, 132, 188, 191, 203–4
curriculum,
   of mission schools, 20
   diversification, 74–77
   reform, 165–74

D

Daily Comet, 47
Daily Times, 67, 129, 139, 161, 163, 167
debt, 153, 167, 169–70, 198
decentralization, 193
decolonization, 4, 12, 36–37, 46–48, 55, 156
decree, 93–94, 109, 114, 126, 167, 174, 196, 202, 204–5
defense, 191
democratization, 5, 15, 50, 80, 111
dependency, 141, 193
deregulation, 16
development, 6, 10, 28
   Colonial, 31, 71
   Economic, 34
   National, 113
   Overseas, 62
dictatorship, 131, 136, 198, 208
Dike, Kenneth, 25, 28, 40, 64, 75, 84, 89, 91–92, 97
Dimka, B.S., 121
Dina, I.O., 98
Dingyadi, Sani, 39
diplomas, 141, 201
Direct Entry, 125
disadvantaged states, 190
discrimination, 6, 132, 176, 206
Dominions, 12
Dominions, British, 49
Durkheim, Emile, 5–7, 103

E

earmarked, 80, 113, 195
Echeruo, M.J.C., 152
ecology, 3
economic meltdown, 150
editorial, 34, 90, 108, 129, 139, 163, 180, 206
Edo, 146
education
   colonial, 17, 19, 21, 23, 25, 27, 29, 31, 33, 35
   free, 135
   higher, 3, 6, 10, 28, 33, 63, 71, 79, 82, 119, 148, 188, 190, 195, 199
   secondary, 152

university, 69, 71, 73, 75, 77, 79, 81, 83, 85, 87, 89, 91, 93, 95, 97, 99, 101, 107
Western, 18, 26
Education Scheme, 124
educational
   disparity, 27
   expansion, 207
   imbalance, 26
Educationally Disadvantaged States, 144–45
Education Tax Fund, 196
Egbe Omo Oduduwa, 27
Egypt, 12, 181
Eke, A.Y., 107–10
Ekiti, Ado, 149
Ekpoma, 148
Ekpu, Ray, 154, 180
Ekwueme, Alex, 140, 153
Eliagwu, 108
elitism, 46, 50, 58, 87
Emir of Zaria, 40
emirs, 26, 42
employment, 6, 42, 66, 74, 106, 116, 120, 135, 165, 182
Enahoro, Anthony, 51
Endowment Fund, 195
enrolment
   course, 9
   primary school, 57–58
   regional statistics at UCI 1948–1959, 7
   students in universities, 105–7, 113–15, 130, 132–33, 142
entrants, 85, 91, 105, 165
Enugu, 72
equality, 45, 121, 132
Esau, E.E., 35
Etiti, 149
Exclusive Legislative List, 110
Eyo, Ita, 45–46
Eze, Nduka, 47–48

F

faculty, 34–35, 64, 77, 81, 179–81
Fafunwa, Babs, 36, 58, 88, 99
Fagbamiye, E.O., 101
Fagbulu, T., 146
Fagerlind, 8
Fascism, 31
federal control, 107
Federal Executive Council, 114
Federal Ministry of Education, 81, 89, 162
Federal Universities Development Sector Adjustment Credit, 178
Federal Universities of Technology, 174
Federation, 40, 43, 53, 81, 92, 108, 135
fellowships, 81
Fergusson, John, 65
Fieldhouse, Roger, 47
Fine Arts, 141
First National Development Plan, 80, 106, 142, 153, 170
First National Rolling Plan, 182–83
Folarin, Bamidele, 201
forestry, 82, 84, 122
Foundations, 49, 81
   Ford, 48
   Rockefeller, 48, 81
Fourah Bay, 28
Fourth National Development Plan, 142, 153
Freeman, Thomas Birch, 19
Fulani, 23, 40

G

Gaskiya Ta Fi Kwabo, 7, 28
Gboyega, Alex, 115
General Certificate of Education, 87–88, 90–91, 125
GDP, 113, 128

Germany
  West, 81
  East, 46
Ghana, 30, 132, 181
Gills, Malcolm, 208
Gold Coast, 30
Goma, Lameck K.H., 12
Gongola, 139–40, 144, 149
Government
  British, 30, 40, 54,172
  Federal, 4, 15, 53, 148, 183
  National, 10
  Nigerian, 55
  Regional, 79
  State, 110
Governor General, 56, 61
Governor, 2, 21, 23, 29, 38, 40, 53–54, 56, 62, 86, 93, 148–49
Gowon, Yakubu, 8, 93–94, 96–97, 99, 104–5, 107–16, 119–20, 122, 124, 131
Greater Nigerian People's Party (GNPP), 136
Grey, Ralph (Sir), 56, 61
Guardian, The, 151, 192, 200
Guatemala, 181
Gulf War, 15, 137, 184, 191
Guobadia, Abel, 140
Gwagwalada, 177

H

Hailey, Lord, 29
Hallett, Robin, 53
Halliday, F.J., 2
Harare, 171
Harbison, F.H., 8, 72
Hardyman, N.T., 172
Harvard, 64
Hausa, 23, 27, 40
Horton, James, 28
Houphouët–Boigny, Félix, 69

House
  Eastern, 44, 46
  Federal, 22
  Western, 41
HSC, 74, 80, 91
Human Capital Theory, 8
Humanities, 65, 88–89, 96–97, 151, 165, 179
Hungary, 46
Hussey, E.R.J., 30
Huxley, Julian, 33

I

Ibadan
  university college, 2–3, 56, 123–24, 146, 161, 166, 200
ICSA, 116
Ife, 78, 83–85, 87–88, 96, 105, 107, 114, 118, 166, 180
Igbo, 23, 27, 40, 92–94
Ijeomah, B.I.C., 176
Ikoku, Alvan, 39
Ikoku, Chimere, 189
Ilorin, 114, 166–67
Imo, 139–40, 143, 148–49, 193
Imoudu, Michael, 47
implementation
  Ashby Commission Report, 68, 82
  IMF-Structural Adjustment Program, 186
  Jamaican resolution, 50
  massification program, 101
  quota system, 143, 189–90
India, 2, 52, 90, 188
indigenes, 105, 115, 149, 157
intellectual, 75, 111, 120
intellectuals, 28, 95, 180
intelligentsias, 131
Interim Joint Matriculation, 126
International Baccalaureate, 12
International Monetary Fund, 13, 15, 156, 159–60, 167–70, 177, 179, 186, 197, 203–4, 207

Inter-University Council for Higher Education in the Colonies, 108, 115
Investment, 71
Iran, 137
Iraq, 137, 191
Ireland, 9
Islamic, 18, 25–26, 60, 166
Israel, 78
Ita, Eyo, 42, 46
Ivory Coast, 132, 181
Iyayi, Festus, 175

J

Jamaica, 50
Joint Admissions and Matriculation Board, 125–28, 132, 141, 143–46, 181–82, 194
Japan, 188
JCC, 65
Johnson, Ampah, 12
Johnson, George, 77
Jones, Creech, 33
Jones, Jesse, 20
Jones, Mouat, 30–31
Jos, 114, 127, 200–201
Jubilee, Silver, 171

K

Kaduna, 48, 52, 144
Kaita, Isa, 65
Kampala, 3
Kano, 78, 94, 114, 144, 187, 193
Katsina, 187
Kenya, 9, 181
Kepple, Francis, 64
Kilson, Martin, 54
Koranic, 25, 42
Kosemani, J.M., 27, 146
Kwara, 94, 123

L

Lagos
  Colony and Protectorate, 21–23
  Federal Capital Territory, 43–44
Lagos Daily, 34
Lebeau, Y., 206
Liberia, 181
Littlewood, V.H.K., 60
Lockwood, John (Sir), 52, 60–61, 63
Longe, Gray, 188–90, 192, 195
Lowe, J.B., 172
Lugard, Frederick (Sir, Lord), 21, 25–26
Lyttleton, Oliver, 43

M

Macaulay, Ogedegbe, 47
MacDonald, 31
Macpherson, John (Sir), 38, 40
Maiduguri, 114, 168
Makurdi, 162, 176–77, 182
management, 72, 84, 104, 132, 173, 176
Manchester, 3
manpower
  national, 81
  regional, 76
massification
  concept, 1–5
  implementation, 101
  of university education, 36, 66, 104, 137
Maxwell, Dan, 50–51
Mbakwe, Sam, 148–49
Megaforce, T., 146
Mellanby, Kenneth, 29
Mexico, 78
Middle Belt, 187, 191
Middle East, 113
Midwest, 94, 121
military dictatorship, 191
Milverton, Lord, 53
missionaries, 7, 17–20, 22–23, 25–26, 42

modernization, 8, 13, 61, 68, 86, 140
Mohammed, Murtala, 15, 104, 109, 119–21, 131, 178

N

Naira, 152, 169, 181, 196
National
  Assembly, 142
  Certificate, 125
  Concord, 146
  Curriculum Conference, 99, 110
  Electric Power Authority, 138
  Implementation Committee on the Report of the Review of Higher Education in Nigeria, 195
  Institute of Strategic Studies, 142
  Minimum Standards and Establishment of Institutions, 167, 204
  Open University, 15, 137, 156, 161–62
  Union of Nigerian Students, 131
  Youth Service Corps, 112
nationalism, 45–46, 54–55, 61
nationalists, 3, 7, 11–12, 14, 17, 22, 28–29, 31, 35–38, 41, 43, 47, 49, 66, 104
  leftist, 47
nation building, 4–6, 15, 41, 68–69, 87, 94–95, 108, 112, 128, 135, 186, 210–12, 215
National Convention of Nigerian Citizens, 40–42
National Council on Education (NCE), 110, 125
National Curriculum Conference, 99, 110
National Development Plan, 80–82, 96, 106, 110–11, 113–14, 119, 142–43, 152–53, 170
National Implementation Committee on the Report of the Review of Higher Education in Nigeria, 195

National Manpower Board, 81–82
National Open University, 137–39, 161
National Party of Nigeria (UPN), 136
National Youth Service Corps (NYSC), 112
nationhood, 185, 187, 189, 191, 193, 195, 197, 199, 201, 203, 205, 207
Nayaya, Adamu, 178
Nazism, 31
Ndayako, Umaru Sanda, 199
New Nigerian, 126
New York, 38, 49
New Zealand, 90
newspapers, 35–36, 47, 53, 66, 153, 200
Newswatch, 146, 185, 222
Nicaragua, 181
Niger, 139–40, 144, 149
Niger Coast Protectorate, 21
Nigeria, 1–16
  colonial administration, 20
  division into regions, 23, 25
  Eastern, 46
  foreign debt, 153
  leftist elements, 47
  modern, 21
  Northern, 25–26, 85
  threat of communism, 48
  Western, 19, 79
Nigerian Association of University Teachers (NAUT), 131
Nigerian citizens, 40
Nigerian Civil War, 8, 103–4
Nigerian College of Arts, Science and Technology, 72, 82–83
Nigerian Educational Research Council, 99
Nigerian Tribune, 126
Nigerianization, 36, 51–53, 58
Northern Civil Service, 93
Northern People's Congress, 40
Northernization, 53

Nigerian People's Party (NPP), 136
Nigerian Universities Commission (NUC), 26, 81–82
  duties and assignment, 84–85, 90–91, 114
  empowered by Buhari administration, 167
Nsukka, 72, 77, 83–84, 88, 105, 107, 118, 167
Nwachukuwu, Aja, 11, 56–57, 62
Nwagwu, N.A., 154
Nwauwa, Apollos, 12, 23, 31, 45
Nyerere, Julius, 69
Nzeogwu, Kaduna, 92, 94

O

Obanikoro (Chief), 39
Obasanjo, Olusegun, 15, 104, 121, 123–25, 128, 130–31, 133, 136, 164, 187, 208
Odufuwa, J.J., 47
Odupitan, J.A.O., 67
Ogun, 139–40, 149
Ojike, Mbonu, 45
Ojo, G.J. Afolabi, 138
Ojukwu, Odumegwu, 93–94
Okada, 205
Okafo, Achike, 154
Okar, Gideon, 187
Okeowo, Segun, 131
Okigwe, 193
Okija, 205
Okusami, O.F., 166
Olusanya, G.O., 142
Oluwasanmi, 4
Omo, Egbe, 27
Onabamiro, 65, 67, 73, 77, 150
Ondo, 20, 139–40, 149
Onuaguluchi, G.O., 127
Onyeka-Ben, Victor, 201
Ordinary Level, 87–88, 90, 214

Organization of Petroleum Exporting Countries, 113
Orizu, Nwafor, 45
Orkar, Gideon, 187–88, 191
Osadolor, O., 21
Owerri, 162, 193

P

Paris Club, 170
Parliamentary, 92, 135
Petroleum Profit Tax (PPT) Act, 196
Pettipiere, W.H., 119
Philosophical Society, 56
Pifer, Alan, 11–12, 49–51, 54–58, 60–63
Plateau (state), 94, 144
political instability, 185
politicization, 13, 186
Polytechnics, 164, 182, 196
Port Harcourt, 114, 149
Portuguese, 19, 166
Post-War Reconstruction, 95
pre-colonial, 18
Presidential Planning Committee, 138
private university, 185, 204
Program
  Colonies, 12, 49
  Fulbright, 49
Protectorate, 21, 25–26
  Northern, 21
  Southern, 21
Provinces, 22, 29
Psacharopoulos, 8
Puddah System, 25
Puerto Rico, 50

Q

Quota System, 115, 135, 143

R

Rationalization Policy, 161, 163, 165, 167, 169, 171, 173, 175, 177, 179, 181, 183
rationalization, 13, 15, 159–61, 163, 167, 169–75, 181–83, 185, 204
recession, 30, 128, 152–53, 155–56, 161, 165, 174, 203
recovery
    economic, 198
    national, 179
reform
    admission, 115, 123–24
    curriculum, 64, 88, 167, 169, 173, 178
    higher education, 11–12, 14, 46, 50, 56, 121
    university, 172
regimes, 13, 15–16, 131, 160, 185, 199
Region
    Eastern, 39–41, 44–45, 51–52, 56–58, 66, 77–78, 94
    Midwest, 94
    Northern, 39, 52–53, 58, 60, 78, 94, 107, 151
    Western, 33, 39–40, 52, 57–58, 66, 73, 77–80, 83, 94
regionalism, 69
registrar, 125–27, 146, 172
Remo, Ilishan, 205
Renan, Ernest, 5
Report
    Dina, 108
    Elliot, 50
Republic
    Democratic, 9
    Federal, 187, 190
    First, 92, 135
    Second, 135, 137, 139, 141, 143, 145, 147, 149, 151, 153, 155–57
Residual List, 44, 110
Restoration Grant, 195
Revitalization, 208
Revolution, 37, 41, 48, 187
    Green, 140
Richards, Arthur, 53
Robbins' Principle, 4
Robertson, James Wilson (Sir), 56, 62
Roden, Charles, 29
Russians, 54

S

sabotage, 124
Sada, Pius, 201
Sadique, 179
Saharan, 13, 83, 178
salary, 150, 155, 195
Salim, Bello, 82, 119, 126
Salisbury, 54
Samo, 70
São Thomé, 19
Sarduana of Sokoto, 51
scholarship, 5, 52, 75, 81, 85, 87, 91–92, 101, 165
School Certificate, 67, 71, 79, 88, 91, 125
schools
    community, 27
    private, 27
    unity, 112
secession, 94
secessionist, 94
Second World War, 3, 11, 29–31, 38, 41, 46, 48–49
Secretariat, 81
Selassie, Haile, 70
self-government, 32
Seminar on National Policy on Education, 110–12
Shagari, Shehu, 15, 136–40, 142–43, 145–46, 149–50, 155–57, 159–60, 164
Shehu, Emman, 188
Shonekan, Ernest, 198
Shrent, Elias, 20

Sierra Leone, 28
Singapore, 3
Sklar, Richard, 6
Sokoto, 51, 114, 144, 187, 189
Solarin, Tai, 34
Southernization, 53
stabilization, 195
Stackpole, Steve, 49–50, 56
Stalin, Joseph, 46
Stanley, Oliver, 31
State
    Abia, 149, 193
    Anambra, 148, 193
    Bendel, 148
    Benue, 193
    Central, 107, 118
    Delta, 193, 201
    Eastern, 107
    Enugu, 201
    Gongola, 149
    Ibom, 193
    Imo, 148–49, 152, 193, 200
    Kano, 107
    Lagos, 149, 200–201
    Midwestern, 94, 105
    Ogun, 149, 201
    Ondo, 149
    Participation in Higher Education, 148
    Plateau, 107
    Rivers, 107, 149, 200
    West, 109
    Western, 107, 118
statesmanship, 154
Structural Adjustment Program, 159, 168–69, 171, 173–74, 177, 179, 186, 195, 197–98, 203, 207
Studies
    African, 56, 83
    Strategic, 142
Study Group, 180
Supreme Military Council, 110

T

Ta, Gaskiya, 7, 28
Taggart, Glen, 81
Tahir, Ibrahim, 95
Tanzania, 9, 69
technology, 72, 82–83, 105, 135, 141, 148–49, 165, 175, 193, 200–201
    agricultural, 141
    engineering, 141
Territory, Federal, 86
theory, human capital, 8–9
Thomas-Ogboji, 186
Transitional Provision, 94
Trow, Martin, 4
Trust Deed, 195

U

Udoji, Jerome, 66
UK. *See* United Kingdom
Umudike, 193
University of Abuja, 177
University College of Ibadan (UCI), 2, 18, 37, 56, 211
University Grants Committee (UGC), 172
University Matriculation Examination (UME), 125–26, 144, 194
Unification Decree, 93
Union, Nigerian, 35
United Kingdom, 36, 52, 55, 63, 65, 84, 88, 90, 119, 171
United Nations Educational, Scientific, and Cultural Organization (UNESCO), 18, 81–82, 112
United Nations (UN), 82, 110
United States, 11, 29–30, 45–46, 48–50, 52, 55, 57, 63, 66, 74, 78, 88, 90, 135, 144
Universal Primary Education Scheme, 124
University
    of Abuja, 177

Ahmadu Bello, 116, 126, 215
Andrews, 172
autonomy, 119
Babcock, 205–6
Bagauda, 193
of Benin, 105, 107, 117,147,154
College of Ibadan, 2, 18, 37, 43, 50, 56, 78, 115
College of the West Indies, 50
of East Africa, 9
Federal, 78
finances, 130
grants, 172
of Ife, 78, 83, 96, 105, 180
Igbinedion, 205–6
of Lagos, 82–83, 88, 106–7, 118, 131, 171, 201
of London, 32–33, 51, 63, 83
Madonna, 205–6
matriculation, 125, 144
of Nigeria, 44–46, 51, 56, 72, 77, 80–81, 85, 88, 90, 96, 106, 130, 171, 189, 214
Programme, 162
Regional, 78
resources, 173
Rice, 208
of Salford, 172
unrest, 29, 89, 132, 164, 186, 191
Universal Primary Education, 124
Unity Party of Nigeria, 136
USAID, 80–81
Union of Soviet Socialist Republics (USSR), 11, 46–48, 54
Uzoma, R.I., 41–42

V

Vice-Chancellor, 89
of Ahmadu Bello University, 95, 215
of Delta State University, 201
of Imo State University, 152, 223
of the University of Benin, 117, 147
of the University of Jos, 127
of the University of Lagos, 106, 118, 152, 171
of University of Nigerian Nsukka, 189

W

Wachukwu, Jaja, 149
Watts, G.E., 64
Waziri, Ibrahim, 136
Welfare Act, 31, 71
West African School Certificate, 125
West Indies, 50
Western educated, 20
West Virginia, 5
White Paper, 171–72, 174, 176
Wolfensohn, D. James, 208
Wood, Charles, 2, 29
World Bank, 13
structural adjustment, 160, 170–71
World Federation of Trade Unions, 48

Y

Yaba, 28, 30, 33, 36
Yesufu, 81, 117, 120, 147
Yola, 149, 162, 176–77
Yom Kippur, 113
Yoruba, 23, 27, 40

Z

Zaire, 9
Zambia, 9, 181
Zaria, 40, 66, 72, 82–84, 105, 114, 116, 118
Zikist Movement, 47–48
Zikists, 47

www.ingramcontent.com/pod-product-compliance
Lightning Source LLC
Chambersburg PA
CBHW052013290426
44112CB00014B/2221